IGNATIUS de LOYOLA

Powers of Imagining

IGNATIUS DE LOYOLA

A PHILOSOPHICAL HERMENEUTIC OF IMAGINING
THROUGH THE COLLECTED WORKS OF
IGNATIUS DE LOYOLA
WITH A TRANSLATION OF THESE WORKS

Foreword by
Patrick Heelan, S.J.

ANTONIO T. DE NICOLAS

STATE UNIVERSITY OF NEW YORK PRESS

Published by State University of New York Press, Albany
© 1986 State University of New York
All rights reserved. Printed in the United States of America
Text and cover design by Sushila Blackman
For information, address State University of New York Press,
    State University Plaza, Albany, NY 12246

Library of Congress Cataloging in Publication Data

De Nicolas, Antonio T., 1932-
    Ignatius: a hermeneutic of St. Ignatius de Loyola using a new
      translation of his Spiritual exercises, his Spiritual diary, his Autobiography
      Autobiography, and some of his letters.

    Bibliography: p.
    Includes index
    1. Ignatius, of Loyola, Saint, 1491-1556.
1. Ignatius, of Loyola, Saint, 1491-1556.   II. Title:
BX4700.L7D36   1986   248'.092'4   85-2739
ISBN 0-88706-109-5
ISBN 0-88706-110-9(pbk.)

10 9 8 7 6 5 4 3 2

IN MEMORIAM

Ignatius de Loyola
Juan de la Cruz
Teresa de Avila
Juan Ramón Jiménez
Ortega y Gasset
George Santayana
My mother

Contents

IGNATIUS DE LOYOLA

In a world
splintered by diversity
constrained
by theoretical uniformity,
hierarchical ladders
you broke the fences
of the human spirit
planting the coordinates
of the soul
in the fields
of the divine will.

When the world
around you
exercised thoughts
to conform to the norms
of logic
and propositional law
you turned the soul
around
to exercise remembering
through memories
of the fall, the angel,
the hell of human choice,
the fields of Galilee,
the death at the Cross,
the resurrection,
the love of God.

Memories glued
to the ancient soul
of human forgotten
by thought relieved
in orginial imaginings
away from concepts,
sensuous feelings,
obedience to the law,
to steal the light

of the horizon
outside the limits
of human thought
by creating
pure images
while enlarging
the size
of a human body
habituated to the small
pleasures of familiar
objects
taking the will adrift
like a boat
in a surging tide
of dark waters
surrounding the soul.

Imaginings of the pure image
uncontaminated by thought,
repellent to the outside,
bent only on the Will of God
stretching the bounderies
of the human body
to the outer horizons
of the human will
to a region of intimacy
where human will
and the Will of God meet.
Imaginings of the pure image
uncontaminated by the human
encircling the earth
with a ring of human flesh
sensitive only
to the touch of God
for the love of men.

ANTONIO T. DE NICOLÁS

Foreword

MANY OF THE UNIVERSITIES AND LIBRARIES of Europe bear
the IHS monogram of the Jesuit order, more properly called the
"Society of Jesus". Such buildings were once owned by the Jesuits,
among the greatest scholars, educators, patrons of the arts of their
time. The first members of the order belonged to the generation of
Nicholaus Copernicus, the generation that saw the beginnings of
the scientific revolution, the generation that discovered infinite space
and created the new sciences of the cosmos and of nature. This
same generation paralleled the exploration of nature with the exploration of the earth sending ships beyond Europe to extend the discoveries that had begun in the previous century. Such voyages were
also missionary endeavors bringing both the new sciences and
Christianity to the "new" lands. Even before the pilgrims landed in
Massachusetts, the missionary and educational effort of the Jesuits
had spread in this way to India, China, Japan, Mexico, and was
soon to extend to Brazil, Paraguay, Canada, the Midwest of the
United States, and California. The founder of this learned and powerful society was Saint Ignatius de Loyola.

Ignatius was born into a Basque family of minor nobility with
no great wealth or important connections. His education was not
extensive. He never rose to any high rank in the Church. He was
not a charismatic preacher. Yet he became one of the great leaders
and organizers of Counter-Reformation Europe. The instrument of
his success was the *Spiritual Exercises*, a set of brief instructions
for spiritual renewal that he composed during his convalescence
after the siege of Pamplona and polished laboriously in the ensuing
years.

The *Spiritual Exercises* do not teach doctrine nor morals. When used by an experienced master, they prepare a person to experience and to discern the affects that accompany the practice of living the "memory" of Christ's life, death, and resurrection. Such "memory" is not the memory of the scriptural scholar, nor of the scientist or historian, nor even that of the theologian or church fathers. The "memory" in question is of a special kind that is now largely forgotten though it flourished for millenia when European culture was predominantly oral. This is the "memory" that Antonio de Nicolas calls the "powers of imagining."

The "powers of imagining" consist in calling on the sensuous imagination with great intensity—*exercising* the sensuous powers—in order to reenact, as it were, in ones's own life the symbolic narratives of the past, so as to feel the affects of one's imagined present participation in the lives and events, in this case, of the founder of Christianity and of his disciples. Ignatian meditation, then, is not a form of rational (formal logical) analysis, nor does it seek historical and scientific accuracy. It is rather a manner of experiencing and then discerning, that is, evaluating, the spiritual affects of (what Ignatius called) "consolation" and "desolation," first in the course of such imaginative exercises, then in contemplating the world around that God made, and finally at the heart of daily human living. By the correct use of such discernment, one was enabled autonomously to come to those decisions that were (to use the motto of the Jesuit order) "for the greater glory of God."

Such a claim was rightly feared by some as tending toward a form of heterodox anti-ecclesiastical mystical "illuminism." However, unlike other forms of religious enthusiasm within and outside of the Roman Catholic Church at that time and later, Ignatian freedom to discern what was "for the greater glory of God" did not aim at replacing church authority in its own legitimate domain, but at supplementing the public administration of the church by training suitable people in the arts of spiritual discernment. Such people were taught to become aware of the inner life of the Holy Spirit shared by all Christians and to learn to respond autonomously to its demands. Such was the aim and the promise of the *Spiritual Exercises*. This little book moulded the first companions of Ignatius and made possible the extraordinary expansion of the Jesuit order in the fifty years after Ignatius' death, and the effects of its pedagogy formed a worldwide bond such that, despite isolation from one another on five continents, the first generations of Jesuits seemed to be responding to a common, still, but commanding voice.

How is one to understand the claims to knowledge that are made by Ignatian meditation for the power of enactment (or reenactment) of our memories, particularly of our religious memories?

Such practices, though they have long passed out of common use in scientific and academic circles, have nevertheless an important and respected place in the history of our culture and even in the development of modern science.

Modern science emerged in the seventeenth century as the creation of several quite different traditions. The view that nature was to be best understood as a machine or set of machines—the mechanical tradition—was the one that came to dominate nineteenth century scientific thinking. In this view, a machine is something made up of interlocking (atomic or molecular) parts that perform cyclic motions, itself devoid of intrinsic purpose, in an otherwise empty space-time container. The mechanical view denies that there are in nature spiritual, rational, religious, or preternatural powers other than, perhaps, the human spirit.

Mechanical explanation, however, was scarcely used in antiquity. Both antiquity and the Middle Ages conceived the cosmos holistically as a living thing, full of finite powers and limited rational purposes. Such was the model defended, say, by Aristotle, whose authority was paramount in high culture during the period just before the scientific revolution. The holistic organic model persisted after the development of mechanical science right into the nineteenth century particularly in the "lower sciences" such as biology and medicine and is a second ingredient of development of modern science. Something of the holistic and purposive character of this model is presently being rediscovered in physical cosmology and in some other branches of modern science.

Both organismic and mechanical models of explanation are naturalistic models in that they do not rest on claims either to preternatural knowledge or to the existence of preternatural powers in the world. Although today we think of science as exclusively naturalistic, it would be a serious mistake to think that modern science sprang entirely from such roots, or continues in its most creative moments to spring from such roots.

The third important ingredient of the scientific revolution was the Hermetic tradition stemming in part from the Neoplatonic literary revival of the fifteenth century Renaissance with its interest in numerology, and in part from even older Christian and non-Christian Gnostic sources in antiquity, particularly in Egypt and the Middle East.[1] Greatly dependent on this tradition were alchemy, astrology, and the science of mnemonics or memory. All of these sciences touched religion at one extreme and magic at the other. Their practitioners conceived themselves as operating in some way as agents of divine or preternatural powers in nature, either constraining such powers to serve private purposes (magic) or working in holy complicity with such powers for the greater glory of God (religion). Among the great figures of the scientific revolution, Copernicus, Kepler, Gilbert, and Newton saw themselves as such *magi*—that is, as engaged in solving the cosmic riddles which God uses both to display subtly and at the same time to guard the secret formulae to know which give control of nature's powers. Many others, from Francis Bacon to the Puritan divines who patronized science, were deeply under the influence of this tradition.

More important then than the division between the rival mechanistic and organismic explanations of nature, was the division between the purely naturalistic and the Hermetic traditions of scientific inquiry. To the extent, for example, that Protestantism favored the new sciences, it favored those with a strong Hermetic component such as chemistry or alchemy, while it distrusted mechanical explanations as dangerously antireligious.[2]

Among the sciences closely related to the Hermetic tradition was mnemonics or the science of memory, or—to use de Nicolás's words—the science of the "powers of imagining." The art or science of memory has roots both in ancient rhetoric and in religion.[3] The ancient treatises on memory from classical Roman antiquity, such as those by Quintilian and Cicero, described techniques for storing in memory and retrieving whatever could be useful in argument or for persuasion. One is advised to build in imagination, for instance, a "memory palace," where each room is the repository of information to be remembered. This was stored under the symbolic forms of pictures, statues, number diagrams, and other Hermetic displays, often exaggerated in tone or in caricature, placed at strategic locations in the rooms and corridors so as to facilitate recall.

Information, however, is power to act or to reenact, and in so being is feeling, sharing, learning from, and commanding in a mysterious way the powers that fill the cosmos. Here memory touches religion. For God makes plans for people and things—God's will, as it is called—and these seek fruition through the powers and gentle influences—the actual graces—that suffuse the universe. It was the practice of spiritual, mystical, or Hermetic disciplines associated with these beliefs that as, for example, in the case of Copernicus, Kepler, and Gilbert directed much of their scientific work. The abuse of such discipline was magic, or black magic to distinguish it from the proper use of such discipline which was called white magic. Magic—or black magic—was the use of memory to constrain the cosmic powers for selfish interests regardless of God's will.

The method of Ignatius belongs to the old tradition of mnemonics or the cultivation of memory.[4] Such a discipline was not exercised just for the sake of recall but—in its religious use—in order to learn God's will. God's will was communicated through reenacting, through making live in one's own experience, those mysterious memory symbols that spoke of salvation, of the cosmos, and of human history. Such a reenactment was directed in the first place toward feeling the affects that accompanied it, then toward learning to interpret these affects correctly, and then toward making life decisions in accordance with their guidance. Following Ignatius, after a suitable spiritual preparation, one started with the Christian memory of the life, death, and resurrection of Christ. From these one learned to recognize the true affects of "consolation" and "desolation." Then, one moved on to the natural and cosmological environment, learning to recognize the same spiritual affects in reenacting the mysteries of nature. And from there, one carried the principles of discernment into daily life.[5]

What is recovered by Professor de Nicolás in his work is the radical flavor of the original sense of the *Spiritual Exercises*. This radical flavor was lost gradually in the seventeenth century in the interests, perhaps, of adapting the Ignatian spirit to the environment of large institutional responsibilities. It was not until the 1950's, after a century and a half of persecution and repression that afflicted the Jesuit order in Europe, that the radicality of the Ignatian *Exercises* was rediscovered. Among the pioneers in this rediscovery with whom I came in contact when I worked on the early directories of the *Exercises* in the late fifties were Karl and Hugo Rahner, Joseph Pegon and Jacques Guillet. The latter authored the article "Discernement des esprits," in Volume III of the *Dictionnaire de Spiritualité Ascétique et Mystique* (Paris: Beauchesne et Ses Fils, 1957).[6]

De Nicolás' "powers of imagining" suggest that there is a deep fraternal bond among members of the human race, as well as an affective "sympathy" among people, nature, and historical circumstances made alive by "memory." At the birth of all original newness, such as a new religion, a new science, a new philosophy, a new art or poem, there the "powers of imagining" are at work exploring and "tasting" some new found "memory." Like Ignatius, like Plato, such creative persons choose to obey the demands of this inner "memory" rather than the established practices of their times. The lesson de Nicolás wants us to learn is that unless we discover how to use and develop our "powers of imagining," we surrender our own freedom; that is, we fail to know how to innovate while preserving the continuity of our "memories" which are ourselves.

Antonio de Nicolás has collected in this volume the text of the *Spiritual Exercises* together with other writings of Ignatius that show how he himself used the methods of discernment and how he applied them in the case of other people. Principal among these are

Ignatius' *Spiritual Diary*, in which he recorded the spiritual affects ("movements") on which he based some important decisions for the governance of the Jesuit order, his *Autobiography*, and some letters, the most important of which is the *Letter on Obedience* to the members of the order at Coimbra that lays out the ecclesial (or collegial) dimension of decision making under the influence of spiritual movements. All of these documents are newly and beautifully translated by Professor de Nicolás, and accompanied by narratives and explanations that add immeasurably to our understanding of Ignatius and of the essence of Ignatian prayer.

I have known Professor de Nicolás for many years and seen this project ripen so lovingly over those years. There is a lifetime of experience with the *Spiritual Exercises* behind this witty, poetic, and brilliant work. Nevertheless, for all the insightful commentary that Professor de Nicolás provides, the *Exercises* remain a mystery unless they too are "memorized" and reenacted in the life of prayer. I am very happy to introduce this wonderful book to all interested in the "powers of imagining," but especially to prayerful readers who want to live *Ad Majorem Dei Gloriam*, that is, who seek the "greater glory of God."

PATRICK A. HEELAN, S.J.
STATE UNIVERSITY OF NEW YORK
STONY BROOK, NEW YORK

Acknowledgements

I WISH TO THANK THE JESUITS on three continents. They shaped my inner life. This volume is my small way of saying thanks.

I wish to thank first those fathers from Spain who assembled the complete works of St. Ignatius. Without them my one-man's work would have been impossible.

Thanks, forever, to Fr. Victor Blajot, who gave me the *Spiritual Exercises* several times, once for a whole month, and introduced me to Ignatius' *Spiritual Diary*. Thanks, also, to his brother, Jorge, a Jesuit, who convinced me I could forsake Spanish and write in English, but forgot to mention the labor involved. I want to bring from the memories of my youth my professor of rhetoric, a Jesuit who embodied humility almost to the point of oblivion; I cannot remember his name. From India I wish to remember Fr. Richard DeSmet, who introduced me to the philosophies of East and West and was not offended when I abandoned Louvain for the temples of Khajuraho; Fr. Pedro Arrupe, who reminded me in Spain and Japan that the first rule of the Jesuits is the law of charity and love; and my blood brother, Fito, Adolfo, a Jesuit in Japan, who has made philosophy and theology for us a family affair. From America I wish to remember aloud Patrick Heelan, colleague and friend. No one respects the decisions of others more than this Jesuit. He has made it possible, with his quiet presence, for me to continue and conclude the most solitary task of my life: the writing of this book.

To my family Mimi, Rachel, Tara, for their patience and understanding. This they know. What they do not know is that during this snowy winter they kept feeding the birds by my window

and that at least two cardinals, maybe the same one, on two different occasions, chose to cast their flaming, perdurable colors on the
white pages of my typewriter rather than on the snow outside.

I also wish to thank my students at the State University of
New York at Stony Brook, who showed me the need to recall the
technologies of invention.

My deep thanks to John and Jamie Maniatis, friends from
heaven, who by resurrecting for me a contemporary community in
tune with divine origins set free the sails of my becalmed inspiration.

My thanks to Mary Bruno, who found time and patience to
edit and type the last draft of this manuscript and to Joseph Blackman
for his masterful copyediting of this volume.

Introduction:
The Neural Connection.

This body is the field.
Bhagavad Gītā,XIII,1.

I WOULD BE LESS THAN CANDID IF I were to keep to myself the fact that it was only after I finished translating his writings and writing this study on Ignatius' use of imagining that the actual "text" of this book became visible. The visible appeared only when the intelligible act of writing ended. A long journey came thus to a close. The search for this visible and intelligible text began in my adolescence in Spain, was interrupted in India, and was taken up again in America. Why I feel compelled to set it down here in such biographical detail is not easy to explain. Perhaps others will read in these lines their own agonic search. Perhaps there is a community that needs these lines in order to discard the isolation of the search for the company of communal acting.

It was at the end of this writing that a memory of my past dissolved, through the writing, into a continuity of living. While a student of philosophy at Poona (India) I used to spend long hours in a solitary chapel at the time of day when the Indian landscape was most drenched with sun and human silence. I was always alone there, at that time of day. It was, perhaps, the total human silence at that time of the day that made that voice sound so loud and clear: "Too distant to be God; not close enough to be human" it said in English, when my mother tongue was still Spanish. The voice seemed to come from the tabernacle, and mysteriously my body seemed also to be there.

That incident changed the course of my life in many ways. I never ventured an explanation, nor could ever find one, but the memory would never go away; not until I finished writing this book did the pieces of the distant message came together, as if a puzzle had been solved or a mysterious koan had been suddenly decoded. My body and soul had then violently rejected an artificial

xvii

organ which through theoretical manipulation had tried to substitute the original organs through which I was and had always been making my life. I had no way, then, of connecting this body/soul rejection with the powers of imagining.

Remembering and imagining as practiced by a sixteenth century man like Ignatius de Loyola are very distant mental acts for someone reading these lines in contemporary America. But the same acts are much closer in intelligibility and visibility to someone, like the present writer, born in Spain in the thirties and sharing the life of a Castilian village. Remembering and imagining was our daily life. Cognitive skills, Newtonian physics, and Descartes were as much in the future in the village as they were in the sixteenth century. From my village the sixteenth century did not feel distant. Ignatius de Loyola, Teresa de Avila, and Juan de la Cruz were as close at hand in the village as unleavened bread, Moorish folk songs, and the Christian catechism. Many of the stories of the past I learned at the knees of my two grandmothers, who did not know how to read or write. To this day I remember not only the stories, biblical or folkloric, but above all the rhythm, the bouncing of the knees, the cadence of the voice, the heaving of the warm breasts, the smell of thyme and coriander. My worlds are still surrounded by horizons of tall wheat, as the village was framed by seas of waving wheat. A young child's imagination would burn like the wheat fields in the setting sun and row majestically through red and yellow seas towards vividly close, imaginary goals. For a child in a Spanish village, the main occupation seemed to be to remember and imagine. The men of the family, meanwhile, were busy administering law, teaching medicine at the University of Valladolid, harvesting, hunting, or playing music on the church organ. This is how I remember my grandfather. On the surface the village was unified as a Christian village by the hand of the priest, Don Salvino. With a firm hand and a loud voice he would tell everyone what to wear, what it should cover, how we all should talk, how we all should behave, for we were all Christians. But in the street fights the names of diversity would ring loud: "marrano," "moro," "bruja," "judío." The names would also enter our home when we four brothers would start a fight. My mother's voice would rise above all the noise and would remind us: "We are old Christians; let there be harmony."

Modernity came timidly into the village. Its arrival was more symbolic than real. When my grandfather died, he left the village some money to build bathrooms in the school—the only school in the village; also the only bathrooms. When in one of my summer visits, some years later, I visited the school, I remarked to my aunt how extremely clean the bathrooms were. "They should be," she answered, "the children are not allowed to use them." My family donated money to the village to build a canal to irrigate the fields. The village built a canal right there in the village itself; as a consequence, the only fields it could benefit were those away from the village, or those belonging to other villages but not our own. And so life proceeded as if it were happening somewhere else.

One day, however, a new fury shook the village and darkened the daily routine like a large shadow. Don Salvino, the priest, had been removed from the village by the bishop because, so the rumor went, he slept with his maid and put the land of the parish in her name. Don Salvino was placed in a convent in Palencia, and the village—why?—was punished without a priest for two years. None of us will ever forget those two years. The seeming unity of the villagers came tumbling down like a tree felled by lightning. Instead of a universal identity the villagers broke into myriad little clans. At the center of every clan there was a sorcerer, a witch, a healer, a shaman, a midwife. Sorcery and immorality broke down the old barriers and the old village confines. People lived more and more in the shadows. A group of young men banded together to remove any vestiges of virginity from among humans or animals. (They built a wooden stool to reach the mules.) There were shrines built to the devil in the bark of trees. The village resembled more a suburb of Ixtlan than a Christian village in Spain. Christianity never returned to the village in the old form. The new priest, when he took over the village, was never the authoritative, distant figure of old. He became a friend, one more man in the village. He succeeded in gathering the whole village in his house every night, even the men; but this time no longer because he was a priest but because he owned the only television in the village.

Though I have travelled so far and wide, the village has never left me. The sixteenth century seems not so distant to a Spaniard born in the twentieth in a Spanish village.

The "communion of saints" is perhaps the best kept secret of Christianity. Saints are often presented as if their lives had been lived in a vacuum, historical and human. But the saints lived their lives like us, having to make decisions about the circumstances surrounding them. Not only did they have to make decisions, but, as in the case of Ignatius de Loyola, they devised models to make decisions in a public domain often hostile, sometimes even dangerous to their lives, physically and spiritually. Because they risked so much to be fully human, their humanity is exemplary, and it should be studied as such; not, however, to imitate the external details of their lives, but in order to uncover our human capacities for creation. For such is the human condition: once a member of the species performs the extraordinary, the rest of the species, either singly or as a body, becomes capable of performing the same kind of extraordinary deed. Humans are neurophysiologically connected, they form a neural community, and each one of us has the power and the inheritance of such a community. My task, therefore, in what follows, is not so much to teach anyone new tricks, or new theories, but rather to lift the veils that cover human memories so that the original and common mental processes of originality and creation may become visible again. Let us make public the communion of saints.

Philosophy is the discipline I follow in trying to make intelligible and visible those mental processes by which we access Ignatius' texts. But philosophy is itself a problematic activity and has a problematic history. There are several "styles" of doing philosophy today and the history of philosophy is not something we have had from the beginning. Philosophy is constituted as philosophers "make" philosophy. History appears as history is uncovered. For this reason I take philosophy as originally hermeneutical, that is interpretative, in so far as it not only interprets but forms the tradition of philosophy as it interprets. Interpretation is simultaneously a constitution of history that makes itself as it uncovers the history of the philosophical act in history. Philosophy is not just, therefore, thinking, but rather, thinking-in-community. The same act of thinking needs to be at the same time contemporary and historical. Imagining, equally, is not just imagining, but rather imagining-in-community; the same act of imagining must be equally contemporary and historical. The coincidence of these two interpretative acts, in the present and in history, constitutes the community and the tradition of hermeneutics. It constitutes also the justification of what we understand as philosophy. The identification of these two acts, the hermeneutical and the historical, however, is not as problematical as it appears if we link this identification to the languages through which they are put into use. Language, then, will take into account not only the *external* tokens of sound, gesture and word, but also the *internal* tokens of intentionality, conceptualization, and purposive action, in short, the technologies of their use.

It is precisely the history of these mental acts in philosophy that makes the study undertaken here more difficult. Words like *text, technology, sign, imagining, thinking* are familiar to all readers. But these words have a different history, therefore, meaning, in different historical periods. *Imagining*, for example, has a history as distant as Plato in our tradition, and what he meant by this act and what the contemporary reader might suppose are not coincident. For this main reason I wish to clarify the terms we are going to use in this study even if at this stage they are only intelligible and Plato would frown on defining what has not been seen. The word *text* is used in this study in a technical sense. A distinction is made between a primary text and a secondary text. The primary text is here understood as identical with the body. The body being none of the empirical bodies we see but rather the human body as the recipient and store of all human habits and behaviors which individual bodies may repeat. In this sense the primary text/body is the field, the origin, the source. A secondary text is neither in the body nor the body itself but rather a set or sets of signs and sign-like material organized for reading, or interpreting.

A primary text is formed through the use of a primary technology. A primary technology is the habituation in the ordering and repetition of certain mental acts and languages to extend the human sensorium as far as the technology is able to reach. Because of the habit-forming character of a primary technology and its imprinting of those habits in the primary text/body, primary technologies are embodied technologies, movable organs, that make possible certain worlds for those trained in them or adept in using them. A secondary technology is the technology used for the reading of signs organized by the primary technology. What, for example, for an untrained layman is just a flash of light, for a trained physicist adept in the primary and secondary technologies of operating within the context of modern physics will be an electron, or some other particle, something real in his world of technology. What for the untrained reader is a "light" or "three musical notes of an organ" for Ignatius is God and the Trinity.

Primary technologies define for us the kind of signs to look for in reading. Reading is simply the ability of using the secondary technology to follow the path of the signs. Reader and user of technology must coincide in the kind of signs they select for reading. Cognitive skills, as primary technology, define for us the semiotic text for reading and the kind of meaning that is possible within that secondary text. Imagining, on the other hand, will give us different signs for reading, emotions, tears, a whole new world alien to cognitive skills, and that the reader must be able to identify as signs, on condition that he/she be trained in the technologies of those signs.

The acts themselves of imagining, thinking, and fantasy need initial clarification. Thinking is done according to some rules of logic. Fantasy, in all its manifestations, includes always a subject as the beginning, middle and end of that act. In contemporary practice this act is also called imagining. But in this study Ignatius' use of imagining and what imagining implies is of a very different kind. For Ignatius imagining is making images. Therefore one cannot borrow them, one must make them out of nothing, though the starting point is always memory. In its strictest sense imagining is a mental act that does not restrict itself to the mind, but includes also the body and is capable of producing a type of experience where all, except the subject is present. That is, the subject witnesses the process by which the consciousness of imagining extends as far as the body limits reach. These body limits are also part and parcel of the act of imagining as described in this study.

It is not my intention in the following chapter to trace the chronology of Ignatius' life. I will follow, instead, the strategy of dropping clues about the sixteenth century as background to piece together those features of Ignatius' native background needed to understand the emergence of the *Spiritual Exercises* and their powers of imagining. To the traditional sketch of the circumstances of the time, with its reformist, interioristic politics and theology, I will add a new feature: the oral/audial tradition which Christianity in general and Spain in particular had been counting on for so many centuries. In adding this last interpretative clue, I know I am not in line with the traditional efforts to make Ignatius intelligible only by the criteria of a literary tradition that mostly followed him. No one in Spain, in his time or even as close to us as ours, has stood on that literary tradition as the exclusive ground of human understanding. Philosophical reflection is needed to describe the whole range of possible and actual influences affecting the actual circumstances of the period and the documents under scrutiny.

With these introductory notes in mind we may now proceed with the rest of the book.

BIOGRAPHICAL DATA

Loyola, Iñigo de, Ignacio de, Ignatius de. (He used three names, but for practical purposes we will use only the last one.)

1491   Born in Loyola, probably before the 23rd of October.

1505   October 23—Azpeitia. Acts as witness on the sale of a horse (*MI, Font. doc.* n.32).

1506   Travels to Arévalo as the page of Juan Velázquez de Cuéllar, main accountant of the Catholic King Ferdinand. (*Archivum Historicum* 26(1957) 230-251).

1515   February 20—Azpeitia. Brought to court by the magistrate of Guipuzcoa Hernández de la Gama, on what was considered a serious case against him (*MI, Font. doc.* n.48).

1517   Joins as a gentleman the service of Antonio Manrique de Lara, duke of Nájera, viceroy of Navarre.

1520   Participates in the military occupation of Nájera.

1521   May 17-18—Leads a garrison of auxiliary troops to Pamplona.

      May 19—Does not allow for the fortress to be surrendered to the French troops.

      May 20.—Is wounded in the right leg defending the castle and receives medical care from the French doctors.

      May 23—The castle of Pamplona surrenders.

      June 2—5—Is taken to Loyola.

      June 24—Receives the last sacraments.

      June 28—Begins to recover.

      August-September—Asks for reading material, exciting romances about knights, which were then fashionable reading. They give him, for lack of these books, the lives of the saints. From now on he aims to imitate them. Conversion.

      October-December—Looks for signs in the readings of *Vita Christi*, by the Carthusian Ludolph of Saxony, which had been translated into Spanish and given a preface by the Franciscan Fray Ambrosio de Montesino. He also came across some lives of the saints (*Flos Sanctorum*) written by the Dominican Bishop Jacobus de Voragine, with an introduction by the Cistercian Fray Gauberto Maria Vagad.

1522   February—Leaves for Aránzazu, Navarrete, and Montserrat.

      March—Reaches Montserrat.

      March 22-24.—General confession.

      March 25.—Descends to Manresa, where he dedicates himself to a life of prayer and penance.

      August-September—Has vision by the Cardoner River. Inner transformation. Begins to write the *Exercises*.

1523   February—Arrives in Barcelona on his way to Jerusalem.

      September 4—Arrives in Jerusalem.

1524   Returns to Barcelona at the beginning of February.

1525   Spends the whole year in Barcelona studying grammar.

1526   Travels to Alcalá to study humanities.

November 21—Juan Rodríguez de Figueroa, Vicar-General of Alcalá, dictates sentence against Ignatius.

December—Ignatius and his three companions are asked to wear different clothing and shoes.

1527   March 6—The Inquisition goes against him.

April 18-19—Goes to jail.

May 2-21—Third bout with the Inquisition.

June 1—Sentence of Figueroa against Ignatius. Ignatius leaves jail about the 21. Leaves Alcalá.

July, early.—Arrives in Salamanca.

July, towards the end.—Encounter with the Dominicans. Goes to jail after three days.

August 20-22—Is absolved by the Inquisition but is forbidden to teach theological matters without studying theology. Leaves jail.

September—Leaves Salamanca and via Barcelona leaves for Paris. His companions abandon him.

1528   February 2—Arrives in Paris. Lives in a hospital. Studies Latin at Montaigu College.

April, past the 12—Moves to the pilgrim hospice of St. Jacques for lack of money.

1529   Lent—First trip to Bruges, where he met with Luis Vives, Erasmus' best disciple.

May-June—Gives the *Exercises* to Peralta, Castro, and Amador.

September—Moves to the College of Sante-Barbe in Paris.

October 1—Starts his studies in philosophy and becomes friendly with Peter Faver and Francis Xavier.

1530-1531—Travels to Antwerp and London.

1532   Becomes a Bachelor of Arts.

1534   April—Obtains his Master of Arts degree, and is known as Master Ignatius.

August—Ignatius and his friends, Nicolás Bobadilla, Peter Favre, Diego Laínez, Simón Rodríguez, Alfonso Salmerón and Francisco de Xavier met in the Chapel of the Martyrs in Montmartre to take their vows and lead a radically apostolic life according to the Gospel. The vows they took were of poverty, chastity, and to make a pilgrimage to Jerusalem. If the pilgrimage proved impossible, they proposed to put themselves at the direct service of the Pope, for in their opinion, he had the best overall view of the needs of Christendom.

1535   Returns to Spain to recover his health.

1536   Goes to Venice to study theology and give the exercises.

1537   His companions from Paris arrive and work at the hospitals.

June—Becomes a priest.

November—Has the vision at La Storta. Enters Rome.

1538   June-August—Persecution in Rome is resolved in Ignatius' favor.

November 18-23—Unable to go to Jerusalem, the first companions put themselves at the service of the pope.

1539 March—Deliberation to form a religious order.
      May 4—First decision about the society.
      June-August—The first draft of the society is prepared.
      September 3—Paul III approves the new society.
1540 March 4—Simón Rodríguez leaves on his way to India.
      March 16—Francis Xavier leaves for India.
      September 27—The Society of Jesus is officially approved with
      the bull *Regimini militantis Ecclesiae*, limiting the number of
      members to 60.
1541 March 10—The constitutions of the society are drafted.
      April 8—Ignatius is unamimously chosen as general of the new
      society.
      April 19—Ignatius accepts.
1544 February 2-March 13—Writes the *Spiritual Diary*.
      March 14—New bull *Iniunctum nobis* reconfirming the society
      and removing the limitation of 60 members.
1544-1552—Runs the society spreading all over the world and finishes
      writing the constitutions.
1554 April—Is ill and his health deteriorates.
      October 26—Accepts as a member of the society the daughter of
      King Charles V, Doña Juana de Austria, the only woman Jesuit.
1556 July 30—Ignatius dies.
      August 1—He is buried.
1622 March 12—He is canonized by Gregory XV.
1922 July 25—Ignatius is proclaimed Patron of all Spiritual Exercises
      and works related to them by Pius XI.

ABBREVIATIONS

The over one hundred volumes that have appeared so far of the Monumenta Historica Societatis Iesu are indicated by the following abbreviations:

MHSI: *Monumenta Historica S.I.*

MI: *Monumenta Ignatiana*, in the following four series:

MI,I: *Epistolae et Instructiones S.Ignatii*, 12 Vols. (Madrid, 1903-11) Letters and Instructions.

MI,II: *Exercitia Spiritualia S. Ignatii eorumque Directoria*, 2 vols. (Madrid and Rome, 1919 and 1955) Spiritual Exercises

MI,III: *Sancti Ignatii Constitutiones Societatis Iesu*, 4 vols. (Rome, 1934-8) Constitutions and Rules.

MI,IV: *Scripta de Sancto Ignatio* 2 vols. (Madrid, 1904, 1918) Documents about Ignatius' canonization and contemporary.

MI, *Epp: Monumenta Ignatiana Epistolae* (MHSI)

MI, *Exer.: Exercitia* (MHSI)

MI, *Const.: Constitutiones* (MHSI)

MI, *Scripta*: (MHSI)

MI, *Font.narr.: Fontes narrativi* (MHSI)

MI, *Font.doc.: Fontes documentales* (MHSI)

Mixtae.: Epistolae Mixtae (MHSI)

RAM.: *Revue d'Ascetique et de Mystique*, Toulouse

RazFe.: *Razón y Fé*, Madrid

MANR.: *Manresa*, Madrid: magazine of research and information on ascetics and mysticism

CIS.: Centrum Ignatianum Spiritualitatis, Borgo Santo Spiritu S.C.P. 6139,00100 Rome (Italy)

CBE.: Collection de la Bibliotèque des Exercices, Enghien-Paris

Exer.: Exercises

One

Text of
Imagining

1

The Native, General Background of Ignatius de Loyola

And I listen *with my eyes*
to the dead.

—Quevedo

We are old Christians; let
there be harmony.

—My Mother

GNATIUS DE LOYOLA CAME INTO THIS WORLD with the Spanish *Siglo de Oro*, the "Golden Age" of Spanish life, which extended from the sixteenth century to the first part of the seventeenth. Under the monarchs Fernando (Ferdinand) (1452-1516) and Isabella (Isabel) (1474-1504) Spain had grown from a collection of feudalistic dukedoms into the most powerful nation in Europe. With Charles V and Philip II Spain reached the height of its power in Europe and the New World. The sun never set on the Spanish Empire. The Spanish skies were filled with bright luminaries: El Greco, Velázquez, Teresa de Avila, Lope de Vega, Luis de Góngora, Francisco de Quevedo, Miguel de Cervantes, Juan de la Cruz (John of the Cross), Luis de León, Ignatius de Loyola.

Just one year after the birth of Ignatius, 1492, marked the beginning of the Golden Age. This was the year when Columbus landed in Hispañola, opening the Americas to Spain and Europe. The Moors had just been defeated at Granada, ending 800 years of *reconquista* and national humiliation. The Moors that remained in Spain, as well as the Jews, had converted to Christianity and become the new Christians, though some converted back to the old religion as soon as the new Christians were persecuted. Castilian had become the national language, gaining dominion over Catalan, Galician, Latin, Hebrew, and Arabic. The humanist Antonio de Nebrija published at this time *Arte de la lengua castellana*, the first Spanish grammar and the first systematic grammar of any modern European language. The first polyglot Bible appeared at this time under

3

the auspices of Cardinal Cisneros. The intellectual life of the country, reversing the trend of the previous century, moved from the convents to the new universities. At least twenty new universities were founded in the sixteenth century. Politically, at last, the nation seemed to be united:

> Un Monarca, un Imperio, una Espada
> (One Monarch, One Empire, One Sword)

This was also the age of vast dreams:

> la edad gloriosa en que promete el cielo
> una grey y un pastor solo en el suelo.
> (the glorious age when the heavens promise
> one flock, and on the earth only one shepherd)[1]

The dreams of Spaniards, however, were limited by the Spanish realities. The running of the country and the wealth were in the hands of the nobility, the first born of every noble family. The other children, even those of noble birth, had only two choices left: the army or the church. With the explosion of literature and art some found their way into writing or painting.

Those who chose the church had to make a further choice. They could follow the ordinary way and become clerics under the jurisdiction and financial patronage of a bishop, or they could try to go the way of the Counter-Reformation. Cardinal Jiménez de Cisneros, confessor of Queen Isabella since 1492, primate of all Spanish lands since 1495, grand inquisitor since 1507, twice the regent of Spain, had started the counter-reformation of the church in Spain at least fifty years ahead of the rest of Europe (Bataillon, 1950, p.1). Thanks to Cardinal Cisneros few countries or periods of history are as rich as sixteenth century Spain in religious reformers. Where there arose a human need, there arose simultaneously a saint with a community to take care of that need. Itinerant mendicants exemplified evangelical poverty, as did the reformers of old orders. The hopelessly ill found a champion in St. Juan de Dios; the priests a community of saintliness in St. Juan de Avila; and so did the slaves, fallen women, religious converts and laxed religious communities. But no amount of religious fervor and mystical exuberance could destroy the daily confrontation, at the hands of the Inquisition, with an equally religious bigotry obsessed with purity of blood and doctrinal conformity. It was a common experience of religious reformers to be asked to write down their thoughts and to present these to the Inquisition. None of the Spanish mystics— Ignatius, Juan de la Cruz, Teresa de Avila, Luis de León, Luis de Granada—was spared. Most of them served jail sentences or had their works expurgated or both. For a sixteenth century Spaniard with mystical experiences and dreams of reformation, the battle to be fought was not only between his/her soul and God, but also between the mystic's writings and the Inquisition. The Spanish Inquisition issued an *Index of Prohibited Books* in 1547 and another in 1551 so complete that hardly any writer of the sixteenth century was spared, from Erasmus to the translators of the Bible and the New Testament in the vernacular. The reading of scripture was, according to the Inquisition, an inexhaustible source of heresy (Bataillon, 1950, pp. 715-724).

TECHNOLOGIES AND THE NATIVE BACKGROUND

The present study tries to isolate the native background of Ignatius the mystic. It must then, of necessity, ignore other less pertinent backgrounds, such as the political, economic or even artistic. The present study is a systematic focusing on the Christianity of the times to single out the particular background the mystic embodied and the technologies he or she employed.[2] Throughout this study the words *technology, text, signs, body* and *history* will be used. Equally the words *imagining, fantasy, cognition, intelligible,* and *visible* will appear and reappear throughout. Each one of these words has a history and a local meaning depending on the origin of its use. In a world with such diverse technologies as the sixteenth century—magic, mysticism, reading, oral/audial, deductive logic, etc.—it is obvious there would be a power struggle based on some theoretical need in order to unify or reduce this multiplicity to only one technology; the winner would then offer one all-embracing image to unify experience and one language as the proper means of communication. Every culture and every period of history witnesses such a struggle. Contemporary America, for example, accepts as primary the scientific image, so that language, training in education, and image coincide in the wake of a tradition that follows the language of nature or science as the the unifying image. The manifest image—the non-scientific image—must seek from the primary image whatever legitimacy it has. Present continental—European—tradition acts the other way around. The manifest image is the primary image, and to it the scientific image must answer. In the sixteenth century theology enforced by the Inquisition created the scientific image of those times, and to it all other images and languages were forced to account and to find an adequate translation.

Inquisitions, however, are not only a fixture of public domains but are also present in the private habits of reading, writing, and interpreting. Inquisitional habits, such as those found in reading, writing, or interpreting are hard to break. They are not just wrong ideas, or even stubborn ideas. They are the result of the repetition

of certain acts or techniques which have become embodied in the
executing subjects to the point of total transparency. It is only
through a separate reflective act that the transparencies are made
visible or intelligible, and hopefully bias free. The techniques of
reading, for example, become transparent to the reader of this page.
This page may be read only on condition that the techniques the
reader uses to read disappear while he or she is reading. The same
applies to cognitive, imaginative, volitive acts that together form a
language, and the images of that language form the inner transparencies through which humans act, think, imagine and communicate.

Philosophical reflection and description of those transparencies are able to show their positive, acquisitive power. For it is only
through them that humans are able to open fields of discovery,
fields of creation and eventual communion. Human transparencies
are originally a series of actions, of mental and bodily extensions,
through which humans extend the reach of their sensations. Mental and bodily acts extend through these operations to make intelligible or visible a common structure which borrows from both the
world structure and the structure of those operations through which
the world appears intelligible or visible. The world of every particular
historical period is more than the sum of things facing our senses.
It is also the place of their creation, the determination of the identity of their shapes, the connection of our perspectives, which are
the instruments through which it is created, reached, seen or
understood. Human instrumentality is primarily our ability to create through the extension of our senses the sensible aspect of the
world. Human instrumentality, as opposed to external instrumentality, is the instrumentality humans use to extend their inner organs
through language to the most distant recesses of the universe.
Through language, the language of images as much as the language of propositions, its articulation, its repetition, its materiality, and its intentionality, humans have been able to extend their
lives and sensations to the degree that this structure of extension
and those of the worlds so discovered have come together. External
instrumentality, external technology, has never been as far-reaching
in human acquisitiveness and extension as those inner technologies,
those inner instruments through which humans have extended their
humanity to the heavens, the earth, and those other regions where
human emotions and presence are possible. Our human organs, in
such human extension, are not properly organs. On the contrary,
as Merleau-Ponty has pointed out: "Our instruments are detacha-
ble organs" (1964, *The Primacy of Perception*, p.178). Through
them we inhabit the world from the inside, through them we inhabit
that fissure between creation and manifestation, sight and seeing,
sense and sensation. The human body and the world recede as pre-

suppositions to make room for the more concrete human body and for the worlds of history: the origins of sensation and their visible and intelligible organization. Where the world ends and humans begin it is not possible to say. There is no historical break in this circuit.

One alternative left to us is to try to capture through philosophical description and reflection those structures of creativity, identical with inner technologies, that exemplify for us the effort at extension of the human, and that through this effort organize a public world and a public society.

For this reason we shall use the term *primary text* to refer to the human body in so far as it is the source from which meaning flows to human action through what I call a *primary technology*. A primary technology is an instrumental extension of the sensory systems, like language, that makes a particular inner ordering of mental and bodily functions available to others. A primary technology issues, then, in a system of public signs. Those signs are a *secondary text*. The primary text is the original text, and the secondary text is simply one of the commentaries, clarifications, or mediations through which the existence of the primary text's historicity is publicly known. The primary text lies hidden and is associated with some forms of bodily structures and behaviors that are not reached by reflective analysis. A commentator or reader of the secondary text, however, can come to know the primary text as the origin of the secondary text and correct the interpretation of one by the interpretation of the other. Third party readers of the secondary text(s) may be able to decipher it because they were trained in the use of the primary technology.

These clarifications will appear strategically more useful as we proceed. The need for such strategy appears clear when we note how the sixteenth century, background to the documents of this study, is a historical coincidence of multiple technologies which earlier or later on appeared separated or did not exist. What separates the sixteenth century from the previous history of Christianity is the appearance of reading, writing, and the printed word as technologies of reading different from the oral technologies of reading, writing, and recording. No dogma or theoretical definition had more power to define a sixteenth century man or woman than the technologies of reading practiced according to the cognitive criteria of the theologians of the time. The history of this period is best interpreted by describing the technologies it was able to master best. These technologies define history and historical periods better than any theory can. They define the history of Christianity as well as the history of mankind. These are the technologies the interpreter needs to embody before making the interpretation of any text, for these are the technologies by which the texts were written or transmitted in the first place. Let us imagine for a moment how the history of Christianity might have changed had this human fact been heeded by someone as influential as St. Augustine. Had Augustine been successful at developing the technologies of imagining as used in the mystery religions, rather than having been a failure at them, we might have had a different interpretation of the Trinity, and of the human, and even of the divine will. We would have had a different Christianity. In his work *De Trinitate*, Book XIV, he introduces chapter four with the following thesis: "The image of God is to be sought in the immortality of the rational soul. How a Trinity is demonstrated in the mind." Then he proceeds to identify the Trinity with the operations of the mind. Such is precisely the kind of identity that the mystics rejected, not for theoretical reasons but because they had other technologies of imagining that originated beyond the rational soul or mind, and yet were in the soul. Some of these same criticisms apply to Scholastic philosophy in particular and contemporary academic philosophy in general. They are products of a literary culture that takes the eye as the primary sense for the organization of sensation. Sensation is organized by the criteria of a semiotic model that considers its texts as based upon the properties of sentences as embodied in grammar, two-valued logic, mathematics, natural science, and classical physics. Such texts and interpretations tend to reduce all issues, all languages, to one or another form of logomachy: disputes about words, their meanings, relationships and implications. Invariably, the best entry through which all listening or reading should be done is none other than the originating technologies out of which the texts were constructed—a language, a logic, plus the repetition of certain acts until the whole technology became transparent to the users (de Nicolás, 1982, pp.27-271). The problem with technologies, however, is that when one is being used, all the others are excluded. Interpretative technologies involve not only the mind, but the whole body. They are embodied technologies, and sudden conversion from one to the other is impossible. Technologies are developed through practice, or are uncovered in the recesses of the body as possible historical uses of the body. The human body, apparently, carries these determinations in the neuro-physiological system as a code for possible users, as we shall see later on. The main problem with technologies is that one may exclude or cancel all others while one is in use. Most times we follow what is best accepted in the public fashion. Our educational systems seem conducive to the teaching of one and only one technology at a time. Thus we seem to create illiterate experts. Nowhere is this problem more urgently felt than in the technologies of the will, or technologies of decision making, and technologies of interpretation, or the ability to embody other texts' originating technologies. For this reason alone the documents here presented should be an exercise in hermeneutics and human mobility at least to remind us that our bodies are the depositories of many other human possibilities. To recall them is an effort to make them vividly present.

EARLY CHRISTIANITY

Christianity separated itself from the many groups and mystery religions of the times through two principal points: a) its historical relation to a crucified Jew, and b) its assertion that this historical event, like the life of every human, was part of a plan of a non-natural or supernatural will.[3] This will beyond nature operated by laws neither visible nor apparent and at times contrary to the visible laws of nature. Though that will was absolute, it was also absolute love, and in the exercise of that love it had limited itself so as to allow all humans to act against that will at will. That will had created out of nothing, but this act of creation was at the cost of a self-sacrifice in the Second Person of the Trinity, the historical Jesus. That act of creation was performed by breaking the original unity of God at the cost of his own incarnation. Men and women were free to repeat that act of creation at the cost of cancelling their own natural worlds, through the mediation of Christ. None of this, as practice, was repugnant to the spirit of the age. Mysteries abounded and some of them made similar or even weirder claims. Furthermore, technologies of the will were common among mystery religions (Williams, 1941, p.27). What really separated Christianity from the rest of the world was its need to define, cognitively and dogmatically, the Christian mysteries. Paul was the initiator of this movement when he placed theology above ecstasy, since it is the former which builds the church more effectively (I *Cor.* 14:5,19). The rise of the Inquisition was just one step more in the need to fix belief. In the beginning and throughout it was the fight against heresy as identical with sorcery and witchcraft. Later on, with the mass conversion of the barbarians in the twelfth century, it was the need to fix belief in order to avoid heresy. The Inquisition dealt only with theoretical deviations from dogma. At times it dealt with those deviations directly; at others it remitted the cases to the bishop's courts or the secular courts. The Inquisition tried to preserve a uniformity and conformity to dogma not only in external propositional communication but also in its *belief* that the sacramental and dogmatic life of the church was sufficient to guarantee the "security" of salvation. The people of the Inquisition were deeply fearful of the damnation of Christian souls. They believed they had a sure way of passage for Christian souls to follow if they only followed the rules. If these men tormented, tortured, and persecuted other Christians, it was not for lack of faith. Just the opposite: they had unlimited faith in the sacramental system they helped to define. Sorcerers, magicians, mystics, saints, and inquisitors all claimed that their powers of decision came only from God, the same God. What, then, separated them? Not being able to call the supernatural as their witness, we are forced to return to our common focus, their embodied technologies, or those natural links of causality that through repeated use became a transparent causal chain in their decision mechanism. What separates theologians, inquisitors, magicians, sorcerors, and mystics from one another is nothing more nor less than the means by which they perform their mental and human acts: their embodied technologies. For this reason the study of a saint such as Ignatius is important, for he carries for us those technologies that both separate and unify Christianity, those technologies that are the origin and the growth of Christianity, that resurrect Christianity from the dead.

The sixteenth century looks like a mosaic of technologies in constant conflict: the technologies of mysticism and theology, and the technologies of those lesser "wills"—the devil, magic, witchcraft, divination, and our own sinful will. But perhaps before we focus narrowly on them, we should describe them more explicitly as they surrounded Ignatius de Loyola in the sixteenth century.

IGNATIUS' CONVERSION

Manresa, 1522

At the age of thirty-two Ignatius left the family home at Loyola a new man. The old man, the brave captain, the friend of gamblers and women had given way to a new man with a new resolution: "feeling within himself the powerful urge to serve our Lord" (*Autobiography*, 11).[4] He made his way on a mule to the shores of the Mediterranean Sea. He spent the night of March 24, 1522, in a vigil of arms in the chapel of the Benedictine abbey at Montserrat, his resolution becoming firmer to dedicate his life irrevocably to God. But once this resolution has been made, where does one turn, where does one begin? Ignatius made his way down the mountain of Montserrat to a little town nearby called Manresa. There he stayed until February, 1923. He found the seclusion of a cave overlooking the river Cardoner and facing the high, sawed-off mountain of Montserrat some twenty miles away. There he experimented in prayer, meditation, and penances. It was a slow, painful process but also a time of new discoveries and new joys. It was a time of fierce reflection on a path that was eventually going to become the path he would give to others as the *Spiritual Exercises*. "At this time," he dictated in this *Autobiography*, "God dealt with him just as a schoolmaster treats a little boy when he teaches him" (*Autobiography*,27). It was here that for Ignatius a spiritual path was opened. It was also here, while traveling the path, that a long string of mystical experiences accompanied the journey. His *Autobiography* or *Diary of a Pilgrim*, which he dictated in 1555, and which is part of the translations included in this volume, summarizes this period, linking the exercises to the signs that appeared with those exercises.

First: Ignatius' spiritual journey would lead him outside of time, to an experience original to time and human history, the Trinity.

> One day while he was reciting the Hours of Our Lady on the steps of the same monastery, his understanding began to be lifted up so that he was perceiving the Most Holy Trinity as a musical harmony in the shape of three organ keys (*en figura de tres teclas*). This was accompanied with so many tears and sobbings that he could not control himself.
>
> (*Autobiography*, 28)

Second: He came to understand the Christian image of God the Creator, and the way of this creation.

> Another time it came to his understanding with great spiritual relish the manner in which God created the world. It seemed that he saw something white, out of which rays were coming, and that from this God was making light. But he did not know how to explain these things, nor did he remember well the spiritual illuminations which God impressed on his soul at that time.
>
> (*Autobiography*, 29)

Third: The mysteries of Christian life which Ignatius used for meditation in his initial stages became finally centered around the Christian mandala of the Mass and the Eucharist, where the whole of Christian life arose simultaneously for Christian memory to "re-member."

> One day. . .when he was hearing mass in the Church of the monastery already mentioned, while the Body of the Lord was being raised, he saw with his inner eyes something like white rays coming down from above. Although he cannot explain this after so long a time, yet what he clearly perceived with his understanding was to see how Jesus Christ Our Lord was present in that Holy Sacrament.
>
> (*Autobiography*, 29)

Fourth: He gained at this time an understanding of the role of the mediators, Jesus and Mary, on the path to the Trinity. This understanding is essential in turn to understanding the function of images in meditation and the "reading" of signs in the *Spiritual Diary*, included in this volume.

> When he was at prayer he often saw for a long time with his inner eyes the humanity of Christ. The shape that appeared to him was like a white body, not very large or very small, but he did not distinguish any distinction of members. He saw this many times in Manresa. . .He also saw Our Lady in similar form, without distinguishing the members. These things which he saw confirmed him then, and gave him thereafter such great confirmation of his faith, that he often thought to himself: Even if there were no Scripture to teach us these matters of faith, he would be determined to die for them merely because of what he saw.
>
> (*Autobiography*, 29)

Fifth: Contrary to the fashion of the previous century, when a convert to a spiritual life would find a propitious environment only in a monastery, Ignatius realized at Manresa that his cosmic vision had to find a community in the world, that it fitted the plan of the will of God as a means to bring that will to the world. The discoveries he made while in his imaginative meditations had a way of pouring knowledge and certainty into his cognitive speculations and learning. His vision by the river Cardoner seems to put an end to speculation that meditation does not instruct the intellect and vice versa.

> The road ran long next to the river. Moving along intent on his meditations, he sat down for a while with his face towards the river which there ran deep. As he sat, the eyes of his understanding began to open; not that he saw a vision, but (he came) to understand and know many things, matters spiritual and those pertaining to faith and to studies. This took place with such great clarity that these things appeared to be something completely new. It is impossible to explain the particulars he understood at that time, though they were many, other than by saying that he received great clarity in his understanding. This was such that in the whole course of his life, through sixty-two years, even if he put together all the many gifts he had had from God and all of the many things he knew and added them all together, he does not think they would amount to as much as he had received at that one moment.
>
> (*Autobiography*, 30)

By the time he left the little town of Manresa he had a whole plan of human and divine action. This cosmic plan included the will of God, the way to bring it into the world, and the method of the ascent and descent of that will through the mediators, the instrumentality of the whole human being. He also had the resolve to carry out this cosmic plan. For this he felt in need of two things: The cognitive skills necessary to make this plan part of the public domain and a community of men to carry out the plan with him. For these ends he had to study.

Loyola 1521

While recovering from his wounds, at the age of thirty, at Loyola, Ignatius read two books: the *Life of Christ* by the Carthusian Ludolph of Saxony (d.1370) in the Spanish translation of the Franciscan Ambrosio de Montesinos, and the *Flos Sanctorum*, a Spanish version of the short life of the saints or *Leyenda Aurea*, written by the Dominican Jacobus de Voragine (Varazze) (d.1298) and containing a preface by the Cistercian Fray Gauberto Vagad (*Obras Completas*, 1977, abbr. *O.C.* p.94, note 5.). Christian literature reached Ignatius through the medieval devotional writings of the Franciscan, Carthusian, Dominican, and Cistertian schools.

Ludolph's *Life*, expanding the *Meditationes Vitae Christi*, long attributed to St. Bonaventure (d.1274), enshrined the Franciscan tradition of poverty and love, especially the love for Christ in the crib and the cross. Ignatius, like Francis, saw in poverty the perfect antidote to the widespread avarice of the clerics. Ludolph presented in order meditations on the Incarnation, Nativity, stay in the temple, hidden life, public life, Passion, Resurrection, risen life and Ascension. Ignatius would later make his *Spiritual Exercises* a string of memory-points in the history of salvation using the images of the life of Christ. In reading Ludolph he also was confirmed in the practice of imaginative contemplation of Christ in the Gospel mysteries and many of the methods of praying which he later taught in the *Exercises*.

Gauberto Vagad, formerly a soldier in the declining age of chivalry, told in his preface to the Spanish *Flos Sanctorum* about the "knights of God," the saints, who did resplendent deeds in the service of the "Eternal Prince, Jesus Christ," and whose ever "victorious flag" these knights were following. Gauberto's preface contained a fundamental idea we find again in Ignatius' *Exercises*: to give an outstanding service to Christ under the banner of this King who has the saints as his knights. This desire to be an outstanding knight of Christ replaced his fantasies of chivalrous service to women (*Autobiography*,6,7). From Jacobus' medieval hagiography Ignatius found other fantasies to chase: "St. Dominic did this, therefore, I must do it. St. Francis did this, therefore, I must do it" (*Autobiography*,7). In the alternating lows of boredom or highs of joy which Ignatius experienced while fantasizing about dedicating his life to the service of a particular woman or the service of Christ by following the deeds of the saints, Ignatius "came to recognize the difference between the two spirits that moved him, the one being from the evil spirit, the other from God" (*Autobiography*,8). This discernment or testing of spirits was to become the main criterion for reading signs in his spiritual life, as may be clearly seen from the *Spiritual Diary* included in this volume.

Ignatius developed a habit which he never gave up, that of keeping spiritual notes. "He found much relish in these books, and it occurred to him to excerpt in brief form some of the more essential matters from the life of Christ and of the saints. So he began to write a book with much diligence. . .writing the words of Christ in red ink and those of our Lady in blue" (*Autobiography*,11). Since this copybook is lost, we do not know which passages he transcribed. We may summarize this period by noting that even when Ignatius read books and transcribed passages, it would be inaccurate to suppose for a moment that his reading was a proper reading of texts, the way we read today, or that in reading Ignatius was using the skills for reading we presuppose for such activity. Ignatius was surrounded by an oral culture in which focusing, in reading or looking or listening, was done the way oral people read, look, and listen. Their primary focus is not information, and memory is not used to store and recall that information. In an oral culture information becomes secondary, the involvement with the present primary, and reading is a memory activity to make present the past or in some ways to predict the future. From Ignatius' own description of those readings we see him giving them to his memory to fantasize, perhaps daydream, even imagining with a closeness the written word does not have in literary cultures, at least not in prose and certainly not in all poetic writing. In other words it is likely those written books did not teach Ignatius anything he did not already know from other sources. They did, however, remind him of memories forgotten.

Formal Studies, 1524-1535

A literary culture like that of the sixteenth century defines itself by technologies more sophisticated than the skills of reading. Reading, after all, may be done by oral criteria. A whole new system of communication is at work and one must embody it in order to belong to it. This is the task of education. As we read from the *Autobiography*, Ignatius found himself surrounded by pious people ready to follow him and his instructions. They were not literary people, they were "beatas," pious women and men who find in him the encouragement to keep doing what they were already doing. It is perhaps symptomatic of the precarious beginnings of any new religious movement how easily people are converted to it, and yet how little the movement picks up until it finds its legitimate place in the public domain, with the public tools. In Ignatius' case, of the followers that first surrounded him, none joined the society he founded, and most of them caused Ignatius problems, either personal or public, with the Inquistion (*Autobiography*,61). Therefore, on his return from the Holy Land to Venice in 1524 his mind was made up "to study for a time to be able to help souls" (*Autobiography*,50). Thus he began a long and laborious task of education. At the age of thirty-three he went to Barcelona and started the study of Latin. From Lent of 1526 to June, 1527, he studied arts at Cardinal Cisneros' great University of Alcalá. There he studied "the logic of Soto, the physics of Albert the Great, and the Master of the Sentences (Peter Lombard)" (*Autobiography*,57). While he was at Alcalá, he also worked at giving spiritual exercises. He apparently took many notes while giving them and reflecting on his own experience. Twenty-two years later, in 1548, it became the little book we know as the *Spiritual Exercises*. He often took leave from his studies either to give spiritual exercises or to follow his spiritual life, for he found himself very often dry inside because of his studies. He also found many spiritual temptations to distract him from studying (*Autobiography*,55).

Harassed by various officials and doctors of the Inquisition, Ignatius left Alcalá in June 1527 for Salamanca. He found the same difficulties there, so he decided to turn over to the examiner Bachelor Frías "all his papers, which were the *Exercises*, for examination" (*Autobiography*,67). He was again forbidden to help others by preaching. So he decided to continue his studies at Paris. There he arrived in February, 1528.

At the University of Paris, he studied humanities and philosophy. At the age of forty-two, on March 13, 1533, he graduated with a Licentiate in Arts. This prepared him to receive the degree of Master of Arts in April, 1534. Meanwhile he had also been winning his first permanent followers, all fellow students, brilliant men: Favre, Xavier, Salmerón, Laynez, Bobadilla, Rodríguez, Jay, Bröet, and Cordure. He did not win them over through literary exchanges, but by guiding them individually through his spiritual exercises. Then, for about a year and a half, beginning probably close to March, 1533, he studied theology under the Dominicans on the Rue St. Jacques. His professors had already made the substitution of the *Summa Theologiae* of St. Thomas Aquinas for the *Sentences of Peter Lombard. Ignatius obviously liked the change, for twenty years later, in Rome, he ordered his Jesuits to substitute the Summa Theologiae* of St. Thomas for the *Sentences*. Ignatius gives us a veiled reason for this change in his "Rules for Conforming with the Church" rule 11, "for they are the last to come on the scene."

We may summarize this period, however, by stating that Ignatius did not become a literary man, or fall into the trap of thinking that the rules of discovery through deductive logic are the same for men and women as for God. As far as Ignatius was concerned, the whole system of Scholastic philosophy was heuristically ineffective. It did not operate through observation, nor had it a system of apodictic verification. Ignatius' heuristic system, his system for decision making, would have a different origin, as we shall soon see. But since Scholastic philosophy was part of the public system of social communion and was also the public speech of the church, he made it a rule for his Jesuits to praise it always. There is no doubt, however, that Ignatius, after his formal training, felt a peer among peers. Others among his Jesuits were better theologians or literary people, better or more scrupulous scholars, but none had the no-nonsense clarity of mind Ignatius achieved in his letters or in the formulation of the constitutions.

ERASMUS

In literary cultures and intellectual circles there is always the temptation of grouping around a central figure or a current style. The members of the group rise or fall with the fortunes of the central figure. Few people had more intellectual influence in the sixteenth century than Erasmus. Erasmus became Cardinal Cisneros' favorite reformer. He invited Erasmus to visit Spain, an invitation Erasmus declined, for "in Spain there are hardly any Christians" (Bataillon, 1950, p.78). Yet Erasmus did not need to appear personally in Spain. His books were widely read, and his good name and fame came in the company of none other than the Emperor Carlos (Charles) V. The Spanish king was more influenced by Erasmus than any other Spaniard. He even named Erasmus his counsellor (Bataillon, 1950, p.81). It was difficult in sixteenth century Spain to ignore him or his influence. Neither Ignatius nor Cervantes could avoid it. Ignatius was a student at Alcalá when the *Enchiridion* of Erasmus, translated into Spanish, was making a furor among faculty and students. It seems that Ignatius was asked by his confessor to read the book. According to Ignatius' first biographer, Ribadeneyra, Ignatius picked up the book to read it but gave it up when he realized that his "spiritual fervor was becoming tepid and his devotion was cooling off." But according to Bataillon, who presents the two versions of the incident (Bataillon, 1950, p.213), the advice of the confessor was that Ignatius should read the book by Erasmus as his daily spiritual reading. Ignatius refused to do such a thing and kept using the *Imitation of Christ*, which was his daily devotional reading. His devotion to Erasmus, however, ran deeper than it appeared from Ribadeneyra's version. Ignatius' confessor at the time was Miona, a Portuguese priest and friend of Bernardino Tovar, leader of the followers of Erasmus in Alcalá (Bataillon, 1950, p.213). This priest, Miona, by the way, eventually made the *Spiritual Exercises* and became a Jesuit (see *Letters* in this volume). It is also known that Ignatius kept contact with Erasmus' disciples, especially Luis Vives (*O.C.* 135 n.). And it is well known that Ignatius followed in his own way Erasmus' pronouncement that *Monachatus non est pietas* ("the monastery does not guarantee piety") by founding an order very different from those of the fifteenth century, not bound to bishop, cloister, or choir. From this and other instances of Ignatius' relations with the intellectuals and the famous of his time, a picture emerges clearly. Ignatius followed a straight path that started in the Trinity, went through the Gospels and the fathers of the church, ended with the accepted forms of theology the church accepted as such, and avoided at all costs linking up with controversial figures, too new or too intransigent. It is a curious irony of history that Ignatius the mystic would choose the study of pagan humanities as the core course of Jesuit education, while Erasmus, the humanist, would rather have Christianity preached from the pulpit, in the classroom, the universities, and by the mouths of the European kings. If one were to compare "native backgrounds" as an exercise in hermeneutics, these two would appear irreconcilable. But Ignatius the mystic was a man of enormous political sagacity. He discarded nothing in his method of exercises (for he understood education to be also an exercise, not a search for content and information), and thus we will find in his *Exercises* a summary and new synthesis of the whole sixteenth century native background.

ALUMBRADOS AND OTHER SPIRITUALITIES

Ignatius was born Inigo de Loyola, and he used this name while in Spain and for a time after his conversion. Then he changed to the Latin "Ignatius," and he continued signing in this manner all his correspondence. In the beginning of his preaching at Manresa and Alcalá, he and his band of followers were named "Iñiguistas," a way to let people know he was a dangerous mystic. Thus the group was identified with "*alumbrados, beatas*, sorcerors" (Bataillon, 1950, p.546), and became an easy target of the Inquisition. When Ignatius was brought in front of the Inquisition at Alcalá and Salamanca, he was always asked the same initial question: "What you preach, is it the result of a learned doctrine or of the Holy Spirit?" The Inquisition knew the doctrines it was looking for were those of the *alumbrados*, principally, then those of Jewish and Islamic origin, later on Erasmus, Luther, and finally interpretations of the New Testament derived from any of those sources (Bataillon, 1950, pp.62-71).

The *alumbrados*, or illuminists, consisted of small groups of both clerics and laymen, mostly new Christians, who appeared in New Castile during the first two decades of the sixteenth century and practiced a form of interior Christianity. They opposed exterior and visible works and preached mental prayer. Four or five people would come together and read from the book of Job or the Gospels and would compare that reading with the translations of St. Jerome or Erasmus as a counterpoint (Bataillon, 1950, pp.62-77). These people did form a sect or cult or religious group. They gathered together spontaneously and thus were difficult to control by the Inquisition (Ibid.). Persecutions were mostly individual. Ignatius, who developed a spirituality on the most traditional lines of the Church, suffered through this comparison and tried to shed that initial image by which he was identified. The differences are as instructive as the similarities.

Franciscan monks had popularized mental prayer in their convents. A Franciscan by the name of Fray Melchor is identified as the leader of this movement and to him, for the first time, is given the name of *alumbrado*: "*alumbrado* (illumined) by Satan's darkness" (Bataillon, 1950, pp.62-72). It is another Franciscan, one who had earlier been a friend and participant in *alumbrado* conventicles, Fray Francisco de Osuna, who becomes the most influential exponent of a particular form of mental prayer. He published in 1537 his *Tercer Abecedario Espiritual* ("Third Spiritual Alphabet").[5] There he taught what he called *recogimiento* or recollection. This practice required no special aptitude and could be easily practiced by anyone. The goal was to empty one's mind from all thought during the space of one to two hours, so that then it could be occupied by God. If followed through, this practice would lead to what St. Teresa de Avila later called Prayer of Quiet, and perhaps to ecstasy, called Prayer of Union. The essential technique consisted in emptying the mind, like a yogi, of all thought, for "Este no pensar nada es pensarlo todo" ("not to think anything is to think everything"). By 1559 the book was put in the Index of the Inquisition.

Teresa de Avila, however, read this book, and her copy, which has come down to us, is heavily underlined and scored with crosses, hearts, and pointing hands drawn in the margin. It was as a result of reading this book that Teresa launched her spiritual career.

The *alumbrados* practiced also another form of mental prayer called *dejamiento* ("letting go") as opposed to *recogimiento* ("recollection") (Ibid.). In this form of meditation the soul remained passive, without effort or striving, in surrender to the love of God. Those who practiced this form of prayer did not look for ecstasy, but rather concentrated on the love of their fellow humans: "El amor de Dios en el hombre es Dios" ("the love of God in man is God") (Ibid.).

The *alumbrados* insisted on always showing a happy face. They were energetic and confident people. They were confident of their own salvation and did not believe one should feel sad with the sad mysteries of the Christian faith—death and sufferings of Christ; after all, the Resurrection was around the corner. Happy experiences were the clue to a happy life and women played a large part in their conventicles (Ibid.).

Their doctrines, their lack of compassion and fear at the mysteries of the faith, and also the fact that they could organize themselves without any church control brought the Dominican Melchor Cano and the powers of the Inquisition upon them. From 1524 through 1616 the persecution continued.

Other sources of Spanish mystico-literary authors may be found amongst Jewish and Islamic authors. They did not touch Ignatius fundamentally, but they express the climate of the times and the different technologies available.

Jewish mystical sources were most obviously predominant in authors like Teresa de Avila, Luis de León, and Juan de la Cruz. They all were connected or came from a "converso" background. A knowledge of Jewish mysticism came to them surely through their families—Teresa and Luis de León to some extent; Juan de la Cruz probably died without knowing his origins.[6] They all, however, knew such key intellectual documents as León Hebreo's *Diologui d'amore* (1533) (*"Dialogues of Love"*) published first in Italian and then in Spanish. In this volume Hebreo, a Spanish Jew exiled to Naples, proposes a philosophy of love as a means of obtaining union with God. The book is Neoplatonic and reveals familiarity with Philo the Jew and Plotinus. It also contains references to Ben Gabirol, Maimonides, and the Cabala. With the exception of the biblical Song of Songs, no book was more in the climate of Spanish mysticism than León Hebreo's *Dialogues of Love*.

Islamic influence came to Spanish mysticism via the Neoplatonic thought of the Alexandrians, especially Plotinus. This form of thought and expression was preserved and transformed in Persian and Arabic mysticism during the European dark ages, then transmitted to Spain through the Moors. Ibn Arabi (1163-1240), writing in Spain, is central to Spanish mystical poetry. But probably of greater significance was his Egyptian contemporary, Ibn al-Farid, and his long work, *The Poem of the Way*. The speaker in Ibn al-Farid's poem seeks union with God. The metaphor for attaining divine union is human love, the love for a woman. First, however, the speaker must divest himself of himself, of all ties with the phenomenal world, in order to find the woman (God) with whom he ultimately identifies. Juan de la Cruz's lines, "I die because I do not die (muero porque no muero)" are a commonplace of Spanish mysticism anticipated in Islamic poetry, as in Ibn al-Farid's line, "If I do not die/in love, I live for ever in death" (Brenan, 1973, pp.108-115).

THE ORAL AND AUDIAL TRADITIONS

The reading of signs is causally determined by the technology the reader uses in such reading. The appearance of the written word did not alter the reading of the written page by the criteria of oral/audial technologies. Other technologies had to be embodied for the "visual" criteria to submerge the oral/audial ones. One peculiarity of the Spanish mystics not as evident in the Flemish and German counterparts, and also one hardly touched by scholars, is the influence of oral and audial cultures in the sixteenth century. Scholars have assumed consistently that the reading of signs was always done by the technologies they had learned when they were in graduate school. The fact that a man like Ignatius was "little read" but of "great culture" was due primarily to his immersion in the oral/audial tradition of his period, which happened to be also the tradition of the church.

An oral culture organizes itself by criteria of sound and uses its oral creations to transmit its own technologies of listening and remembering. By these same technologies all signs are interpreted and information transmitted. But beyond the information there is a whole world of experience measured as proportion by the rhythms of the oral chant, verse, and voice cadences. People are instructed in the norms of experience by listening to the rhythm of the measure of proportion as it appears in sentences, poetry, and speech (Turner, 1983).

An audial[7] culture is the internal—epistemological—map the oral culture follows, knowingly or simply as the basic presupposition of the culture (de Nicolás, 1982). An audial culture takes the ear as a primary sense, and all its texts are ruled by the correspondence between the innate auditory sense of harmony and tone, and certain arithmetic properties and ratios; for example, of the vibrating string. Language within such a culture is primarily a language about wholes, frames, contexts, systems and only secondarily about things. It also possesses inner mandala, or protogeometries homologous with musical arithmology charting the path of memory and imagination. In fact, imagining as language marks the path the culture followed from its origin to the present moment.

A very peculiar feature of meditation in general and the *Spiritual Exercises* in particular is that ideally it requires conditions of silence more easily found in an acoustic laboratory than in a church. All the mystics, and Ignatius more so than others, insist on ideal conditions of silence for meditation so that the voice of God may be heard. Contemporary experiments in acoustics confirm that the perception of tone takes time and it is only possible under ideal conditions, which include quiet surroundings, good volume, and so on. To organize perception appropriate to the signal frequency takes even more time. (This might explain the careful selection Ignatius made of the candidates for meditation in view of their stamina to endure such prolonged tests and their sensibility to listen to the "signs" of meditation.)

Another feature which has remained a puzzle to interpreters of the *Exercises* is their division into four weeks. This division does not fit the tripartite division of mystical theology by cognitive criteria but it fits the audial character of tuning theory and of the classical (Platonic, Pythagorean, and more so Asian cultures) description of imagining (de Nicolás, 1976a, 1976, 1982).[8]

354

Through the Christian mystics and church fathers, and the tradition revived by Boethius,[9] the sixteenth century Spanish mystic shares with the Greeks an ancient semantic and technological text inseparable from the text of music as world harmony. This tradition, besides, was written down. It is to the harmonizing thought of the Greeks that the church fathers owe the first image of the world seen as a harmony patterned on music. We do not have the space in this study to retrace the musical grammar of the Greeks to audial cultures from India or Babylon. This I and others have done elsewhere (de Nicolás, 1976a, 1976, 1982 and McClain, 1976, 1978, Heelan, 1979). Plato is a large footnote to these cultures, as we shall soon see. In his footsteps, through Boethius, the church fathers turned a proto-scientific musical world into a microcosmic plan of salvation.

THE GREEK MODEL

For the Greeks the world resembled Apollo's lute. This was a visible image because for the Greeks *idea* and *eidos, thinking* and *representation*, were one inseparable act, a text in our sense. It was probably not only the so-called Pythagoreans, but Pythagoras himself who assumed a fourfold harmony in the world: the harmony of the strings, of the body and soul, of the state, of the starry sky. This idea and image of harmony has been alive wherever the influence of Pythagoras was felt, from Plato, Ptolemy, Cicero, Kepler, Athanasius Kircher, Leibniz to the church fathers and the workings of the imagination and memory of the mystics and the people of oral cultures.[10]

Plato needs to be studied anew from the perspective of a dialectics conceived on a musical map that preserves not only the musical model of the past but contributes a clear description of the technologies involved in the use of such a map. He is the one that divided the "divided" line classifying the different kinds of knowledge by musical proportions.[11] Through this division different types of technologies are applied to the lower part of the line—knowledge through abstraction and by the development of cognitive skills, and to the upper part, the epistemic part—knowledge through the skills of the imagination. While the lower part of the divided line provides knowledge, this knowledge is only "a shadow" of knowledge. True knowledge, wisdom, is the attribute of the technologies of the upper part, of the imagination.

The dialectics of the upper part of the divided line imply these four moves: a) Turning the soul in a new and opposite direction; b) using a different faculty than in the lower part of the divided line; c) through "recollection" finding different objects that are experientially different, like the Forms, as light is to shadow; d) producing as a result a different kind of knowledge, that is, wisdom. These four moves are made in the *Republic* 508e-511e, and 532a-534e. Furthermore, Plato describes in the *Phaedo* 67c-d, also 79e-81e, how the knowledge so acquired equals the experience of the Forms and how this knowledge is independent from the normal kind of knowledge derived from body sensations. The Forms may be known only after death or by "practicing death," by accustoming the soul to "withdraw from all contact with the body and concentrate itself on itself. . .alone by itself."

In the *Symposium* Plato seems to relish the musical vision of a world mapped by music when he describes the progeny of humans as Eros, love. Our parents are *poros* and *penia*, "abundance, exuberance, and necessity" (*Symposium*,203a). Consequently we live in mid air, in a region as vast as it is endless; we are the homeless seekers (*Symposium*,203a-d); never entirely full, never entirely empty (Ibid.,203e); we are always between complete wisdom and complete ignorance (Ibid.); neither mortal nor immortal (Ibid.); always mediating between heaven and hell (Ibid.,202e). Because we have no home, we need to make one every time we act, and because we lack nature, we make one on our decisions to love. Only when we give birth to goodness (*Symposium*,206b) do we experience immortality (Ibid.,207a). It is only in this act of creating goodness that we experience the immortal and become free from the doubts and indeterminedness of the middle ground, the homeless ground (Ibid.). For, in his own words:

> the divine does not mingle with humans; but through Eros, Love, the intercourse of the divine and the human transpires. The wisdom of this is spiritual; all other wisdom, that of the mechanical arts, is mundane.
>
> (*Symposium*, 203a)

When Plato sets down the technologies by which this inter-course with the divine takes place (Ibid.,210a-212a), he is, to say the least, intriguing. These technologies are not logical acts, thinking acts, but rather resemble the activities of the mystery religions; in the words of Diotima "the mystery of Eros and the initiation into this mystery" (Ibid., 209a-210a). Candidates focus on—visualize —beauty in one body, then, on the vocalized experience of that beauty, rise to larger beauties, all bodies, human institutions, sciences, the journey to Err, the cultural images. Candidates experience a state of passivity after these meditations; no longer are they able to control the course of their experiencing, but rather, a vision of beauty comes to them independent of any object: "This revelation will not take the form of a face, or of hands, or of anything that is of the flesh. It will neither be words, nor knowledge, nor something that exists in something else, such as a creature, or the earth, or the heavens, or anything else that is. . ." (Ibid.,210a-211a). This revelation is the child of exuberance (Ibid.,212a) and it makes the mortal one with the immortal (*Phaedo*,64a-84b).

In the *Timaeus*, by contrast, Plato uses music for speculative purposes, trying to build a new cosmogony around the exact schemes of Greek music and numbers, like those of Archytas. There he puts together how the world soul (a religious concept), the regulation of the cosmos (a concept of physics), world harmony (a musical concept), and the soul of man (a psychological concept) are fused. It is precisely this need to put together so many diverse elements present in the earlier Greek speculations of Heraclitus and Democritus, that leads in the musical harmony of the Greeks to an explanation of the differences of sound, of movement, celestial or human, and of the measure of that movement by mathematics and quantitative celestial bodies (Spitzer, 1963, p.11). The scientific dream appears exhumed by Kepler in 1618 and the whole musical world and its map reappears almost whole in the church fathers (Ibid.).

THE CHURCH FATHERS

While in Plato the musical map eventually became the *Laws*, in the hands of the church fathers the model underwent some transformations. For the Greeks the musical model was born from the lute, but they projected the model to the stars from which the processes of nature flowed. Furthermore, the Greeks became involved in the problems created by such a model; whether differences of sound were due to the physiological perception of the ear (Aristotle), of the senses (Aristoxenus), or to the ratio and proportion of mathematical data (Pythagoreans). The church fathers, on the other hand, used the model as a carry over of the oral/ audial tradition in order to express how antagonistic political forces are brought into "harmonious unification" to "avoid a discordant manifoldness"; for they aimed at the ultimate goal of "thinking together", making the discordant subject to the concordant.

The idea of musical harmony is prevalent in Christian Latin literature. Quotations from the Scriptures (Job 38:7) putting together matutinal stars and the children of God with musical harmony and angelic choirs are commonplace. Christians, in line with the Greek tradition, insist on *feeling* and place it at the center of all harmony, as the feeling of love. St. Paul in Cor.23,1, makes it a law, the law of love, that will be the cornerstone of Christian harmony. Only through charity may we reach true music. Augustine also established love, as the order of love—*ordo amoris*—as the center of what evidently is a mixture of pagan and Christian images: order becomes love, but only musical order is true love.

The same theme is present in Origen (*Comm*, to John,5:5) when, in trying to explain the transcendence of the monotheistic God that is incorporeal and unidentifiable with any part or the whole of creation, he calls God the "Symphony that is." Gregory of Nissa (*De hominis opificio* 12; dialogue with Macrina, p. 95) uses the same image for the soul of man "present everywhere in the body just as an artist is present in his musical instrument"; the soul informs different organs of the body as a musician elicits different tones from different strings. The soul is the invisible harmony in the contrasting elements of this world, either ours of that of the whole creation.

St. Ambrose's *Exaemeron* is a perfect example of this tradition and of the language of images about images. There he describes in a beautiful prose hymn the creation of the sea: image after image exemplifies the musical model until a successive transformation of one perceptible picture into another achieves a new fusion. One image mounts on another until they all converge in the transcendental reality, the background, of the one God. Christian art repeats the same method where earthy images may appear, then melt away and vanish. To the Christian eye they are not valuable in themselves, but only as memory points to lead to their original background, the Creator. Metaphors, as in the old Greek and Latin authors like

Cicero, lose their double directions. Metaphors for a Christian are realities of true fusion. And this technology of transforming the normal into the creative spills over to Christian writers in what Leo Spitzer calls "poetics by alchemy." He brings in the examples of the Spanish poet Góngora, who may lead us through metaphors from a maid adorning herself for marriage to Egyptian tombstones; or the famous passage in which Proust, through the use of metaphors, transforms lilacs into fountains; or of Valery's *Cimetier marin*, that "sea cemetery" reminiscent of the Ambrosian sea, which becomes successively a roof covered with white pigeons, a temple of time, a flock of sheep with a shepherd dog, a multicolored hydra. All this is based on the same Christian technology of kaleidoscopic transformation of images. The mystics will use the same technology internally, and make the Christian mystery a kaleidoscope for the mobility of their imaginations. The fathers of the church—Basil, Clement of Alexandria, St. Paulinus—will use the same technology to add dance and song to the Christian ritual. In all these cases we witness the same idea of harmony applied to all human acts in such a way that all the senses converge into one harmonious feeling (Spitzer, 1963, pp.22-24). Ignatius' *sentire cum Ecclesia* ("conforming with the Church") has this sense rather than one of humble intellectual subservience.

Augustine introduces into world harmony the same ideology he introduces in the Trinity: both are at the service of the operations of the mind. But even then, he is not able to depart from the tradition. Where Ambrose is polyphonic, Augustine is monodic. Augustine emphasizes the one pervading order as it reveals itself in the linear succession of time. Borrowing the laws of numbers (*numeri*) from the Pythagoreans and experienced as he was in the fall and rise of civilizations, he thought in terms of a creation taking place in time and developing through time: a creation with a beginning, a middle and an end; a creation paraphrasing history. Memory, therefore, will remember to read events in this frame. How can numbers that rule over man in history be reconciled with God? By showing that both agree through numbers. The death and resurrection of Christ is the one historical fact that is in "musical" harmony with the parallel event in the history of men (*De Trinitate*, 4,2,4 and 4,3,6). The cithara of Augustine is a monocord, i.e., a one-string instrument, for everything moves towards monotheism (*De civitate Dei*, XVII,xiv). The treatise *De Musica* mounts upwards like a gradual and slow psalm in steep consistency and imperturbability towards the One (*De Musica*, 6,17,56-58). The Augustinian hierarchy is a pyramid: at the bottom are the bodies which "are as good as high is their number"; then come the souls which "are changed by the wisdom of divine numbers," if they turn away

from earthly sin toward the Creator. For Augustine man's consciousness rests on temporal-rhythmical grounds; music is the field
of investigation, according to him, for the inner senses by which,
and by which alone, world harmony and God can be intuited; the
terrible mystery of how the different parts *aliqua copulatione ad
unum rediguntur* ("through a certain copulation become one") is
to be understood only by the spiritual senses of a man with inner
eyes able to see the invisible (*vir intrinsecus oculatus et invisibiliter
videns*); this seeing, however, is not a sensuous seeing, but an operation of the mind (*mente igitur videmus*) (*De religione vera*,32,
59-60).

Johannes Scotus Erigena, in the ninth century, uses musical
harmony in a way similar to Augustine's. Erigena's theodicy is based
on musical proportions rooted in man's inner senses. Erigena links
man's creation, fall, and redemption to the rising and falling of the
scale. Man's history is only a sign of his ultimate return to his
harmonious origin, the end of the world being the return to the
origin. Similarly, the seven liberal arts, in a circular movement,
come from God and return to Him; this is particularly true of
music, which starts from its origin, its tone—*tam dulcis sonus*—
moving through consonances (symphonies) only to return to tone,
in which the music is virtually comprehended (Spitzer, 1963,
pp.41-42). This is a very clear antecedent in this tradition of Ignatius' "Origin and Foundation" and the division of the four weeks of
the *Exercises*.

This tradition of musical harmony reappears in the biblical studies of the Middle Ages as a hermeneutics of musical concordants.
Church fathers tried to harmonize pagan and Christians' texts, saints
with saints. St. Bonaventure, the thirteenth century church doctor,
writes: "The whole of Scripture is like a cithara, and the low string
does not make harmony by itself, but with the others; in the same
manner one place in Scripture depends on the other, even more
thousand places look to one place" (*Hexaemeron collatio*,XIX,7,
in *Opera Omnia*, Quaracchi, 1891,V,421.).

This musical model and the tradition that followed it together
with its technologies would necessarily overflow into the language
of the period and provide a musical vocabulary which today makes
no sense unless we remember music. For example, music equalled
concord, which equalled temperament, which equalled temperance,
which equalled moderation; namely, response, agreement, harmonic
feeling, conformity. This might explain why in the sixteenth century mind of Ignatius he did not perceive that there could be a
tension between his mystical experience and the propositions of
cognitive theology, and he sums up this musical resonance in his
"Rules for conforming with the Church."

THE SIXTEENTH CENTURY

The linguistic equations derived from music, and their links to the Christian origins and tradition, so vital to the mystic, are to be found only in the written texts of oral/audial cultures. There the mystic found the embodied technologies of meditation for tuning the souls to have music in themselves. It is in this tradition and this music that sixteenth century Spain finds its expression with Ignatius, Luis de León, Teresa de Avila, Juan de la Cruz, Quevedo, Góngora, and so on. This is the time when "eyes are vocal, tears have tongues, and there are words not made for tongues" (Crashaw, quoted by Spitzer, 1963, p.134). The world harmony, destroyed by original sin and the fall of the angels, was restored by Christ, the "new string" on the world lute. The sacrifice of Christ restores the harmony of the universe. With the death of Christ all the opposing elements become reconciled, and so it must happen in each of our lives.

It is not surprising, therefore, that when sixteenth century Spain turns literary, it simultaneously explodes with a musical rebirth. Lope de Vega, Calderón, Luis de León, Cervantes, and Quevedo, to name a few, are clear examples of a tradition that has always been alive. They, however, are "reading" those literary texts by the criteria of their origin: silence as a source of knowledge reminds them of the *música callada* ("silent music") of the Pythagoreans and the church fathers. To one degree or another these literary superstars followed the advice of Quevedo when reading the texts from the past:

> y escucho con mis ojos a los muertos
> (and I listen with my eyes to the dead)[12]

The written simplicity of the *Exercises* is a testimony to the audial echoes of the tradition. Ignatius does not describe, argue, exhort. He weaves a text to engage memory, and this in turn to engage the imagination. His *Exercises* is just that, point by point exercises. This simplicity does not come either from ignorance or from knowledge. It comes simply from the technologies he aimed to exercise. Cervantes summarized this attitude with his own approach to the classical tradition of music in *Don Quijote*,II,26. There the protagonist and the puppeteer give the following advice to the boy whose role it is to accompany the puppet show with a story which he himself has to put into words: "Boy, boy, follow your story in a straight line, and do not tackle curves or transverse lines. . . .Young man, don't get into elaborations. . .; follow your *plain chant* and avoid counterpoints, which, being subtle, break up. . . .Young man, be plain: avoid the heights, for all affectation is bad" (italics added).

But this story would not be complete if we did not indicate that this musical model was so pervasive that some refused to follow it. One need only remember the scene in *Hamlet* (III,2) in which dealing with the human soul as an instrument of music is seen as a violation of the individual:

> You would play upon me; you would seem to know my stops; you would pluck out the heart of my mystery; you would sound me from my lowest note to the top of my compass; and there is much music, excellent voice, in this little organ, yet you cannot make it speak. 'Sblood, do you think I am easier to be played on than a pipe? Call me what instrument you will, though you can fret me, you cannot play upon me.

The past and the future of Europe rests more on these two attitudes about the musical model than on any other images, fears, or threats the sixteenth century had to offer.

SUMMARY OF DESCRIPTIVE STRATEGIES
TO BE FOLLOWED

We have tried to outline, in a general manner, the different regional backgrounds which together form the native background from which the writings of Ignatius de Loyola emerge. As texts of that period, these writings need to be read with the technologies of the period. Those written texts originate from different technologies, and by recalling them we will recall our own familiarity with those technologies.

Ignatius de Loyola wrote several texts; therefore, reading them demands that we separate the technologies of their reading. *The Constitutions*, for example, were written by the criteria of a cognitive technology and so are to be read. The *Spiritual Exercises* and the *Spiritual Diary*, on the other hand, were composed with a different original technology in mind. To the degree we are able to describe it, or embody it, make it visible or intelligible, to the same degree we will be able to read those texts.

The *Spiritual Exercises* is a prescriptive text, a how-to text, of meditation. Following the rules prescribed in this text an original, or primary technology is embodied. This technology articulates a language of images, organizes memory, and re-sensitizes the body of exercitants to the will of God. This will of God is opened to exercitants through their ability to prepare the conditions of imagining and the act of imagining so that certain signs appear—certain sensations—through those imagining exercises. The exercitant, together with some one else, has then to be able to read those signs and separate the right signs from the wrong ones in the secondary text—the readable text—derived from imagining, in the commentary text. This second, accompanied, reading is a necessary condition for the will of God—the signs of meditation—to become public, become decision in human society.

The upcoming chapters will develop these strategies in detail. We shall consider separately the primary text and the primary technology, then the secondary text(s) and secondary technology or reading technology, and then their appearance in the public domain. We shall conclude this study with a consideration of the consequences of hermeneutics. These strategies, the body of this study, and its style, are all dictated and held together by the special kind of imagining act Ignatius prescribes in his *Exercises*. This act of imagining is the primary focus—the background and foreground—of this hermeneutical study.

2

Imagining:
Primary Text, Primary Technology

OLLOWING ORTEGA'S LEAD THAT "clarity is the good manners of the philosopher," we shall retrace our steps before proceeding to state with more accuracy the leading differences between the two reading technologies of cognition and imagination. The kind of clarity we are aiming for here is one of design, or image, at the expense, perhaps, of propositional details.

When we talk, in general, of cognition and imagination, our talk is rather empty because they are not objects. They are nowhere to be found so that we may submit them to our examination. What we find instead are certain operations (embodied habits) and languages through which we identify cognition or intellect and imagination and will. When we look for the intellect, we find certain cognitive skills we learn, use, and repeat. In practice, these skills "read" perception, sensuous imagining, and what is called reason as a result of certain original or primary reading technologies. These "reading" skills are the skills that use the deductive method, or inductive and transcendental methods, or some form of dialectics in its idealist or material forms. Sensuous imagining and reason are subservient to those cognitive skills. Such cognitive skills are at the top of a hierarchical ladder of faculties and knowledge. Anyone acquainted with contemporary philosophy will notice how these skills, or reading technologies, determine also the varieties of contemporary "styles" of doing philosophy: analytic, phenomenological, systematic, dialectical. In every case the reading technology causally determines the kind of signs that are to be read and the kind of text which is considered to be primary. These reading technologies, besides, are so embodied in the subjects using them that the more transparent they are, the more they are identified with philosophy itself.

The kind of reading technology we are looking for in this description is that of imagining as prescribed by Ignatius de Loyola. We take this technology of imagining as being the kind of imagining which heralded Western culture in the form of Plato's dialectics. We mentioned in the previous chapter that this kind of imagining was the one Plato chose as his primary epistemology and the ground of his dialectics. This kind of imagining has the special feature that it is not based on images derived from sensuous objects. It is rather an imagining which builds images to the degree it is able to cancel the sensuous world. The images of this kind of imagining are non-sensuous. Aristotle, Plato's disciple, made a different choice, and images derived from sensuous objects became for him the epistemo-logical ground of his philosophy. The rest of philosophy followed in his tracks in a deliberate effort to explain, or describe, as much as possible—possibly everything—through natural means without any appeal to the extra-natural. This effort at universal explanation by one model of reason, by one cognitive reading technology, by one particular habit of thinking, has had, as a consequence, fatal deviations from reason. Power and reductionism have had more prominent exercise than reason in philosophical circles. This is nowhere more evident than in the reading of texts from our, or even more obviously, from other cultures. Historically, cognitive and imaginative technologies have had a long, irreconcilable oppo-sition. Since both, however, have been used by humans to create conditions for making decisions in the world, and since both are embodied technologies, both need to be presented. Amputations are unhealthy actions against human memory. Each technology, however, has its own domain of competence and may not be de-stroyed in the name of better reason or better imagining without amputating human possibilities.

Historically, cognitive technologies derive from cognitive episte-mologies, and their specific task is to read the book of nature. Imagi-native technologies derive from oral/audial epistemologies—sound criteria, and their primary task is to read the will of God.

Cognition rests on principles, imagining on origins. Principles rest on axioms or logic; origins rest on memory and are made by imagining. Cognition stands on abstraction, theory; imagining on experience. Through cognitive skills, models may be devised to apply to humans without any recourse to history. Cognitive models are ahistorical or fictive; imagining, on the other hand, rests wholly on history as its witness. It is the history of how humans transformed imaginings into human lives, and thus history becomes the count or description of those human embodiments.

These two primary texts do not divide the human psyche. Rather, whichever one we choose to operate through carries the whole human psyche with it. In practice, however, these two texts are complementary. What may be truly said in one, or done in one, may not be truly said, or done, in the other. Any attempt at mixing them up, or reducing one to the other, or simply translating one into the other, gives rise either to a hybrid text foreign to both, or to a futile exercise in power rather than reason.

These two primary texts originate and are originated through language; cognition originates languages based on some logic or another; imagining originates the language of images, especially the language of the image of creation. Cognitive languages give rise to beliefs; the language of the imagination to faith. Beliefs are handed out freely, at no cost; they are easily interchangable and their supply is unlimited. Faith guarantees mobility, even in the dark, that is, in the absence of beliefs and their concomitant sensations. This inner mobility is the hidden spring we all need to travel the discontinuous paths of life. This is the kind of faith the retreat-ant, in Ignatius' *Exercises*, needs to cover the distance from his own self as origin and foundation to the Trinity as the genetic origin and foundation of Christian life. Faith and beliefs need to be kept separate to make human mobility possible. One may have or not have beliefs, one may lose them, but one cannot afford to have a life, any form of life, without faith and the mobility of faith that guarantees human sensitization. Faith is like life: one has to make it to receive it. It takes effort and dedication and affects the soul as much as the body.

The condition of embodiment that these primary texts acquire in actual use makes them transparent to those using them, and for this reason a separate act of hermeneutics is needed to bring these texts to the foreground.

THE IMAGE OF CREATION OUT OF NOTHING

Phenomenology aims for a presuppositionless philosophy. Yet, philosophers in that tradition—Husserl of the *Crisis of European Sciences*, Heidegger, Ricoeur, Merleau-Ponty and others—following habits of reason as old as Aristotle, take as legitimate the manipula-tive control that scientific models have over people and things. In short, their whole philosophical project rests on a hidden mythic image that has organizing value for their activities as philosophers. A mythic image operates on the assumption that it is a necessary and sufficient condition for the organization of the whole of life.

These philosophers, on the wings of that image, take for granted the pragmatic goal of science to control natural phenomena and that therefore this end justifies the means of a fictive—non-historical—reconstruction of nature according to model systems of science that make the achievement of these goals possible. The *eidos* (essence) Husserl is looking for remains always an invariant in manifold profiles. This mythic, hidden image that has made much of phenomenology possible, creates at the same time the main reason to doubt phenomenology's claims about the suspension of the "natural attitude," or the possibility of performing, by this method, a radical "epoché." It is also for this reason that Ortega rebelled against Husserl for not allowing himself to go far enough. Ortega believed in a phenomenology and a hermeneutics practiced as "the sport of transmigration," or justifying itself by being able to get to the roots of other people's reasons. Philosophy should examine the roots, the origins of reason as they appear historically, not only one method of defining reason. Reason is plural and needs justification to be philosophy; it does not equal a "habit of reason." Reason, to be philosophy and justify itself, needs to be able to catch the differences, not only the similarities.

As mentioned earlier what originally separated Christianity from the many mystery religions, moral reformers, free-lance worshippers, and groups that followed specific rites, was the will of God, the epistemology of the will of God.[2] This will (the Father) created the world out of nothing, became human flesh in the Second Person of the Trinity (the Son), and performed these deeds out of love (the Spirit). This Trinitarian experience is the origin of Christianity. It is also an experience that has already happened. It can only be recovered by another act of love. Imagination, memory, and love form the cornerstone for gaining this experience which, because it does not appear in time requires the ability to create out of nothing, to fire the imagination with images not yet born.

The epistemology of the will of God did imply, besides, that the world was, and therefore could be, created out of nothing. Conversely, it also implied that the act of creation, human or divine, required, as a first step, the cancellation of the existing world, or worlds, of God and created /interpreted by humans. Furthermore, this will of God so humbled and limited itself in the act of creation that it gave free will to the humans it created. While the original state of the created human was God's image and was seen by God to be good, the subsequent choice by humans of knowing differently introduced in the world and themselves a rift in the act of knowing itself: it introduced the fall. This was a different and lower form of knowing dependent on human criteria of rational principles and cultural usages, dependent on humans away from God.

While knowledge of the original image is unitary, knowledge of the fall is diverse and multiple and stands on the ground of human abstractions, not God's will. Historically and originally both grounds of knowing are in opposition: their first historical reconciliation is through the death of Christ at the Cross. The second historical reconciliation is through the way of the mystics and the technologies they devised for the passage from knowing through cognitive skills and ideologies that humans invented, to knowing which is identical with or close to the original act of creation out of nothing.

The mystic's sense of humility is more than a virtue. It is a systematic condition needed to embody certain technologies, languages, and habits of reading, sensing, feeling, and acting that will make the act of creation, the new birth, possible. These technologies are radical, yet they are a revolution against nothing. They simply prepare the fertile ground where the will of God will make itself manifest. These technologies, however, are not the cause of God's manifestation and mystical signs. But without them the manifestation of God and those mystical signs do not appear.[3]

Understanding the mythic image gives meaning and organization to the whole life of the mystics and accounts also for their faith and language. It is always within mythic contexts that the life and action of people gain ultimate meaning. Without them, the descriptions that follow would be futile and meaningless.

SUSPENDING THE NATURAL ATTITUDE

In order to proceed more rapidly in this description, I also take it that there is a primary text for each mystic, in particular for Ignatius, and therefore for anyone who performs the full spiritual exercises with some proficency.

Humans are creatures of habit. Habits are not only ideas but also a whole range of operations that act through the human body with complete transparency to the subjects. The human body abhors a vacuum; it must be active at all times. Habits, therefore, can only be changed through other habits. The more radical and transparent the habit, the more radical and difficult the change, and the deeper the concentration and dedication needed for the implementation of the new habit. Habits of thought are the most difficult to change. Other thoughts, good or bad, sublime or stupid, only reinforce an already existing habit of thought. Psychologizing will not do. A complete philosophical overhaul is needed.

In the first Annotation to the *Spiritual Exercises* (abbr. *Exer.*) Ignatius de Loyola describes what this philosophical overhaul consists of. It consists of exercises, and he also describes the purpose. By spiritual exercises he means any discipline that will exercise the spirit, like meditation, vocal and mental prayer, devotions, examination of conscience, just as walking, running, or jogging are physical exercises (*Exer.*1). These exercises are primarily for only one purpose: to transform the will of the subject from attachment to his own self, as center and origin of action, to attachment to the will of God, as origin and foundation of all action, and in this manner to guide one's life (*Exer.*23).

Many people have had these general aims, but no one has had the audacity and systematic insight to develop strategies that would turn good wishes into realities. Simultaneously, no one has dared the divinity in such concrete and human terms as Ignatius did. He truly believed these exercises were the patrimony of every Christian. Ignatius gathered all his strategies (and God's eventual participation in them) within the short exercise period of four weeks, a short month considering the stakes. (As we may see from his *Spiritual Diary*, Ignatius never did meditation as he describes in his *Exercises*. It was his experience, and optimistically he foresaw that after a whole month of exercises everyone would have such powers of concentration and be on such friendly terms with the divinity that they would be able to elicit, on the spur of the moment, the powers of those technologies they so laboriously cultivated. Ignatius did just that. We see him in his *Diary* concentrating for ten minutes before Mass, or walking to it, and then using the Mass like a mandala to reach his decision.)

It is a common complaint of the mystics, and of those who take up meditation seriously, that the beginnings are the most difficult. It is a time of trial, of meandering about looking for new ways, of disorientation, of aridity.[4] Ignatius, on the other hand, does not seem to want to take those difficulties too seriously. From the beginning of the exercises he sets the retreatant into a sort of assault on the divinity.

Ignatius is convinced that that inner space may be revealed, opened, touched, by that unique act of creation, meditation, and by no other creature, object, or sensation. Only God, he believes, owns the human center (*Exer.*, 316,322,329,330). But this center is covered by a communications system, a natural attitude, a self-indulgence, that impedes human access to it. Ignatius' initiation into this mystery is a definite effort at breaking down this communications system and building a new one through which the soul and God may communicate. Since the external communications system has also, through language and its repetition, through the use of the faculties and the repetition of this use, sensitized the subject into a series of body sensations and their habitual comfort, the new system of communications will aim precisely at destroying, suspending, this habitualization. The exercises start in the human body and end in the transformation of this same human body. A new language is given the retreatant, a new memory and a new imagination. Through this retraining, a new will might emerge in harmony with the will of God.

The first week of the exercises is one of trial and training. It is a time of testing the will of the retreatant and the body of that will. Not everyone's body is ready for meditation at the particular time chosen for the exercises. Ignatius wants to single out those who might continue from those who should proceed no further. Though the exercises carry so much promise, they could also be dangerous to one's health if not done under the best physical conditions. Ignatius says of those with *poco suiecto* ("little temperament, lack of stamina and preparation") that "they should not proceed any further" (*Exer.*,18). This first week is one of violence to the body habits of the retreatant. He is asked to search for a "place" (*Exer.*, 20) away from the ordinary place to which he/she is normally accustomed: the cave of Manresa, a lonely room, a room different from the one usually inhabited, a different house, a monastery in the country, an unaccustomed place with controlled lighting where the retreatant has to invent new body habits and where outside communications systems do not reach. The retreatant is instructed about lights: less in the first and third weeks, more in the second and fourth (*Exer.*,79). The retreatant's body is subjected to new and calculated positions: kneeling, prostrating oneself face down, standing with the head bent down, pacing, walking, sitting rigidly (*Exer.*, 74,75,76,77), lowering the eyes, raising the eyes, closing out sounds, listening to special rhythms as the meditation dictates (*Exer.*,81,258). The whole body of the retreatant must be reeducated until it becomes like a repellent to the familiar external communications systems and habits. All gestures, facial expressions, and bodily movements must be painstakingly gone over as if in slow motion so that the body becomes impervious to the outside and begins to learn the technologies of facing and gathering within.

The will of the retreatant is now used as a surgical knife to cut some openings into that interior world. The whole attention is now away from the world—even if in order to achieve this, the different moments of life, of a day, of a prayer, of a meditation, of an examination of conscience, of an act, a look, or a thought—must be cut to pieces, one by one (*Exer.*,24,25,26,27,33,34,38,42,43). But on the trail of these acts of the will a language is being formed: "intense pain and tears" (*Exer.*,55); "ugliness and evil. . .of sin" (*Exer.*,57);

comparisons of God's attributes and one's own, wisdom and ignorance, omnipotence and weakness, justice and inequity, goodness and selfishness (*Exer.*,59); *esclamación admirative con crescido afecto* ("amazed exclamations filled with a growing emotion") (*Exer.*,60); self-pity, gratitude, amazement, disgust, consolation, desolation (*Exer.*,62). These are the signs of this language the will has started to create by turning the entire life and every minute of it into an interior timetable in which only the "chimes of eternity" are heard. By the time the will becomes habituated to those exercises, there will no longer be room for external and familiar languages. The clock of the "solitary region" is now running. Waking up is determined by this time table (*Exer.*,74), and so are the time and kind of prayer; examination of conscience (*Exer.*,43), the type of examination of conscience; meditation; conversations with the guide of the exercises; what to bring to those conversations; relaxation of emotion by changing the type of prayer to a lighter form (*Exer.*,238); rhythmic breathing (*Exer.*,258); contemplation on the ten commandments (*Exer.*,238), on the seven deadly sins (*Exer.*, 244), on the three powers of the soul (*Exer.*,246); or when to slow the meditation by considering every word pronounced (*Exer.*,249), or just the opposite, concentration only on those points of meditation "where I felt the most intense spiritual feeling" (*Exer.*,62). And, of course, we must not forget, a new diet has to be included (*Exer.*,84), and one should sleep with less comfort than one is used to and cause sensible pain to the body (*Exer.*,85). Even while going to sleep there is no stopping this clock: one should prepare oneself for the coming day by going over the memory-points of the meditation one is going to make in the morning (*Exer.*,73), but not for too long, for one must sleep. But as soon as awake, while dressing, one should already bring to mind what one is about to meditate upon. Neither the clock of the "solitary region" nor the timetable of eternity allow for any external language to come in; there are no cracks between exercises: *No dando lugar a unos pensamientos ni a otros* ("not to make room for this kind of thoughts or any other") (*Exer.*,74).

Spiritual exercises, however, do not compare to an army "boot camp." Ignatius is very sensitive to that: "If the one giving the exercises sees that he who makes them is in desolation or tempted, he should not be harsh or severe with him, but rather gentle and soft. . ." (*Exer.*,7). And if at times Ignatius recommends acting against natural inclinations (*agere contra, Exer.*,13,16), as when he says that if one feels like not going the length of a whole hour in meditation one should therefore at once decide to go for one hour and a half, he also makes the exercitant aware that all those things are only means to an end. One should use, therefore, those things only *tanto. . .cuanto* ("as much as") (*Exer.*,23) one needs to in order to achieve those ends. For in the end the exercises are for the soul to get ready to receive the will of God, not just to follow suggestions from the guide of the exercises, or confessors, or friends, or enemies: ". . .it is much better, in searching for the divine Will, to let Our Creator and Lord communicate Himself to the devout soul. . ." (*Exer.*,15).

The exercises of the will and the hint of the language that emerges build around the inner space of the retreatant a scaffolding of inner habits ready to sustain the new emerging body of meditation. Soon the drama unfolds: the retreatant experiences the excitement of the new, and the bereavement of the familiar. The retreatant is not guaranteed that the divinity may enter the solitary space, while the familiar will no longer feel the same. The retreatant can never anticipate what is about to happen or even if it will happen. One needs to give up everything, and yet, one cannot anticipate that the empty spaces are going to be filled. This journey needs raw human faith. Except for one thing: the exercises themselves, which keep opening horizons of language. And another thing: memory and its predictability. The exercises in time become established in memory.

MEMORY AND PREDICTABILITY

The origin of Christianity was an experience that had already happened. It originated outside of time with the Trinity and entered time in the Second Person of the Trinity through the mystery of the Incarnation and Redemption. It is precisely because of the fact that this experience has already happened that for every Christian to know is to remember. Memory makes of Christians communities and religion; it is the common ground of memories, on which all stand, that joins them as community. Without memory Christianity could not be articulated. Christ had already set down the internal law of the community: "Do this in remembrance of me" (*Luke* 22:19). And even when the Father will send, in Christ's name, the comforter, the Spirit, he will do it to "bring all things to your remembrance" (*John* 14,25). To be a Christian is primarily to live on memory, to turn memory around, to store memories, to turn every sign, whatever its origin, into a memory-point, and to articulate those memories so that memory remains active. Those memories are the remembrance of the will of God in operation. They are of a past actively present and therefore, being God's will, with a future. It is memories that predictably organize the future—but not without human effort and participation.

Strictly speaking the spiritual exercises are a string of memories, of memory-points. Even as written, the exercises are not to be read only for information or edification or content. Each and every word is slowly and carefully chiselled out so that it becomes a memory-point for action, or for making memory.

On its journey, the retreatant's will searches life for sins, the day divided into exercises of the will to discover and remove flaws, exercises primarily in memory: memories that travel back and forth, up and down, within the perimeters of a human life. Meditation begins by "bringing to memory" the first sin of the angels (*Exer.*, 50); "by bringing to memory" the sin of Adam and Eve (*Exer.*,51); "by bringing to memory" our sins (*Exer.*,52), all the sins of a life time (*Exer.*,56), year by year, place by place, looking at the places lived, conversations held, work done (Ibid.); by bringing to memory the souls in hell (*Exer.*,71); etc. He uses memory to instruct the intellect: "so that the intellect, without meandering, may reason with concentration going over the reminiscences (memories) of the things contemplated in past exercises. . ." (*Exer.*,64). Ignatius literally means, through the *Exercises*, "to bring all things into remembrance."

To bring all things into remembrance, however, demands from us certain shifts in technologies. In every case human effort is needed.

Ignatius de Loyola shared with the other mystics of his time habits of reading different from ours. Early in his *Autobiography* (*Autobiography*, 6 and 7), he lets us know how he used reading in order to fix memory points and visualize the things the saints did and that he could also do. With these memories he would then dream of doing greater things for the service of God. In this manner Ignatius kept his mind well-occupied. Ignatius' knowledge came through the experience of meditation, not through reasoning out the mysteries of Christianity. It is true that the *Exercises* use the three potencies or faculties of the soul, but it is by turning all things into remembrance or memory that they are held together. The flight of the soul will eventually take place through imagining.[5]

Turning all things into remembrance is not an easy task, however. The memories of Christianity are not factual history, are not human deeds. In order to turn all things into remembrance one must perform a radical hermeneutical act. How does one remember "the souls in hell" or the Trinity before Creation, or angels sinning, or how Christ used his five senses, or even one's sins without a radical reinterpretation of those cognitive ciphers? Those are living memories to a Christian and therefore recoverable. To recall them is to call them, and, therefore, they may be articulated in language. They are the language in which imagining takes place.[6] On these memory units imagining will act. This memory bank is the only security the retreatant has that the system works; it is the lifeline, the communications system, of Christianity. It is in this sense, of memory in use, that memory acts with an element of predictability in the system. Memory, by turning back, vivifies the retreatant and guarantees the future. Memory mediates all human action: it is language, and it is divine human life.

IMAGINING AS INDIVIDUAL DISMEMBERMENT

Language, in order not to be a dead language, must be used, spoken, written down. Memories would become dead if not activated through acts of imagining.

Contrary to contemporary practices in psychology in which imagining is guided so that individuals and groups share and are guided in imagining the same image,[7] or in which archetypal images are the object and goal of imagining,[8] Ignatius, astonishingly enough, leaves retreatants entirely to their "own abilities" (*Exer.*,18) when it comes down to guiding them in the act of imagining. Ignatius provides memory points, describes how to imagine, but the images to be imagined are absent from the *Exercises*. Actual imagining is the retreatants' exercise. But this may be understood since Ignatius cannot draw on any existing subjective reservoir of images with which the subject may be more or less familiar, even though through some of those images individuals have experienced transformations, even creations. Ignatius displaces retreatants from any subjective or objective pool of images and vigorously transplants them to an imageless field where the absence of images will force the exercise of creating them. This kind of imagining is the more powerful because it does not rest on images anyone ever before created: The images are to be born from a sheer power of imagining.

This strategy of Ignatius, then, which is so demanding, rests more on the actual technologies of imagining than on any images. Thus his insistence on technology: concentration in order to bring out the pure image, the uncontaminated image, the image in perfect solitude, the original image, the divine image. One cannot borrow it, one must create it. The image created in meditation is the only image that will gain currency. In this creation all other images are automatically excluded. The whole technology developed in the *Exercises* has one aim: the perfect image, for it is in it and through it that God's signs will appear. The image will turn to language and return to the public domain.

The pure image, the original image, will penetrate the public domain if first it penetrates the material body of the retreatant. This material body is always set facing the scene, the image, to be imagined. But this material body is a fluid body which through imagining may become a slave in the Nativity, a knight in the two kingdoms, a sinner facing the Cross; or may change sizes if compared to other men, the angels, God (*Exer.*,58); it may become a vermin worth "many hells" (*Exer.*,60) or the temple, the image of God, animated by God, sensitized by him (*Exer.*,235).

Technically, however, this fluid material body of the retreatant becomes dismembered through the act of imagining. Ignatius conceives imagining as an act of dismembering the senses by running them in isolation through the image being made.[9]

Retreatants are placed in front of a scene and asked to make their own *contemplación viendo el lugar* ("contemplation seeing the place"). They are asked to make up the scene with exhausting detail: the road: how long, wide, flat, whether running through valleys or hills; the cave: how big, small, how high, how low, how furnished (*Exer.*, 112). Imagine hell, the width and depth and length (*Exer.*,65), or imagine the synagogue, villages, and castles (*Exer.*, 91), or the Three Divine Persons (*Exer.*,102), or Mary riding a donkey or Joseph pulling an ox (*Exer.*,110). But for Ignatius the image alone is not the source of signs or of the system of signs. The image on recall may be called to memory, but the actual birth of the signs or the system of signs does not take place until the retreatant proceeds, through imagining, to read the image through his own dismembered sensorium. The perfect image, the solitary image, the divine image is set into motion through the sensuous motion of the retreatant's senses as he or she runs them, one at a time, through the image. It takes the reading of an image by each sense for it to become a mediation between the exercitant and signs of God's will. The efficacy of the image is made possible on condition that the subject as a fixed unity be kept elusively absent in the act of imagining. What retreatants are asked to do is to lend sight, sound, smell, touch, and movement to the image. They vitialize the image through their dismembered sensorium. Each sense must read the image separately, each sense must sensitize the image separately, each sense must read/write its separate movement on the image separately. What is done through visualization must be repeated through hearing, smelling, touching, moving. This applies to the exercises on hell, the Nativity, the Cross, and Resurrection; in short, to any exercises where images are to be imagined.

It is the exercise of imagining that makes possible the appearance of images and signs and the articulation of both as a language. Images, of themselves, do nothing. The retreatant must exercise them by reading/writing sensation on them. In its preparatory stage imagining is a technology that if performed in all its purity will create signs and articulate itself into a language. It will force sensible signs to appear in the act of sensitizing the image of meditation.

As a consequence, and because it is an embodied technology, it will also desensitize subjects to their original unities and attachments while sensitizing them to fresh and new sensations. Imagining, therefore, with its preliminary organization of bodily acts, memories, and sensitizing of images is the primary text through which a language appears and may be articulated. Without this primary text, this technology of habituation, written in the human body, neither signs nor the language of their articulation will appear. This primary text becomes through imagining the primary technology, causal origin of the diacritical system of signs that are to be read. Those signs will have several readers: The retreatant, his director or confessor, his spiritual guide, whoever is trained to reach such text. The readers must be acquainted with the primary technology and the primary text. They must be so expert in such reading that they may read the signs even if they are not the authors of the primary technology or the reader/writer of the primary text. It is on this condition that the primary text and primary technology produce not only a language but also the possibility of its articulation, either as a private articulation to a spiritual guide, or as a public articulation for the public domain. We shall leave these points for a later development. Meanwhile let us continue with imagining.

MEDIATION, DEATH, TRANSFORMATION

The story of imagining is, as yet, an unfinished one. Ignatius de Loyola is not concerned with texts, semiotics, or language. The purpose of his *Exercises* is to bring about a transformation in human bodies in such a manner that they will be able to make decisions in conformity with the will of God. It is true that the first condition for such a transformation is the existence of a communications system through which the transformation takes place and becomes public. But this is only the beginning. Most of the inner transformations remain hidden and, for lack of a language, ineffective, not able to reach the public domain. But the fact that these transformations are not always articulated does not mean that they are completely futile, wasted, or actually of no use to the rest of humanity. We must remember that these technologies of imagining operate at a level that, because it is original, neuro-physiological, affects the rest of humanity, even if they do not know it—activities become more easily performed by others once they have become embodied, made flesh, in someone else. It is obvious from the exercises of the first week alone that they set in motion a pattern of transformation that becomes more and more clear as the other weeks roll along. The meditator's body and senses are systematically dismembered while imagining. This in turn produces new objects, attachments, and sensitizations. While the exercises start with two frames, the retreatant's and God's, facing each other, the distance becomes slowly less pronounced. Frames intermingle through imagining, and the retreatant's frame-size changes as the actual signs of meditation begin to occur. The mediator of these two distances is the image. All imagining is a mediation. The unity and size of the image is identical with the identity the retreatant keeps receiving and shedding. This fluid mobility eventually desensitizes the retreat ant to any images of self except those it discovers while imagining. While the meditator keeps building horizons, frames, in meditation, new signs and sensations eventually appear on those horizons.

As the exercises progress, in the second through the fourth weeks, the structure of imagining persists. The two frames keep facing each other in every meditation: the retreatant's and God's. The images of the life of Christ—without any theological squeamishness—become, as chosen by Ignatius, the mediation between those two frames. The results are similar to those of the first week. Now, however, sensations, language, and sensitizations become suddenly stronger. A taste for imagining anticipates the meditation and makes it fly. Imagining is produced with much greater ease. The retreatant begins to separate the right signs of meditation and becomes adept at articulating them to the guide. Ignatius believed that by the end of the second week the retreatant should be strong enough to start making decisions on those signs, with the advice of his guide.

There is a moment in the exercises, some time around the third week, when all the striving, the careful, agonic dedication to sharpening the will, remembering, and imagining accumulate on the retreatant with such force that all the habits of the past, the expectations of the familiar, seem to collapse. Death seems to invade every corner of the retreatant's body and soul. The "old man," as Ignatius used the expression, suddenly dies. Most people stop short of this death, the most brutal episode and powerful act of these technologies.[10] One is careful never to burn all the boats. At its most successful, this death is a complete death to all the habits of the original unity. A new life takes over now that sensitizes the retreatant from the inside out, rather than from the outside in. This is a painful bereavement for the body, which is not sure what will come next. This is the dark night of the soul. In the dawn of a new life it is not clear if life as we knew it will happen again, and it is even less clear that what happened while doing the exercises will ever happen again, in or outside of them. One needs to be very humble to be original. It is better to imitate. The fight within the soul that wants both the old way and the new is a continuous fight between two loves starting at last to recognize a common origin.

While the meditator has been busy building frames and imagining, what started as such innocent activity suddenly turns into experience and life: the image, through imagining, has become alive, and imagining stops, at last, the moment this life begins.

The fourth week of the *Exercises* is a new song of confirmation. The transformation has taken place, and the whole cycle of Creation, Redemption, and Resurrection gives place to "meditation to gain love" (*Exer.*,230). The book of life, history, humans, the stars, angels, and mountains become now the secondary text, so many extraordinary signs, of the original act of Creation and love. Imagining has now gone full circle: from the original Creator to man and from man back to the original Creator. Matter and spirit have found the middle ground where the divine and the human share a language.

How this language is articulated is the scope of the next two chapters.

3

A Text for Reading, A Text for Deciding

In whatever way men approach me,
in the same way they receive
their reward.

—Bhagavad Gītā,4.11.

HILOSOPHY IN GENERAL AND HERMENEUTICS in particular remind me so often of a magic show. The magician is able to pull the rabbit out of the hat not because the rabbit was there in the first place, but because the magician or the assistant put it there. A magic trick like this takes place when the philosopher reads texts without having embodied the primary technologies of those texts. The philosopher keeps pulling out rabbits he has inserted and keeps doing this again and again.

As we have seen in the previous chapter, reading in general depends among other things on a particular input fed into the neurophysiological system. The invention of the press was a type of input that made possible a program of action, a definitive technology of composing and reading. This program of action, through repetition, resulted in a crystallized neural hardware that in turn incorporated a definite cultural loop into the functioning human nervous system. This new habit, this technology of composing and reading, changed both the internal and external environments and both became, in turn, reinforced through a system of education that was itself the result of the new technology.

When a new system of reading becomes the standard technology of a period, it does not mean that it destroys the previous systems through which reading was done. The old technologies become temporarily forgotten, ready to use any time the subject decides to do so. Technologies, that is, inner technologies concerning body actions, are not completely forgotten; they just need to be revived through exercise, as is the case of riding a bicycle.

The primary text of the *Exercises*, as we have seen in the previous chapter, is identifiable through a technology that transforms the human faculties to operate in a manner different from, say, "reading for information." This primary technology is the necessary and sufficient condition for a series of signs to appear so that we may have a readable text; that is, a text for reading. The primary technology is not itself, in whole or in part, a sign, nor may it be read as a sign. It is, rather, a series of acts that through repetition form an input into the human body. This input crystallizes into neural hardware and incorporates a cultural loop into the human nervous system. The whole species may now act on this habit made possible through an individual or collective exercise. This neural hardware in meditation is not causal of the signs that appear in meditation, but it is causal of the text offered for reading, that is, the text as articulated.

Since these signs, as articulated, depend on as many texts as there are people who enter meditation, it will be near impossible to speak of "one" text. While the primary text and primary technology are one and apply to all those entering meditation, the secondary text, in contrast, is a multitude, and we cannot offer generalities that apply to all. For this reason in examining the secondary text one must go case by case. For the purposes of this study in hermeneutics and imagining we shall refer exclusively to Ignatius' secondary texts; that is, the signs that appear in the "Rules for discerning spirits" and the *Spiritual Diary*. This being the secondary text of Ignatius, we also cannot separate it from the purpose Ignatius had for it: making decisions. Thus the secondary text will serve us not only as an exercise in reading, but also as a deliberate plan for making human decisions.

The secondary text needs several simultaneous readers to lead to decision making or even to decipher. The first reader is the exercitant. The other reader is the spiritual guide. These first readings might eventually place the secondary text in the public domain, as a text for public scrutiny, a readable text, or as decisions affecting the public domain.

EXPERIMENTING WITH A MULE

When Ignatius de Loyola was only Iñigo de Loyola, a soldier recovering from his wounds, he discovered to his astonishment that what used to sensitize him, fantasizing about women, had come to an end. Gone were the days of carousing about, gambling, and bringing illegitimate children into this world. He had had a conversion. But then the problem became what to do with his life. He soon discovered in his fantasies that thinking of doing the things the saints did for Christ would bring him more lasting pleasure than fantasizing about women, or the woman he had chosen for his fantasies (*Autobiography*,1:6,7,8). He held to that more lasting pleasure as a sure sign from God and decided to dedicate his life to the service of Christ. But how would he do that? Would he go to the Holy Land and preach to the infidels, or move to a monastery and become a Carthusian? (*Autobiography*,1:12). While in these deliberations, a sign came to him in the form of a vision "with such excessive consolation that it left him with such disgust for the whole of his past life, and especially for anything concerning the flesh, that it seems to him his soul had been deprived of all sense-impression previously printed in it" (*Autobiography*,1:10).

Strengthened by these signs, he sets out in search of a final shape for the adventure of his new life. Montserrat, where he intends to become a knight-in-armor for Christ, is the first step. On his way to the mountain he comes upon a Moor on horseback, and both ride together for a while. In the course of the conversation the Moor disagrees with Ignatius on the virginity of Mary, mother of Jesus. The Moor explains that he does not negate Mary's virginity *before* the birth of Jesus. But how could she remain a Virgin *after* giving birth? Ignatius is enraged. The Moor, cautiously, takes off and rides ahead. Ignatius does not want to act on impulse; nor does he want to make a decision on rational principles; and so, as a test of his new life, he lets the mule decide. If the mule were to take the left fork of the road, he would chase after the Moor and kill him. If the mule were to take the right fork, he would let the Moor go in peace, take the road to Montserrat, and spend the night in knightly vigil. The mule took to the right; the Moor was safe. Ignatius took this as a sign from God that the Moor should not be killed and that God took pleasure in his knighthood for Christ (*Autobiography*,2:14-15).

This raw interpretation by Ignatius of these early signs already gives us a clue to the direction he is going to take when he becomes more sophisticated. Still, Ignatius seemed prone to oversimplifications. When Ignatius made it to Jerusalem with a group of pilgrims, he ran away from the group at great personal and diplomatic risk in the hope of staying behind. A friar found him, took him by the arm, reprimanded him severely, and delivered him to the ship with the others bound for home. Ignatius took this as a sign that God did not want him to remain in Jerusalem (*Autobiography*,4:44-48).

Ribadeneira, his official biographer, recounts the story of how Ignatius, already an old man, used to keep the whole community of Jesuits in the refectory after dinner, longer than usual, in order to read to them his latest notes on obedience. One night, as he was doing this reading against the will of many of those present, the roof fell on the spot in the garden where they would have been sitting, as was their custom, had he not detained them reading about obedience. This Ignatius, obviously, took as a sign of how pleased God was with his notes on obedience. And so on.

But this same Ignatius is the one who discovered, through his own reading of the signs that came to him while doing the exercises, the true inner signs of meditation accompanied by joy, consolation, desolation, visions, and other material that convinced him that he and God were on the same communications system. With the meticulousness of an accountant he noted them, examined them, and instructed the exercitant and the spiritual guide on how to read them and use them to make decisions. His vision by the Cardoner River also convinced him that the knowledge from these signs was more lasting, exact, and definitive than any form of knowledge derived from human cognitive devices (*Autobiography*,3:30). It was a legitimate basis for making decisions.

THE SECONDARY TEXT(S): PRIVATE ARTICULATION

The test that the primary technology is functioning is that it gives out certain signs. The second test is that these signs must be such that they can be read simultaneously by the retreatant and another person, usually the spiritual director. Both must find themselves reading the same text.

What for the retreatant is one thing, namely the deciphering of the signs produced by the exercise of the primary technology, for the spiritual director or any other external reader is a different thing. For the spiritual director or external reader have first to establish the secondary text. However, both retreatant and external reader must agree as to what the secondary text is. What makes such an agreement possible is the fact that both share the same primary text, the same bodily unity of being experts at using an embodied primary technology. The reading of the secondary text(s) is not dependent on the actual, immediate, use of the primary technology. It is dependent, however, on the primary text to the extent that those participating in the reading share a common, embodied, primary technology. The external reader, besides, carries the advantage of having read many such secondary texts besides his own. All readers are reading a commentary text, derived and secondary.

It does not take much effort to read in the *Autobiography* the agonic task Ignatius placed upon himself in discerning the diverse movement of the different spirits afflicting or consoling him while doing the exercises at Manresa: Consolation, desolation, tears, visions, scruples, sightings, joy, depressions; simultaneously these were penances to force the signs, changes in penances to force the signs, and articulation of those signs in writing, in conversations, in confessions, and in decisions (*Autobiography*,3:19,25,33,34; 10:96-97).

A man so experienced about signs, through his own meditations, would be meticulous in bringing this knowledge to others. The structure of this secondary text, or signs of meditation, is found early in the *Exercises*. The annotations instruct the one giving the exercises not to embellish the story, but simply to mention the points for meditation (*Exer.*,2). In this same annotation Ignatius sets the "style" which both retreatant and guide are looking for: "For to know much does not fill and satisfy the soul, but rather to feel and taste things interiorly."

Since to feel things interiorly implies the use of the will, Ignatius cautions the retreatant: "In all the exercises that follow we use of the acts of the intellect to reason and of the will to feel; one must be careful, when using the will. . .to use more respect on our part than when we use reason to understand" (*Exer.*,3). What then, will the text appear? Ignatius took it for granted that it should, but if it does not appear as "spiritual motions in the soul of the retreatant, like consolations, desolations, or not shaken by different spirits," then the one giving the exercises should question the retreatant about the way he/she makes the exercises (*Exer.*,6). Ignatius, through the spiritual guide, sends the retreatant to the minor leagues for retraining: back to basics. In listing those basic conditions Ignatius gives us the structure of the secondary text, too:

Does the retreatant (a) make the exercises the primary text? b) follow the times assigned for them? c) follow the additions diligently (*Exer.*,73-90)? Both the retreatant and guide should go over these points carefully.

It will clarify matters for the reader if again we summarize these additions insofar as they constitute the "basics" on which the primary text is put into practice: 1) Summarize points for meditation before going to sleep; 2) Revise those points on waking up; 3) Take one or two steps before the place of meditation considering how God looks at one; lower the head in sign of reverence; 4) Look for the body positions that best helps and stay in it; 5) After the exercise, for about fifteen minutes, reflect on what happened, how the meditation went—if badly, look for the cause and repent; if well, give thanks; 6) Avoid joyful thoughts in the first and third weeks, thinking of sad and painful things instead; 7) Darken the room, except for reading and eating; 8) Do not joke or say things to make people laugh; 9) Keep eyes down; 10) Do penance—of diet, sleeping, punishing the flesh. The reasons for penance are a) to pay for past sins, b) to conquer oneself, c) to find what one is looking for in meditation. The rule for making penance should be to find what we are looking for in the exercises; therefore, if we do not, then we should change the diet, sleeping penances, or flesh penances, either doing more or less, alternating days or several days doing penance and others abstaining (*Exer.*,73-90).

But what are we looking for in the exercises? Each exercise has a second prelude which constitutes the secondary text of the exercise (*Exer.*,48) where what one wants to find in the exercise is demanded or requested: "according to the subject matter, that is, if the exercise is on the Resurrection, we should ask for joy with Christ rejoicing, if it is on the Passion, we should ask for pain, tears and suffering with Christ suffering. In the present meditation one should ask for shame and confusion, for I see how many souls have been damned for one single mortal sin and how many times have I deserved to be damned for the many sins I have committed" (*Exer.*,48).

Ignatius de Loyola is, once again, at the heart of Christian tradition. In the absence of the Father and the Son, the Spirit is the only text Christians are left with. "It is to your advantage that I go away, for if I do not go away, the Counsellor will not come to you; but if I do, I will send him to you" (John,16:7). The Father, who remains always hidden, appears through the Son, who comes from heaven and returns to heaven. Only the Spirit remains with Christians, and the Spirit needs to be interpreted, too. There is no immaculate perception for Christians. Paul, once again, comes to the rescue with his classification of the signs of the Spirit: "The fruit of the Spirit is love, joy, peace, patience, kindness, goodness, faithfulness, gentleness, self-control" (Gal.5:22).

In practice, however, the reading of these signs created many problems for Christians. In the case of Ignatius the movements of his soul were so intense and confusing that he was led more to scruples and even a temptation of suicide (*Autobiography*,3:24). As a consequence of this incident and on its resolution Ignatius came to note "the way by which that Spirit had come upon him" and how God's way of handling him at that time was "as a teacher a child" which was as well, for "he had no one to instruct him" (*Autobiography*,3:27). The vision by the river Cardoner changed for Ignatius his way of discerning the signs, for it was after this vision that he was able to distinguish another vision in the form of a serpent with radiant light and many eyes as not coming from God but from the devil (*Autobiography*,3:31). The ability to read these signs, which Ignatius acquired with such pains and agonic effort, is what he tries to share with the guide of the exercises and the retreatant. These reading guides appear in separate annotations and series of notations worth noticing: there are the preliminary annotations we have already mentioned (*Exer.*,1-20); the additions (*Exer.*,73-90); preambles on elections (*Exer.*,169-189); rules for discerning spirits (314-327); rules "for greater discernment of spirits" (328-336); rules for reading the signs of the enemy (345-351); and finally rules to "keep our true place in the Militant Church" (352-370).

Through the preliminary annotations he warns retreatants and guides that signs are normal in the course of the exercises. If there are no signs, retreatants should be questioned. It is not important for the guides of the exercises to question or know anything about the sins of retreatants, but it is very important that they learn about the signs of the exercises. Only on this data will guides be able to judge whether retreatants should be led on to an election and to the end of the *Exercises*, or whether they should keep retreatants in the program of the first week only (*Exer.*,8,9,18).

The most extraordinary innovation in Ignatius' *Exercises* is that he links signs with elections or decisions. These decisions involve a choice between different possible states of life: married, single, religious life, etc.; and also elections or decisions about two alternate choices within that chosen state of life: study or prayer, poverty or riches, Carmelite or Dominican, etc. These decisions are reached in several stages, but in the end they rest on our ability to read certain signs. In order for us to be able to make a "judiciously" sound decision, Ignatius presupposes three different situations, each one related directly to our ability to read signs.

The first situation is the perfect one, when God so moves the will that there is no doubt whatsoever as to what to do. Secondly, "when one finds much light and information through the experience of consolation and desolation and the ability to read these signs"; and finally, when there is a "period of calm when the soul is not agitated by diverse spirits and when it exercises its natural faculties freely and tranquilly" (*Exer.*,175-177). Even in the third situation, when we have reached the "greatest rational motion," the election should be submitted for approval to God in meditation for consent and verification (*Exer.*,182-183), which involves further reading of signs.

For our purpose here, however, the most interesting scenario is the second one: when the ability to read consolation and desolation determine also our ability to decide. For it is in this ability that our hermeneutical activity here rests. How complicated can reading get? I wish to summarize here the whole process as given in the *Exercises*, for these are going to be our working criteria for reading the *Spiritual Diary*.

The series of criteria for reading the first week's signs set the retreatant and the guide on the lookout for only those signs derived from the primary text. The program of this reading may be summarized as a dedication to continue the reading, regardless of how many contradictory signs appear in that reading. Although addressed to beginners, the reading criteria presuppose a "person working with fervor to purify the self from sins"; that is, persons bent on a vocation looking for the will of God (*Exer.*,315). Consolation and desolation are the signs to be looking for, even when at this stage they come mostly from natural causes (*Exer.*,316-317).

Desolations, as signs, appear on account of three main reasons: a) the exercises are not properly made; b) they are a trial allowed by God to show we do not need the constant bribery of joyful signs to persevere in the goal; c) they are signs to show us the dependence of all signs, in particular the joyful ones, not on us but on "a gratuitous gift of God" (*Exer.*,322). The result of those readings will be to encourage us to keep on reading; that is, making the text, by not changing the original orientation; by not changing the resolutions already made, unless it be to counter with generosity the signs of desolation themselves (*Exer.*,318-319); by continuing reading in the certainty that the signs from God are present, though not experienced (*Exer.*,320); by learning to wait for the signs to appear, for all signs are transitory (*Exer.*,321).

On the other hand, the signs that appear as consolation are to be read awaiting the signs of desolation, so that we learn that all spiritual success comes from God (*Exer.*,323-324). This is not too complex a program for reading. The only addition is Ignatius' remarks on the tactics of signs appearing from the devil. Like a scheming woman, he makes those signs appear strong if because of the anxieties and hesitations of the reading person he is not opposed. Like a seducer, he tempts the reader to keep his deceitful signs secret, for if they were articulated to the guide of the exercises, they would never end even in a sentence, much less into a resolution. Like a military strategist, he aims those signs at the weak spots in our resolutions (*Exer.*,325-327).

The guides to reading consolation, in particular those in the second week, introduce new, more sophisticated variations. Though the signs of consolation are presented as "proper to the good spirit," they may not be always read as such. The bad angel may disguise signs to appear as good. They are joyful, and yet may lead to bad resolutions. Ignatius here introduces a new kind of reading. The retreatant and the guide should be looking for signs as consolation that appear without previous cause, or that may not be attributed to any other external cause (*Exer.*,330). Consolation signs must be submitted to rigorous reading through examination: separate the time of reading the present consolation from the time the soul is over it. In this period the soul might be making wrong decisions inspired by a wrong reading. All consolation signs must be examined carefully (*Exer.*,336). If they come from the bad angel, the signs of "his serpentine tail" (*Exer.*,334) will soon appear.

THE SUBTLE READING

If the primary text of the *Exercises* has been duly embodied by the retreatant and the guide of the *Exercises* is an expert in sign reading, we would then have the following situation: Both are simultaneously reading the same set of signs. Both are looking for the same signs that would enable decisions to be made. Both would know that retreatants should be, by this time, indifferent to all types of choices. In fact, both know that retreatants should not, of themselves, make any choices. What they do instead is to present to God two equally valid choices for confirmation or verification. The choice will depend on the nod of God to either one of those alternatives. But that nod will have to be read carefully from the signs. Since the signs come from the good as well as the bad angel, and good signs may be produced by either, other reading criteria must be discovered to be sure the reading is correct.

Ignatius de Loyola summarizes a life of experience in reading those signs in the *Exercises* 333-336. This is the text for reading:

333. We must examine with great attention the sequence of our mental life. If the beginning, the middle and the end is all good, leaning to the good, this is the sign of the good angel. But if the series of thoughts suggested end up in some bad thing or distraction, or less good than what the soul had already planned to do, or the soul becomes weak, or disturbed, or agitated by losing its peace, tranquility and quietude it previously had, this is a clear sign that all this comes from the evil spirit, the enemy of our advancement and eternal salvation.

334. When the enemy of human nature is thus felt and known by his serpent's tail and bad end it leads to, it is then useful for the person so tempted to examine at once the sequence of the good thoughts the devil suggested to that person, and from the very beginning and how little by little the enemy set about lowering that soul from the sweetness and spiritual joy it had up to that point to his perverse intention; in this manner thanks to this experience understood and remembered the soul may in the future guard against the devil's accustomed tricks.

335. For those who travel from good to better, the good angel touches the soul quietly, lightly, pleasantly, like a drop of

water entering a sponge. The bad angel touches it sharply, with noise and agitation, as when a drop of water falls on a stone. In those who are going from bad to worse, the same spirits act in contrary manner. The reason for this is that the dispositions of the souls are contrary or similar to the said angels; thus, when they are contrary the spirits enter noisily and with disturbances that are easily noticed; when they are related, the spirit enters silently, as coming home through an open door.

As we see from the above descriptions, Ignatius is not asking us to read words and sentences, but rather the signs of motions. In this particular case the subtlety of the sign, a change in interior balance, is rather a *symptom* that needs to be read as a *sign*. It takes long experience in reading to be able to detect these signs. Yet, the more subtle reading depends on this ability, or the text collapses into jibberish.

THE SPIRITUAL DIARY

All the promissory notes Ignatius has been distributing along the path of the *Exercises* find a textual bank, where all are cashed at once, in the *Spiritual Diary*.

The *Spiritual Diary* is one of the most remarkable documents ever written in any language. It covers the period of one year, February 2, 1544 - February 27, 1545, and shows the master, Ignatius, at work in the art of reading signs. The *Diary* is his own account of different signs that come to him in meditation and that he needs to read in order to come up with the right decision. In short, it is the verification of the primary text: the *Exercises*. The choices Ignatius puts up for election in the meditations that we witness in the *Diary* are these: should the Jesuit houses have full income, partial, or none at all? In modern terms, should the Jesuit houses accept endowments or not? For a whole year we witness Ignatius presenting this election to the nod of God. By being able to discern signs, Ignatius eventually reaches the decision that the Jesuit houses should have no endowments whatsoever.

The *Spiritual Diary* clearly shows the working of Ignatius' spirituality. It verifies for us the causal connection between the primary and secondary texts as we have described them here and embodies in a few pages the criteria for reading the secondary text we have outlined in this chapter and regathered from the *Exercises* and the *Autobiography*. It also has the implication that the favors Ignatius received during his lifetime are all linked to the fact that the primary text of meditation was readying him to receive those favors. Thus we see how many of the favors narrated in the *Auto-*

biography did actually happen in the context of meditation. We have carefully outlined those passages so that the thesis stands complete. In reading the *Diary* one has a better idea of how the other documents were compiled and how all together form the communications system Ignatius outlined for Christian practice.

The *Spiritual Diary* has remained practically unknown until very recently and of course unpublished. This is the first time the complete *Diary* is offered in English translation with the codes deciphered and passages included that appear in other documents. The early Jesuits were cautious to the extreme, aware as they were of the ever present Inquisition, and decided to keep the mystical *writings* of Ignatius under wraps. A few fragments were included by Ribadeneyra and Bartoli in their life of the saint. It was not until 1892 that Fr. Juan José de la Torre published the first part of the *Diary* in the *Constitutiones S.I.* (Madrid). In 1922, Fr. Feder brought out a German translation of the same. Only in 1934 was the *Spiritual Diary* published in its totality in the first volume of the *Constitutions* in *Monumenta Historica*. This edition is the basis of the translation presented in this volume—including the words Ignatius erased or added on the margins, plus the study of Fr. de Guibert in 1938 and the latest details to decipher the abbreviations of the *Diary* as they appear in *Obras Completas de Ignacio de Loyola*, Biblioteca de Autores Cristianos, Madrid 1977. This edition by the Spanish Jesuits has made it possible for a single man to translate and put together a work that had occupied generations of scholars for many centuries.

The *Spiritual Diary* is the verification system, the secondary text, of the *Spiritual Exercises*, of the primary text. It would be trivializing the *Diary*, now available, to describe it at greater length. This sequence of documents also makes the *Spiritual Exercises* a different kind of document than it is normally taken to be. The description made of the primary text in the previous chapter is made possible with greater normative power once the *Diary* is read. The text of imagining is more vigorously prominent than it was believed to be. The connection between imagining and the will is richly established. The *Diary* opens clearly the way to those secrets of Christianity that up to recent times were only whispered as possible or lost. But above all it clearly establishes the exhaustive detail of the act of reading the signs. In the short span of one year the *Diary* records the following different signs: in the first forty days alone, Ignatius has tears over 125 times, an average of four times a day, and 26 times tears with sobbing. Other signs he meticulously reads: joy, spiritual rest, intense consolation, rising of the mind, divine impressions, illuminations, intensification of faith, hope, charity, knowledge, spiritual flavor and relish, spiritual visitations, rapture, etc. Of these kinds of signs is the *Diary*'s reading made.

THE QUESTION OF OBEDIENCE

Obedience appears again and again as a question mark in this text of signs to be read.

The human tension of cognition and imagination, of the image and the origin, of theology and experience, of the two wills—God's and the retreatant's—of the two texts and two technologies, primary and secondary, of the two readers, the retreatant and the spiritual guide, is finally resolved in the unity of a decision taken. Through decision, the signs that appear in the act of imagining while meditating, become flesh in the world, become the world. God's desire for the world and the world's for God are reconciled in the deciding body of the retreatant through the decision made. In Ignatius' spirituality the primary and secondary texts, the primary and secondary technologies, have as their goal to make decisions, to bring the will of God to the world. Other founders of religious orders used meditation differently; John of the Cross, Teresa de Avila for example used meditation more as a goal in itself. But in Ignatius' communications system the rule of *tanto. . . cuanto* ("as much. . .as") applies to all things including meditation. The articulation of the secondary text must return as language to the world. Private articulation is not sufficient. The will of God must be turned to language and join the public domain.

We have established earlier that the secondary text has at least two readers: the retreatant and the spiritual guide. A bond must be established between those two readers as to whether a reading is to make it to the public domain and if so which reading is the final one.

At the beginnings of a conversion we see any mystic looking around for someone to help read those signs. Nobody seems to understand them till someone arrives with help. The mystics become attached to the reader who helps them decode the coded messages. The second reader contributes with the mystic to the formation of the readable text. The method is always the same: the second reader becomes a severe editor of the text. He points out the true readings, edits messages not pertinent to the text, moves the mystic to keep on creating new signs when stuck by a writer's block or by scruples, or to return to the fundamentals of writing when other interests distract. The confessor, the second reader, is also the writer of the text. He helps build the text as an expert reader. But only on one condition: that the mystic obey him blindly and follow his instructions without hesitation, without even mental reservations (see letter on obedience). In the beginnings things seem to work out under this arrangement. We see Ignatius, as he narrates in his *Autobiography*,3:24-27, struggle with scruples and jump ahead by following the instructions of the confessor. The second reader seems to be imperative in the making of the secondary text, at least in the beginnings.

Soon, however, the mystic begins to experience in the flesh such certainty, such knowledge, "more than putting together all the help received from God in a life time, all the knowledge even if gathered in one pile, as in that one only time," (*Autobiography*, 3:30), as happened to Ignatius in the vision by the Cardoner River, that the advice of others becomes a torment, if not a nuisance and perhaps unnecessary. However, there is always the danger that what started as the search for the will of God might turn out in the world as the imposition of the will of an individual. The remedy, in Ignatius' hands, was again obedience to the superior. The second reader must always contribute to the reading of the text, must always be present.

A different kind of challenge to Ignatius' spiritual economy came in the opposite direction. Ignatius founded the Jesuits on a spiritual program that would not only be spiritual but would enter the public domain and influence it in competition with the established public institutions in Europe, Asia, Africa, or the ends of the world. Within this program his spiritual proficiency was seen as a means to an end. The secondary text was all he required of his Jesuits. If, by any chance, or God's gifts, some of them received extraordinary graces, they should not interfere with this universal program of public service. The Jesuits should be able to read those signs and those signs only in collaboration with their superiors and confessors that would make the whole project of universal efficacy possible. Spirituality was a necessary condition for the society but only if it also contributed to reading the will of God in the world.

Some Spanish and Portuguese Jesuits discovered that while studying their spiritual life was at a low ebb. They decided to use the exercises as an end in themselves—to the detriment of their future efficacy in the public domain. They wanted to meditate more and deal with the world less. Ignatius wrote to those young Jesuits the "Letter on Obedience" (included in this volume), trying to remedy this misunderstanding of the true goals of the society. One of the leaders of this movement was a co-founder of the society, Simón Rodríguez, and Ignatius used all possible ways to make him understand. When Ignatius was convinced there was no way to bring him under obedience, he dispatched Fr. Nadal, his secretary, with letters of discharge asking the offender to leave the society. Fortunately, Fr. Rodríguez died a Jesuit, before Fr. Nadal could catch up with him. The young Jesuits of Coimbra understood obedience, and the crisis was over. But not the question of obedience, which to this day remains a large question in the text of reading the signs.

Ignatius, of course, found some form of solution, suggesting that if one is turned down, after following all the conditions of the primary and secondary text, in anything proposed to the superior, one should bring it up again and again if the election receives the nod of the divinity in subsequent presentations. In practice, however, obedience works differently, much as finding favorable readers for a manuscript prepared for publication. Mystics were forced to keep on changing readers, confessors, not so much looking for a good editor as someone who would favorably read their text. At one given time a religious person is under several superiors. There is always a chance that one of them would make a good reader. The common objection against obedience, however, does not remove the fact that without it the secondary text, the reading of signs, technically cannot be formed. And if it is not formed, then any projects of world information are doomed to failure. Though obedience is not part of the readable text, it presumes the embodiment of the text as an integral part of the historical world to be informed. Obedience is part of sharing in the hardware of the primary text. A share in the company of the best, the saints, the creation. It affirms the faith that the primary text is already in the world. It is only for this reason that private articulation is possible, that there is a community of embodied subjects, and that the public domain may be newly informed. Were this not the case, the articulation of the acts of imagining could only be psychologized—made exclusively private—but they could never find a place in the public domain through a philosophical hermeneutics.

4

Imagining and the Public Domain

It was the dawn that joined the dewdrop
to the drop of blood,
and made them tremble
under a forest of memories.

And thus to release chance,
pure and new, into the hands
of the one who was arriving.

—Laureano Albán[1]

HE PATH OF IMAGINING IN SEARCH of experiential origins, we identified, earlier on in this study, with structures marked by audial/musical criteria. The parameters of the oral/audial world were tone and number—memory and imagination—as Plato testified. (The Greek atomists displaced this cosmology by introducing the parameters of space and time). In Plato's *Republic*, as in Tennyson's Camelot, this text bears the form of the desire of the world:

> . . .the city is built
> to music, therefore never built at all.
> And, therefore, built for ever.

Imagining, like music, provides quantity, that is numbers of memories, and quality precisely and spontaneously so that sense impressions can be measured, accounted for, and so that proportion can be experienced. The eternal polarity between growth and limit, contraries and contradictories, silence and speech, is resolved in imagining through the continuous unities of embodiment and discontinuous plurality of decisions. This discontinuous plurality inevitably leads to problems of compatibility, which music resolves, as does imagining, with a universal "tempering" of every system, a universal sacrifice shared by everyone involved. Where cognitive theologies emphasize a monodic propositional agreement, the audial tradition, of which Christianity is a part, gives us a polyphonic symphony of experience. For this reason a hermeneutics of mystic

texts is primarily a hermeneutics of the collective form of the collective desire of the world. The experiences and signs of the mystic
are just language, either as primary or secondary text, and this
language is precisely the form of that human desire. The mystic,
by identifying in his own body, through imagining, through language and feeling, language and sign, speaks simultaneously the
deeper language of the world's desires. Through the mystic the
world and the divinity communicate. They share a common ground,
the "dawn that joined the dewdrop to the drop of blood." This
common background is the field of imagining and simultaneously
the language of imagining. Because this language is the text, it is
recoverable through hermeneutics. But because this text is a transformation of language, hermeneutics needs to transform itself to
be able to interpret. This transformation consists in performing
the embodiment the text requires before the act of interpretation
takes place. To reduce the text to a biographical entity or to an
imitation of a text is not only to banish the author to "social
isolation" but also to fail in the hermeneutical act we propose to
perform as philosophers.

No biographical account can do justice to the plurality of texts
the "prose" of any of our lives can freely fit. Ignatius is a clear
example similar to so many other mystics. Ignatius was so many
pedestrian and imaginative people: sinner, soldier, gambler, lover,
priest, founder, superior, mystic, saint, suspect of the Inquisition,
doer of spiritual exercises, writer, dreamer, director of women's
consciences, director of men's consciences; he was short in theology,
sharp in philosophy, a guide of souls, at times a lost soul himself.
Even after his conversion, while he declares himself a passionate
servant of the church, Ignatius and his Jesuits formed an order
under the jurisdiction of no bishop, without cloister or choir, subject to no human hierarchy; he and his Jesuits made a vow of obedience to the Pope, but this originally applied only in the eventuality
that he or any of the Jesuits taking the vow (not all do) were sent
to different geographical places. Of the church's practices and teachings he wanted all to be praised ("Rules for Conforming with the
Church"), but his own teachings and practice stressed grace, faith,
and recollection in a way that made him suspect to the Inquisition.
He praised cognitive skills but followed imagining; he founded an
order for men, but one of its first members was a woman (see
Letters in this volume); he founded an order for priests, but some
men were accepted who were not; he asked and was granted dispensation from Rome not to attend to the spiritual guidance of women,
and yet he never stopped directing them and even had some under
vow to him (*Letters*); he found homes for prostitutes, and allowed
conversos (new Christians from Judaism) to share his house and

food; he invented a way of contemplation but dismissed Jesuits because they liked contemplation too much (*Letters*); he reprimanded everyone (*Letters*), praised only the most weak and fired the disobedient; he preferred to work with the nobility but opened his society to all social classes, including "new Christians," and made the *Exercises* accessible to all. Ignatius avoided controversy and controversial Christians (St. Juan de Avila, Erasmus) but without fear aligned himself with pagan humanism in his program of education. When all religious orders were so sensitive to admitting "new Christians" that they wrote constitutions to make it impossible, Ignatius discriminated against no one, and he even professed in public that he would take it as a special grace from our Lord to come from Jewish lineage: "Why imagine! That a man could be a kinsman by blood (*secundum carnem*) of Christ Our Lord and of Our Lady the glorious Virgin Mary."[2] He lived for others and through his Jesuits his language spread over the face of the earth, even while he was alive; yet he died alone. The little book *Spiritual Exercises* has had more than 4,500 editions in nineteen languages and sold more than five million copies. More than two million people make the exercises annually for a period of at least a week and within closed quarters. Another seven million make the so-called open exercises through evening lectures and public missions (*Obras Completas*, 1977).[3] Popes, saints, and Christians attest to the power of this little book to transform ordinary lives into extraordinary ones. St. Francis of Sales, who died in 1622, summarized the power of this little book by saying: "It has performed more conversions than it has words" (Ibid.,p.170). Pope Pius XI declared Ignatius de Loyola Patron Saint of all spiritual exercises and of all forms of Christian meditation.

If Ignatius had not made the exercises and willed them to the public, what human silence there would have been!

But perhaps it is Juan de la Cruz (John of the Cross), another Spanish mystic, who best and most memorably summarized the whole transformation as the collective desire of the body and the world in his poem: "Love's Living Flame" (my own translation):

Love's Living Flame
Song that the soul sings in the intimate union with God, her beloved bridegroom.

1. O Love's living flame,
   tenderly you wound
   my soul's deepest center!
   Since you no longer evade me
   will you, please, at last conclude:
   rend the veil of this sweet encounter!

2. O cautery so tender!
   O pampered wound!
   O soft hand! O touch so delicately strange
   tasting of eternal life
   and cancelling all debts!
   Killing, death into life you change!

3. O lamps of fiery lure
   in whose shining transparence
   the deep cavern of the senses,
   that was blind and obscure,
   warmth and light, with strange flares
   gives next to the lover's caresses!

4. How tame and loving
   your memory rises in my breast,
   where secretly only you live
   and in your fragrant breathing,
   full of goodness and grace,
   how delicately in love you make me feel!

Had John not been a poet, what a silence!

Even the excesses of mystical experience transform language and with it the desire of the world. Mystic aphasia is only a momentary lapse of memory. It always translates into language. There is no better example of this than that passionate, excessive woman: Teresa de Avila. She knew better than anyone that transformation begins in the will: "Without knowing how, it becomes captive; it merely consents to God, allowing Him to imprison it as one who well knows how to be captive of its lover" (*Live*,14:2). And it is this will that suddenly becomes more than life and yet must be held in her heart:

> I saw close to me an angel in bodily form. . .not very large, but small; very beautiful, his face aflame, he must have been one of the highest angels. . .In his hand I saw a golden dart, long, the tip of the dart red with some fire. This dart would enter my heart many times and reach my insides; in drawing out the dart it seemed he was taking them with it; he left me all inflamed in great love for God. The pain was so deep that it made me moan; and it was so excessive the sweetness this unbearable pain plunged me into, that there was no way for me to wish it to stop, nor was the soul satisfied with any less than God Himself.
>
> (*Life*,29:13)[4]

Had Teresa not been a woman-mystic, what a silence there would have been!

This is the secret of the "communion of saints" many thought was lost. The hermeneutics of discovery may yet turn this secret into the coin of public currency. But first we should clear up a few historical problems with the kind of hermeneutics we need to revive in order for this transformation to occur.

THE HYBRID TEXT

Only in writing may we find the whole testimony of humanity. What is not written is dead. Writing, however, is the sediment of many texts. We are able to find hiding, in writing, texts that were not originally written. They are not literary texts. For this reason the first rule of hermeneutics is that no literary text may substitute for the original text, whether literary or audial/oral. An original hermeneutical act of embodiment is demanded from the interpreter before interpreting texts. If this act of embodiment is missing, we turn out either trivial or marginal texts, or use any text as an exercise in power rather than reason. One of the most gallant efforts in contemporary semiotics—the study of texts—to liberate Ignatius de Loyola from the fate of banishment as a biographical entity has been carried out by Roland Barthes (1976).[5] Barthes' reading of Ignatius' text is Marxist, and though it appeals to many scientific sensibilities of contemporary intellectual audiences, it misses the primary text. I should, in all fairness, add immediately that it has been the analysis of the text in Barthes' sense that has legitimized the use of the writings of the saints and mystics in public and academic institutions. To achieve this where literature and theology failed is not a small feat. But this achievement is not without a high cost in reductionism. Ignatius' contribution to humankind is, in Barthes' reading of the text, Ignatius' contribution to semiology, to the science of signs; Ignatius' sainthood is thus replaced by a system of communication, a logothesis; faith is displaced by language; experience by neurosis; history by future research. Roland Barthes' text of Ignatius is the ultimate reduction, through cognitive skills, of the spirit to the sheer materiality of discrete signs. All this, however, is not as deplorable as the fact that this reader of texts misses Ignatius' primary text completely. The text Barthes is so successful at dissecting, and which he calls Loyola's text, is only one of the secondary texts, and he substitutes for it a Marxist's semiotics that determines such a reading. This primary text of Barthes is not Ignatius' primary text. Barthes, of course, did not miss the text of Ignatius because he was a Marxist. It is precisely Barthes' Marxism that more than any other factor contributed to his sympathy for Loyola's text. There is an affinity, in both cases: the primary texts share in an original effort of imagining that, unknowingly perhaps, brought Barthes to Ignatius' text. What misled Barthes in identifying the text he was examining was rather a "habit of thought" in which texts that are primary and the product of imagining must be reduced to texts that are cognitive and the product of cognitive skills. This habit of thought has its origins with Christian theology and goes all the way back to the neo-Platonist St. Augustine. Barthes is here in good company. It proves that the embodiment of habits of thought or reading is deeper than political colorings.

Writing, we stated earlier, does not give us any text. We have to decipher and interpret one or another text. Which one we succeed in interpreting will depend on our reading abilities, our primary reading technologies. Barthes' reading of Ignatius' text is, perhaps, not as revealing as the example of Augustine creating, out of the text of Christianity, a hybrid text that would haunt Christianity for centuries. The effects of Augustine's reading of texts still causes unbreakable habits of reading in contemporary hermeneutics.

Augustine's ultimate quest was identical with the ultimate form of the desire of the soul: *desiderium beautidinis* (desire for happiness). Soon, however, this desire of the soul was translated by him as the "desire to be" or *desiderium essendi*. The history of this reduction, from the desire of the soul to the desire of the mind, is worth dissecting. In this mutation of texts lies the history of the Christian hybrid text.

Augustine, in search of that experience of "being with God" (*esse cum Deo*), remained with the Manicheans for several years, adept at their doctrines and imaginative practices. But Augustine was a total failure at imagining. No experience came to him through imagining. He never mastered the technologies of imagining. As Augustine narrates in *Confessions* IV:16-31, he moved on, trying to reconcile the Manichean doctrine of two substances, spiritual and material. Ambrose's preaching started him on the track of an ultimate principle, even when Augustine was incapable of conceiving a purely spiritual reality (*Confessions*, V:10-20). In moral desperation he tried to look for help in the Gospel. Then the new text was born (*Confessions*, VIII:12,28-29).

Augustine "enters philosophy" the way one enters religion, for the salvation of one's soul, as he narrates in *De Vera Religione*. This project of salvation, however, in Augustine's hands, undergoes several transformations. First, it becomes an exercise in reading the Scriptures in order to replace the discipline of the sciences (Zum Brunn, 1978).[6] Second, this exercise of reading the Scriptures is made possible thanks to the "books of the Platonists" which Augustine found to replace the Manichean exercises (Ibid., p.2). Third, this intellectual quest of Augustine was for the sake of understanding his faith, the Old Testament and the New: *Exodus* 3:14 ("I am who am"), and *John's* 8:58,8:24, and 8:28 ("Before Abraham was, I am.). As Augustine summarizes in the *Dialogues*, the quest is to "have God" (*habere deum*), and to "be with God" (*esse cum deo*) since He is "Being Itself" (*ipsum esse*) (Zum Brunn, 1969).[7] Thus Augustine's journey leads him from faith to the understanding of faith and this finally to a state of intellectual intuition. Thus for Augustine the primary text of Christianity will become the understanding of faith that grounds faith: *sic sum ipsum esse ut nolim hominibus de esse* ("I am Being itself in such a way as not to wish to mislead men") (*Sermon*, 7). In this manner the intellectual acts of the mind become the primary technologies, in Augustine's vision, of health and salvation. Once this was established, the role of the mediator, Christ, had to be reduced to the salvation of Greek reason, or Augustine's understanding of it since Christ had come down to teach us the doctrine of reason (Zum Brunn, 1978).[8] Thus Augustine does not even blink when, in his work *De Trinitate*, XIV, he introduces chapter four with the following thesis: "The image of God is to be sought in the immortality of the rational soul. How a Trinity is demonstrated in the mind." Thus Augustine reduces the whole text to the natural operations of memory, understanding, and will; this thesis is a reformation of *Confessions* IX and X, and *De Musica* VI. If the soul has any hope, it is not in the here and now but in its immortality. Augustine cannot forget his own failure in imagining and relates it to the orthodox doctrine of the Church: "There are few who attain this knowledge here below, and even after this life it is impossible to surpass it"; or even more radically:

> Whoever thinks that in this mortal life a man may so disperse the mists of bodily and carnal imaginations as to possess the undoubted light of changeless truth, and to cleave to it with the unswerving constancy of a spirit wholly estranged from the common ways of life...he understands neither what he seeks, nor who it is who seeks it.
> (*De Ordine*,1:8,24)

The impact of this hybrid text (Greek and Hebrew sources) on Christianity will not escape the reader. It is a form of reflection joined with prayer, of thinking and salvation unified in a common project of transformation, a clear and hybrid mixture of reason and will, thought and tears, intellection and occultism, at the service of a particular human technology of reading the text of Christianity with only those tools accepted under a definition of rational acts and mortal faculties and experiences. Transcendence lies only in a hope of immortality that becomes hopeless once it is realized that the conditions for that kind of knowledge disappear with death through the disintegration of those same faculties and the conditions for their operation. And yet, this is a hybrid text most used and encouraged in the making of spiritual exercises and Western types of meditation, and ironically, it has survived as the "habit of thought" of contemporary hermeneutics. Contemporary practitioners of hermeneutics take up this hybrid text and project it on any text, hoping to interpret through hermeneutical circles the "essence of being itself." For these philosophers philosophy is also a project of salvation, where "to save is to redirect essence with the aim of making it reappear, for the first time, in the manner that is proper to itself" (Heidegger, 1958).[9] No one acquainted with phenomenology will fail to recognize this as its own project.

THE BIOLOGICAL FOUNDATIONS OF IMAGINING

The mystics in general and Ignatius de Loyola in particular share that "secret of human communion" that the sciences and philosophies grounded in cognitive skills have denied us. The natural sciences were created as an effort in human emancipation. They embody a model of interpretation in which the natural is sufficient to explain; one need not bring in the supernatural, or better still the natural displaces the supernatural as not necessary. Ironically, it is the mystics with their talk of supernatural entities that center the whole human through acting on the human body, while the natural sciences appeal to a disembodied mind. Furthermore, this mind, as history moves on, becomes less and less potent to the point of surrendering its powers of creation to external agents, like mathematical models, external technologies, experts, and social and biological engineers. The mystics worked on the assumption that human capacities were historically embodied, and therefore present, enabling humans to share with others the reading of their own experiential texts. Natural science, on the other hand, demands from us what we ideologically ought to be, regardless of what we have been. It demands that we stop living a life already in progress, that we cancel it, or suspend it, or put it on hold, on the tacit promise that we will be better off for that amputation. The mystics share the secret of how life is and has been. Because of that secret, human life is primarily human history; it is a life already lived. For this reason it may be repeated, at the level of the primary text, as our own originality. Natural science and its external technology, on the other hand, with its unexplained demand that it become a universal ideological model necessary and sufficient for the organization of human life, demands from all of us a surrender to one particular form of life, to become a passing commentary, a substitution of what is already happening. In no way does natural science and its technology represent the form of all the desire of the world. This substitution of the primary text by fictive secondary texts has

proven costly in terms of human living. Too many human memories have been chemically buried in the flesh of the young to their
loss.

The mystics, on the other hand, show a deeper faith in the
biological basis of the human communion more in line with recent
studies in perceptual psychology, brain chemistry, psychology, brain
evolution, brain development, ethology, cultural anthropology, and
biology in general, than studies derived from traditional models of
natural and social sciences. For the sake of brevity I will simply
note some of these characteristics as derived from the study in
which we have been engaged in this book.[10]

Imagining, as described in this study and exemplified in the
practice of the mystics, provides a better *model* of human images
and the power of imagining. This model is more complete and biologically continuous, being historical, than the unextended rational
substance of Descartes, the *tabula rasa* of Locke, the association
matrix of Hume, the passive reinforcement-driven animal of Skin-
ner, and the genetically hard-wired robots of the sociobiologists.
Imagining, as a model, includes not only the elements which made
those other natural models work, but also the elements those models left behind in order to include the form of the whole desire and
capacity of the world.

The total image of the origin has always remained hidden as a
model. Yet it has been created originally and continuously. The
reason is historically simple. The images of the act of creation and
of the human species are an original and potential unity, linked to
each other from the birth of the species. These paradigmatic images,
however, appear collectively to give birth and articulation to different cultures. These cultural paradigms appear *distributively* in each
life individually as the embodiment of a cultural primordial image.
The manifestation of these paradigmatic images, collectively and
distributively, is what makes possible the kind of public articulation
we are involved in here. As a model, it also explains the unity of
the first acts of wo/men—Adam/Eve, etc.—as involving not only
individuals but the whole species.

The primordial images of creation are encoded in our brain
and tissues in such a manner that imagining involves always a transformation that is holographic or holomoving in power. Imagining,
as a model, is primarily based on human biology: sensitization follows the image, the image is a total holomovement of sensation.
Each part contains the total image and the total image appears in
each part. What is already an embodied existing power in the species may be exercised by each individual distributively through the
technologies of the primary text.

This distributive exercise is the one that accounts for imagining as an autonomous activity, already present in human biology. The sensitization that takes place through imagining is systematically and methodically transformed into a human decision, through repetitions and original acts of imagining, by turning all experience into memories, by impregnating the intellect with those memories, by training the will to act in accordance with those original memories. The knowledge thus gained through imagining is not only autonomous but of a different kind than the knowledge derived from the technologies of thinking gained through cognitive skills based on cognitive epistemologies.

From a distributive perspective, human focusing, either in search of information or paying attention, is selective and therefore bound by limits. The primary text operates not by recalling knowledge already held, but rather by bringing about a new articulation of a language always present as origin, either through the creation of pure images—non-sensuous—or by transforming the old ones in view of the primary text. The operation of the primary text is to open horizons already present and yet newly articulated.

Imagining is fully determinative: it cannot stand ambiguity. We need to make decisions on such information, and therefore, we cannot tolerate doubt. Total coordination between the ability to read signs and to make decisions on that ability is required.

Imagining flourishes in a system of several readers, or community of embodied subjects, to share in that reading and process of decision making. The materiality of the human body and sensuous biases gives way to the communal presence of embodied subjects with abilities to interpret the signs of new articulations.

Imagining is innovative; it renews human sensation. The human nervous system seems to be designed with an enormous capacity to register *differences*; that is, it becomes what it is through repetitions that become biological habits. The nervous system is the acknowledged presence of these habits. The nervous system tends to ignore the expected and responds more excitedly to new and unexpected stimuli. For this reason there is the continuous striving of the human body, always more intrigued by the odd than by the expected. It is more inspired by movement and change, contrast and borderlines, than by any other characteristics of time and space.

Imagining is fundamentally synthetic. It creates unions, holographic marks, even in the absence of such marks. Silence is turned, in imagining, into a sign of decision making.

Imagining is primarily active. It builds scenarios to be tested and painfully rebuilds them when they prove false. All human faculties are involved in this activity as much organs of action as they are of knowledge. The knowledge of imagining spreads to all human organs, faculties, and sinews in an inverse relation to the knowledge of cognitive skills.

Imagining proceeds by gathering knowledge hierarchically. Simpler operations of motor organs inform higher cells with more complex operations and even more complex and decipherable stimuli.

Imagining is primarily a social function. Arousal, orientation, attention, motivation, transmission, and reading of signs are primarily social actions within social and cultural contexts. Successful imagining is identifiable only as social transformation. The invention of the press, for example, made it possible for the act of reading to become a synthetic-social transformation. A particular input became a program of action, which in turn crystalized into neural hardware, which incorporated a cultural loop into the human nervous system. In turn this new synthesis changed the environment within which humans were programmed or educated.

In short, the generative image is also a generative power outside of time. It enters time in the actual act of imagining and transforms time by infiltrating and transforming the public domain made by humans, because it was already there.

CLOSING REMARKS

Ignatius de Loyola has been praised, and hated, for many extraordinary deeds: founding the Jesuits, the Society of Jesus, leading the ill-named Counter Reformation; opening the church to all the corners of the world. He has been less noticed for the smaller and less extraordinary deeds: his praise for everybody else's path; his insatiable quest for knowledge; his reconciliation of so many diverse practices in the church. I have my own memories and my own gratitudes: the sense of adventure he instilled in the human body through his *Exercises*; the tangibility of faith against the false security and distrust of beliefs; the path of imagining as a secure way to return home, knowing that home would be any place the imagination chose; the dedication to clarify the acts of imagining through a common reading with others, to study the public domain and interact with it, to keep on learning even when one already knows, to try public articulation as the measure of one's knowledge and ignorance. I prefer, however, to remember Ignatius writing— committed to his writing, clarifying his writing in the absolute conviction that others with him and before him had already read his lines, if not his written lines. Ignatius' writing is like the Japanese haiku:

To hear
the sounds of the breeze
in the pine wood tree
in the ink painting.

Our lives, at best, are like Ignatius' writing, memory points for others. The rest is up to the powers of imagining.

While world conquest and the quest for social position or individual advancement have always been clear paths for humans, the conquest of the Spirit, of the will of God, may be considered at best a messy affair. While for the former pursuits the models are clear at any given period of history, for the latter the models are so hidden that human action has always turned out to be inadequate. And this is, of course, the primary cause of the inadequacy: Christians, above all young Christians, do not believe that the kingdom of the Spirit functions under human models; they take theological statements as factual happenings that to them "grace" alone may remedy, correct, or improve. As far as Christians are concerned, the facts of the Spirit are clear and indisputable. But this is not the case. The world of the Spirit labors as much under interpretative human models as do physics or economics. The only difference is that in physics or economics people work on the assumption that those models might be fallible and are ready to remake them. In the case of the model governing the Spirit, on the other hand, the model, by remaining tacit, supplants the source of Revelation with only human ignorance and pride and inflicts despair. The belief that humans are radically and "naturally" fallen creatures is not so much a fact of revelation as of its lack. This belief is linked to a human model of the God/man relationship in which Revelation in many respects is missing. St. Augustine is the most obvious preacher of that original fall, yet the concept of "nature" to which he linked it is not Christian, but Greek. The fact of the fall, besides, has nothing to do with "nature" but with the human will, a will that may deviate from God's, but was not necessarily created to do so. Augustine placed evil in the "nature" of men and women. He could not imagine the desire of the human body as the legitimate and necessary desire and embodiment of the whole desire of creation rising, or with the possibility of rising, through the human body, to the will of the Creator. But then again, Augustine closed the gates of revelation once he closed the gates of non-sensuous imagining, as the place where the "dawn. . .joined the dewdrop and the drop of blood, and made them tremble under a forest of memories." Augustine did not model man on God's image; instead, he modeled the Trinity on man's mortal faculties. Augustine's way out, which Protestantism took later on in history, was hope in a great and continuous dose of "grace" to overcome an impasse in fact created by man, not by God.

The other model of God with the same Trinitarian shortcomings is the one best represented by St. Thomas Aquinas in his *Summa Theologiae*. Though the *Summa* has a triadic form, the model is not Trinitarian but Christological, and this has opressive consequences for the young soul of the believer. On this model the Trinity is reduced to the formula, "God becomes man." Jesus, the mediator, becomes identical with God/man. But this is not exactly the Trinitarian origin of Jesus. In the Trinity, Christ is the Second Person, not the whole Trinity. It is not the case, therefore, that God became man; rather, that the Second Person of the Trinity became man. Through his mediation the other two Persons are made present; revelation may thus be opened to humans through Christ. But then certain other actions, besides guilt and grace, are required and made possible for humans. Thus the Trinitarian model (or its absence or substitutes for it) has influenced Christians by determining not only their beliefs but also, in different ways, their public and private behaviors. For those following the Augustinian model, the image of God coincides with the actions of their human faculties as a mirror coincides with its image; life is close, individual, agonic, and passionate, but this image is closer to human models than to models of God. The images supporting this model are borrowed from the external world, not from the inner world of imagining. Revelation is thus closed, and the hope for "grace" is a must in the face of such a hopeless situation.

For the Thomists, on the other hand, humans and "nature" are an *analogy* of God, a model-at-a-distance, from which, again, participation in Revelation has been subtracted. In this model cognition is dependent on the external world, and the best styles of life, that is, Christian life, are equated with individual perfections, individual super-heroes, celibate isolation, avoidance of the world, and theoretical contemplation.

The model of the Trinity, however, as it emerges from the inner workings of mystics like Ignatius de Loyola, Teresa de Avila, and Juan de la Cruz (John of the Cross) starts by placing the Trinity at the center of Christian life and of life as a total project. By turning all things into remembrance, this model returns Jesus to the wholeness of the Trinity, away from the near idolatry of ideologies and the subtle clouding of vision on human ego-centeredness. The incarnate Son is one-third of the revelation. Through him the whole Trinity may be set to work to open revelation, as it was in the beginning. Through him the whole of Creation returns to its origins in the human body. It is not revelation that gave us Christology, but rather Christology, as a reduction of the Trinity, that cut off revelation. We have been, after all, in the grips of models "too distant to be God and not close enough to be human." In the Trinitarian model that Ignatius offers us through his practice and writings, as presented in the documents of this volume, the fancy of a young man of any age could easily be turned into a human project encompassing a whole life time. The human will may be corrected, may even be trained to move synchronically with the will of God in a repetition of that original act of creation-out-of-nothing that cancelled the Creator so that the world might appear. The human body may shamelessly embody the whole desire of the whole of creation as a rite of passage for its divine restoration. No greater sign of love may be performed than the one that cancels one's self so that others may live. On this faith Christianity has become the hidden text of people we call mystics. Ignatius de Loyola is, perhaps, the most systematic exponent of this Christian text. The text remains opened still: "Let us make man to our image and likeness" (Gen. 1:26). What a man has done in his own flesh makes it easier for the rest of us to repeat in ours.

5

Consequences of Hermeneutics

> *Now, here my dear Glaucon, is the whole risk*
> *for a human being. . . And on this account each one*
> *of us must, to the neglect of other studies, above*
> *all see to it that he is a seeker and a student of*
> *that study by which he might be able to learn and*
> *find out who will give him the capacity and the*
> *knowledge to distinguish the good and the bad life,*
> *and so everywhere and always choose the better*
> *from among those that are possible. . . (underline added)*
>
> —Plato/Socrates/*Republic*,618b

 WENT DOWN TO PEIREUS. . ." With these enigmatic words[1] in the *Republic* Plato launches the listener and the generations of philosophers that followed into one of the most astonishing quests of the human spirit: the search for philosophic wisdom. This philosophic wisdom, however, would inform decisions regarding the good life. The philosopher would be trained in such a manner that he/she could always and everywhere choose the better life from among those that are possible. In short, the general project of philosophic wisdom came down to a training in particular habits that would lead the philosopher to a habitual practice of "virtue." Philosophic wisdom as project meant also the visible aspect of performing "virtue by habit." The intelligible and the visible form the complete project of what philosophy was understood to be in the beginning of Western culture. [See illustrations 1 and 2]

"I went down. . ." Socrates says, or even more accurately "down-went-I," and if *then* down-he-went, then *now* he must be "up," or is the writer neither "up" nor "down" but in a third unnamed place?[2] Does writing take place "up," "down," or in neither of the two places? And if in neither place, then, where does philosophic writing take place?

"Peiraeus" answers Socrates. In the original Greek the definitive article is missing. It does not say "the Peiraeus" but "Peiraeus' " "the land beyond," the land beyond the limits, not in Athens and "yet within the defensive walls of Athens" (Bremer, 1984,p.3). "Peiraeus" is both in and not in Athens; it is the place that gives common interests to the assembled speakers; it is the writing and the margins, it is the page.

As the narrative of the *Republic* develops, we find other clues that aid us in the present study. In book five of the *Republic* we discover that the young people conspire to hold Socrates with them to make him talk. Socrates agrees to this "robbery", and in this manner a "community" of speakers is formed. Polemarchus, Adei-

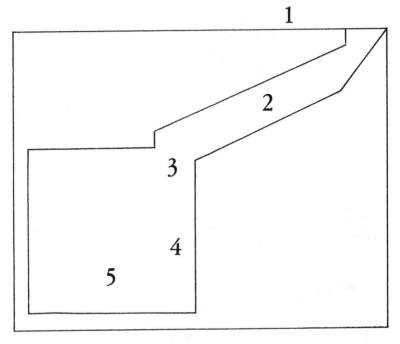

1. THE REPUBLIC:

ACT I:
The physical place of Peiraeus in relation to Athens: 1. Athens; 2. the way of the descent; 3,4,5 Peiraeus.

ACT II., and III.
The Divided line and the Cave. 1. The Sun; 2. "..the rough, steep way up." 3, . . "the fire burning far above and behind them."; 4, "human beings carrying all sorts of arifacts"; 5, "the prisoner, facing the wall of shadows." The intelligible casts shadows only, and it is seen such.

ACT IV.
The narrative of Er. All life, human life, takes place in the cave. There are no humans who make human life in the Sun region. Therefore the descent into the Cave which now becomes the ground of death. Out of the death of the past new life emerges through the technologies of imagining. One must, however, be adept at "practicing death." Memories and imagining are capable of resurrecting the past to make it present life. Through this practice the technologies of the visible are kept alive.

mantus, Glaucon, and even Thrasymachus agree to be part of this community. The same individuals with interests as diverse as they appeared to have in the earlier books of the *Republic*, in particular book one, by agreeing now, in book five, to form a community, bring a new beginning to the discussion of justice. The new beginning will appear in book six with the "divided line," subsequently "the cave," and finally the "journey of Er." But without this com-

The Visible	IDEAS	WISDOM
	Imagining: The Making of Images	Certain Knowledge
The Intelligible	Objects of Science and Art. Theoretical Thought	Shadow of Knowledge
	Opinions, Beliefs	
	Images from Objects	

II. THE DIVIDED LINE AS EMBODIED TECHNOLOGIES

Nowhere in the *Republic* does Plato say which part of the divided line is the intelligible and which is the visible. The fact, however, that Plato describes in detail the acts by which objects and mental operations are performed makes it impossible on hermeneutical grounds to identify the larger part of the line as corresponding to objects and acts of just thinking. The technologies of thinking are identifiable with the other parts of the divided line. The upper part and longest part is the world of Er and the technologies connected with "practicing death," "remembering" and "imagining" as described in this study.

This interpretation sets the history of philosophy on its head. No lesser an authority than Kant in his *Critique of Pure Reason* A 313/B 384 writes:

> Plato made use of the expression 'idea' in such a way as quite evidently to have meant by it something which not only can never be borrowed from the senses but far surpasses even the concepts of the understanding. . . For Plato, ideas are archetypes of the things themselves, and not, in the manner of categories, merely keys to possible experiences. In this view they have issued from the highest reason, and from that source have come to be shared in by human reason.

Kant, however, modifies Plato's 'ideas' and reduces mental life to sets of concepts of pure reason. And he adds:

> The absolute whole of all appearance . . .is only an idea. Since we can never represent it in images, it remains a problem to which there is no solution. (*Critique,* A 327-328/B 384)

munity Socrates' vision "up there" would have never become public domain.

The spaces of discourse in the *Republic* keep shifting as the "community" moves. Each space provides diverse communication systems, diverse expectations on the listeners and participants, diverse intellectual activities, diverse intelligibilities, diverse visibilities or lack of them. The spaces of these discourses are all in "Peiraeus," first in what seems to be Polemarchus' home. This is the space where Polemarchus joins Socrates in a communal relationship, as later on the others do. Polemarchus is the first to join in community with the project of Socrates (Bremer, p.14). He is also the one responsible for initiating the "robbery" of Socrates through his slave and who assumes direct and public responsibility for Socrates' arrest. As the dialogue proceeds, Polemarchus comes from "far off" to only a "little distance from Socrates" (Bremer, p.14). In the end he is even ready to let Socrates go, only Socrates is there to stay.

What begins as the space of "Peiraeus," as the *Republic* unfolds becomes Polemarchus' home, the divided line, the cave, Hades, the journey of Er. Each space demands a different orientation in the listener and the participants, each space commands a new language, each language a new and different technology. Each language and each technology individually demand a different training for their use. Each use requires a different embodiment in the practitioner. These different embodiments form our human history. This history is the history of that essential activity we recognize as philosophy, the history of the omnipresent philosophical Greek aorist in action: the action of hermeneutics, the perennial act of interpreting. Ortega y Gasset summarized this vision with his usual eloquence:

> The Universe was not discovered by philosophy, (but rather philosophy) has been a series of trials during twenty-five centuries to deal with the Universe through the mental procedure that is philosophy. In this experiment divers ways of making that instrument function have been tried. Every new try takes advantage of the previous one. Above all it takes advantage of the errors and limitations of the previous ones. In this sense it is proper to talk of the history of philosophy being the description of the progress of philosophizing. This progress may end up by being in the end that some good day we may discover that not only this or that 'way of thinking' philosophically, was limited and therefore, wrong, but in absolute terms, to philosophize, any kind of philosophizing, is a limitation, an insufficiency, an error, and that there will be a need to invent another way of intellectually facing the Universe; a way different from any of the previous to philosophy and from philosophy itself.[3]

In trying to introduce into the public domain of philosophic discourse Ignatius de Loyola's use of imagining I am aware that a description alone is not sufficient. Imagining itself is part of the philosophical activity of hermeneutics from the beginning of Western culture, and as such its history needs to be brought out. Communities need to be formed before a project and its success are possible.

This study was started with the seemingly simple task in mind of "reading" several connected and disconnected "texts" from the writings of a mystic, Ignatius de Loyola. Though the main focus of this study was the description of how Ignatius used the act of imagining, we found ourselves involved very rapidly in developing the technology of imagining itself. Imagining led us to those inner orderings of our mental life through which imagining takes place. We described imagining by describing how to imagine within the context of Ignatius' writings.

The difficulties surrounding this project accumulated as soon as writing was started. Writing from the center of the page gives out a different reading than writing from the margins. The act of imagining, as practiced by Ignatius de Loyola, is of such a variety that it has only seldom been part of the prose of center-page. It can only be read from the margins, regardless of the violence to writing/ reading this might do to both writer and reader.

Ignatius, as much as Plato, belongs to oral-audial cultures, in which writing and reading performed other functions than the same acts perform for us today. They were both linked to an orality more fundamental than we make room for today in center-page writing. Today we are radically biased against orality, to the point of denying it the full-fledged citizenship of rationality. For this reason we are prone either to suppress whatever traits of orality they might show in their writings, or translate their orality into intelligible terms by our own criteria. Traits of orality have been labeled "residual orality," as if suddenly fully-developed humans had discovered in their less-developed ancestors the tail of their atavistic irrationality, like an undesirable illness, a weakness to be removed through contemporary models of the rational.

It was only after I finished writing this study on imagining and proceeded to descend to Peiraeus that what had been done "up there" seemed to show its most rational face. It could be possible, after all, to list the different spaces of discourse, the different communities, languages, and technologies in use, and to show the inner, philosophical orderings of those acts as constituting the contemporary and historical dimensions of philosophical hermeneutics.

IMAGINING AND WESTERN PHILOSOPHY

It is not a difficult task to gather a community of speakers from the history of philosophy at Polemarchus' house to talk about imagining. Besides the fact that, contrary to the habit of philosophers to disagree on most things, they all seem to agree that without images there are no intelligible judgments of facts. Outside of this, the community seems to disintegrate. The varieties of imaginary acts, how they are performed, which are essential to the common good, which are only individual, which are used for decisions, which to avoid and which to use to pass the time—and what the difference is between fantasy and imagination—these pass unsaid or unclarified. In short, the history of imagining waits to be articulated. A study like the present one may aid in that direction.

Plato is the first philosopher from the West in this tradition to be named as setting the norm of a general ambivalence towards imagining. In the divided line, the image abstracted from empirical objects is placed almost at the bottom of the line. (Mute within the tradition is the fact that the longer part of the divided line, the epistemic part, is a long journey, Er's journey, of imagining, a journey through cultural frames. This journey may only be undertaken on condition that we drink from the "river of forgetfulness" and cancel the worlds and sensations we are familiar with. But about this more later on.)

It is this image from empirical objects that has held center-page as imagining in the West. Aristotle raised it from the low place Plato set it in to the lofty realms of epistemology, where thinking "will not exist without images" (*De Anima*,432a 14), even though "imagination is for the most part false" (*De Anima*,428a 11). Through the medieval philosophers Hume accepts the same tradition, when on the one hand he calls for a "resolution to reject all the trivial suggestions of the fancy, and to adhere to the understanding" (*A Treatise of Human Nature*, p.267), but then he defines understanding as "the general and more establish'd properties of the imagination" (Ibid.p.267). He goes even further by stating that "the memory, senses, and understanding are, therefore, all of them founded on the imagination" (Ibid.p.265). Kant distinguishes two types of imaginations, the "visionary" one which "produces empty figments of the brain," and the "inventive" imagination, which operates "under the strict surveillance of reason" (*Critique of Pure Reason*, A770,B798). Though for Kant imagination is blind, it turns out that "it is an indispensable function of the soul, without which we should have no knowledge whatsoever," for it provides a synthesis in the understanding and it is such synthesis "that gives rise to knowledge" (Ibid. A78, B103, A77). In short, without imagination there is no philosophy.

Descartes is perhaps the best classic example of ambivalence about imagining. The *Meditations* would not be possible without a hard dose of imagining, for Descartes has to *imagine* every belief so that he might "imagine the least doubt" (*Meditations*, 1961, p.23). Descartes' *Treatise of Man* is again an imaginative exercise on how a mechanistic model for men would "resemble us." And yet he concludes that imagining is "in no way necessary to my nature or essence, that is to say, to the essence of my mind" (*Meditations*, p.69).

Fichte's *Grundlage of 1794* turns the tables around and proposes a systematic formal analysis of imagining as the transcendental ground of all human acting and human temporality. "All reality. . ." he writes, "is brought forth solely by the imagination. . . this act of the imagination forms the basis for the possibility of our consciousness, our life, our being for ourselves. . ." (*Grundlage*, 59). Fichte's analysis of the act of imagining is the best formal link phenomenology has to the philosophical past. Some phenomenologists are tapping this forgotten source (Hohler, 1982).

Ambivalence about the varieties of imagining endures in the tradition; in no one is the case more evident than in Husserl, and through him in the tradition that followed.

While in many respects Husserl shares with the past the biases of a non-historical reconstruction of nature and takes as legitimate the manipulative control over people and things that scientific models have (and with him Heidegger, Ricoeur, Merleau-Ponty and others in the same tradition), it is at the hands of Husserl that imagining regains a more central foundational role. Phenomenology without imagining is not possible and this on account of two strategies, both philosophical. The first consists in phenomenological reduction, that is, the technique to bracket objects or even reality. The second is the technique of free variation, that is, the use of actual acts of imagining to let the imagination "have free rein" (*Phänomenologische Psychologie*, p.71). According to Husserl "freedom in the investigation of essences necessarily requires that one operate on the plane of the imagination" (*Ideas*, sec.70).

The tradition that followed Husserl, despite this auspicious send off, has dealt with the imagination and imagining with ambivalent results. Confusion as to which description is of imagining and which of fantasy, confusion about day dreaming, reverie, cultural typologies and how the different uses of imagining operate is prevalent. But despite these shortcomings, a history of imagining is being built while the dialogue continues.

Notable efforts are those of Edward Casey, *Imagining: A Phenomenological Study* and Robert Neville's *The Reconstruction of Thinking*. Though both take the imagination as the faculty that abstracts from empirical objects, still both make substantial contributions to the history of imagining. Casey's study establishes the autonomy of the imagination, while Neville's argues that it is through images that all perception is mediated. Both studies together are an important contribution in line with the present study on Ignatius in the sense that what we normally call interpretation, or hermeneutics, is originally a basic image that holds together cosmic worlds or empirical objects. In short, the first original human act is that of imagining.

The most remarkable studies on imagination by contemporary philosophers come from Gaston Bachelard and his disciple Gilbert Durand. Though both are different in sensibilities and even projects, both contribute to the dialogue by keeping history opened. Bachelard is the closer to the interests of the present study. "There is," as he says, "no phenomenology of passivity. . . . The description of the image requires that we participate actively in the creating imagination" (*The Poetics of Reverie*, p.4). As in this present study, Bachelard focuses on the act of creation itself. But unlike this study, his act of imagining is that of reverie. The images he imagines are those of some poets and some scientists or philosophers. His focus gives us a new variety of imagining through which we learn to do phenomenology. Simultaneously he introduces a new kinesis, movement, into the phenomenological act that was missing earlier. Through the discovery of the images that created certain worlds, present there, worlds at hand, we discover what it is that we do when we do phenomenology. Furthermore, he has the ability to separate the philosophical act from the psychological act in the same act of phenomenological reduction. "Psychological acts make a man out of a poet, but how to make a poet out of a man, in spite of life?" (*Poetics of Reverie*, p.10) is Bachelard's challenge as a phenomenologist. Echoes of the same problem appear in the study of world modellings in science as may be seen in the recent study by Alex Comfort, *Reality and Empathy*, 1984.

Bachelard's disciple Gilbert Durand has aimed for a universal typology of images in his study *Les Structures Anthropologiques de L'Imaginaire*. This study is closer to Fichte's dream of a transcendental imagination than to a Bachelardian phenomenology. Still, the primacy and autonomy of the imagination is obvious in intent, even when one does not learn its use, or one is left wondering if the images one classifies are the same concepts one reads. How does phenomenology deal with the difficult task of translating the image to the public domain? Is it sufficient to translate the image into a concept?

This short list of characters dealing with imagining in our history of philosophy has, at least, helped us to establish a tradition to enter into dialogue with it, and to point out the points of ambivalence about the tradition and the act of imagining itself. How do we proceed from the problem to a continuation of the dialogue, to actually building the tradition in its own historical acts of imagining? Where do we go from Polemarchus' house? Is there any other communal space where the continuation of the dialogue would be possible?

The first five Books of the *Republic* are separated from the remaining five by the divided line. The community of young men and Socrates have reached a point of communal agreement to talk about "justice." Definitions abound. Every one of the speakers tries a new one. All except Socrates. Socrates refuses to do so because "justice has not yet been seen." Only on condition that "justice be seen" will Socrates define it. Similarly with "imagining." Though the history we have outlined previously seems to talk about "imagining", the act of "imagining" does not appear anywhere as a visible feature. The intelligible features of justice or of imagining are not sufficient if we are to account for justice in the *Republic* or for imagining in the writings of Ignatius de Loyola. We are not suggesting a difference of degree in justice or in imagining but a difference in kind.

In appearance the prose of the *Republic* (when focused upon the external tokens of language) leads the listener/reader along a smooth and easy pathway; there are changes of direction, delays in the journey but all in all there appears to be a progressive development, an intimation to the listener/reader that home is near. But suddenly Socrates takes over, introduces sudden shocks and abrupt discontinuities, and familiar expectations are set on their head. These shocks, these discontinuities draw attention to themselves and force a "new listening", a "new reading" of what now appears totally strange. These shocks, these abrupt discontinuities are introduced at the end of book six with the divided line, and followed with the cave and the journey of Er.

The divided line ought to be a simple exercise in reading (509b-511e). How difficult can it be to divide a line into two unequal segments? One must be larger than the other; one must be labelled *intelligible*, the other *visible*. (We mentioned in chapter one of this study the difficulty of such a division and the problem it has created for philosophers). Are opinions, images from empirical objects, objects of art, and science visible or intelligible? Is the epistemic part, the larger part, visible or intelligible? A decision must be made. Or must it? If the philosopher makes no decision, then he has no ground on which to stand. If he does make a decision, then his philosophy will suffer.

Every philosopher after Plato has read the *Republic* knowing *a priori* which part of the divided line was the visible and which the intelligible. Opinions, images from empirical objects, objects from science and art are all visible; ideas, models, theories are intelligible. But here lies the problem and the different kind of philosophy Plato intends as a project. Plato does not say which part is which (Bremer, pp.82-114). It would have been easy for him to do so. But he does not do it. He refuses. A commitment to either side would have ruined his hermeneutical project. It did so for others. The fact that Plato/Socrates continue the dialogue without commitment to such a division and identification requires the philosopher to proceed without such a previous commitment.

As the dialogue continues, it is obvious Plato/Socrates meant for the philosopher to invert the tables and make the visible the origin of the intelligible and not vice-versa. As we see in the cave, the intelligible produces only shadows. And the journey of Er makes visible a world, several possible worlds, otherwise hidden by the intelligibles. With Plato the memories of the past become visible, are visible, and are the origin of the intelligible. With Ignatius de Loyola, Christ and the mysteries are visible and the origin of the intelligible.[4]

THE TECHNOLOGIES OF THE VISIBLE

Before we return to the cave and the journey of Er we need to make a slight detour. This delay is demanded by the distance of reading habits between texts like the *Republic* or Ignatius de Loyola's writings and our own. Mixed with those reading habits there are a few presuppositions that need clarification to make the reading possible.

Natural evolution ends with the appearance of humans. With humans cultural evolution takes over. The cultural becomes the natural in humans. Hence the need for philosophy. The primary technology of culture is language. Through language, its materiality, its measures, its rhythms, its repeatability, its orderings of mental life, humans extend themselves as far and as wide and deeply as language is able to reach. Language, as much through its internal tokens as the external ones, is a technology. It not only creates the visible and the intelligible aspects of human life but sensitizes individuals to those aspects of the visible and the intelligible it can reach. In this creation of the visible and the intelligible language and technology become coextensive. The visible and the intelligible adapt to a language and its inner mechanisms that unfold, repeat, and may be taught and learned. The only condition for this human fluidity, for the fluidity of the human body, is that these technologies be kept alive, be "re-membered."

Contemporary studies in several disciplines have lately emphasized the different technologies or languages used by oral and literary cultures. Authors like Parry, Havelock, Lord, Jousse, Goody, Peabody and particularly Clanchy (1979) and Walter Ong (1967, 1982) have done an exemplary task in warning contemporary readers of the dangers of reading oral cultures by the criteria of contemporary literacy. From Plato (*Seventh Letter*) to Walter Ong cautionary notes have been issued as to the dangers of writing. The technologizing of the word has been seen as a danger against thought. Writing, printing, and electronics are seen as in some indefinite way causing thought to be biased, narrow, arbitrary, imperialistic. What is not clear, in this criticism, is why writing and not reading is the guilty activity in contemporary culture. The written page may be read in many ways. The reader makes decisions, not the written page. Furthermore, all texts as much from oral as from literary cultures are written down. We only deal with those that are written down. We cannot blame the only access we have to the past. The dream of an innocent reader using a "natural" language is still alive. The fact of the matter, however, is that language and technology are coextensive. Language, oral or written, printed or electronic is an inner technology that organizes mental life, orders its acts, decides by its sheer power and materiality while extending externally the visible, auditive, tactile, sensuous and intelligible world of humans. Language is neither natural nor instrumental; language is radically, biologically, originally a technology organized through cultural habits, needs, and repetitions. Thought is not possible outside of language; imagining is not possible outside of language; fantasizing is not possible outside of language. The intentional ordering of our mental life follows the cultural ordering of our linguistic technologies. The fact that there are several such technologies accounts for the shifts in cultural and bodily habits, the supression and forgetfulness of some, and the possible revivification of all.

It was Plato who first conceived of philosophy and the philosopher as the ones to keep alive these multiple technologies. The way to keep them alive was to develop in the body itself a sustained, constantly exercised habit of recollection, so that when called upon, philosophers would be ready and able to make decisions for the rest of us. That is, philosophers, to be philosophers, needed as a primary condition to have within themselves—not in a written tablet, not in print, not in electronic soft or hardware (hence his opposition to writing)—those technologies, plural languages, that need be applied in decision making (*Gorgias, Phaedrus*). All technology can be taught. Language makes that possible; it is repeatable. Repetition makes the possibility an embodied reality. Since we hold historically a plurality of languages, technologies, we also hold a plurality of choices. Depending on how we choose our training, even the best life or virtue can be learned. One may actually learn to perform "virtue by habit," or the philosopher may actually chose the best life, "by habit", as Plato dreamt.

A technology, however, is more than a mere technic. A technology embraces a common system of communication and commerce among the people of a culture. This system of communication is held together by a language interiorized as technology and, therefore, it can be repeated distributively within a common bodily intimacy of understanding and dialogue. Everyone within the communication system knows what is being said, for all order their faculties and linguistic habits to listen to the same things. The external tokens of language as well as the internal ones of decision, conceptualization, purposive action, are ordered, included or excluded in the dialogue according to the technology in use. Any form of conversion and transformation implies the simultaneous use of a different technology. If the technology is not developed, the greatest vision, the greatest insight, the greatest experience does not reach the public domain as what it originally is, but rather as a continuation of what it already was.

For this reason language viewed as technology and since it is an embodied technology, includes in its expression a general native background: a biographical immersion of the writer in the technologies described and a biographical writing in which the philosopher shows his proficiency in the acts and technologies described. Language is primarily biographical. It is inner technology, which is primarily transparent, made visible.

Hermeneutics demands of the philosopher that all human possibilities be first held evident, made evident and remembered. This effort of memory required by hermeneutics entails that the philosopher practicing it must not be committed *a priori* to any one particular technology. He must be familiar with each one of them, remember them, and repeat them when needed, so that the memory remains alive. He cannot be a common mortal, take a philosophical position, and read the world through that technology. The philosopher needs stay in constant exercise and must be a constant "reminder."

The knowledgeable reader will by now have anticipated the use of the word *text* throughout this study to be coextensive with language as technology. Antecedents of this use may be found in the large literature of post-phenomenological hermeneutics, semiotics, structuralism, deconstruction, etc. Some other readers might find the use of the term in regard to illiterate mystics in illiterate cultures, or even contemporary illiterate mystics, inappropriate. They will term my use of the word *text* an example of chirographic bias. By this is meant an opposition between "natural" thought and thought that has built into itself the technology of writing, printing, or electronics.

This present study on imagining addresses both groups of readers in different ways. This study criticizes the use of the word *text* as the ultimate source of reference for analysis and proceeds beyond intelligibility to the embodiment of technology in the human body, the primary text. This embodied text is the referential text of all analysis. The present study takes the study of texts to be coextensive with the embodied habits of humans found in the human body, therefore with human history. This is the reason why remembering texts in the present is simultaneously building history.

This study also criticizes the belief that we can get outside of language and use it as a tool. Man is language, its use, and the habits accumulated through that use. My own studies about oral cultures (de Nicolas 1971,1976a,1976,1982) and those of others— Ernest McClain (1977,1978,1981), Patrick Heelan (1979,1983), John Bremer (1984), and Leo Treitler (1984)—suggest that language, technology, culture, and text are coextensive. Where literary cultures use some logic to map the technology of language, oral cultures used music and the criteria of sound to map the technologies of its use. They used meters of music and their measures as the model and measure of proportion, and these were coextensive with language and its measures and proportions. Oral language, if it can increase human rationality, needs to be shown as autonomously rational, and not simply the victim of literacy and its current technology.

The present study, however, because it takes its stand on hermeneutics, proceeds beyond the issues mentioned above and abandons the common place for a unique place: a place of indeterminedness. In order to be hermeneutical this study does not take sides on issues; it cannot take sides because of intelligible philosophical principles on the adequate or inadequate interpretation of texts. Strategically this study looks for the original acts that make texts visible; thus, it is beyond industrial cultures, deconstruction, Marxism, Freudianism, structuralism, even phenomenology. This study is simply hermeneutical. Thus, it does not issue principles of interpretation, it simply presupposes them. It presupposes them in the text. Therefore no interpretation is possible, on this hermeneutical stand, unless certain technological embodiments are present in the interpreter and become the guide for reading. If those technological embodiments are not present, then no amount of philosophical principle or description will replace them and do the philosophical job. Hermeneutics works on the assumption that the interpreter is capable of identifying as reader those acts, and no others, that create the text in the first place. Since all the material

we interpret is written down, printed out, or recorded on electronic
screens—even that from oral cultures—the text is all we now have.
Communications, even those from God to the soul, lead only to
possible texts. Texts become actual only when written; only then
do they join the public domain. The interpreter needs to uncover
the acts by which the text is to be read and thereby help readers
reorder the acts of their mental lives for them to coincide with
those of the text. Reading acts and composing acts need to coincide
for the text in its interpretative context to become visible. The
initial task of hermeneutics is to bring out the multiplicity of those
acts and thus let the plurality of texts exemplify the plurality of
historical-human-mental-bodily-life.

THE RETURN TO THE CAVE

Plato's *Republic* remains to this day the primer of hermeneutics.
The plurality of texts coincides in the *Republic* with the plurality
of technologies. Each place of discourse entails a different technology in use. The philosopher is the embodied exemplar of such
embodied acts.

After Socrates introduces the divided line in the dialogue, the
house of Polemarchus is transformed into a new "place." It becomes
the cave. The Sun is now "up," the cave is now "down" and in
between there is the mid-region of the "fire," where the "intelligible"
is *seen* as being the cause of the shadows in the walls. All the
previous discourses and speakers are now *seen* waving their "intelligibles" in front of the fire to produce shadows. The prisoners and
even the speakers live by them, are sensitized by them, and shortly
will feel their emptiness. The region of the sun is obviously the
"solitary region," where no one dwells. Life is in the cave. Prisoners,
guardians, and Socrates live there together. The intelligible con-
trols the life of the city. Discourse has now a different place: the
middle region in front of the fire.

This middle region is the constant place of writing. Socrates
not only rewrites "justice" as his community defined it, but he also
rewrites Homer in the *Republic* the same way Ignatius rewrites
Augustine. Homer was a bad poet who took images from discreet
objects and made them the prototype of the behavior of the gods.
He was also the bad poet that buried the human dead and made
them obsolete for posterity. The Hector that Homer buried is not
dead in the *Republic* of Socrates/Plato. Hector/Er becomes alive at
the hand of Socrates and brings from the dead the history and
images —visible—from the past to rebuild the present. Hector does
not die, as in Homer, at the hand of Achilles. Plato rewrites the
end of the Iliad by not naming Achilles, thus holding back forever

the hand that killed memory, and brings Hector/Er back from the dead in order to "save the story." Er does not die in the *Republic* and, therefore, never dies (Bremer, pp.115-152).

No birth, however, takes place without great pain. The joys and overwhelming sensitizations at the sight of the sun are only proportionate to the bereavement and desolation we feel when we learn our life was guided, and we see the familiar theory die in front of our very eyes. The theoretical magicians in front of the fire die hard, for they live in us as embodied theory. The bereavement for the death of the customary is much harder to take than the consolation of the sun. A whole range of possible technologies from the accumulations of history need to be kept alive if we are not to collapse completely. To save humans from the fate that the collapse of theories like those of Homer, Augustine, or Aquinas might inflict in their lives is the primary aim of an education like that of the *Republic*; it insists on a plurality of technological texts for human survival.

The model of those technological texts is the journal of Er. Once more Socrates/Plato relocates us to another place where the dialogue is continued.

Er's place is Hades, a place of total human bereavement. None of the familiar sensations are present. The worlds, as we know them, are forgotten, cancelled. We have drunk from the "river of forgetfulness", and the only visible things are images of the past. This is the time to see colors as they are, images through images, total lives through total lives at a glance. Choices are made on the ability to see in this manner. This is the place of the visible only. The place of choice.

Er is a man of "every tribe." He is neither a Greek, nor an Aethenian, neither Thracian nor Persian. He is a *Pamphylian*, a man who makes his home everywhere. He is every man. He is also Socrates, he is Plato. He is the lone witness, he chooses alone, is judged alone, rewarded alone, punished alone, alone born again, alone he gives his testimony. He is the warrior for whom every place is all the life there is. He is always in the presence of death, his place is the death of the worlds around him. (He is also the chosen messenger, with no freedom to refuse.) It is on Er that Plato/Socrates use a journey of twelve days to describe in detail how the visible is brought to human kind, the cave, again. Er is systematically dismembered, as witness-to-be, into a plurality of sights, sounds, smells, touches, tastes, and movements. This dismemberment is the condition that he will deliver his "message" to those in the cave. What he tells is the following: What happened to other men is "empirically dead;" for the dead to live again among the living, it needs to be remembered by re-telling. Homer, the intelligibles, are wrong burying the dead for ever. Plato/Socrates/Er resurrect the dead by turning them first into living memories, so that the living may stay alive by the technologies of resurrection. Not to let them be surrendered to something less poetic such as realism, empiricism, positivism, or idealism, to what is visible or intelligible as dictated by those intelligibles, is the corrective of hermeneutics.

Hermeneutics, however, in its effort to make visibility out of life, is a humble, obedient exercise. The vision of the sun may give us worlds, but not yet communities, societies, or cultures. That vision needs to be shared with others, mediated through others, lived in the company of others. The vision needs to be read in the company of some other human who has had the experience of such reading and that of the sun. Plato found Socrates, Socrates Er, Er the historical past. Ignatius found other mystics, reading confessors, the historical past, including the one of Plato. Plato as much as Ignatius is an exemplar of how to choose the better life from among those that are possible, each within his own historical horizons and the possibilities of his own faith. In either case the past is the only guide. Though our futures are many, the past is common. There is always that "other" from the past that joins hands with us in this same act of reading.

Against this project of philosophy as hermeneutics, which Plato dreamt, the philosophy that followed, given that the past is always made from our present, made a commitment to the intelligible side of the divided line as the ground of philosophy. Those secure grounds did not turn out as secure as they seemed. Contemporary efforts at hermeneutics do not find it easy to disengage themselves from past habits of thinking.

THE FUTURE OF PHILOSOPHY

The future of Philosophy is necessarily linked to Philosophy's origins. Originally, as embodied in Plato's doing of philosophy, Philosophy is concerned—motivated in its own activity—with the quality of all the acts it performs. Quality of performance concerns itself with directing the will to select, sort out, those acts that are historically capable of being re-membered and therefore executed. The distinctions and divisions leading to the selection of these acts are to be found in the quality itself of the act performed, not in the external properties of objects and their external relations. Thus we may distinguish between "things" and images, originals and copies, models and fictions (simulacra). Divisions are made for the sake of an inner genealogy that identifies the pure from the impure, the authentic from the inauthentic, and is not at all concerned with classification of genus and species. This is a philosophy primarily concerned with the sorting of gold, as in the *Republic*, or the sorting of claims ("I am the shepherd of men", "I am the possessed, the lover") as in the *Statesman* or the *Phoedrus*.

The selection of the pure act works in Plato under the strict necessity of the model. The model of musical operations performed in books 8, 9, and 10 of the *Republic* through the marriage myth, the myth of the Tyrant, the Myth of Er, and equally in the circulation of souls in the *Phaedrus*, the myth of archaic times in the *Statesman*, or the World-Soul in the *Timeaus*,—is the internal criterion of selection itself in the total narrative of foundation according to which selectivity may be applied. The mythical grounds the philosophical. And the philosophical has to deal with the selection of foundation, the object of claims and claimant; in Platonic terms, the unsharable, the shared, the sharer, (the father, the mother, the offspring).

Plato's philosophical corpus divides into those texts that establish the foundations for the claims (authentic claims) and those *that hunt down the false claimant (Timeaeus, Critias, Republic, Laws,* and *Phaedrus, Statesman, Sophist*). Plato is as rigorous in establishing the positive path of and for Philosophy as he is in predicting the possible false (fictive) path of the same. Plato is aware from the beginning that the fictive is not only the negation of the original, but also that it has the power to cover any original from emerging. Philosophy may be done not only as a false copy of philosophical activity but even more the false copy may (has the power) to put into question the very notion of copy and of embodied models.

For a copy to be like the original, that is, well grounded in an identity of acts, the copy must retain both the image and the likeness of the original. In the *Sophist* Plato distinguishes between iconic copies (likenesses) and phantasmatic simulacra (semblances) (*Sophist* 236b, 264c). Icons are good images, they are endowed with resemblance, that is, relations and propotions (as in the musical model) that constitute inner performance. The claimant conforms to the real only in so far as the operations through which he/she reaches it conform to the operations modeled by the Idea, the ground and claim of all copies. It is a lineage of qualities on how the derived semblances equal the original modeling.

The similacrum, on the other hand, is not just that it is a copy of a copy, a degraded icon, but rather an image without a resemblance. A fallen angel, or a fallen creature, retaining the image of God while loosing the resemblance. This is the state of sin of Philosophy. We have internalized a dissimilitude. The simulacrum includes within itself the power to cover and exclude all originality, all history, by forming those constructions that include within them the angle of the observer. This blind center, this decentered self perspective, this point of view occupied by the observer is the real flight from the original image, a process of progression towards the unbound, a gradual subversion of history, an avoidance of the limit, the Same and the Like. It is also the negation of both original and copies, model and reproduction, it is the birth of *simulation*, the inauthentic, together with no criterion for negating the false claimant. Philosophy has thus entered the Modern Age and the sin of modernism.

We as philosophers need to keep the *whole* story alive.

THE FUTURE OF HERMENEUTICS

This study on imagining was undertaken with a sense of alarming urgency. The habits of intelligibility inherited from the past have introduced into practically every area of human education and action fictive—non historical—models of manipulating the cultural. The manipulative control over people and things that scientific models have is taken for granted. The pragmatic goal of science to control natural phenomena is also taken for granted, and this end justifies the means of a fictive reconstruction of nature according to models of science that make this achievement possible. In a recent study entitled *Space-Perception and the Philosophy of Science*, Patrick Heelan (1983) shows how from the beginnings of Western culture with Aristotle, later on Augustine, Aquinas, Galileo, Spinoza, and in our times Einstein, there has been the belief that Nature is a book "written" from the start in its complete form, final and original, and that science, be it theology, as the science of the past, or the natural sciences of the present, is the actual form of that reading. Heelan shows in his exemplary study that hermeneutics are performed on embodied technologies that make visible the transparencies of intelligible technologies. We hope his model may serve others to do hermeneutics rather than talk about them.

Similarly, the external technologies created by science are taking a form that is being denied to humans by the same criteria that all technology is expected to be only an external extension of the human body. External technologies have a way of interiorizing themselves and becoming the software of inner mechanisms in humans. Eventually software may become hardware and form a cultural loop, the way printing did with reading. Through external technology man is displaced as the bearer of thought, imagination, and other mental operations; he is being displaced by the machine, which by now not only 'thinks,' 'counts,' or "imagines', but in certain cases perhaps also decides. A hormone made through genetic engineering, for example, brings science and technology so close that they are indistinguishable. Learning how a foreign protein can be made by bacteria (science) and the production of a functional hormone (its application, its technology) were realized simultaneously. Science and technology are in this case inseparable. How can technology not escape detection when it masquerades as science? Who is there to supervise? If humans are deprived of the legitimate operations that constitute them as humans, especially their will, what kind of humans are we educating? Inner technologies are linked to the human will. If we deprive humans of the exercise of these technologies, we deprive them of their own will. To the degree we succeed in our machines to imagine, or to think, to that same degree we deprive our population of those exercises. The problem, obviously, is not the machine. The problem is the models we humans select for our training.

No other voice from the recent past has been more eloquent than that of Ortega y Gasset to turn hermeneutics into a program of education:

> Whoever aspires to understand man—that eternal tramp, a thing essentially on the road—must throw overboard all immobile concepts and learn to think in ever shifting terms.[5]

This inner mobility is the way of hermeneutics:

> If primitive humanity had not possessed this ability to inflame itself with far off things in order to struggle against obstacles it encountered close at hand, humanity would continue to be static.[6]

But according to Ortega this task is impossible unless we change our habits: "We need a new technique of invention."[7] Ortega understood this need in the fact that man is bodily linked to his past. Man and history are the accumulation of those internalized habits: "The historical past is not just a simple past because it is not the present. . .but because it has happened to other men of whom we have a memory and, therefore, it keeps on happening to us who are constantly re-membering it."[8] Ortega aimed at returning philosophy to its hermeneutical origins, its own history. Intelligibility has not always been full and immutable; it has also been empty and deficient. Knowing has not been the exercise of a faculty that produced knowledge when used. Knowing is meditated through multiple technologies that men and women may use as their birth right, but it is not permanent. Knowing, rather, is a historical form humans reached in view of certain failures in their lives.[9] Ortega's reformulation of hermeneutics is closer to our own interests in this study, and I bring it here to separate it from the formulations of hermeneutics of Dilthey (1958), Gadamer (1975), Ricoeur (1981), and Heidegger (1962). Unlike Dilthey, Ortega would focus on the primary decisions of history, rather than its ideas. As against Gadamer, Ricoeur, Heidegger, and others, Ortega would insist on the primary condition of embodied technologies, habits of thought, linguistic habits of the text etc. before the text may be analyzed. It is only after this technological embodiment, not before, that philosophical reflection is possible. Otherwise, what we call hermeneutics is only a bridge of passage for foreign texts to migrate into our own hospitable but imperialistic soil.

The documents that follow in translation are the actual texts of this study. Imagining is described as made in the *Spiritual Exercises*, annotations and other documents of the *Exercises*. The reading of the signs of imagining is taken from the *Spiritual Diary*. The public domain and the hybrid presentation of the primary text of the *Exercises* and the secondary text of the *Diary* appear in the *Diary of a Pilgrim*. Since the whole life of a man or a woman is not just imagining, we felt, for the sake of balance, the need to add some other documents from Ignatius' writings under the section of *The Letters*. The mystic is also many other people, able to make other decisions and deal with the world in more diverse situations and through diverse mental skills. For this reason we have added those documents that show the plurality of texts in Ignatius. Some relate directly to imagining, others do not. All together balance the picture of a man through a wider choice of his prose. The man is his whole prose. We hope, through this study, to make it also ours.

ANTONIO T. de NICOLÁS
SETAUKET, N.Y. 1984

Two

A PLURALITY

OF

TEXTS

IN TRANSLATION

SPIRITUAL EXERCISES

Contents

THE "PAPERS" LATER KNOWN AS THE *Exercises* which Ignatius de Loyola gave to Martín Frías in Salamanca, at the request of the Inquisition, for his examination, and the "writing" which Ignatius gave in Paris to the Inquisitor Valentín Lievin have all been lost. What we know as the *Exercises* is the so-called "Autograph" in Spanish, a text of the *Exercises* with about forty-seven handwritten marginal notes by the hand of Ignatius. It is on this text, as edited in 1928 by Father Codina in Turin, that the present translation is based. This full text appears in the Spanish edition of the *Obras Completas* of San Ignacio de Loyola, Biblioteca de Autores Cristianos, Madrid, 1977.

I have tried to follow the Spanish text as closely as possible, including the Spanish annotations, but trying to preserve Ignatius' language in English usage. I should make, perhaps, a few remarks on the translation itself, in particular on those points where I have chosen a different English word rather than the accustomed English usage of the same word.

Previous English or American translators have tried to pick out the sense of every paragraph rather than the "language" of the text. I have aimed for the latter and found it thus possible to avoid several mistakes repeated in the past. I have at times, often, changed the punctuation of the long Spanish sentences to make the reading easier. But these improvements are small compared to other more serious issues I will now mention.

English translations of Ignatius' *Exercises* share a cognitive bias absent in the saint. This bias is spread around in such a subtle manner that the exercitant is perhaps not aware that what he or she is given as meditation or spiritual exercises has little to do with what Ignatius meant or did with the same activities. The key word in contention here is the word *principio*, which Ignatius uses to establish the kind of exercises that are to follow in meditation. This word he uses in describing his *Principio y Fundamento* (23) or the foundation of all the exercises that are about to follow. The usual English translation of this word *principio* is *principle*, and thus the phrase is translated as *Principle and Foundation*. In Spanish and Latin, however, the word *principio* means both origin and principle. Philosophers agree on few things, and this is one of the few. The word *principle* stands for origins of cognition, or for logic as principles and origin of cognition. Thus logic, or reason, is the skill needed to act according to those principles. On the other hand, origins have nothing to do with cognition and cognitive skills: in order to discover one's origins in their most radical, original sense, the faculties to use are imagination and memory. Feeling is the criterion used for knowing that one is dealing with origins and not principles. The *Spiritual Exercises* are closer to imagining than to an intellectual quest. The intellect acts on principles, the imagination on origins. The origins the imagination and memory work on, in the *Exercises*, are the origins of the most original experience of Christianity, the frames of the life of Christ, and originally and ultimately, the frame of the experience of the Trinity, of which the Christian experience was born, according to the traditions Ignatius follows. On this simple philosophical clarification the history of Christianity of the last four centuries is summarized. And it is on this question of the supremacy of the intellect over the imagination and vice versa that cultures and individuals have been divided, internally and externally, since the beginning of cultures. Furthermore, while in English we may say of someone that he is a "man of principle" in the singular, we could not say the same in Spanish. In Spanish the sentence would be "*un hombre de principios*," in the plural. Therefore, "Principle and Foundation" is totally wrong as a translation. For this reason I have used the native meaning: Origin and Foundation.

These points are made more explicitly clear in the main body of the text of this volume.

Readers of this text not acquainted with the traditional language of the *Exercises*, which I have tried to preserve as much as possible, might find some English expressions odd if not incorrect. I would like to address them now.

We are used to hearing people talk about "doing" meditation, or "doing" exercises to lose weight, or to run in the Olympics. Tradition, however, has kept the Spanish *hacer ejercicios*, or the Latin *exercicia facere* as the English "to make" the meditation, or to "make the exercises", and so I have kept these expressions in the English version of this text. This tradition goes back to the sixteenth century, and there is no point in breaking it.

For further research on the origin of the *Exercises* and other related documents I add an up-to-date, comprehensive bibliography in several languages at the end of this volume. I hope with this to encourage research in an area that needs it desperately. It was to me a shock to find that the only copy available in this country of Fr. Gagliardi's commentary on the *Discernment of Spirits*, a commentary approved by Ignatius and essential to the understanding of making the exercises, had never been opened by anyone. I had to do so with a knife, for the pages were still sewn together when it came to me.

One last note on the style of the *Exercises*. In the *Exercises*, and even more so in the *Spiritual Diary*, Ignatius seems to be writing not with a pen but with a hammer. I have tried to make the style a bit more readable. The reader should be aware, however, that the dry and abrupt style is fitting to a text that as "written" is a false text, and as a guide to meditation is no more than memory points to let the imagination weave the real texts—much more beautiful and not written—of what is soon going to feel like real life, and not imagination.

Following the same method, images could be constructed from narrations of the Old Testament, Hindu and Buddhist mandalas, or even, in a smaller scale, the corporation, the nation, the community.

—ANTONIO T. de NICOLÁS

ANIMA CHRISTI

Soul of Christ, sanctify me.
Body of Christ, save me.
Blood of Christ, inebriate me.
Water from the side of Christ, wash me.
Passion of Christ, strengthen me.
O good Jesu, hear me;
Within Thy wounds hide me;
Suffer me not to be separated from Thee;
From the malignant enemy defend me;
In the hour of my death call me,
And bid me come to Thee,
That with Thy Saints I may praise Thee
For ever and ever. Amen.[1]

Spiritual Exercises

NNOTATIONS FOR OBTAINING SOME understanding of the following Spiritual Exercises and thus help the giver of them as well as the recipient.[2]

[1]　The first annotation is that this expression, Spiritual Exercises, embraces every method of examining one's conscience, of meditation, of contemplation, of praying mentally or vocally, and of other spiritual activities that will be mentioned later. For just as strolling, walking, and running are bodily exercises, so spiritual exercises are methods of preparing and disposing the soul to free itself of all inordinate attachments, and after accomplishing this, of seeking and discovering the divine will regarding one's life orientation for the health of one's soul.[3]

[2]　The second is that the person who gives another instruction in the method and procedure of meditation or contemplation must faithfully narrate the story pertaining to such contemplation or meditation. He should limit his discourse to a brief, summary statement of its principal points; for then the person making the contemplation, by reviewing the true foundations of the story, and by personal reflection and reasoning may find something that will make it a little more clear—or touch him more deeply. This may happen as a result of his own reasoning or through the enlightenment of his understanding by divine grace. This is a greater spiritual satisfaction and produces more fruit than if the one who gives the exercises were to discourse at great length and amplify the meaning of the subject matter, for it is not an abundance of knowledge that fills and satisfies the soul but rather the feeling and savoring of things internally.[4]

[3]　In all of the following Spiritual Exercises, one uses acts of the intellect for reasoning and those of the will for eliciting affections. We should realize, however, that in acts of the will, when we are speaking vocally or mentally with God our Lord or His saints, more reverence is required of us than when the intellect is used for reasoning.

[4]　Four weeks are assigned to the following Spiritual Exercises corresponding to the four parts into which they are divided: the first, which is the consideration and contemplation of sin; the second, the life of our Lord Jesus Christ up to and including Palm Sunday; the third, the passion of Christ our Lord; and the fourth, the Resurrection and Ascension, to which are appended Three Methods of Prayer. This does not mean that each week must cover of necessity seven or eight days. It may happen that some exercitants in the first week are slower than others in finding what they are seeking, i.e., contrition, sorrow, and tears for their sins. In like manner some may be more diligent than others, or be more disturbed or tried by different spirits; it may be necessary sometimes to shorten the week and on other occasions to lengthen it. The same is true for the following weeks as the subject matter requires. However, the Exercises should be completed in about thirty days.

[5]　Anyone making the Exercises will benefit greatly if he enters into them with great courage and generosity with his Creator and Lord, offering Him his entire will and freedom, that His Divine Majesty may make use of his person and of all that he possesses in accordance with His most holy will.

[6]　When the one who is giving the Exercises feels that the soul of the exercitant is experiencing neither consolation nor desolation nor any other spiritual movement, or that he has not been troubled by different spirits, he should question him closely about the Exercises; whether he is making them, making them at the appointed time,[5] and in what manner he makes them. He should in like manner question him about the additions, if he makes them attentively, and he should require particularly a detailed account of each of these points. Consolation and Desolation are treated in nos. 317-317. The additions are given in nos. 73-90.

[7]　If the one giving the Exercises sees that he who makes them is in desolation or tempted, he should be careful not to be severe or harsh with him but rather gentle and kind. He should give him courage and strength for the future, helping him to see the wiles of the enemy of human kind, and having him prepare and dispose himself for the consolation to come.

[8]　If the one who is giving the Exercises perceives a need for instruction of the exercitant regarding desolation and the snares of the enemy, as also with respect to consolation, he may explain to

him the rules of the first and second week on the discernment of several spirits, nos. 316-324, 328-336.

[9]   It is well to observe that when the exercitant is making the Exercises of the first week, if he is a person not well versed in spiritual matters and is tempted crudely and openly, for example, by showing obstacles to further advancement in the service of our Lord, such as, hardships or shame or fear of worldly honor, etc., then the one giving the Exercises should not talk with him on the rules for discerning different spirits, which are found in the second week. This matter is too subtle and too advanced for him to comprehend, and the rules of the second week are as likely to do him harm as the rules of the first week are likely to be of assistance to him.

[10]   When the one giving the Exercises feels that the exercitant is being shaken and tempted under the appearance of good, then it would be well to speak with him about the rules of the second week already mentioned. For ordinarily it is more usual for the enemy of human kind to tempt under the appearance of good when a person is exercising in the illuminative way, which corresponds to the Exercises of the second week, than in the purgative way, corresponding to the Exercises of the first week.[6]

[11]   It is to the benefit of the person making the Exercises of the first week to know nothing of what is to be done in the second week. He should rather work in the first week to acquire what he is seeking, as though he expected to find nothing more in the second.

[12]   The one giving the Exercises should impress upon the exercitant that since he must devote one hour to each of the five Exercises or contemplations that are to be made each day, that he should always be completely satisfied in his conscience that he has spent a full hour at the Exercise, and rather more than an hour rather than less; since the enemy often tries to have us shorten the hour for such contemplation, meditation, or prayer.

[13]   It should be noted also that just as in time of consolation it is simple and light to remain in contemplation for an entire hour, so it is quite difficult in time of desolation to complete the hour. Therefore, to overcome desolation and to conquer temptation, the exercitant should continue a little beyond the full hour. Thus he will accustom himself not only to resist the adversary, but even to defeat him.

[14]   If the one giving the Exercises sees that the exercitant is full of fervor and in consolation, he should prevent him from making any hasty or unconsidered promise or vow. The more aware he is of the exercitant's impulsive character, the more he should warn and admonish him. Even though one may rightfully urge another to embrace the religious life, where it is understood that he will

take vows of obedience, poverty, and chastity, and although a good work done under vow is more meritorious than one done without vow, still one should consider carefully the individual circumstances and character of the person concerned, and what help or obstacles he would meet in accomplishing what he wishes to promise.

[15]   The one giving the Exercises should not move the one making them more towards poverty, or to make any other promise rather than its contrary; neither should he encourage him to choose one state of life rather than another. For though outside of the Exercises it would be both lawful and meritorious to urge all who are in all probability suited for it to embrace continence, virginity, religious life, and all other forms of evangelical perfection, in these Spiritual Exercises it is much better and more convenient in seeking the Divine Will, that our Creator and Savior should communicate Himself to the devout soul, embracing it with His love and praise, and disposing it to the way in which it can best serve Him in the future. Thus, the one who gives the Exercises should not show bias nor lean either to one side or the other, but standing in the middle like the balance of a scale, he should allow the Creator to work directly with his creature, and the creature with its Creator and Lord.

[16]   For this purpose and in order that the Creator and Lord may work with more certainty in His creature, if such soul had any inordinate inclination or attachment to anything, it will be most useful for it to move, putting all energy to attain the contrary of that to which it is at present ill-attached. For instance, if a soul is inclined to seek or keep some office or benefice,[7] not for the honor and glory of God our Lord nor for the spiritual health of souls, but for its personal convenience and temporal gain, the soul must wish for the contrary of its affections. By earnest prayer and other spiritual exercises it must ask the contrary of God our Lord. That is to say it should desire to have no such office or benefice, nor anything else, unless the Divine Majesty, restoring order to the soul's wishes, change its first inordinate affection so that now the reason for desiring or holding one thing or another is solely the service, the honor, and the glory of his Divine Majesty.

[17]   The one giving the Exercises need not inquire into, nor know the personal thoughts and sins of the one who is making the Exercises, but it will be very useful for the latter to be faithfully informed of the various movements and thoughts which the different spirits bring to him. In this way, depending on whether the exercitant progresses little or much, the director can give some spiritual exercises most in conformity with the needs of the soul so moved.

[18]   The Spiritual Exercises should be adapted to the require-

ments of the persons who wish to make them, that is to say, according to their age, their education, and their capacity. A person who is uneducated or of narrow comprehension should not be given exercises which he could not bear without strain or from which he could get no profit. In like manner to each should be given those exercises which will be of the most profit and help to him depending on his disposition and the amount of progress he wishes to make. Thus one who wishes to be helped only to get instruction and to reach a certain degree of spiritual contentment, may be given the Particular Examination (n.24) and afterwards the General Examination (n.32) together with the Method of Prayer on the Commandments, the Deadly Sins, etc., for a half hour in the morning (n.238). Weekly confession of his sins is also to be recommended, and if possible, Holy Communion every two weeks, or better, if he is so inclined, every week. This method of giving the Exercises is best suited to those who are illiterate or poorly educated: each commandment should be explained, and also the Deadly Sins, the precepts of the Church, the uses of the five senses, and the *Works of Mercy*. Equally, if the director of the Exercises sees that the exercitant has little aptitude, or little natural ability, or that he is one from whom little fruit could be expected, it is better to give him some of the lighter, easier exercises until he has gone to confession, and then to give him some methods of examination of conscience and a program for more frequent confession than has been his custom, so that he may preserve what he has gained, without going further into the matter of the election nor into any other exercises beyond those of the first week, especially when greater profit may be gained with others, since there is insufficient time for everything.[8]

[19]   A person engaged in public affairs or proper business, if he is educated and has ability, can make the Exercises by taking an hour and a half for them each day. First, the end for which man is created should be explained to him; then he can also be given the Particular Examination of Conscience for half an hour; and afterwards the General Examination of Conscience and also the method of confessing and of receiving the Blessed Sacrament. He can make each morning for three days, one hour of meditation on the first, second, and third sins (n.45). For three more days, at the same hour, the meditation should be a review of his sins (n.55). Three more days, at the same hour, he should meditate on the punishment due to sin (n.65). With all three meditations he should be given the Ten Additions (n.73). He should use the method described at length following Exercises for meditation on the mysteries of Christ our Lord.[9]

[20]   One who is not involved in worldly affairs and who wishes to make the greatest possible progress,[10] should be given all the

Spiritual Exercises in the manner in which they are here set forth. In these Exercises, as a general rule, he will profit all the more if he is separated from all of his friends and from all worldly cares; for example, if he moves from the house where he lives and chooses another home or room where he may dwell as privately as possible, so that he may be free to go to Mass[11] and Vespers every day, without fear of hindrance from his friends. There are three principal advantages, among many others to be gained by such seclusion: the first is that the person who withdraws from many friends and acquaintances and from distracting businesses in order to serve and praise God our Lord, gains no little merit from His Divine Majesty. The second is that being thus separated, not having his mind divided by many things but giving all his care to only one, which is the service of his Creator and the profiting of his own soul, he is more at liberty to use his natural faculties in searching more diligently for what he so desires. The third advantage is that the more the soul finds itself alone and away from men, the more apt it is to approach and be united with its Creator and Lord. The closer the soul coming near Him, the more it is disposed to receive graces and gifts from His divine and sovereign goodness.

SPIRITUAL EXERCISES

[21]   to conquer oneself, and to organize one's life without influence in one's decisions by any inordinate attachment.[12]

PRESUPPOSITION

[22]   In order that the one who gives these Exercises and he who makes them may receive more assistance and profit from them, they should begin with the presupposition that every good Christian ought to be more willing to give a good interpretation to the proposition of another than to condemn it.[13] If he cannot give a good interpretation to his proposition, he should ask the other how he understands it, and if he is in error, he should correct him with charity. If this is not sufficient, he should seek every suitable means of correcting his understanding so that he may save the proposition of the other by understanding it properly.

[FIRST WEEK]

[23]   ORIGIN AND FOUNDATION[14]

Man is created to praise, make reverence, and serve God our Lord[15] and by these means to save his soul.[16] All other things on the face of the earth[17] are created for man to help him in the pursuit of the goal for which he is created. From this it follows that man is to use these things as much as[18] they will help him attain his end. Likewise, he must rid himself of them as much as they prevent him from attaining it. Therefore, we must make ourselves indifferent[19] to all created things, in so far as it is left to the choice of our free will and is not forbidden; in such manner we should not prefer health to sickness, riches to poverty, honor to dishonor, a long life to a short one, and so in all things; we should desire and choose only those things which will best help us attain the end for which we are created.

PARTICULAR AND DAILY EXAMINATION OF CONSCIENCE[20]

[24]   This Exercise is performed at three different times, and there are two examinations to be made.

1st. As soon as he arises in the morning the man should resolve to guard himself carefully against the particular sin or defect which he wishes two correct or amend.

[25]   2nd. Before lunch[21] he should ask God our Lord for what he desires, namely, the grace to remember how many times he has fallen into the particular sin or defect, and to correct himself in the future. Following this he should make the first examination demanding an account of his soul regarding that particular matter which he proposed for himself and which he desires to correct and amend. He should review each hour or period of the time elapsed from the hour of rising to the exact hour of this examination, and he should make note on the first line of the letter g=,[22] a mark for each time that he has fallen into the particular sin or defect. He should then renew his resolution to improve himself until the time of the second examination that he will make.

[26]   3rd. After the evening meal he will make a second examination, reviewing each hour from the first examination to this second one, and on to the second line of the same diagram he will again make a mark for each time that he has fallen into the particular sin or defect.

FOUR ADDITIONS FOLLOW

[27]   to help remove more quickly the particular sin or defect.

1st. The first addition is that each time that one falls into the particular sin or defect, he should place his hand on his chest, repenting that he has fallen. This can be done even in the presence of many people without them noticing it.

[28]   2nd. The second addition is that since the first line of the diagram with the letter g= represents the first examination, and the second line, the second examination, at night the exercitant

should observe whether there is an improvement from the first line to the second, that is, from the first examination to the second.

[29]   3rd. The third addition is that he should compare the second day with the first, that is to say, the two examinations of the present day with the two examinations of the preceding day, and see if there is a daily improvement.

[30]   4th. The fourth addition is that he should also compare one week with another and see if there is greater improvement during the present week than in the past week.

[31]   Note: It may be noted that the first large G denotes Sunday. The second is smaller and stands for Monday, the third, for Tuesday, and so fourth.

G

g

g

g

g

g

g

GENERAL EXAMINATION OF CONSCIENCE

[32]   to help the exercitant purify himself and make better confessions.[23]

I presuppose that there are three kinds of thoughts in my mind. The first is a thought which is my own and which comes solely from my own liberty and will; the other two come from without, the one from the good spirit and the other from the evil one.

[33]   *About Thoughts*:[24] 1st. There are two ways of gaining merit from an evil thought which comes from without: the thought comes to me to commit a mortal sin. I resist the thought and immediately it is conquered.

[34]   2nd. When the same evil thought comes to me and I resist it, and it returns again and again, but I continue to resist it until it is vanquished. This second way is much more meritorious than the first.

[35]   One is guilty of venial sin if the same thought of committing mortal sin comes to him, and he gives it some attention or takes some sensual pleasure in it, or when there is some negligence in rejecting it.

There are two ways of sinning mortally:

[36]   1st. The first exists when one consents to an evil thought with the intention of carrying it out later, or with the intention of doing so if he could.

[37]   2nd. The second way of sinning mortally is to put the thought of the sin into action. This is a more grievous sin for three reasons: first, because of the greater length of time; second, because of the greater intensity; third, because of the greater injury done to both persons.

[38]   *About Words*: One must not swear by the Creator nor by any creature unless it were with truth, necessity, and reverence. By necessity I mean, not when any truth whatsoever is affirmed under oath, but when it is of real importance, for the profit of the soul or the body or for the protection of temporal goods. By reverence* I mean that when naming the Creator and Lord one will innerly express the honor and reverence due Him.

[39]   It should be noted that when we take an unnecessary oath we sin more seriously if we swear by the Creator than if we swear by a creature. Still, it is more difficult to swear in the proper manner, that is with truth, necessity, and reverence, by a creature than by the Creator, for the following reasons:

1st. The first reason is that when we want to swear by some creature, in the naming of that creature we are not so attentive and prudent in telling the truth, or considering whether it is necessary to swear, as we would be when we use the name of the Creator and Lord of all things.

2nd. The second is that when we swear by any creature, it is not so easy to show reverence and respect (*acatamiento*) to the Creator as when we swear in the name of the Creator and Lord Himself; for to use the name of God our Lord carries with it a greater respect (*acatamiento*) and reverence than to take an oath in

---

Acatamiento in Spanish has a richer meaning than our English equivalent. The act of acatamiento includes inner expression, acceptance, surrender, affectionate communion, and joyful fear all in the same act. See also *Spiritual Diary* nos. 84,103,128,156-178 and passim. *Trans. note.*

the name of a creature. This is why it is more permissible for those who are perfect than for those who are imperfect to swear by a creature. Due to their continued contemplation and the enlightenment of their understanding, the perfect are more able to consider, meditate, and contemplate God our Lord as existing in all creatures by his essence, presence, and power. Thus, when they swear by a creature, they are more likely to be disposed to show respect (*acatamiento*) for their Creator and Lord than those who are imperfect.

3rd. The third: in frequently swearing by a creature, idolatry is more to be feared in the imperfect than in the perfect.

[40] Idle words should not be spoken. By idle words I mean words which serve no good purpose, and do not profit me or anyone else, nor are they intended to do so. Words spoken for a useful purpose or words intended for the good of one's soul or that of another, or for the good of the body, or for one's temporal welfare are never idle words. Neither are words idle because one speaks of matters which are foreign to his state, for example, when a religious man speaks of wars or of commerce. In all that has been mentioned there is merit if the words are directed to a good end, and it is sinful if they are directed to a bad end, or spoken idly.

[41] Nothing should be said to defame another or gossip of others. If I reveal a hidden mortal sin committed by another, I sin mortally. If I reveal another's hidden venial sin, I sin venially. In revealing the defects of another I thereby make known my own defect. If the intention is good, the defect or sin of another may be spoken of:

1st. The first manner is when the sin is public, as in the case of a woman openly engaged in prostitution, or a sentence passed by a court of justice, or a known error which is corrupting the souls of those with whom we are conversing.

2nd. The second is when the hidden sin is made known to someone to help him rise from his own sin. There must, however, be some grounds or probable reasons for expecting that this will help him.

[42] *About Actions*: The subject matter is the Ten Commandments, the precepts of the Church, and the recommendations of superiors. Any action committed against any of these three groups is a more or less serious sin according to the gravity of the matter. By recommendations of superiors I mean, for example, the Indulgences attached to the Crusades and other Indulgences, such as those for peace, requiring confession and reception of the most Holy Sacrament. For we would not sin lightly if we acted or caused others to act against such pious recommendations and exhortations of our elders.

METHOD OF MAKING THE GENERAL EXAMINATION

[43]　　This examination contains five points:

1st. The first point is to render thanks to God for the favors we have received.

2nd. The second point is to ask for grace to know my sins and to free myself from them.

3rd. The third point is to demand an account of my soul from the moment of rising until the present examination; either hour by hour or from one period to another. I shall first make an examination of my thoughts, then my words, and then my actions in the same order as that given in the Particular Examination of Conscience.

4th. The fourth point is to ask pardon of God our Lord for my failings.

5th. The fifth point is to resolve to amend my life with the help of God's grace. Close with the "Our Father".

GENERAL CONFESSION AND HOLY COMMUNION

[44]　　Anyone who of his own accord wishes to make a general Confession[25] will find, among many other advantages, these three:

1st. Although anyone who confesses once a year is not required to make a general confession, by doing so he will gain much more profit and merit because of the greater sorrow he will have for his sins and for the wickedness of his whole life.

2nd. Just as during the Spiritual Exercises a person gains a more intimate knowledge of his sins and their malice than at a time when he is not occupied with his interior life, so now because of this greater understanding and sorrow for his sins, he will find greater profit and merit than he would have had before.

3rd. After making a better confession and being better disposed, he will be more worthy and better prepared to receive the most Holy Sacrament, which will help him not only to avoid sin but also to preserve and increase grace. It would be best to make this general confession immediately after the Exercises of the first week.

THE FIRST EXERCISE

[45]　　is a meditation made with the three powers of the soul, and the subject is the first, second, and third sins.[26] It contains the preparatory prayer, two preludes, three principal points, and a colloquy.

[46]　　*Prayer*: The purpose of the preparatory prayer[27] is to ask of God our Lord the grace that all intentions, actions, and works

may be directed purely to the service and praise of His Divine Majesty.

[47]   *The first prelude* is composition* seeing the place.[28] It should be noted at this point that when the meditation or contemplation is on a visible object, for example, contemplating Christ our Lord during His life on earth, for He is visible, the composition will consist of seeing with the imagination's eye the physical place where the object that we wish to contemplate is present. By the physical place I mean, for instance, a temple or mountain where Jesus or Our Lady is, depending on the subject of the contemplation. In meditation on sins, the composition will consist of imagining and considering my soul imprisoned in its corruptible body, and my entire being in this vale of tears as an exile among brute beasts. (By entire being) I mean the whole composite of body and soul.

[48]   *The second prelude* is to ask God our Lord for what I want and desire.[29] The request must be according to the subject matter. Therefore, if the contemplation is on the Resurrection, I shall ask for joy with Christ rejoicing; if it is on the Passion, I shall ask for pain, tears, and suffering with Christ suffering. In the present meditation I shall ask for shame and confusion at myself, for I see how many souls have been damned for a single mortal sin, and how often I have deserved to be damned eternally for the many sins I have committed.

[49]   *Note.* The preparatory prayer without change, and the two preludes mentioned above, which may be changed at times if the subject matter requires it, are to be made before all contemplations and meditations.

[50]   1st. The first point will be to recall to memory the first sin, which was that of the angels, then to apply the understanding by considering this sin in detail, then the will[30] by seeking to remember and understand all, so that I may be the more ashamed and confounded when I compare the one sin of the angels with the many that I have committed. Since they went to hell for one sin, how many times have I deserved it for my many sins. I will call to memory the sin of the angels, remembering that they were created in the state of grace, that they refused to make use of their freedom to offer reverence and obedience to their Creator and Lord, and that through pride, they fell from grace into sin and were cast from heaven into hell. In like manner my understanding is to be used to reason more in detail on the subject matter, and thereby move more deeply my affections through the use of the will.

[51]   2nd. The second point is to do the same, that is, to employ the three powers of the soul to consider the sin of Adam and Eve. Call to memory how they did such long penance for their sin and

---

*Note: Composition: internal ordering to proceed to meditation.

what corruption fell upon the whole human race, causing so many to go to hell. I say to call to memory the second sin, that of our first parents. Recall that after Adam had been created in the Plain of Damascus and placed in Paradise, how Eve had been formed from his rib, and how they were forbidden to eat the fruit of the tree of knowledge, and how by eating it they committed sin. After their sin, clothed in garments of skin and cast out of Paradise without the original justice which they had lost, they lived all their lives in much travail and great penance. The understanding is likewise to be used in considering the subject matter in greater detail, and the will is to be employed as already explained.

[52]   3rd. The third point is to call to memory the third sin. This is the particular sin of any person who went to hell because of one mortal sin. Consider also the innumerable others who have gone to hell for fewer sins than I have committed. I say to consider the third particular sin. Call to memory the grievousness and malice of sin against our Creator and Lord. Let the understanding consider how in sinning and acting against Infinite Goodness, one has justly been condemned forever. Close with acts of the will, as mentioned above.

[53]   *Colloquy*.[31] Imagine Christ our Lord before you, hanging upon the cross. Speak with Him of how from being the Creator He became man, and how, possessing eternal life, He submitted to temporal death to die for our sins.

Then I shall meditate upon myself and ask, "What have I done for Christ? What am I now doing for Christ? What ought I do for Christ?" And as I see Him in this condition, hanging upon the cross, I shall meditate on the thoughts that come to my mind.

[54]   The colloquy is made properly by speaking as one friend speaks to another, or as a servant speaks to his master, now asking some favor, now accusing oneself for some wrong deed, or again, communicating one's affairs to Him and seeking His advice concerning them. Conclude with the "Our Father".

THE SECOND EXERCISE

[55]   is a meditation on sin. It consists, after the preparatory prayer and two preludes, of five points, and a colloquy.

Prayer: This is the same as in the first Exercise.

The first prelude is the same composition (as in the first Exercise.)

The second prelude is to ask for what I desire. I shall here ask what I want, an ever-increasing and intense sorrow and tears[32] for my sins.

[56]   1st. The first point is the review of my sins. I shall bring

to my memory all the sins of my life, looking at them year by year, and period by period. Three things will help me to do this: first, I shall recall to mind the place and house where I lived; secondly, the associations I have had with others; thirdly, the positions which I have filled.

[57]   2nd. The second point is to weigh my sins, considering the ugliness and the malice that every mortal sin committed has in itself, even though it were not forbidden.

[58]   3rd. The third point is to consider who I am and abase myself by these examples:

1.) Who am I in comparison to all men?   2.) What are men in comparison with the angels and saints of heaven?   3.) What is all creation in comparison with God? Then myself alone, what can I be?   4.) Let me consider all my own corruption and foulness of body.   5.) Let me see myself as a sore and an abscess from whence have come forth so many sins, so many evils, and the most vile poison.

[59]   4th. The fourth point is now to consider who God is against whom I have sinned, recalling his attributes and comparing them to their contraries in me: His wisdom to my ignorance; His omnipotence to my weakness; His justice with my iniquity, His goodness with my sinfulness.

[60]   5th. The fifth point is to be struck with amazement and filled with a growing emotion as I consider how creatures have suffered me to live, and have sustained me in life. How the angels, the swords of Divine Justice, tolerated me, guarded me, and prayed for me. How the saints have interceded and prayed for me. How the heavens, moon, and stars, and the elements; fruits, birds, fishes, and animals have all served my needs. How the earth has not opened and swallowed me up, creating new hells that I might suffer eternal torment in them.

[61]   *Colloquy.* I will end this meditation with a colloquy directing my thoughts to God's mercy. I will give thanks to Him for having granted me life until now, and I will resolve with the help of His grace to amend my life for the future. Close with an "Our Father".

THE THIRD EXERCISE

[62]   is a repetition[33] of the first and second Exercises, with three colloquies.[34]

After the preparatory prayer and the two preludes, the first and second Exercises are to be repeated. I will note and dwell upon the points in which I have felt the greatest consolation or desolation, or the greatest spiritual relish. I will then make these colloquies in the following manner:

[63] *1st. Colloquy.* The first colloquy is with our Lady, that she may obtain grace for me from her Son and Lord for three things: 1) That I may have a thorough knowledge of my sins and a feeling of abhorrence for them. 2) That I may comprehend the disorder of my actions, so that detesting them I will amend my ways and put my life in order. 3) That I may know the world, and being filled with horror of it, I may put away from me worldly and vain things.

Conclude with the "Hail Mary".

2nd Colloquy. The second colloquy is with the Son of God. I will beg Him to intercede with the Father to obtain these graces for me. Conclude with the "Anima Christi."

3rd Colloquy. The third colloquy is with our Eternal Father. I will request that He Himself grant these graces to me. Conclude with the "Our Father".

THE FOURTH EXERCISE

[64]   is a resume of the third Exercise.[35]

I have called this a resume because the intellect, without digression, is to recall and review thoroughly the reminiscenses of matters contemplated in the previous Exercises. The same three colloquies should then be made.

THE FIFTH EXERCISE

[65]   is a meditation on hell. It contains after the preparatory prayer and two preludes, five points, and a colloquy.

Preparatory prayer: The preparatory prayer will be as usual.

The first prelude is the composition of place. Here it will be to see in imagination the length, breadth, and depth of hell.[36]

The second prelude is I will ask for what I desire. Here it will be to ask for a deep awareness of the pain suffered by the damned, so that if I should forget the love of the Eternal Lord, at least the fear of punishment will help me to avoid falling into sin.

[66]   1st. The first point is to see with the eye of the imagination the great fires, and the souls enveloped, as it were, in bodies of fire.

[67]   2nd. The second point is to hear the wailing, the screaming, cries, and blasphemies against Christ our Lord and all His saints.

[68]   3rd. The third point is to smell the smoke, the brimstone, the corruption, and rottenness.

[69]   4th. The fourth point is to taste bitter things, as tears, sadness, and remorse of conscience.

[70]   5th. The fifth point is to feel with the sense of touch how the flames surround and burn souls.

[71]   *Colloquy*: Enter into a colloquy with Christ our Lord. Recall to mind the souls in hell. Some are there because they did not believe in His coming; others, though they believed, did not act according to His Commandments.

These souls may be divided into three classes:

1st. Those who went to hell before the coming of Christ.

2nd. Those who were damned during His lifetime.

3rd. Those condemned to hell after His life in the world.

I will now give Him thanks for not having permitted me to fall into any of these classes, thus putting an end to my life.

I will also thank Him for the great kindness and mercy He has always shown me until this present moment. Conclude with an "Our Father."

[72]   *Note.* The first Exercise will be made at midnight; the second, immediately on rising in the morning; the third, before or after Mass but before dinner; the fourth, at the hour of Vespers. It is understood that this arrangement of hours, more or less, is to be observed during the entire four weeks, in so far as age, disposition, and physical constitution enable the exercitant to make five exercises or fewer.

ADDITIONS[37]

[73]   to help the exercitant make the Exercises better and to assist him in finding what he desires:

1st. The first addition is after going to bed, as I am about to go to sleep, for the space of a "Hail Mary," I should think of the hour when I have to rise, and for what purpose, summing up the Exercises I have to make.

[74]   2nd. The second: when I wake up, I will not permit my mind to wander to other things, I will turn it at once to the subject that I am going to contemplate in the first Exercise at midnight. I shall be filled with confusion for my many sins, thinking of such examples as that of a knight who finds himself in the presence of his king and the entire court and is filled with shame and confusion for having so greatly offended him from whom he had already received so many gifts and favors.

In like manner, in the second Exercise, I will see myself as a great sinner, bound in chains, who is about to appear before the supreme, eternal Judge; and I will take as an example how prisoners in chains and worthy of death appear before their earthly judge. As I dress, I will think over these thoughts, or others, according to the subject matter.

[75]   3rd. The third is, a step or two from the place where I am going to meditate or contemplate, I will stand for the space of an

"Our Father," and with my mind raised on high, I will consider that God our Lord sees me, etc. I will then make an act of reverence or humility.

[76]   4th. The fourth: I will enter into the meditation, at times kneeling, at times prostrate on the ground, at other times supine, or seated or standing, always intent on seeking what I desire. Two things should be noted:

The first one is that, if I find what I am seeking while kneeling I will not change my posture, and if prostrate, I will continue in that position, etc.

The second is that as soon as I find that which I desire, I will meditate quietly, without being anxious to continue further until I have satisfied myself.

[77]   5th. The fifth: after I have finished an Exercise I will examine for the space of a quarter of an hour, either while sitting or walking, how I have succeeded in the meditation or contemplation. If I have performed the Exercise poorly, I will seek out the cause, and when I have found it, I will be sorry, so that I may make amends in the future. If I have performed the Exercise well, I will thank God our Lord, and following the same method next time.

[78]   6th. The sixth: I will not think of pleasant and joyful things as heaven, the Resurrection, etc., for such consideration of joy and delight will hinder the feeling of pain, sorrow, and tears that I should have for my sins. It would be better for me to bring to memory that I want to feel sorrow and pain, remembering death and the judgment.

[79]   7th. The seventh: for the same reason I will deprive myself of all light, closing the shutters and doors when I am in my room, unless I need the light to say my prayers, to read, or to eat.

[80]   8th. The eighth: I will neither laugh nor say anything that will provoke laughter.

[81]   9th. The ninth: I will restrain my eyes except in looking to receive or dismiss the person with whom I have to speak.

[82]   10th .The tenth: this direction is concerned with penance, which is divided into interior and exterior. Interior penance is sorrow for one's sins, and a firm resolution not to commit them or any others. Exterior penance is the fruit of interior penance, and is the punishment we inflict upon ourselves for the sins committed. We perform this penance in three ways.

[83]   1st. The first is regarding food. It will be noted that when we deny ourselves what is superfluous, it is not penance but temperance. It is penance when we deny ourselves what is proper for us to have, and the more we deny ourselves, the greater and better is the penance, provided we do not harm ourselves or cause ourselves serious illness.

[84]   2nd. The second is regarding sleeping. Here again it is not penance when we deny ourselves the superfluity of delicate and soft things. But it is penance when we deny ourselves what is suitable for us. Again, the more we deny ourselves the greater the penance, provided we cause ourselves no injury or serious illness. Nor should we deny ourselves our due amount of sleep unless we have the bad habit of sleeping too much. It may then be done to arrive at a proper mean.

[85]   3rd. The third is by chastising the flesh, thereby causing sensible pain. This is done by wearing hairshirts, cords, or iron chains on the body, or by scourging or wounding oneself, or by other kinds of austerities.

[86]   What seems the most suitable and safest thing in doing penance is for the pain to be felt in the flesh, without penetration to the bones, thus causing pain but not illness. Therefore it seems more fitting to scourge oneself with light cords, which cause exterior pain, than in another way that might cause internal and serious infirmity.

[*Four Observations on Penance*]

[87]   1st. Note. The first note is that exterior penances are performed principally to produce three effects: 1st. To satisfy for past sins. 2nd. To overcome ourselves, so that sensuality will be obedient to reason and our lower inclinations be subject to higher ones. 3rd. To seek and find some grace or gift that we wish to obtain, as for instance, a deep sorrow for our sins, or to grieve for them or for the pains and sufferings that Christ our Lord endured in His passion, or for the solution of some doubt that is troubling us.

[88]   2nd. The second note is that it is to be noted that the first and second additions should be applied to the Exercises at midnight and at daybreak, and not to the Exercises that are made at other times. The fourth addition will never be followed in Church in the presence of others, but only in private, as at home, etc.

[89]   3rd. The third is that when the exercitant still does not find what he is seeking, for example, tears, consolations, etc., he will often find it advantageous to change his penance in the matter of food, sleep, or the other acts that he has been performing. Thus we may alternate, doing penance for two or three days, and then for two or three days omitting it. For some it is better to do more penance and for others less. We often fail to do penance also out of love for what pleases the senses and through a false conviction that human nature cannot bear it without notable illness. Sometimes, on the contrary, we may do too much penance, thinking that our body can bear it. Since God our Lord knows our nature infinitely

better than we do, often in such changes He grants us to understand what best suits each of us.

[90]   4th. The fourth is that the Particular Examination will be made to remove defects and negligences relating to the Exercises and the Additions. This will also be done in the second, third, and fourth weeks.[38]

[SECOND WEEK]

[91]   The call of the earthly king helps us to contemplate the life of the Eternal King.[39]

Prayer: The preparatory prayer will be as usual.

First prelude: This is composition seeing the place. Here it will be to see with the sight of the imagination the synagogues,[40] villages, and castles[41] where Jesus our Lord preached.[42]

Second prelude: I will ask for the grace that I desire. Here it will be to ask of our Lord the grace that I may not be deaf to His call, but prompt and diligent to fulfill His most holy will.

[*Part One*]

[92]   1st. The first point is to place before me a human king, chosen by God our Lord Himself, to whom all princes and all Christians pay reverence and obey.

[93]   2nd. The second point: I will consider how this king speaks to all his people, saying, "It is my will to conquer all infidel lands. Therefore, whoever wishes to come with me must be content to eat as I eat, drink as I drink, dress as I dress, etc. He must also be willing to work with me by day, and watch by night, etc. He will then share with me in victory as he has shared in the toils."

[94]   3rd. The third point: I will consider what the answer of good subjects ought to be to such a generous and human king, and consequently, if anyone would refuse the request of such a king, how he would deserve to be despised by everyone, and considered an unworthy knight.[43]

[*Part Two*]

[95]   The second part of this Exercise consists in applying the above mentioned example of this earthly king to Christ our Lord, in the following three points:

1st. As to the first point, if we heed such a call of an earthly king to his subjects, how much more worthy of consideration is it to see Christ our Lord, the Eternal King, and before Him, all of mankind, to whom, and to each man in particular, He calls and says: "It is My will to conquer the whole world and all My enemies, and thus to enter into the glory of My Father: therefore, whoever wishes to come with me must labor with Me, so that following Me in suffering, he may also follow Me in glory."

[96]   2nd. The second point: I will consider that anyone with judgment and reason will offer their whole persons for this work.

[97]   3rd. The third point: those who wish to show the greatest commitment and to distinguish themselves in every service of their Eternal King and Universal Lord, will not only offer their persons for the work, but by going against their own sensuality and carnal and worldly love, will make offerings of greater value and importance, saying:

> [98]Eternal Lord of all things, I make this offering[44] with your love and help, in the presence of your infinite goodness and in the presence of your glorious Mother and of all the Saints of your heavenly court, that it is my wish and desire, and my deliberate resolve, provided only that it be for your greater service and praise, to imitate you in bearing all injuries, all abuse, and all poverty both physical and spiritual, if your most Sacred Majesty be willing to choose me for such a life and state.

[99]   1st.Note. This Exercise is to be made twice during the day: in the morning when we rise, and an hour before dinner or supper.

[100]   2nd. Note. It will be very profitable to read for short periods some passages from the *Imitation of Christ* or from the Gospels and the Lives of the Saints, during the second week and thereafter.[45]

FIRST DAY

First Contemplation[46]

[101]   This contemplation is on the Incarnation.[47] It contains the preparatory prayer, three preludes, three points, and a colloquy.

Prayer: The usual preparatory prayer.

[102]   *The first prelude* is to recall the history of the subject I am about to contemplate. Here it is how the Three Divine Persons were looking down on the whole expanse or roundness of the earth, filled with human beings and how on seeing that all were going down to hell, they decreed, in their eternity, that the Second Person should become man to save the race of humans. When the fullness of time then came, they sent the Angel St. Gabriel to Our Lady, (no. 262).

[103]   *The second prelude* is composition seeing the place. Here it will be the great capacity and space of the world, where dwell so many and different peoples; equally, then, the particular city of Nazareth in the province of Galilee, and the house and room where our Lady lives.

[104]   *The third prelude* is to ask for what I desire. Here it will be to ask for an inner knowledge of our Lord, who has become man for me, that I may better love and follow Him.

[105]   *Note*. It is well to observe here that the same preparatory prayer without change, as was mentioned in the beginning, and the same three preludes, are to be made during this week and the following weeks. The form may be changed to conform to the subject matter.

[106]   1st. The first point is to see all the different people on the face of the earth, so varied in dress and in behavior. Some are white and others black, some at peace and others at war; some weeping and others laughing; some well and others sick; some being born and others dying, etc.

       Second, to see and consider the Three Divine Persons seated on the royal throne of the Divine Majesty, how they behold the entire face and vastness of the earth and all the people in such great blindness, and how they die and go down into hell.

       Third, I will see our Lady and the angel who greets her. I will reflect, that I may draw profit from such sight.

[107]   2nd. The second point will be to hear what the people throughout the world are saying, how they converse with one another, how they swear and blaspheme, etc. Next listen to what the Three Divine Persons are saying, that is, "Let us work the redemption of human kind," etc. Then listen to what the angel and our Lady are saying. Then reflect to draw profit from their words.

[108]   3rd. The third point will be to consider what the people throughout the world are doing; how they are wounding, killing, and going to hell, etc. Next consider what the Three Divine Persons are doing, namely accomplishing the most Holy Incarnation, etc., also what the angel and our Lady are doing, as the angel fulfills his office of ambassador, and our Lady humbles herself and gives thanks to the Divine Majesty. Then reflect to derive some profit from each of these things.

[109]   *Colloquy*. Finally the colloquy thinking of what I should say to the Three Divine Persons, or the eternal Word Incarnate, or to His Mother and our Lady, asking help according to the need that I feel within myself, so that I may more closely follow and imitate our Lord who has just become Incarnate. Close with "Our Father."

Second Contemplation

[110]   The second contemplation is on the Nativity.
       Prayer: The usual prayer.

[111]   *The first prelude* is the history of the Nativity; here it will be how our Lady, almost nine months with child, set out from

Nazareth, seated on an ass, as may be piously imagined, together with Joseph and a servant girl leading an ox and going to Bethlehem to pay the tribute that Caesar had imposed on the whole land, (no. 264).

[112]   *The second prelude* is composition seeing the place. Here I will see with the sight of the imagination the road from Nazareth to Bethlehem, considering its length and breadth, and whether it is level or winding through valleys and over hills. I will also behold the place or the cave of the Nativity, how large or how small, how low and how high it may be and how it was furnished.

[113]   *The third prelude* will be the same and in the same manner as in the preceding contemplation.

[114]   1st. The first point is to see the persons, that is, our Lady and Joseph, the servant girl, and the Child Jesus after his birth. I will make myself a poor and unworthy slave looking upon them, contemplating them, and ministering to their needs, as though I were present there, with all possible modesty and reverence. I will then reflect within myself in order that I may derive some benefit.

[115]   2nd. The second point is to observe, consider, and contemplate what they are saying and to reflect within myself that I may derive some profit.

[116]   3rd. The third point is to observe and consider what they are doing: the journey and hardships which they undergo in order that our Lord might be born in extreme poverty, and after so many labors of hunger and thirst, heat and cold, insults and injuries, He is to die on the cross, and all this for me. I will then reflect in order to gain some spiritual profit.

[117]   *Colloquy.* Conclude with a colloquy as in the preceding contemplation and with the "Our Father."

Third Contemplation

[118]   This is repetition of the first and second Exercises.

After the preparatory prayer and the three preludes, repeat the first and second Exercises. Always make note of some of the more important parts in which one has found some understanding, consolation, or desolation. Conclude in the same manner with a colloquy and the "Our Father."

[119]   In this repetition and in all those that follow, the same order of procedure will be observed as in the repetition of the first week, changing the subject matter but following the same form.

Fourth Contemplation

[120]   This is a repetition of the first and second exercises in the same manner as in the repetition given above.

Fifth Contemplation

[121]   The purpose of this contemplation will be to apply the five senses[48] to the first and second contemplations.

Prayer. After the preparatory prayer and the three preludes, it will be profitable to apply the five senses of the imagination to the first and second contemplations in the following manner:

[122]   1st. The first point is to see the persons with the sight of the imagination contemplating and meditating in detail upon the circumstances surrounding them, and then draw some spiritual profit from this scene.

[123]   2nd. The second point is to hear what they are saying, or what they might say, and then reflect within myself to draw some benefit.

[124]   3rd. The third is to smell and taste with the sense of smell and taste the infinite fragrance and sweetness of the Divinity, and of the soul, and of its virtues, and of all else, according to the person I am contemplating. And I will reflect within myself to draw profit from it.

[125]   4th. The fourth is to use the sense of touch, as by embracing and kissing the place where the persons walk or sit, always endeavoring to draw some profit from this.

[126]   *Colloquy.* Conclude with a colloquy, and with the "Our Father," as in the first and second contemplations.

Notes

[127]   1st. The first note is to observe that during this week and the following I should read only the event concerned with the contemplation that I am about to make. Thus, for the present, I should not read any event which I am not going to consider on that day or at that hour, so that the consideration of one mystery may not interfere with the consideration of another.

[128]   2nd. The second: the first Exercise on the Incarnation will be made at midnight, the second at daybreak, the third at the hour of Mass, the fourth at the hour of Vespers, and the fifth before supper, spending one hour in each of the five exercises, and the same order shall be observed in all that follows.

[129]   3rd. The third: it should be noted that if the exercitant is old or weak, or even if he is strong, if he has been left somewhat weak, it is better that in this second week, sometimes at least, he should not rise at midnight. He could then make one contemplation in the morning, another at the time of Mass, and another before dinner, with one repetition of these at the time of Vespers and the application of the five senses before supper.

[130]   4th. The fourth: in this second week, of all the ten addi-

tions mentioned for the first week, the second, sixth, and seventh, and part of the tenth, are to be changed.

The second addition will be to place before me, immediately on awaking, the subject of contemplation which I am going to make, desiring to know more thoroughly the eternal Word Incarnate, so that I may better serve and follow Him.

The sixth addition will be to bring frequently to memory the life and events of Christ our Lord, from the Incarnation to the place I am now contemplating.

The seventh addition will be that the exercitant should take care to make use of darkness or light, of good or bad weather as much as he feels that it can be useful in helping him to find what he desires.

The tenth addition will be that the exercitant must conduct himself according to the demands of the events that he is contemplating, for some of them require penance and others do not. And so all ten additions are to be observed with great care.

[131]   5th. The fifth note: in all the Exercises, except the one at midnight and the one in the morning, something equivalent to the second addition should be adopted in the following manner:

As soon as I remember that it is time for the Exercise which I am going to make, before entering into it, I will call to mind where I am going and into Whose presence, briefly recalling the Exercise I am about to make, and, observing the third addition, I will begin the Exercise.

SECOND DAY

[132]   Take for the first and second contemplations, the Presentation in the Temple (no. 268) and the Flight into Exile in Egypt (no. 209). Two repetitions should be made of these contemplations, and the application of the five senses, as was done the preceding day.

Note

[133]   Even though the exercitant be strong and well-disposed, sometimes it will be profitable to make some changes, from the second day to the fourth inclusive, in order that he may more readily find what he desires. Thus he may make only one contemplation at daybreak, and another about the time of Mass, and make a repetition of them at the time of Vespers, and the application of the senses before supper.

THIRD DAY

[134]   On this day use as subject matter how the Child Jesus was obedient to His parents at Nazareth (no. 271), and how after-

wards they found Him in the temple (no. 272). Then make the two repetitions and the application of the senses.

[135]   *Prelude* to the Consideration of the States of Life. We have already considered the example which Christ our Lord has given us for the first state of life, that is the observance of the commandments, being as He was under obedience to His parents. We have also considered the example that He gave us for the second state of life, that of evangelical perfection, when He remained in the temple, leaving His foster father and His natural Mother that He might devote Himself entirely to the service of His heavenly Father. We will begin now, while contemplating His life, to investigate and to ask in what kind of life or state His Divine Majesty wishes to make use of us. Thus, as an introduction to this subject, in the first following Exercise we will consider the intention of Christ our Lord, and on the other hand that of the enemy of human nature, and we will also consider how we ought to prepare ourselves to seek perfection in whatever state or kind of life that God our Lord shall grant us to choose.

FOURTH DAY

A Meditation on Two Standards

[136]   The one of Christ our supreme Captain and Lord; the other of Lucifer, the mortal enemy of human kind.[49]

Prayer: The usual preparatory prayer.

[137]   *The first prelude* is the history of the subject matter. Here it will be how Christ our Lord calls and wants all men under His standard, and how Lucifer, on the contrary, wants all men under his.

[138]   *The second prelude* is composition seeing the place. Here it will be to see a vast plain covering the entire region of Jerusalem, where the supreme Leader of the good people is Christ our Lord; and another plain in the region of Babylon, where the leader of the enemy is Lucifer.

[139]   *The third prelude* is to ask for what I desire. Here it will be to ask for a knowledge of the deceits of the evil leader and help to guard myself against them, and a knowledge of the true life which the supreme and true Leader reveals, and for the grace to imitate Him.

[140]   1st. The first point is to imagine how the evil leader of all the enemy is as if seated in that vast plain of Babylon, as on a great throne of fire and smoke in a horrible and frightening figure.

[141]   2nd. The second point is to consider how he calls together countless demons, and how he scatters them, some to one city,

some to another, throughout the whole world, missing no province, no place, no state of life, nor even any single person.

[142]   3rd. The third point is to listen to the harangue which he delivers to them, how he spurs them on to ensnare men and to bind them in chains; how he bids them first to tempt men with the lust of riches (as he is most accustomed to do), that they may thereby more easily gain the vain honor of the world, and then come to unbounded pride. The first step in his snare is that of riches, the second, honor, and the third, pride. From these three steps he leads them on to all other vices.

[143]   By contrast we are to imagine, on the other hand, the supreme and true Leader, who is Christ our Lord.

[144]   1st. The first point is to consider how Christ our Lord takes His place in that great plain of the region of Jerusalem; and how he chooses an unpretentious, beautiful, and gracious spot.

[145]   2nd. The second point is to see how the Lord of the entire world chooses so many persons, apostles, disciples, etc., and sends them throughout the whole world to spread His sacred doctrine among men of every state and condition.

[146]   3rd. The third point is to listen to the discourse which Christ our Lord makes to all His servants and friends whom He sends on this mission, charging them that they should seek to help all men; first, by encouraging them to embrace the most perfect spiritual poverty, and if it should please His Divine Majesty, to chose them for it; also, to embrace actual poverty. Secondly, by encouraging them to desire insults and contempt, for from these two things comes humility. So then there are three steps: the first, poverty opposed to riches; the second, scorn or contempt, opposed to worldly honor; and third, humility, opposed to pride. These three steps lead to all other virtues.

[147]   1st Colloquy. It will be addressed to our Lady and I will ask her to obtain for me from her Son and Lord grace that I may be received under His standard; first, in the most perfect spiritual poverty, and should it so please His Divine Majesty to choose me, also in actual poverty; secondly, in bearing reproaches and offenses, thus imitating Him more perfectly, provided only I can suffer them without sin on the part of any other person or displeasure to His Divine Majesty. Afterwards, I will say the "Hail Mary."

   2nd Colloquy. I will ask the Son to obtain for me the same graces from the Father, and I will then recite the "Anima Christi."

   3rd Colloquy. I will also ask the Father to grant me the same graces, and I will say the "Our Father."

[148]   *Note.* This Exercise will be made at midnight and again in the morning. There will also be two repetitions of the same

Exercise at the time of Mass and at the time of Vespers, always ending with the three colloquys, with our Lady, with the Son, and with the Father. The meditation on the three classes of men, which follows, will be made an hour before supper.

The Three Classes of Men[50]

[149]   On the same fourth day a meditation on the three classes of men is to be made, so that we may embrace that which is best.[51]

Prayer: The usual preparatory prayer.

[150]   *The first prelude* is the history. Here it is to consider three classes of men. Each of them has acquired ten thousand ducats, but not purely or properly for the love of God. These men all wish to save their souls and find peace in God our Lord by freeing themselves of the serious impediment arising from their attachment to this acquired money.

[151]   *The second prelude* is composition seeing the place. Here I will behold myself standing in the presence of God our Lord and all His saints, that I may desire and know what is most pleasing to His Divine Goodness.

[152]   *The third prelude* is to ask for what I desire. Here it will be to ask for the grace to choose what is for the greatest glory of His Divine Majesty and the salvation of my soul.

[153]   *The first class.* They would like to free themselves of the attachment they have for the money they acquired, in order to find peace in God our Lord, and to be able to save their souls, but up to the hour of death they do not take the means.

[154]   *The second class.* They want to free themselves of the attachment, but they wish to do so in such a way as to retain what they have acquired. They thus want God to come to what they desire, and they do not resolve to give up the money in order to go to God, even though this would be the better state for them.

[155]   *The third class.* They wish to free themselves of the attachment, but in such a way that their inclination will be neither to retain the money acquired nor not to retain it, desiring to act only as God our Lord shall inspire them and as it shall seem better to them for the service and praise of His Divine Majesty. Meanwhile, they wish to consider that they have already given up all attachments, striving not to desire that thing nor anything else, unless it be only the service of God our Lord that prompts their action. Thus, the desire of being able to serve God our Lord better will move them either to accept the things in question or to give them up.

[156]   *Colloquies.* Make the same three colloquies that were made in the previous contemplation or the Two Standards.

[157]   *Note.* It is to be noted that when we feel opposed to actual poverty or a repugnance to it, when we are not indifferent to poverty or riches, it is of great help in overcoming this inordinate attachment to beg in the colloquies (even though it be against our flesh), that our Lord choose to have us serve Him in actual poverty, and that we desire it, beg for it, and plead for it, provided that it be only for the service and praise of His Divine Goodness.

FIFTH DAY

[158]   The contemplation is on the departure of Christ our Lord from Nazareth to the River Jordan, and how He was baptized (no. 273).

Notes

[159]   1st. This contemplation will be made at midnight and again in the morning. Two repetitions will be made at the time of Mass and at the hour of Vespers. Before supper the application of the senses to the mystery will be made.

Each of these five Exercises will be preceded by the usual preparatory prayer, then the three preludes, as was fully explained in the contemplations on the Incarnation and the Nativity. The Exercise will end with the three colloquies of the contemplation of the three classes of men, or according to the note that follows that Exercise.

[160]   2nd. The particular examination after the noon meal and after supper will be made on the faults and negligences relating to the Exercises and to the additions of the day. This same procedure will be observed on the following days.

SIXTH DAY

[161]   Contemplation on how Christ our Lord went from the River Jordan to the desert and the events that took place at this place. The same procedure will be observed as on the fifth day.

SEVENTH DAY

How St. Andrew and the others followed Christ our Lord (no. 275).

EIGHTH DAY

The Sermon on the Mount, which is on the Eight Beatitudes (no. 278).

NINTH DAY

How Christ appeared to His disciples on the waves of the sea (no. 280).

TENTH DAY

How our Lord preached in the temple (no. 288).

ELEVENTH DAY

The resurrection of Lazarus (no. 285).

TWELFTH DAY

Palm Sunday (no. 287).

Notes

[162]   1st. The first note is that the number of contemplations of this Second Week may be extended or diminished depending on the time which each one wishes to spend or according to the progress he is making. If he wishes to increase them, he may take the mysteries of the Visitation of our Lady to St. Elizabeth, the Shepherds, the Circumcision of the Child Jesus, the Three Kings, and also others. If he wishes to shorten them, he may omit some of the mysteries mentioned above. These are meant to serve as an introduction and method for better and more complete contemplation later.

[163]   2nd. The second: the matter of the elections should be started from the contemplation on the departure of our Lord from Nazareth for the River Jordan and the events included therein, as explained in the following.

[164]   3rd. The third: before entering the elections, and in order to affect within ourselves a love for the true doctrine of Christ our Lord, it is very helpful to consider and ponder on the following three forms of humility, and to reflect upon them from time to time throughout the day. We should likewise make the colloquies that will be mentioned further on.

THE THREE FORMS OF HUMILITY[52]

[165]   The First Form of Humility is necessary for eternal salvation. This requires that I abase and humble myself as much as is possible for me, in order that I may obey in all things the law of God our Lord. Accordingly, I would not give consideration to the thought of breaking any commandment, divine or human, that binds me under pain of mortal sin, even though this offense would make me master of all creation or would preserve my life on earth.

[166]   The Second Form of Humility is more perfect than the first, i.e., if I find myself at such a point that I neither desire nor even prefer to have riches rather than poverty, to seek honor rather than dishonor, to have a long life rather than a short one, provided

that there be the same opportunity to serve God our Lord, and to save my soul. Nor would I, for the sake of all creation or for the purpose of saving my life, consider committing a single venial sin.

[167]   The Third Form of Humility is the most perfect. This exists when, the first and second forms already attained and the praise and glory of the Divine Majesty being equally served and in order to be more like Christ our Lord, I desire and choose poverty with Christ rather than riches, insults with Christ filled with them rather than honor, and desire to be considered worthless and a fool for Christ Who was so considered rather than to be esteemed as wise and clever in this world.

[168]   *Note.* If one desires to attain this third form of humility it will be very profitable for him to make the three colloquies on the three classes of men mentioned above. He should implore our Lord to be pleased to choose him for this third form of humility, which is greater and more perfect, so that he may better imitate and serve Him, provided it be for the equal or greater service and praise of His Divine Majesty.

INTRODUCTION INTO MAKING AN ELECTION OF A WAY OF LIFE

[169]   In every good election, in so far as it depends upon us, the eye of our intention must be simple, looking only to the end for which I am created, that is, for the praise of God our Lord and for the salvation of my soul. Therefore, whatever I elect must have as its purpose to help me to this end, and not to shape or draw the end to the means, but rather the means to the end. Many, for example, first elect marriage, which is a means, and secondarily to serve God our Lord in the married state, which service of God is the end. Likewise there are others who first desire to have benefices (church-related jobs well paid), and afterward to serve God in them. These individuals do not go straight to God, but want God to come straight to their inordinate attachments. Acting thus, they make a means of the end, and an end of the means, so that what they ought to seek first, they seek last. For our first aim, then, should be the desire to serve God, which is the end, and after this, to seek a benefice or to marry, if it is more fitting for me, for these things are but means to the end. Thus, nothing should move me to use such means or to deprive myself of them except it be only the service and praise of God our Lord and the eternal salvation of my soul.

A CONSIDERATION TO OBTAIN INFORMATION ON THE MATTERS IN WHICH AN ELECTION SHOULD BE MADE

[170]   This contains four points and a note:

1st. The first point: it is essential that all matters in which we wish to make an election must be either indifferent or good in themselves. They must meet with the approbation of our Holy Mother, the hierarchial Church, and not be bad or repugnant to her.

[171]   2nd. The second: there are some things that fall within the realm of immutable election, such as the priesthood, matrimony, etc. There are others in which the choice is mutable, as for example, accepting or relinquishing a benefice, accepting or renouncing temporal goods.

[172]   3rd. The third: once an immutable election has been made, there is no further election, for it cannot be dissolved, as it is true with marriage, the priesthood, etc. It should be noted only that if one has not made this election properly, with due consideration, and without inordinate attachments, he should repent and try to lead a good life in the election that he has made. Since this election was ill-considered and improperly made, it does not seem to be a vocation from God, as many err in believing, wishing to interpret an ill-considered or bad choice as a divine call. For every divine call is always pure and clean without any admixture of flesh or other inordinate attachments.

[173]   4th. The fourth: if one has made a proper and well-considered election that is mutable, and has not been influenced either by the flesh or the world, there is no reason why he should make a new election. But he should perfect himself as much as possible in the election he has made.

[174]   *Note.* It is to be noted that if this mutable election is not well-considered and sincerely made, then it will be profitable to make the election anew in the proper manner, if one wishes to bring forth fruits that are worthwhile and pleasing to God our Lord.

THREE TIMES WHEN A WISE AND GOOD ELECTION CAN BE MADE

[175]   The First Time is when God our Lord moves and attracts the will that the devout soul, without question and without desire to question, follows what has been manifested to it. St. Paul and St. Matthew did this when they followed Christ our Lord.

[176]   The Second Time is present when one has developed a clear understanding and knowledge through the experience of consolations and desolations and the discernment of diverse spirits.[53]

[177]   The Third Time is in a time of tranquility. Here one considers first for what purpose man is born, which is to praise God our Lord and to save his soul. Since he desires to attain this end,

he elects some life or state within the bounds of the church that will help him in the service of God our Lord and the salvation of his soul.

I said "a time of tranquility," when the soul is not agitated by diverse spirits, and is freely and calmly making use of its natural powers.

[178]   If an election has not been made on the first or second times, below are given two new methods of making it within the third time.

TWO METHODS OF MAKING A WISE AND GOOD ELECTION DURING THE THIRD TIME

The first method contains six points.[54]

1st. The first point is to place before me the thing on which I wish to make an election, like an office or a benefice to be accepted or refused, or anything else that is the object of a mutable election.

[179]   2nd. Second: I must have as my aim the end for which I am created, which is the praise of God our Lord and the salvation of my soul; and with this in mind I must remain indifferent and free from any inordinate attachments so that I am not more inclined or disposed to take the thing proposed than to reject it, nor to relinquish it rather than to accept it. I must rather be like the poised weights of a scale ready to follow the course which I feel is more for the glory and praise of God our Lord and the salvation of my soul.

[180]   3rd. Third: I must ask God our Lord to wish to move my will and to reveal to my soul what I should do to best promote His praise and glory in the matter of choice. After examining the matter thoroughly and faithfully with my understanding, I should make my election in conformity with His good pleasure and His most holy will.

[181]   4th. Fourth: I will use my reason to weigh the many advantages and benefits that would accrue to me if I held the proposed office or benefice solely for the praise of God our Lord and the salvation of my soul. I will likewise consider and weigh the disadvantages and dangers that there are in holding it. I will proceed in like manner with the other alternative, that is, examine and consider the advantages and benefits as well as the disadvantages and dangers in not holding the proposed office or benefice.

[182]   5th. Fifth: after having thus weighed the matter and carefully examined it from every side, I will consider which alternative appears more reason-able. Acting upon the stronger judgment of reason and not on any inclination of sensuality, I must come to a decision in the matter that I am considering.

[183]　6th. Sixth: after such an election or decision has been reached, I should turn with great diligence to prayer in the presence of God our Lord and offer Him this election that His Divine Majesty may wish to accept and confirm it, if it be to His greater service and praise.

[184]　The second method contains four rules and a note.[55]

1st. The first rule is that the love which moves me and causes me to make this election should come from above, that is from the love of God, so that before I make my choice I will feel that the greater or lesser love that I have for the thing chosen is solely for the sake of my Creator and Lord.

[185]　2nd. The second is to consider someone that I have never seen or known, and on whom I wish to see complete perfection. Now I should consider what I would tell that person to do and elect for the greater glory of God our Lord and the greater perfection of his soul. I will act in like manner myself, keeping the rule that I have proposed for another.

[186]　3rd. The third is to consider that if I were at the point of death, what form and procedure I would wish to have observed in making this present election. Guiding myself by this consideration, I will make my decision on the whole matter.

[187]　4th. The fourth is to examine and consider how I shall be on the day of judgment, to think how I shall then wish to have made my decision in the present matter. The rule which I should then wish to have followed, I will now follow, that I may on that day be filled with joy and delight.

[188]　*Note.* Taking the above mentioned rules as my guide for eternal salvation and peace, I will make my election and offer myself to God our Lord, following the sixth point of the first method of making an election.

HOW TO AMEND AND REFORM ONE'S LIFE AND STATE

[189]　It is to be observed that those who hold ecclesiastical office or who are married (whether they are rich in worldly possessions or not), when they do not have an opportunity to make a decision or are not very willing to do so regarding things that are subject to election, it is very profitable that instead of having them make an election to give to each a form and method of amending and reforming his own life state. This may be done by placing before the person the purpose of his creation, life, and state, which is the glory and praise of God our Lord and the salvation of his own soul.

In order to attain and fulfill this end one should consider and examine thoroughly, using the Exercises and the methods of making an election explained above, how large a house and establishment one should maintain; how one should manage and govern it; how one should guide it by word and example. One ought also to consider what portion of his state one should use for his family and household and how much should be given to the poor and to other pious works. In all these works one should desire and seek nothing but the greatest praise and glory of God our Lord. For each one must realize that he will progress in all spiritual matters in proportion to his flight from self-love, self-will, and self-interest.

[THIRD WEEK]
FIRST DAY

First Contemplation

[190]   The first contemplation at midnight, how Christ our Lord went from Bethany to Jerusalem, including the Last Supper (no. 289), contains the preparatory prayer, three preludes, six points, and a colloquy.[56]

Prayer: The usual preparatory prayer.

[191]   *The first prelude* is to recall the history, which is here how Christ our Lord, while at Bethany, sent two disciples to Jerusalem to prepare the supper, and afterwards He Himself went there with the other disciples. How after they had eaten the Pascal Lamb and supped, He washed their feet and gave His Most Holy Body and His Most Precious Blood to His disciples. How He gave His last discourse after Judas had gone to sell his Lord.

[192]   *The second prelude* is composition seeing the place. Here it will be to consider the road from Bethany to Jerusalem, whether it is broad or narrow, whether it is level, etc. Consider likewise the room of the supper; whether it is large or small, of this shape or another.

[193]   *The third prelude* is to ask for what I desire. Here it will be to ask for pain, compassion, and confusion because the Lord is going to His passion on account of my sins.

[194]   1st. The first point is to visualize the persons at the supper, and reflecting within myself, to strive to gain some profit from them.

2nd. The second point is to listen to what they say, and likewise to draw some profit from it.

3rd. The third point is to observe what they are doing and to draw some fruit from it.

[195]   4th. The fourth point is to consider what Christ our Lord suffers in His humanity or wills to suffer, according to the passage that is being contemplated. Here I will begin with great effort to

strive to grieve, to be sad, and cry. I will strive in like manner through the following points.

[196]   5th. The fifth point is to consider how the Divinity hides Itself. That is to say, how It could destroy Its enemies and does not do so, how It leaves the most Sacred Humanity to suffer so cruelly.

[197]   6th. The sixth point is to consider that all of the suffering is for my sins, etc., and what I ought to do and suffer for Him.

[198]   *Colloquy.* Conclude with a colloquy to Christ our Lord, and at the end say the "Our Father."

[199]   *Note.* It is to be observed, as has already been stated in part, that in the colloquies I must reason and make supplication according to the present subject; that is to say, as I feel tempted or experience consolation, as I wish to have one virtue or another, as I am trying to dispose myself in one direction or another, as I desire to pain or rejoice in the matter of my contemplation. Finally, I shall ask for what I most earnestly desire regarding the particular things that I am considering. In this way I may make just one colloquy to Christ our Lord, or if the subject matter or devotion prompts me to do so, I may make three colloquies, one to the Blessed Mother, one to the Son, and one to the Father, in the manner that was prescribed in the Second Week, in the meditation on Two Standards, together with the note following the meditation on the Three Classes of Men.[57]

Second Contemplation

[200]   The second contemplation in the morning will be on the mysteries from the Last Supper to the Garden inclusive.

Prayer: The usual preparatory prayer.

[201]   *The first prelude* is the history. Here it will be how Christ our Lord descended with his eleven disciples from Mount Zion, where the Supper was held, to the Valley of Josaphat. Leaving eight in one part of the valley, He took the other three into the Garden. He then began to pray, and His sweat became drops of blood. Three times He prayed to His Father, and three times he aroused His disciples from sleep. After His enemies fell to the ground at the sound of His voice, and Judas gave him the kiss of peace, after He restored the ear of Malchus which Peter had cut off, He was made prisoner as malefactor, and He was led through the valley and back up the slope to the house of Annas.

[202]   *The second prelude* is a visualization seeing the place. Here it will be to consider the road from Mount Zion to the Valley of Josaphat, and likewise the Garden; its width, its length, of this shape or another.

[203]   *The third prelude* is to ask for what I desire. In the Pas-

sion the proper thing to ask for is suffering with Christ suffering, a broken heart with Christ heartbroken, tears, and inner pain because of the great pain that Christ endured for me.

Notes

[204]   1st. In this second contemplation, after the preparatory prayer and the three preludes already mentioned, the same procedure is to be followed for the points and colloquies as is found in the first contemplation on the Last Supper. At the hour of Mass and at Vespers, two repetitions will be made on the first and second contemplations. Then before supper, the application of the senses will be made on the subject of these two contemplations, always beginning with the preparatory prayer and the three preludes, according to the subject matter. The form is the same as that prescribed and explained for the second week.

[205]   2nd. As age, temperament, and disposition permit, the exercitant will make each day the five Exercises, or fewer.

[206]   3rd. In the Third Week the second and sixth additions may be modified in part. The second addition shall now be to consider as soon as I awake, where I am going and to what purpose. I shall make a short review of the contemplation which I wish to make. Depending on the subject matter of the mystery, I will strive while rising and dressing to arouse sentiments of sadness and grief within myself because of the great pain and suffering of Christ our Lord.

The sixth addition will now be that I will strive not to permit myself any joyful thoughts, even though they are good and holy, as are those of the Resurrection and the glory of heaven. I will rather awake myself to sorrow, suffering, and anguish frequently calling to mind the labors, burdens, and sufferings that Christ our Lord bore from the moment of His birth up to the mystery of His Passion, which I am now contemplating.

[207]   4th. The particular examination of conscience on the Exercises and the additions as given for this week will be made in the same way as in the past week.

SECOND DAY

[208]   On the second day the contemplation at midnight will be on the events from the Garden to the house of Annas inclusive (no. 291). In the morning the contemplation will be on the events from the house of Annas to the house of Caiphas inclusive (no. 292). Then there will be the two repetitions and the application of the senses, as already stated.

THIRD DAY

The contemplation at midnight will be on the events from the house of Caiphas to that of Pilate inclusive (no. 293). Then in the morning from Pilate to Herod inclusive, (no. 294) and then the repetitions and the application of the senses as above.

FOURTH DAY

At midnight the subject matter will be from Herod to Pilate (no. 295). This contemplation will be on the first half of what took place in the house of Pilate. The morning contemplation will be on the remaining part. Then there will be two repetitions and the application of the senses, as stated.

FIFTH DAY

At midnight, from the house of Pilate to the nailing to the cross, (no. 296) and in the morning, from the raising of the cross to His death (no. 297). Then the two repetitions and the application of the senses.

SIXTH DAY

At midnight, from the taking down from the cross to the burial in the sepulcher inclusive to the house where our Lady was after the burial of her Son.

SEVENTH DAY

A contemplation of the entire Passion in the exercise of midnight and in the morning, and instead of the two repetitions and the application of the senses, consider as frequently as possible throughout the entire day how the most Sacred Body of Christ our Lord remained separated and apart from His Soul, also where and how it was buried. Consider likewise the loneliness of our Lady, her great grief and weariness, also that of the disciples.

[209] *Note.* It is to be observed that anyone who wishes to spend more time on the Passion may consider fewer mysteries in each contemplation, for example, in the first contemplation, on the Last Supper; in the second, the washing of feet; in the third, the institution of the Blessed Sacrament; in the fourth, our Lord's last discourse, and so on for the other contemplations and mysteries.

In like manner, after the Passion has been completed, one may give an entire day to meditation on the first half of the Passion, a second day to the other half, and a third day to the entire Passion. On the other hand, anyone wishing to spend a shorter time on the Passion may take at midnight the Last Supper and the Garden; in the morning at the time of Mass, the house of Annas; at Vespers, the house of Caiphas; in place of the Exercise of the time before supper, the house of Pilate. Thus omitting the repetitions and the application of the senses, he may make five distinct Exercises each day, and in each Exercise contemplate a distinct mystery of the Passion of Christ our Lord.

After he has thus completed the Passion, he may use another day to contemplate the entire Passion in one Exercise, or in several, in the way that he thinks will profit him most.

RULES TO BE OBSERVED IN THE FUTURE IN THE MATTER OF FOOD AS A MEANS OF SELF CONTROL[58]

[210]   1st. The first rule is that there is less need to abstain from bread, for it is not the kind of food over which the appetite is usually inclined to be uncontrolled, or over which temptation is so insistent as with other foods.

[211]   2nd. The second rule: abstinence is more appropriate with regard to drink than to eating bread. Therefore one must consider carefully what would be beneficial to him and therefore permissible, and also what would be harmful, and so to be avoided.

[212]   3rd. The third rule: with regard to foods, greater and more complete abstinence must be practiced because here temptation is likely to be more insistent and the appetite inclined to be excessive. In order to avoid overindulgence, abstinence may be observed in two ways: by accustoming oneself to eat coarse foods, or if delicacies are taken, to eat them in small quantities.

[213]   4th. The fourth rule: while taking care not to become sick, the more one abstains in the quantity of food suited to him, the sooner he will arrive at the mean he should observe in eating and drinking. There are two reasons for this: first, by thus helping and disposing himself, he will more frequently feel the interior directions, consolations, and divine inspirations that will show him the mean that is proper for him. Secondly, if he finds that with such abstinence he lacks sufficient health and strength for the Spiritual Exercises, he will easily be able to judge what is more suitable for sustaining his body.

[214]   5th. The fifth rule: while one is eating, one may consider that one sees Christ our Lord at the table with His Apostles, how He eats and drinks; how He looks and how He speaks, and he will strive to imitate Him. He will thus keep his understanding occupied principally with our Lord, and less with the sustenance of his own body. Thus he may adopt a better method and order in the manner in which he should govern himself.

[215]   6th. The sixth rule: while eating, he may at other times consider the lives of the saints or some other pious contemplation, or he may consider some spiritual work that he has to perform. If he is occupied with such matters, he will take less delight and sensual pleasure in his corporal nourishment.

[216]   7th. The seventh rule: above all, he must take care that his mind is not entirely occupied in what he is eating, and that he is not carried away by his appetite into eating hurriedly. Let him rather be master of himself both in the way that he eats and the amount that he takes.

[217]   8th. The eighth rule: To avoid excess, it is very useful after dinner or after supper, or at another time when one feels no desire to eat, to make a determination for the next dinner or supper, and so for the subsequent days, on the amount of food that is proper for him to eat. Let him not exceed this amount, no matter how strong his appetite or the temptation. Rather, the better to overcome every disorderly appetite and temptation of the enemy, if he is tempted to eat more, he should eat less.

[FOURTH WEEK]
First Contemplation

[218]   How Christ our Lord appeared to our Lady (no. 299).
  Prayer: The usual preparatory prayer.

[219]   *The first prelude* is the history. Here it is how after Christ expired on the cross, and His body remained separated from the soul, yet always united with the Divinity. His blessed soul, likewise united with the Divinity, descended into hell. There He released the souls of the just, then returning to the sepulcher, and rising, He appeared in body and soul to His Blessed Mother.

[220]   *The second prelude* is composition seeing the place. Here it will be to see the arrangement of the holy sepulcher and the place or home of our Lady, noting in detail its different parts, likewise her room, her oratory, etc.

[221]   *The third prelude* is to ask for what I desire. Here it will be to request for grace that I may feel intense joy and gladness for so great a glory and joy of Christ our Lord.

[222]   1st, 2nd and 3rd. The first, second, and third points are the same that we have had in the contemplation on the Last Supper of Christ our Lord (no. 194).

[223]   4th. The fourth point is to consider that the Divinity which seemed to hide itself during the Passion, now appears and manifests itself so miraculously in the most holy Resurrection by its true and most holy effects.

[224]   5th. The fifth is to consider the job of consoler that Christ our Lord exercises, comparing it with the way that friends seem to console one another.

[225]   *Colloquy.* Conclude with one or more colloquies according to the subject matter and then with the "Our Father".

Notes

[226]   1st. The first note: in the following contemplations all of the mysteries from the Resurrection to the Ascension inclusive are to be made in the manner indicated below, observing in other respects throughout the Week of the Resurrection the same form and methods that are followed during the entire Week of the Passion. The exercitant may use this first contemplation on the Resurrection as a guide, for the preludes will be the same, adapted to the subject matter, and the five points will be the same. The additions will be the same, as given below. In all the rest, that is, the repetitions, the application of the senses, the shortening or lengthening of the events, etc., the Week of the Passion may serve as a guide.

[227]   2nd. The second note: ordinarily, it is more suitable in the fourth week than in the other three, to make four Exercises instead of five. The first on rising in the morning; the second at the hour of Mass or before dinner, in place of the first repetition; the third at the hour of Vespers, in place of the second repetition; the fourth before supper, will be the application of the senses to the three Exercises of the day, noticing and slowing down in the principal points and in those parts in which greater enjoyment and spiritual fruition has been felt.

[228]   3rd. The third: although in all contemplations a definite number of points is given, that is, three or five, etc., the one making the contemplation may use more or fewer points, as seems better to him. For this reason it is very useful, before beginning the contemplation, to foresee and determine the number of points that are to be used.

[229]   4th. In this fourth week, the second, sixth, seventh and tenth additions are to be changed.

The second will be that upon waking, I will see in front of me the contemplation that I am about to make, and I will strive to feel joy and gladness at the great joy and gladness of Christ our Lord.

The sixth will be to bring to memory and think things that cause pleasure, happiness, and spiritual joy, for example, the thought of heaven.

The seventh will be to take advantage of light and the comforts of the season, for example, coolness in summer, and the warmth of the sun and of heat in winter, in so far as the soul thinks or can presume that these things may help it to rejoice in its Creator and Redeemer.

The tenth will be, in place of penance, to concentrate on obtaining temperance and moderation in all things, except when fasting and abstinence are required by the Church, for these prescriptions must always be observed unless there is some legitimate impediment.

[230]   CONTEMPLATION TO ATTAIN LOVE[59]

Note. First, two points are to be noted here:

The first is that love ought to be manifested in deeds rather than words.

[231] The second is that love consists in a mutual interchange by the two parties, that is to say, that the lover give to and share with the beloved all that he has or can attain, and vice versa the beloved toward the lover. Thus if he has knowledge, he shares it with the one who does not have it; if riches, they equally share riches, and vice versa.

Prayer: The usual preparatory prayer.

[232] *The first prelude* is the visual representation of the place. Here it is to see how I stand in the presence of God our Lord and of the angels and saints, who intercede for me.

[233] *The second prelude* is to ask for what I desire. Here it will be to ask for inner knowledge of the many blessings I have received, that I may, so enlightened, be filled with gratitude for them, and in all things love and serve His Divine Majesty.

[234] 1st. The first point is to bring to memory the benefits that I have reached from creation, redemption, and the particular gifts I have received. I will ponder with great affection how much God our Lord has done for me, and how many of His gifts He has given me. I will likewise consider how much the same Lord wishes to give Himself to me in so far as He can, according to His divine decrees. I will then reflect within myself, and consider that I, for my part, with great reason and justice, should offer and give to His Divine Majesty, i.e., all of my things and myself with them, as one who makes an offering with deep love, saying:

> Take, O Lord, and receive all my liberty, my memory, my understanding, and my entire will, all that I have and possess. You gave all to me, to you O Lord, I return it. All is yours; dispose of it according to your Will. Give me your Love and grace, for this is enough for me.

[235] 2nd. The second point is to consider how God dwells in His creatures; in the elements, giving them being; in the plants, giving them life; in the animals, giving them sensation; in men, giving them understanding. So He dwells in me, giving me being, life, sensation, and intelligence, and thus making a temple of me, since He created me to the likeness and image of His Divine Majesty. Then I will reflect upon myself in the manner stated in the first point, or in any other way that may seem more beneficial. The same procedure should be served in each of the points that follow.

[236] 3rd. The third point is to consider how God works and labors for me in all created things on the face of the earth; that is, He conducts Himself as one who labors, as in the heavens, the

elements, plants, fruits, flocks, etc. He gives them being, preserves them, grants them growth, sensation, etc. Then I will reflect on myself.

[237]   4th. The fourth point is to consider how all blessings and gifts descend from above. My limited power, for example, comes from the supreme and infinite power from above. In like manner justice, goodness, pity, mercy, etc., descend from above just as the rays from the sun, the waters from the spring, etc. Then I will reflect upon myself, as explained above, and conclude with a colloquy and the "Our Father."

THREE WAYS OF PRAYER[60]

The First Way of Prayer

[238]   The first method of prayer is on the Ten Commandments, the seven capital sins, the three powers of the soul, and the five senses of the body. The purpose of this method of prayer is to give a way, form, and exercises by which the soul may prepare itself and make progress, thereby making its prayer more acceptable, rather than to give a form and method of praying.

[239]   *Additions.* Some exercise equivalent to the second addition of the second week is to be made. Thus, before entering on prayer, I will let my mind repose a little, either by sitting or walking, according as shall seem best to me, and then I will consider where I am going, and for what purpose. This same addition will be made at the beginning of all the ways of prayer.

[240]   *Prayer.* A preparatory prayer is to be made, such as to ask of God our Lord the grace to know how I have failed in regard to the Ten Commandments. I should likewise ask for grace and help to amend myself in the future, asking for a perfect understanding of the commandments so that I may observe them better, to the greater praise and glory of His Divine Majesty.

The Ten Commandments

[241]   For the first way of prayer, it is well to consider and to think over the first commandment, how I have kept it, and where I have failed. For this consideration, I will take, as a rule, the time required to recite three times the "Our Father" and three times the "Hail Mary". If in this time I discover faults I have committed, I will ask pardon and forgiveness for them and say an "Our Father." I will follow this same method for each of the Ten Commandments.

[242]   1st. First note. It is to be observed that when one comes to a commandment against which he is not in the habit of sinning, it is not necessary to delay on it, but according as he realizes that he offends more or less in a commandment, he should spend a greater

or lesser time in its consideration and scrutiny. The same procedure should be observed regarding capital sins.

[243]   2nd. Second note. After I have completed this form of consideration on all the commandments, accused myself where I have failed, and asked for grace and help to amend my life in the future, I will conclude with a colloquy to God our Lord, according to the subject matter.

The Capital Sins

[244]   Regarding the seven capital sins, after the additions, the preparatory prayer is to be made in the manner already prescribed. The only change is that the matter here is the sins which are to be avoided, whereas before it was the commandments to be observed. In like manner the procedure and the rule prescribed above are to be observed, together with the colloquy.

[245]   In order to know better the faults committed relating to capital sins, let the contrary virtues be considered. Thus the better to avoid these sins, one should resolve and endeavor by holy exercises to acquire and retain the seven virtues contrary to them.

The Powers of the Soul

[246]   The same way and rule that were followed for the commandments should be observed with regard to the three powers of the soul, with the addition, preparatory prayer, and colloquy.

The Five Senses of the Body

[247]   Way: the same way will also be followed with regard to the five senses of the body; only the subject matter is changed.

[248]   *Note*: Whoever wishes to imitate Christ our Lord in the use of the senses should recommend himself to His Divine Majesty in the preparatory prayer, and after the consideration of each of the senses say a "Hail Mary" or an "Our Father." If he wishes to imitate Our Lady in the use of the senses, he should recommend himself to her in the preparatory prayer, that She may obtain this grace for him from her Son and Lord. After the consideration of each sense, he should say a "Hail Mary."

The Second Way of Prayer

[249]   The second way consists in contemplating the meaning of each word of a prayer.

[250]   *Addition*: The same addition that was made in the first way of prayer will also be used here.

[251]   *Prayer*: The preparatory prayer will be made according to the person to whom the prayer is directed.

[252]   The second way of prayer is as follows: The person may be kneeling or sitting, whichever suits his disposition better and is

more conducive to devotion. He should keep his eyes closed, or fixed on one position, not permitting them to wander about. He should then say, "Father," and reflect upon this word as long as he finds meanings, comparisons, relish, and consolation in the consideration of it. He should then continue the same method with each word of the "Our Father," or of any other prayer that he may wish to contemplate in this manner.

[253]   1st. The first rule is that he will continue in the prescribed manner for one hour on the "Our Father." When this prayer is finished, he will say the "Hail Mary," the "Creed," the "*Anima Christi*," and the "*Salve Regina*" vocally or mentally, in the customary manner.

[254]   2nd. The second rule is that during the contemplation on the "Our Father," if he finds in one or two words good matter for thought, and relish, and consolation, he should not be anxious to pass on, even though he spend the entire hour on what he has found. When the hour is over, he will say the rest of the "Our Father" in the usual way.

[255]   3rd. The third rule is that if he has spent the entire hour dwelling on one or two words of the "Our Father," on another day, when he wishes to return to the same prayer, he may say the abovementioned word or two in the usual way, and begin the contemplation of the word which immediately follows, as explained in the second rule.

[256]   1st. First note. One must notice that when one has finished the "Our Father," after one or more days, he should contemplate the "Hail Mary" in the same manner, and then the other prayers, so that for some time he is always occupied with one of them.

[257]   2nd. Second note is that when the prayer is finished, he should turn to the Person to whom the prayer is directed, and ask for the virtues and graces for which he feels the greatest need.

The Third Way of Prayer

[258]   *Addition.* The addition is the same as in the first and second ways of prayer.

Prayer: As in the second way of prayer.

The third way of prayer is that, at each breath or respiration, he is to pray mentally, as he says one word of the "Our Father," or any other prayer that is being recited, so that between one breath and another a single word is said. During this same space of time, he is to give his full attention to the meaning of the word, or to the Person whom he is address, or to his own unworthiness, or to the difference between the greatness of this Person and his own lowliness. He will continue, observing the same procedure and rule, through the other words of the "Our Father" and the prayers, namely the "Hail Mary," the "*Anima Christi*," the "Creed," and the "*Salve Regina*" doing as usual.

[259]   1st. The first rule is on another day, or at another hour, when he wishes to pray, he may say the "Hail Mary" in this rhythmic manner, and the other prayers in the same manner.

[260]   2nd. The second rule is that if he wishes to spend a longer time in this rhythmic prayer, he may say all of the above-mentioned prayers, or some of them, observing the same method of rhythmic breathing described above.

THE MYSTERIES OF THE LIFE OF OUR LORD[61]

[261]   *Note.* It will be noted that in all of the following events the words in quotation marks are taken from the Gospel itself but not the other words. Three points are usually given for each mystery, to facilitate the contemplation and meditation.

The Annunciation of Our Lady
(LUKE 1 : 26-38)

[262]   *First Point.* The Angel St. Gabriel greeted our Lady and announced to her the conception of Christ our Lord. And when the Angel had come to her, he said, "Hail, full of grace, ... Thou shalt conceive in thy womb and shalt bring forth a son."

Second Point. The Angel confirms what he had said to our Lady by announcing the conception of St. John the Baptist, saying to her: "And behold, Elizabeth thy kinswoman also has conceived a son in her old age."

Third Point. Our Lady replied to the Angel: "Behold the handmaid of the Lord; be it done to me according to thy word."

The Visitation of Our Lady to Elizabeth
(LUKE 1 : 39-56)

[263]   *First Point.* When our Lady visited St. Elizabeth, St. John the Baptist, in his mother's womb, felt the visitation made by our Lady. When Elizabeth heard the greeting of Mary, the babe in her womb leapt. And Elizabeth was filled with the Holy Spirit, and cried out with a loud voice, saying, "Blessed are thou among women and blessed is the fruit of thy womb!"

Second Point. Our Lady chants the canticle, saying, "My soul magnifies the Lord."

Third Point. And Mary remained with her about three months and returned to her own house.

The Birth of Christ Our Lord
(LUKE 2 : 1-14)

[264]   *First Point.* Our Lady and her spouse, St. Joseph, go from Nazareth to Bethlehem. And Joseph also went up from Galilee to Bethlehem, in obedience to Caesar, with Mary, his espoused wife, who was with child.

Second Point. And she brought forth her firstborn son, and wrapped him in swaddling clothes, and laid him in a manger.

Third Point. And suddenly there was a multitude of the heavenly host praising God and saying, "Glory to God in the highest."

The Shepherds
(LUKE 2 : 8-20)

[265]   *First Point.* The Birth of Christ our Lord is made known to the shepherds by an angel: "I bring you good news of great joy, for today a Savior has been born to you."

Second Point. The shepherds go to Bethlehem. So they went with haste, and they found Mary and Joseph, and the babe lying in the manger.

Third Point. And the shepherds return, glorifying and praising God.

The Circumcision
(LUKE 2 : 21)

[266]   *First Point.* They circumcised the Child Jesus.

Second Point. His name was called Jesus, the name given him by the angel before he was conceived in the womb.

Third Point. They returned the Child to His mother, who felt compassion at the blood shed by her Son.

The Three Magi Kings
(MATT. 2 : 1-12)

[267]   *First Point.* The three Magi Kings, guided by the star, came to adore Jesus, saying, "We have seen his star in the East and have come to worship him."

Second Point. They adored Him and offered Him gifts. "And falling down they worshipped him, and offered him gifts of gold, frankincense, and myrrh."

Third Point. And being warned in a dream not to return to Herod, they went back to their own country by another way.

The Purification of Our Lady and the Presentation of the Child Jesus
(LUKE 2 : 22-39)

[268]   *First Point.* They take the Child Jesus to the Temple to be presented to the Lord as the firstborn, and they offer for Him a pair of turtle doves and two young pigeons.

Second Point. Simeon, coming into the Temple, also received him into his arms, saying, "Now thou dost dismiss thy servant, O Lord, according to thy word, in peace."

Third Point. Anna, coming up at that very hour, began to give praise to the Lord and spoke of him to all who were awaiting the redemption of Jerusalem.

The Flight into Egypt
(MATT. 2 : 13-15)

[269]   *First Point.* Herod wanted to kill the Child Jesus, and so he slew the Innocents. Before their slaughter an angel warned Joseph to fly into Egypt: "Arise and take the child and his mother and flee into Egypt."

Second Point. He set out for Egypt. So he arose, and took the child and his mother by night, and withdrew into Egypt.

Third Point. There he remained until the death of Herod.

The Return from Egypt
(MATT. 2 : 19-23)

[270]   *First Point.* The angel admonishes Joseph to return to Israel: "Arise, and take the child and his mother and go into the land of Israel."

Second Point. So he arose . . . and went into the land of Israel.

Third Point. Since Archelaus, the son of Herod, ruled in Judea, he withdrew to Nazareth.

The Life of Our Lord from the Age of Twelve to the Age of Thirty
(LUKE 2 : 51-52)

[271]   *First Point.* He was obedient to His parents.

Second Point. Jesus advanced in wisdom and age and grace.

Third Point. He seems to have practiced the trade of a carpenter, as St. Mark seems to indicate in Chapter VI: "Is not this the carpenter?"

Jesus Comes to the Temple at the Age of Twelve
(LUKE 2 : 41-50)

[272]   *First Point.* When Christ our Lord was twelve years old, He went up from Nazareth to Jerusalem.

Second Point. Christ our Lord remained in Jerusalem, and His parents did not know it.

Third Point. After three days had passed, they found Him in the Temple, seated in the midst of the doctors and disputing with them. When His parents asked Him where He had been, He replied, "Did you not know that I must be about my Father's business?"

The Baptism of Christ
(MATT. 3 : 13-17)

[273]   *First Point.* After He took leave of His blessed Mother, Christ our Lord went from Nazareth to the River Jordan, where St. John the Baptist was.

Second Point. St. John baptized Christ our Lord. When he wanted to excuse himself, considering that he was unworthy to baptize Him, Christ said to him: "Let it be so now, for so it becomes us to fulfill all justice."

Third Point. The Holy Spirit descended upon Him, and the voice of the Father testified from Heaven: "This is my beloved Son, in whom I am well pleased."

The Temptation of Christ
(LUKE 4 : 1-13; MATT. 4 : 1-11)

[274]   *First Point.* After Jesus was baptized, He went to the desert, where He fasted for forty days and forty nights.

Second Point. He was tempted by the enemy three times. And the tempter came and said to Him, "If thou art the Son of God, command that these stones become loaves of bread . . . . Throw thyself down . . . . All these things will I give thee, if thou wilt fall down and worship me."

Third Point. Angels came and ministered to Him.

The Vocation of the Apostles

[275] *First Point.* It appears that St. Peter and St. Andrew were called three times. They were first called to some knowledge, as is shown in the first chapter of St. John (35-42). They were called a second time to follow Christ in some way, with the intention of returning to the possessions which they had left, as St. Luke relates in Chapter 5: 10-11. The third time they were called to follow Christ our Lord forever, in St. Matthew 4: 18-22 and St. Mark, 1: 16-18.

Second Point. He called Philip, as described in the first chapter of St. John (43), and Matthew, as Matthew himself relates in Chapter 9: 9.

Third Point. He called the other Apostles of whose particular vocation no mention is made in the Gospel.

Three other points are also to be considered:
1) The Apostles were uneducated men, from a low station in life; 2) The dignity to which they were so gently called; 3) The graces and gifts by which they were raised above all the fathers of the Old and New Testament.

The First Miracle, Performed at the Marriage Feast of Cana in Galilee
(JOHN 2 : 1-11)

[276] *First Point.* Christ our Lord and His disciples were invited to the marriage feast.

Second Point. The Mother calls her Son's attention to the lack of wine, saying: "They have no wine," and she tells the attendants: "Do whatever He tells you."

Third Point. He changed the water into wine . . . and He manifested His glory, and His disciples believed in Him.

Christ Drives the Sellers Out of the Temple
(JOHN 2 : 13-16)

[277] *First Point.* He drove all of the sellers from the temple with a scourge made of cord.

Second Point. He overturned the tables and scattered the money of the rich money changers that were in the temple.

Third Point. To the poor who were selling doves, He gently said, "Take these things away, and do not make of the house of my Father a house of business."

The Sermon Christ Delivered on the Mount
(MATT. 5)

[278]   *First Point.* He speaks apart to His beloved disciples, about the eight beatitudes: "Blessed are the poor in spirit . . . the meek . . . the merciful . . . they who mourn . . . they who hunger and thirst for justice . . . the clean of heart . . . the peacemakers . . . they who suffer persecution."

Second Point. He exhorts them to use their talents well: "Even so let your light shine before men, in order that they may see your good works and give glory to your Father in heaven."

Third Point. He shows that He is not a transgressor of the law but a fulfiller. He explains the precept not to kill, not to commit adultery, not to swear falsely, and to love our enemies: "I say to you, love your enemies, do good to those who hate you."

Christ Calms the Storm at Sea
(MATT. 8 : 23-37)

[279]   *First Point.* While Christ our Lord was sleeping in the boat, a great storm arose.

Second Point. His terrified disciples awakened Him; He reproved them for their little faith, saying to them: "Why are you fearful, O you of little faith?"

Third Point. He commanded the winds and the sea to cease; at once the wind ceased and the sea became calm. The men marveled at this saying, "What manner of man is this, that even the wind and the sea obey Him?"

Christ Walks Upon the Sea
(MATT. 14 : 22-33)

[280]   *First Point.* While Christ our Lord remained upon the mountain, He made His disciples get into the boat, and when He had dismissed the crowd, He began to pray alone.

Second Point. The boat was buffeted by the waves; Christ came to them walking upon the water, and the disciples thought that it was an apparition.

Third Point. And Christ said to them: "It is I, fear not." St. Peter, at His command, came to Him, walking upon the waters, but when he doubted, he began to sink, and Christ our Lord saved him, and reproved him for his little faith. Afterwards, when He entered the boat, the wind ceased.

The Apostles are Sent Forth to Preach
(MATT. 10 : 1-16)

[281] *First Point*. Christ called His beloved disciples and gave them power to cast out devils from the bodies of men and to cure all infirmities.

Second Point. He instructed them in prudence and patience. "Behold, I am sending you forth like sheep in the midst of wolves. Be therefore wise as serpents and guileless as doves."

Third Point. He told them how they are to go: "Do not keep gold or silver. Freely you have received, freely give." And He tells them what they are to preach: "And as you go, preach the message, 'The kingdom of heaven is at hand.'"

The Conversion of Magdalene
(LUKE 7 : 36-50)

[282] *First Point*. Magdalene enters the house of the Pharisee, where Christ our Lord is reclining at table. She is carrying an alabaster vessel full of ointment.

Second Point. Standing behind the Lord near His feet, she began to bathe them with her tears and to wipe them with her hair. And she kissed His feet and anointed them with ointment.

Third Point. When the Pharisee accused Magdalene, Christ defended her, saying, "I say to thee, her sins, many as they are, shall be forgiven her, because she has loved much" . . . and He said to the woman: "Thy faith has saved thee; go in peace."

Christ Feeds Five Thousand People
(MATT. 14 : 13-21)

[283] *First Point*. The disciples asked Christ to dismiss the multitude who were with Him, since it was now late.

Second Point. Christ our Lord commanded them to bring the loaves to Him, and ordered the multitude to sit down to eat. He blessed and broke the loaves and gave them to His disciples, and they gave them to the multitude.

Third Point. And all ate and were satisfied, and they gathered up what was left over, twelve baskets full of fragments.

The Transfiguration of Christ
(MATT. 17 : 1-9)

[284] *First Point*. Christ our Lord took with Him His beloved disciples Peter, James, and John. And He was transfigured before them, and His face shown as the sun, and His garments became white as snow.

Second Point. He spoke with Moses and Elias.

Third Point. While St. Peter was saying that they should

build three tabernacles, a voice from heaven was heard, saying,
"This is my beloved Son . . . hear Him." When the disciples heard
this voice, they fell on their faces in great fear. Jesus came and
touched them, and said, "Arise and do not be afraid . . . Tell the
vision to no one until the Son of Man has risen from the dead."

The Resurrection of Lazarus
(JOHN 11 : 1-45)

[285]   *First Point.* Martha and Mary made known to Christ our
Lord the illness of Lazarus. After Jesus heard of this, He remained
two days longer in the place where He was, that the miracle might
be more evident.

Second Point. Before He raised Lazarus, He asked Martha
and Mary to believe, saying, "I am the resurrection and the life; he
who believes in me, even if he die, shall live."

Third Point. He raised Lazarus after He had wept and said
a prayer. The manner of raising him was by the command, "Lazarus,
come forth."

The Supper in Bethany
(MATT. 26 : 6-13)

[286]   *First Point.* Our Lord took supper in the house of Simon
the leper together with Lazarus.

Second Point. Mary poured the precious ointment upon
the head of Christ.

Third Point. Judas murmured, "To what purpose is this
waste of ointment?" But Jesus again excused Magdalene, saying:
"Why do you trouble the woman? She has done me a good turn."

Palm Sunday
(MATT. 21 : 1-11)

[287]   *First Point.* Jesus sent for the ass and the colt, saying:
"Loose them and bring them to me, and if anyone say anything to
you, you shall say that the Lord hath need of them, and immediately he will send them."

Second Point. He mounted the ass which is covered with
the garments of the Apostles.

Third Point. The people came forth to meet Him, spreading their garments and branches along the way, saying, "Hosanna
to the Son of David! Blessed is He who comes in the name of the
Lord! Hosanna in the highest."

Jesus Preaches in the Temple
(LUKE 19 : 47)

[288] *First Point.* And he was teaching daily in the Temple.

Second Point. After His teaching, since there was no one to receive Him in Jerusalem, He returned to Bethany.

The Last Supper
(MATT. 26 : 17-30; JOHN 13 : 1-30)

[289] *First Point.* Jesus ate the Pascal Lamb with His twelve Apostles, to whom He foretold His death: "Amen I say to you, one of you will betray me."

Second Point. He washed the feet of His disciples, even those of Judas. He began with St. Peter, who, considering the majesty of the Lord and his own lowly estate, would not permit it. He said, "Lord, dost thou wash my feet?" Peter did not understand that Jesus was giving them an example of humility by this. Jesus therefore said to him, "I have given you an example, that as I have done for you, so you also should do."

Third Point. He instituted the most Holy Sacrifice of the Eucharist, as the greatest proof of His love, saying, "Take and eat." When the supper was finished, Judas went forth to sell Christ our Lord.

From the Supper to the Agony in the Garden, Inclusive
(MATT. 26 : 30-46; MARK 14 : 26-42)

[290] *First Point.* After they had finished supper and sung a hymn, our Lord went to Mount Olive with His disciples, who were full of fear. He left eight of them in Gethsemane, saying to them, "Sit down here while I go yonder and pray."

Second Point. Accompanied by Peter, James, and John, He prayed to the Father, saying, "Father, if it is possible, let this cup pass away from me; yet not as I will, but as thou willest." And falling into an agony, he prayed the more earnestly.

Third Point. So great was the fear that possessed Him, that He said, "My soul is sad, even unto death," and He sweated blood so copiously that St. Luke says, "His sweat became as drops of blood running down upon the ground." This supposes that His garments were now saturated with blood.

From the Agony in the Garden to the House of Annas, Inclusive
(MATT. 26 : 47-56; LUKE 22 : 47-53; MARK 14 : 43-52; JOHN 18 : 1-23)

[291]   *First Point.* Our Lord allows Himself to be kissed by Judas, and to be seized like a thief. He says to the crowd: "As against a robber you have come out, with swords and clubs, to seize me. I sat daily with you in the temple teaching, and you did not lay hands on me." And when He said, "Whom do you seek?" His enemies fell to the ground.

    Second Point. St. Peter wounded a servant of the high priest. The meek Lord said to him, "Put back thy sword into its place." And He healed the servant's wound.

    Third Point. Jesus is abandoned by His disciples and dragged before Annas. There St. Peter, who had followed at a distance, denied Him the first time. Then a servant struck Christ in the face, saying to Him, "Is that the way thou dost answer the high priest?"

From the House of Annas to the House of Caiphas, Inclusive
(MATT. 26 : 57-75; MARK 14 : 53-72; LUKE 22 : 54-65)

[292]   *First Point.* Jesus is led bound from the House of Annas to the House of Caiphas, where Peter denied Him twice. And when Jesus looked upon Peter, He went out and wept bitterly.

    Second Point. Jesus was left bound the entire night.

    Third Point. And those who held Him prisoner blindfolded Him, and struck Him and buffeted Him, and asked Him, "Prophecy, who is that struck thee?" And in like manner they continued to blaspheme Him.

From the House of Caiphas to the House of Pilate, Inclusive
(MATT. 27 : 1-26; LUKE 23 : 1-5; MARK 15 : 1-15)

[293]   *First Point.* The whole multitude of the Jews brought Him before Pilate and accused Him, saying, "We have found this man perverting the nation, and forbidding the payment of taxes to Caesar."

    Second Point. After Pilate had examined Him several times, he said, "I find no crime deserving of death in him."

    Third Point. Barabbas the robber was preferred to Him. The whole mob cried out together saying, "Away with this man, and release to us Barabbas!"

From the House of Pilate to the House of Herod
(LUKE 23 : 6-10)

[294]   *First Point.* Pilate sent Jesus the Galilean to Herod, the Tetrarch of Galilee.

Second Point. Herod, through curiosity, asked Jesus many questions, but He answered him nothing, even though the scribes and priests unceasingly accused Him.

Third Point. Herod and his entire court mocked Jesus, clothing Him in a white garment.

From the House of Herod to That of Pilate
(MATT. 27 : 24-30; LUKE 23 : 12-23;
MARK 15 : 15-19; JOHN 19 : 1-11)

[295]   *First Point.* Herod sent Him back to Pilate. Because of this, they became friends, although before this they were enemies.

Second Point. Pilate took Jesus and scourged Him, and the soldiers made a crown of thorns and placed it upon His head. They put a purple cloak about Him, and came before Him, saying, "Hail, King of the Jews!" and they struck Him.

Third Point. Pilate had Him brought forth before all the people; Jesus came forth, wearing the crown of thorns and the purple cloak. And Pilate said to them: "Behold the man." When they saw Him, the chief priests cried: "Crucify Him! Crucify Him!"

From the House of Pilate to the Cross, Inclusive
(JOHN 19 : 12-24)

[296]   *First Point.* Pilate, sitting as judge, delivered Jesus to the Jews to be crucified, after they had denied that He was their king, saying, "We have no king but Caesar."

Second Point. He carried the cross upon His shoulders, and as He could not carry it, Simon of Cyrene was forced to carry it after Jesus.

Third Point. They crucified Him between two thieves, placing this title above Him: Jesus of Nazareth, the King of the Jews.

Jesus Upon the Cross
(JOHN 19 : 23-37; MATT. 27 : 35-39;
MARK 15 : 24-38; LUKE 23 : 34-46)

[297]   *First Point.* He spoke seven words on the Cross. He prayed for those who crucified Him; He pardoned the thief; He entrusted His Mother to St. John; He said in a loud voice, "I thirst," and they gave Him gall and vinegar; He said that He was forsaken; He said, "It is consummated!" He said, "Father, into thy hands I commend my spirit."

Second Point. The sun was darkened; rocks rent, graves opened; the veil of the temple was torn in two from top to bottom.

Third Point. They blasphemed Him saying, "Thou who destroyed the Temple . . . come down from the Cross." His garments were divided; His side was pierced with a lance, and blood and water flowed forth.

From the Cross to the Sepulcher, Inclusive
(JOHN 19 : 38-42)

[298]   *First Point.* He was taken down from the Cross by Joseph and Nicodemus in the presence of His sorrowful Mother.

Second Point. His body was carried to the sepulcher, and anointed and buried.

Third Point. Guards were set.

The Resurrection of Christ Our Lord, and His First Apparition

[299]   *First Point.* He appeared to the Virgin Mary. Although this is not mentioned in Scripture, it is considered as mentioned when the Scripture says that He appeared to so many others, for the Scripture supposes that we have understanding, as is written "Are you also without understanding?"

The Second Apparition
(MARK 16 : 1-11)

[300]   *First Point.* Very early in the morning Mary Magdalene, Mary the Mother of Jesus, and Salome go to the tomb. They say to one another, "Who will roll the stone back from the entrance of the tomb for us?"

Second Point. They see the stone rolled back and an angel who says: "You are looking for Jesus of Nazareth . . . he has risen, he is not here."

Third Point. He appeared to Mary, who remained near the tomb after the others had departed.

The Third Apparition
(MATT. 28 : 8-10)

[301]   *First Point.* These Marys go from the tomb with great fear and joy. They want to announce the resurrection of the Lord to the disciples.

Second Point. Christ our Lord appeared to them on the way, and said to them, "Hail!" and they came up to Him, and prostrated themselves at His feet, and adored Him.

Third Point. Jesus said to them: "Do not be afraid; go take word to my brethren that they are to set out for Galilee; there they shall see me."

The Fourth Apparition
(LUKE 24 : 10-12 and 33-34)

[302]   *First Point.* When Peter heard from the women that Christ had risen, he hastened to the tomb.

Second Point. He entered the tomb and saw nothing but the linen cloths with which the body of Christ our Lord had been covered.

Third Point. While Peter was thinking about these things, Christ appeared to him. Therefore the Apostles said, "The Lord is risen indeed, and has appeared to Simon."

The Fifth Apparition
(LUKE 24 : 13-35)

[303]   *First Point.* He appeared to the disciples, who were on the way to Emmaus and were talking of Christ.

Second Point. He reproaches them, and shows them by the Scriptures that Christ had to die and rise again: "O foolish ones and slow of heart to believe in all that the prophets have spoken! Did not Christ have to suffer these things before entering into his glory?"

Third Point. At their entreaties, He remained with them until He gave them Communion; then He disappeared. And they returned to the disciples and told them how they had known Him in the Communion.

The Sixth Apparition
(JOHN 20 : 19-23)

[304]   *First Point.* The disciples, except Thomas, were gathered together, "for fear of the Jews."

Second Point. Jesus appeared to them, the doors being closed, and standing in their midst said, "Peace be to you."

Third Point. He gives them the Holy Spirit, saying to them, "Receive the Holy Spirit; Whose sins you shall forgive, they are forgiven them, and whose sins you shall retain, they are retained."

The Seventh Apparition
(JOHN 20 : 24-29)

[305]   *First Point.* Thomas was incredulous, since he had not been

present at the preceding apparition, and said, "Unless I see . . . I will not believe."

Second Point. Eight days later Jesus appeared to them, the doors being shut, and said to Thomas, "Bring here thy finger and see . . . and be not unbelieving, but believing."

Third Point. Thomas believing, said, "My Lord and My God." And Christ said to him, "Blessed are they who have not seen, and have believed."

The Eighth Apparition
(JOHN 21 : 1-17)

[306]   *First Point.* Jesus manifested Himself to seven of His disciples who were fishing. They had been fishing all night and had caught nothing. At His command they cast forth the net, and now they were unable to draw it up for the great number of fishes.

Second Point. John recognized Him by this miracle, and said to Peter, "It is the Lord." Peter cast himself into the sea and came to Christ.

Third Point. He gave them part of a broiled fish and bread to eat. After he had questioned Peter three times on his love for Him, He commended His sheep to him, saying, "Feed my sheep."

The Ninth Apparition
(MATT. 28 : 16-20)

[307]   *First Point.* At the command of the Lord, the disciples went to Mount Thabor.

Second Point. Christ appeared to them, and said, "All power in heaven and on earth has been given to me."

Third Point. He sent them to preach throughout the world saying, "Go, therefore, and make disciples of all nations, baptizing them in the name of the Father, and of the Son, and of the Holy Spirit."

The Tenth Apparition
(I COR. 15 : 6)

[308]   Then he was seen by more than five hundred breathren at one time.

The Eleventh Apparition
(I COR. 15 : 7)

[309]   After that he was seen by James.

The Twelfth Apparition

[310]   He appeared to Joseph of Arimathea, as may be piously thought, and as we read in the Lives of the Saints.

The Thirteenth Apparition
(I COR. 15 : 8)

[311]   After His Ascension He appeared to St. Paul: "And last of all, as by one born out of due time, he was seen also by me."

He appeared also in soul to the holy fathers in Limbo, and after He had freed them and taken His body again, He appeared many times to the disciples and discoursed with them.

The Ascension of Christ Our Lord
(ACTS 1 : 1-11)

[312]   *First Point.* After Christ our Lord had manifested Himself for forty days to His Apostles, giving them many proofs and signs, and speaking of the Kingdom of God, He commanded them to await in Jerusalem the Holy Spirit that He had promised them.

Second Point. He led them to Mt. Olive, "And He was lifted up before their eyes, and a cloud took Him out of their sight."

Third Point. While they were looking up to heaven, angels said to them: "Men of Galilee, why do you stand looking up to heaven? This Jesus who has been taken up from you into heaven, shall come in the same way as you have seen him going up to heaven."

Rules

[RULES FOR THE DISCERNMENT OF SPIRITS]
[First Week]

[313]   Rules for perceiving and understanding to some degree the different movements that are produced in the soul—the good, that they may be accepted; the bad, that they may be rejected. These rules are more suitable for the First Week.[62]

[314]   1st. The first rule: the enemy is accustomed ordinarily to propose apparent pleasure to those persons who go from mortal sin to mortal sin. He thus causes them to imagine sensual delights and pleasure in order to hold them more and more easily and to increase their vices and sins. The good spirit acts in these persons in a

contrary way, awakening their conscience to a sense of remorse through the habit of their reason.[63]

[315]   2nd. The second rule: the contrary to the first rule takes place in those who earnestly strive to purify themselves from their sins, and who advance from good to better in the service of God our Lord. This way is the opposite of the first rule. It is common, then, for the evil spirit to cause regret, sadness, and to create obstacles and uneasiness through false reasons, for preventing the soul from making further progress. It is characteristic of the good spirit to give courage and strength, consolations, tears, inspirations, and peace, facilitating and removing all obstacles, so that (the soul) may make further progress through good works.

[316]   3rd. The third rule is on Spiritual Consolation. I call it consolation when the soul rises by some interior movement which causes it to be inflamed with love of its Creator and Lord, and consequently can love no created thing on the face of the earth for its own sake, but only in the Creator of all things. Likewise when one sheds tears inspired by love of His Lord, whether it be sorrow for sins or because of the Passion of Christ our Lord, or for any other reason that is directly connected to His service and praise. Finally, I call consolation any increase in hope, faith, and charity and any interior joy that calls and attracts to heavenly things, and to the salvation of one's soul, with quiet and peace in Christ our Lord.

[317]   4th. The fourth rule on Spiritual Desolation. I call desolation all that is contrary to the third rule, as darkness of the soul, turmoil in the soul, inclination to low and earthly things, restlessness resulting from several disturbances and temptations which lead to loss of faith, without hope, and without love, when the soul finds itself completely lazy, tepid, sad, and as if separated from its Creator and Lord. For just as consolation is contrary to desolation, so the thoughts that spring from consolation are the opposite of those that spring from desolation.

[318]   5th. The fifth rule: in time of desolation one should never make a change, but stand firm and constant in the resolutions and decision which guided him the day before the desolation, or to the decision which he observed in the preceding consolation. For just as the good spirit guides and consoles us more in consolation, so in desolation the evil spirit guides us, and with his counsels we never find the way to be right.

[319]   6th. The sixth rule: although in desolation we should not change our earlier resolutions, it will be very advantageous to intensify our activity against such desolation. This can be done by insisting more on prayer, meditation, frequent examinations, and by increasing our penance in some suitable manner.

[320]   7th. The seventh rule: the one who is in desolation should consider that our Lord, in order to try him, has left him to his own natural resources to resist the different agitations and temptations of the enemy. He can resist with Divine help, which is always available to him, even though he may not clearly feel it. Although the Lord has withdrawn from him His great fervor, increasing love, and intense grace, He has nevertheless left him sufficient grace for eternal salvation.

[321]   8th. The eighth rule: the one who is in desolation must work to remain patient, which is contrary to the vexations that have come upon him. He should consider, also, that consolation will soon return, and strive diligently against the desolation in the manner explained in the sixth rule.

[322]   9th. The ninth rule: there are three principal reasons why we are in desolation: the first is because we are tepid, lazy, or negligent in our Spiritual Exercises, and so through our own fault spiritual consolation withdraws from us.

The second is that God may try to test our worth, and how far we may go in His service and praise when we are without such generous rewards of consolation and special graces.

The third is that He wishes to give us true knowledge and understanding, by making us innerly feel that it is not up to us alone to acquire or retain growing devotion, intense love, tears, or any other spiritual consolation, but that all of this is a gift and grace of God our Lord; and so that we do not build a nest on anything else by allowing our intellect to rise up in some pride or vain glory by attributing to ourselves devotion or the other effects of spiritual consolation.

[323]   10th. The tenth rule: the one who is in consolation ought to think of how he will conduct himself during the desolation that will follow later, and thus build up new strength for that time.

[324]   11th. The eleventh rule: the one who is in consolation should take care to humble and abase himself as much as possible. He should recall how little he is worth in time of desolation without such grace or consolation. On the other hand, the person who is in desolation should recall that he is strong enough and has sufficient grace to withstand all of his enemies by taking strength in his Creator and Lord.

[325]   12th. The twelfth rule: the enemy behaves like a woman in that he becomes weak in the presence of strength, but strong if he is not opposed. For it is natural for a woman in a quarrel with a man to lose courage and take flight when the man makes a show of strength, but on the contrary, if the man loses courage and begins to flee, the anger, vindictiveness, and fury of the woman overflows and knows no bounds. In the same manner it is the nature of our

enemy to become weak, lose courage, and take to flight as soon as a person who is following the spiritual life stands courageously against his temptations and does exactly the right opposite of what he suggests. On the contrary, if the exercitant begins to be afraid and lose courage while fighting temptation, there is no wild beast on earth more fierce than the enemy of our human nature as he pursues his evil intention with every increasing malice.

[326]   13th. The thirteenth rule: the enemy also behaves like a false lover who wishes to remain hidden and does not want to be revealed. For when this deceitful man pays court, with evil intent, to the daughter of some good father or the wife of a good husband, he wants his words and suggestions to be kept secret. He is greatly displeased with the contrary: when the girl reveals to her father, or the wife to her husband, his deceitful words and depraved intentions, for he then clearly sees that his plans cannot succeed. In like manner, when the enemy of our human nature tempts a just soul with his wiles and deceits, he wishes and desires that they be received and kept secret. When they are revealed to a confessor or some other spiritual person who understands his deceits and evil designs, the enemy is greatly displeased, for then he cannot succeed in his evil design, once his obvious deceits have been discovered.

[327]   14th. The fourteenth rule: the enemy's behavior is also like that of a military leader who wishes to conquer and plunder whatever he desires. Just as the commander of any army pitches his camp, studies the strength and defenses of a fortress, and then attacks it on its weakest side, in like manner, the enemy of our human nature studies from all sides our theological, cardinal, and moral virtues. Wherever he finds us weakest and most in need for our eternal salvation, there he attacks and tries to take us.

[Second Week]

[328]   Rules for the same effect with a greater discernment of spirits. They are more applicable to the second week.

[329]   1st. The first rule: it belongs to God and His angels to bring true happiness and spiritual joy to the soul and to free it from all the sadness and disturbance which the enemy causes. It is the nature of the enemy to fight against such joy and spiritual consolation by proposing false reasons, subtleties, and constant fallacies.

[330]   2nd. The second rule: it belongs to God alone to give consolation to the soul without previous cause, for it belongs to the Creator to enter into the soul, to leave it, and to act upon it, drawing it wholly to the love of His Divine Majesty; I say without cause, previous feeling, or knowledge of any object from which such con-

solation might come to the soul through its own acts of intellect and will.

[331]   3rd. The third rule: when a cause has preceded, both the good and bad angels may console the soul, but for different purposes. The good angel works for the progress of the soul, that it may grow and rise from the good to the better; the evil one consoles for the opposite purpose, that in time he may draw the soul on to his own evil intention and wickedness.

[332]   4th. The fourth rule: it is characteristic of the evil spirit, when he transforms himself into an angel of light, to go in with the devoted soul's way, but come out his own way. At first he will suggest good and holy thoughts that are in conformity with the disposition of a just soul; then, little by little he strives to gain his own ends by drawing the soul into his hidden deceits and perverse designs.

[333]   5th. The fifth rule: we must examine with great attention the sequence of our thoughts. If the beginning, middle, and the end is all good and leaning to what is entirely good, it is a sign that they are inspired by the good angel. If the series of our thoughts suggested to us end up in something evil, or distraction, or less good than the soul had already planned to do; or the soul weakens, or becomes disturbed or agitated by losing its peace, tranquillity, and quiet which it had before, this is clear sign that all this proceeds from the evil spirit, the enemy of our advancement, and eternal salvation.

[334]   6th. The sixth rule: when the enemy of human nature has been felt and recognized by his colorful serpent's tail, and the bad end to which he leads, it is useful for the person so tempted to examine at once the course of the good thoughts that were suggested to him by the devil. Let him consider their beginning and how the enemy set about little by little lowering that soul from the state of sweetness and spiritual joy it had, up to that point when he finally brought it to his perverse designs. With this experience and knowledge thus acquired and remembered, one may better guard himself in the future against the customary deceits of the enemy.

[335]   7th. The seventh rule: in those who travel from good to better, the touch of the good angel to the soul is gentle, light, and sweet, as a drop of water entering a sponge. The touch of the evil spirit is sharp, noisy, and agitating, like when a drop of water falls on a stone. In those souls that go from bad to worse, the touch of these two spirits is the reverse. The cause for this difference is the disposition of the soul, which is either contrary or similar to that of the spirits mentioned above. Thus, when they are contrary, the spirits enter with noise and disturbances that are easily perceived. When they are related, the spirit enters silently, as into one's own home through an open door.

[336]   8th. The eighth rule: when consolation is without preceding cause, although there is no deception in it, since it proceeds only from God our Lord, as it has been stated above, the spiritual person to whom God gives such consolation ought still to consider and discern with great vigilance and attention the exact time of such consolation from the time that follows, while the soul continues warm and feels the divine favor and the after-effects of the consolation which has passed. For many times in this latter period the soul makes various plans and resolutions which are not inspired directly by God our Lord. They may be the result of its own reflections, in accordance with its own habits, and the relics of its own concepts or judgments, and they may come either from the good spirit or the evil one. It is therefore necessary that they be very carefully examined before they are given full credit, and are put into effect.

[RULES FOR DISTRIBUTION OF ALMS]

[337]   The following rules should be followed in the ministry of distributing alms.

[338]   1st. The first rule: if I am giving alms to relatives or to friends or to persons to whom I am attracted, I must observe four points which have already been mentioned in part in the matter concerning the choice of a way of life. The first one is that the love which moves me and inspires me to give the alms must come from above; that is, from the love of God our Lord. I should feel within myself that the greater or less love that I have for these persons is inspired by God, and that in the motive moving me to greater love of them, God's love must shine.

[339]   2nd. The second rule: I will imagine a man whom I have never seen or known, and whom I consider to possess the greatest perfection in the position and state of life which he occupies. Now the norm I would expect such a person to observe in the giving of alms that would most contribute to the greater glory of God our Lord and the greater perfection of his own soul, I, too, will adopt, doing neither more nor less. I shall observe the same behavior which I considered to be most perfect for him.

[340]   3rd. The third rule: I will imagine myself at the point of death and consider the rules of behavior that I should then wish to have followed in fulfilling the duties of my position. Regulating myself accordingly, I will now observe the same standards in my distribution of alms.

[341]   4th. The fourth rule: I will consider that I am at the Day of Judgment, and I will reflect on how I should then wish to have fulfilled the duties of my position or my ministry. I will follow now the same rules that I shall then wish to have observed.

[342]   5th. The fifth rule: when anyone feels that he is inclined and attached to those persons to whom he wishes to give alms, he should pause and consider well the four rules given above. He should not give alms until he has examined and tested his affections and, in conformity with these rules, removed and cast aside all inordinate attachments.

[343]   6th. The sixth rule: there is no wrong in accepting the goods of God our Lord for distribution if one is called to such a ministry by our God and Lord. However, there may easily be fault or excess in the amount and quantity that one ought to keep for his own needs out of that which he holds to give to others. He should therefore reform his life and his state by the rules given above.

[344]   7th. The seventh rule: for these and many other reasons, it is always better and safer, in matters that concern oneself and one's household, if one cut and reduce one's expenses as much as possible, and thus approach as near as possible our great High Pontiff, our model and rule, who is Christ our Lord. In conformity with this doctrine, the Third Council of Carthage, at which St. Augustine was present, decrees and orders that the furniture of a bishop be plain and poor. The same consideration applies to all states of life, making allowance for the condition and rank of each, and observing due proportion. In the married state we have the example of St. Joachim and St. Anne, who divided their means into three parts and gave first to the poor, the second to the ministry and service of the Temple, and used the third for the support of themselves and their family.

[NOTES CONCERNING SCRUPLES]

[345]   The following notes will be of help in discerning and understanding scruples and the snares of our enemy.[64]

[346]   1st. The first note: the name *scruple* is ordinarily given to that which proceeds from our judgment and free will, i.e., when I take something to be a sin which is not. This might happen when someone, after having accidentally stepped on a cross formed by two straws, of his own accord judges that he has sinned. This is in reality an erroneous judgment and not a real scruple.

[347]   2nd. The second: after I have stepped upon that cross, or after I have thought, said, or done some other thing, the thought comes to me from without that I have sinned, and on the other hand, it seems to me that I have not sinned; nevertheless I am disturbed in this matter, doubting and not doubting that I have sinned. This is truly a scruple and a temptation from our enemy.

[348]   3rd. The third: the first scruple, mentioned in the first note should be much abhorred because it is completely erroneous.

But the second type of scruple mentioned in the second note, is for a certain period of time of no small advantage to the soul that devotes itself to spiritual exercises. It may even greatly purify and cleanse such a soul, separating it far from all appearance of sin, according to that saying of St. Gregory: "It is a sign of good souls to recognize a fault where there is none" (*Epist.* 1.11 ep. 64. *resp.* 10: PL 77. 1195).

[349]   4th. The fourth: the enemy observes very carefully whether one has a delicate or lax soul. If the soul is delicate, he strives to make it excessively so in order to disturb and ruin it more easily. For example, if the enemy sees that a soul consents to no sin, mortal or venial, or even to the appearance of deliberate sin, since he cannot make the soul fall into what has the appearance of sin, he strives to make it judge that there is sin where there is none, as in some insignificant word or thought.

If the soul is lax, the enemy strives to make it still more lax. Thus, if before it took no account of venial sins, he will strive to have it take little account of mortal sins. If, before, it did take some account of them, now he will strive that it care much less or not at all about them.

[350]   5th. The fifth: the soul that desires to advance in the spiritual life must always proceed in a manner contrary to that of the enemy. If the enemy seeks to make the conscience lax, he must strive to make it more sensitive, and if the enemy endeavors to make it delicate to excess, the soul must strive to establish itself solidly in moderation so that it may better maintain in everything its peace.

[351]   6th. The sixth: when such a good soul wishes to say or do something that is acceptable to the Church and to the mind of our superiors, something that may be for the glory of God our Lord, there may come to it from without a thought or temptation not to say or do it because it is motivated by vainglory or some other reason, etc. On such occasions one must raise one's mind to Our Creator and Lord, and if one sees that the action is for God's service, or at least not contrary to it, he ought to act in a manner diametrically opposed to the temptation, as St. Bernard answered a like temptation: "I did not begin this because of you, nor because of you will I end it" (*Legenda Sanctorum*, CXV, Letter G, 1493).

[352]   For the true sense we must have in the Church Militant we should observe the following rules:[65]

[353]   1st. The first: putting aside all private judgment, we should

keep our souls prepared and ready to obey promptly and in all things the true spouse of Christ our Lord, our Holy Mother, the hierarchical Church.

[354]   2nd. The second: to praise the sacrament of confessing with a priest and the reception of the Most Holy Sacrament once a year, and much better once a month, and better still every week, with the requisite and proper dispositions.

[355]   3rd. The third: to praise going to Mass frequently, also the singing of hymns and psalms, and the recitation of long prayers, both in and out of church; also the set times for the Divine Office as a whole, for prayers of all kinds and for the canonical hours.

[356]   4th. The fourth: to praise highly religious orders, virginity, and continence; and also matrimony, but not as highly as the foregoing.

[357]   5th. The fifth: to praise the vows of religion, obedience, poverty, chastity, and other works of perfection. It must be remembered that since a vow is made in matters that lead to evangelical perfection, it is, therefore, improper to make a vow in matters that depart from this perfection; as, for example, to enter business, to get married, and so forth.

[358]   6th. The sixth: to praise the relics of the saints by venerating them and by praying to these saints. Also to praise the stations, pilgrimages, indulgences, jubilees, Crusade indulgences, and the lighting of candles in the churches.

[359]   7th. The seventh: to praise the precepts concerning fasts and abstinences, such as those of Lent, Ember Days, Vigils, Fridays, and Saturdays; likewise to praise acts of penance, both interior and exterior.

[360]   8th. The eighth: to praise the ornaments and buildings of churches as well as sacred images, and to venerate them according to what they represent.

[361]   9th. The ninth: finally, to praise all the precepts of the Church, holding ourselves ready at all times to find reasons for their defense, and never against them.

[362]   10th. The tenth: we should be more ready to approve and praise the directions and recommendations of our superiors as well as their personal behavior. Although sometimes these may not be or may not have been praiseworthy, to speak against them when preaching in public or in conversation with simple people would give rise to gossip and scandal rather than to edification. As a result, the people would be angry with their superiors, whether temporal or spiritual. However, while it does harm to speak ill of our superiors in their absence to simple people, it might be useful to speak of their bad conduct to those who can apply a remedy.

[363]   11th. The eleventh: to praise both positive and scholastic

theology, for as it is more characteristic of the positive doctors, like St. Jerome, St. Augustine, St. Gregory, and others, to encourage the affections to greater love and service of God our Lord in all things, so it also is more characteristic of the scholastic doctors, like St. Thomas, St. Bonaventure, and the Master of the Sentences, etc., to define and explain for our times the things necessary for eternal salvation, and to refute and expose all errors and fallacies. For these scholastic doctors, being of more recent date, not only have a clearer understanding of the Holy Scripture and of the teachings of the positive and holy doctors, but also, being enlightened and inspired by the Divine Virtue, they are helped by the Councils, Canons, and Constitutions of our Holy Mother the Church.

[364]   12th. The twelfth: we must be careful not to make comparisons between the living and those who have already gone to their reward, for it is no small error to say, for example: "This man knows more than St. Augustine"; "He is another St. Francis, or even greater"; "He is another St. Paul in goodness, holiness, etc."

[365]   13th. The thirteenth: if we wish to be sure that we are right in all things, we should always be ready to accept this principle: I will believe that the white that I see is black, if the hierarchical Church so defines it.[66] For, I believe that between the Bridegroom, Christ our Lord, and the Bride, His Church, there is but one spirit, which governs and directs us for the salvation of our souls, for it is by the same Spirit and Lord that the Ten Commandments were given us and who guides and governs our Holy Mother The Church.

[366]   14th. The fourteenth: although it be true that no one can be saved unless it be predestined and unless he have faith and grace, still we must be very careful of our manner of discussing and communicating on these matters.

[367]   15th. The fifteenth: we should not make predestination an habitual subject of conversation. If it is sometimes mentioned, we must speak in such a way that no simple person will fall into error, as happens on occasion when one will say, "It has already been determined whether I will be saved or lost, and in spite of all the good or evil that I do, this will not be changed." As a result, they become negligent of the works that are conducive to their salvation and to the spiritual growth of their souls.

[368]   16th. The sixteenth: in like manner, we must be careful lest by speaking too much and with great emphasis on faith, without any distinction or explanation, we give occasion to the common people to become indolent and lazy in the performance of good works, whether it be before or after their faith is founded in charity.

[369]   17th. The seventeenth: also in our discourse we ought not to emphasize grace too much, for it could turn to poison and destroy

our free will. We may therefore speak of faith and grace to the extent that God enables us to do so, for the greater praise of His Divine Majesty. But, in these dangerous times of ours, it must not be done in such a way that good works or free will suffer any detriment or be considered worthless.

[370]   18th. The eighteenth: although the generous service of God out of pure love should be most highly esteemed, we should praise highly the fear of His Divine Majesty, for filial fear and even servile fear are pious and most holy things. When one cannot attain everything better or more useful, this fear is of great help in getting out of mortal sin, and after this first step one easily advances to filial fear, which is wholly acceptable and pleasing to God our Lord, since it is one with Divine Love.

SPIRITUAL

DIARY

Introduction, Notes
and Translation by
Antonio T. de Nicolás

Contents

THE *SPIRITUAL DIARY* OF Ignatius de Loyola is one of the most remarkable documents ever written in any language. For the period of one year Ignatius de Loyola follows an agonic search for the right signs from the God of his *Spiritual Exercises* in order to make the right decision regarding poverty: should the Jesuit houses have full income, partial, or none at all? In his search for an answer Ignatius uncovers to us the workings of his spirituality as he conceived it. Simultaneously we witness one of the most remarkable testimonies of mysticism. The exercises of the imagination with which Ignatius starts the retreatant in the *Spiritual Exercises* appear now, in the *Diary*, as exercises and imagination turned reality. God speaks back through concrete signs. By being able to discern these signs, Ignatius eventually reaches the decision that the Jesuit houses should have no income at all.

In order to make this document even more evident in its singularity and originality I have added two other documents. The first short document is about the same election on poverty. Ignatius wrote it down trying to reach a decision through cognitive skills — rationally weighing the pros and cons of accepting or not accepting endowments for the Jesuit houses. This is the usual way we understand decision making. The document is apparently inconclusive in Ignatius' own mind, and this opens for us the workings of the *Spiritual Diary*.

The other document I have added is that of the "Letter on Obedience." The reason for doing so is that decision based on noncognitive skills, that is, those decisions arrived at through the signs of meditation, run the risk of either some form of gnosticism or at worst, a subtle way of imposing the retreatant's will on the world in the name of God, using his name in vain. There is obviously a problem as to how the will of God, manifested through the signs of meditation, joins the public domain, becomes incarnate in the world. Ignatius tried to solve this problem through his "Letter on Obedience." The retreatant may be saved from imposing his own will on the world by meditating through a confessor superior the signs he experiences while meditating. Thus, Ignatius found a way of making the private signs of meditation public. Furthermore, if the retreatant is not happy with the superior's decision, he may come again and again to the superior and re-present his case, the same way Ignatius kept coming back again and again to meditation in search of signs.

I have added several known and unknown letters of the saint, with proper introductions to each one, to show the diverse and complicated decisions the saint had to make thus to gain a wider perspective on his method in the *Spiritual Diary*.

The Spiritual Diary

The *Spiritual Diary* of Ignatius de Loyola has remained practically unknown until very recently and of course unpublished. This is the first time the *Diary* is published in English for general consumption, though a couple of semi-private translations have circulated, in mostly unintelligible form and with many errors. No one before has even suggested, as we do here, that the *Diary* represents the verification system of the *Spiritual Exercises* and that without the *Diary* the spiritual exercises would lose their original power of transformation and become just one more spiritual form of reading or thinking.

The early Jesuits were cautious to the extreme, aware as they were of the ever-present Inquisition, and decided at the suggestion of Frs. Nadal, da Cámara and Francis de Borja, to keep the mystical writings of Ignatius under wraps. A few fragments were used by Ribadeneira and Bartoli in their lives of the saint. Not until 1892 did Fr. Juan José de la Torre publish the first part of the *Diary* in the *Constitutiones S.I.* (Madrid). In 1922 Fr. Feder brought out a German translation of the same. Only in 1934 was the *Spiritual Diary* published in its totality in the first volume of the *Constitutions* in *Monumenta Historica*. This edition is the basis of the translation I present in this volume, including the words Ignatius erased or added in the margins, plus the study of Fr. de Guibert in 1938 and the latest details on the codes in the *Diary* as they appear in the *Obras Completas de Ignacio de Loyola*, Biblioteca de Autores Cristianos, (Madrid, 1977). It is this Spanish edition I follow most closely in presenting this first complete English translation.

The Relation of The Diary to Other Writings by the Saint

The *Spiritual Exercises* set for us the technology to guide the imagination in a willing motion within an original communication's system between the soul and God. The *Spiritual Diary* is the *verification*, through signs, that the system is in motion, that it works. Through the *Spiritual Exercises* the soul frames the original horizon, the Christian experience: The Trinity. In the *Diary*, through signs, the will of God appears. Many have considered meditation an end in itself. They do spiritual exercises and rest in them, or record them as the gifts of God to the devout soul, as the attributes of a saint, as an end in themselves. The *Diary* destroys this myth. Ignatius views the *Exercises* as a method of making decisions in the world according to the will of God. The *Diary* shows the discernment of that will, by sifting through the signs of meditation to be able finally to make a decision. The human tension of cognition and imagination, of the origin and the image, of theology and experience, the tension of two wills, God's and the retreatant's, is resolved only in the unity of a decision taken. Through decision the imagination of meditation becomes flesh in the world, becomes the world.

It is only in view of the workings of the *Diary* that other writings of Ignatius, like his *Autobiography* (or *Diary of a Pilgrim*) recover their original context. These writings have to be read as intimately connected to the *Spiritual Exercises* on the one hand, and to the *Diary* on the other. They appear as verifications in Ignatius's spiritual life and not independent of it. They are diaries of, or the results of, other, previous exercises that lead to the making of decisions. Exercises, verification, and decisions are the three willing movements of Ignatius' cycle of spiritual life.

Ignatius fought with his own Jesuits very strongly to preserve this trilogy together. Some Spanish and Portuguese Jesuits wanted to use the exercises as an end in themselves. They wanted to meditate more and deal with the world less. The "Letter on Obedience" tried to remedy that misunderstanding. Ignatius was ready to fire his own Jesuits, including a co-founder of the society, to save the integrity of his method.

For these reasons the *Diary* is a text that deserves close study. It opens wide the secrets of a method that up to recently was lost or only whispered as possible. Now we know it has been canonized and all along was part and parcel of Christianity.

Furthermore, in an age where decision making is mostly in the hands of someone other than the one who should make the decisions, a method that deals with decision making from signs derived from imaginative methods, rather than cognition or private fantasy, should be of interest not only to those making decisions for others, but especially to those who recognize they have lost the power of making their own decisions. No one knows enough cognitively to make decisions. Ignatius devised another method based on the

Spiritual Exercises in which signs are the bases for decision making: the gift of tears, for example. In the first forty days of the *Diary* alone, Ignatius has tears over 125 times, an average of four times a day, and 26 times has tears with sobs. Other signs are listed through the *Diary*: joy, spiritual rest; intense consolation; rising of the mind; divine impressions, illuminations; intensification of faith, hope, charity and knowledge; spiritual flavor and relish; spiritual visitations; rapture, etc. These signs, however, will not appear without proficiency in the *Spiritual Exercises*. Once Ignatius became proficient, he needed only small moments, short prayers, to get himself within the total communication system he devised or recalled from the memories of Christian life.

Editorial Devices and Code of The Diary

Ignatius used the *Diary* to register the signs of meditation while searching for a decision on poverty: Should his houses have income? These were the possibilities:

a) not to have a fixed income (nothing);
b) to have a permanent income (everything);
c) to have some fixed income limited to the churches or sacristies (some).

The election of Ignatius deals with a) and c).

Following the Spanish edition I have added marginal numbers to replace Ignatius' own for the following reason: On certain parts of the text the saint, due to poor sight, changes and repeats numbers, and this creates confusion. The marginal numbers are the standard numbers of the Spanish edition.

Each day is introduced in the *Diary* with the name of the Trinity, Our Lady, Jesus, etc. These introductory names stand for the Mass of the day. It is obvious the liturgy of those days allowed more freedom than today. Thus we find that out of 116 masses celebrated by St. Ignatius, 30 are of the Trinity, 20 of the name of Jesus, 16 of Our Lady, and 9 of the Holy Spirit. Parentheses are the translators. Brackets correspond to the original numbers of the text. Double brackets indicate lines or words suppressed by Ignatius. Certain words or phrases in italics correspond to words or phrases erased first or added later in the margins by St. Ignatius.

There are words, phrases, sentences and whole paragraphs enclosed within bold lines. In this I follow the Spanish edition to indicate partial texts which Ignatius lifted from the *Diary* and were later on added to other texts, *Monumenta Historica S.I., Constitutiones I p. CCXLI*, for example, and the more common text of the *Diary of a Pilgrim* or his *Autobiography*.

Instead of the usual hour of morning meditation we are accustomed to imagine, Ignatius had only three brief moments preparing for Mass:

1) As soon as he got out of bed;
2) A moment of meditation before Mass: His preparatory prayer;
3) While he walked to the chapel and vesting.

A parenthetical note is included where there were certain signs in the *Diary* with special meaning: ≠ and // indicating that he had some form of vision. A line across a page is original to the *Diary*, indicating a new beginning.

Entries in the second part of the *Diary* were introduced with some abbreviations, a.1.d.t. and dots on top of the a. They meant:

a: tears *before* (*antes*) Mass;
1: tears *during* (*durante*) Mass;
d: tears *after* (*después*) Mass;
t: afternoon (*tarde*)

After (366) Ignatius introduced in the *Diary* dots on the top of the letter *a* and some new initials: o.c.y. They meant:

o: prayer (*oración*, 1st prayer);
c: room (*cámara*, prayer in the room);
y: Church (*yglesia*, prayer in the church).
a with three dots on top: tears in the three prayers (before Mass);
a with two dots on top: tears in two of the prayers (before Mass);
a with no dot at all: tears in one of the prayers (before Mass).

These codes are decoded in this translation.

Finally, the text in its original Spanish is very difficult to translate. It is abbreviated as a note, or series of notes, and mixed with Latin and Italianisms. Following the Spanish edition I have broken the text in several cycles or rounds which will appear self-explanatory.

The Society of Jesus adopted, on Ignatius's election, to have no income at all for their houses (*no nada*).

ANTONIO T. de NICOLÁS

Election On Income And Poverty

Deliberations Through Cognitive Skills On Poverty
(OBRAS COMPLETAS, pp. 315-320)

TRANSLATOR'S NOTE

The following short document will help the reader understand in greater depth the need for Ignatius to make a final election on poverty as seen in his *Spiritual Diary*.

This document is earlier than the *Diary* or perhaps even contemporary to the *Diary*. Together with the *Diary* this document forms an election on the same point of the *Constitutions*: should the houses of the Jesuits have fixed revenue or live on the eventual alms of the faithful?

Of interest in this document is that it shows how in St. Ignatius cognition and imagination combined alternatively when making an election (Exer. 177-183).

Ignatius had been deliberating on this point of poverty for a long time. In March of 1541 his companions gathered in Rome and voted: "that the sacristy could have revenues to take care of all the things needed for its maintenance, as long as this income is not used for the father's of the Society." (*Constitutions* of 1541; MHSI, *Const.* I:69-77). Furthermore, this same year of 1541, on the 24th of June, Paul III gave the company the temple of our Lady of the Strada and granted them the income and revenues that this church already possessed.

Apparently Ignatius took part in the vote of 1541 on this matter of poverty, but we have no way to know which way his vote went. He was not yet the general of the Jesuits and his vote was secret like the others. He was obviously not satisfied with his decision, as can be seen from the following document and the *Spiritual Diary*. The whole process is a clear example of how to make elections.

ELECTION ON POVERTY

(AUTOGRAPH. 1544. MI, CONST. I:78-83)

The disadvantages in having no revenue are the advantages in having a partial or total revenue.

1. It seems that the Society will be better maintained if it has a partial or total revenue.

2. Having revenues, they avoid annoying or disedifying others, seeing that for the most part they will have to be clerics who do the begging.

3. Having a revenue they will avoid temptations to an inordinate solicitude in seeking support.

4. They will be able to give themselves with greater leisure and quiet to work, and prayers agreed upon.

5. The time that would be spent in soliciting could be given to preaching, hearing confessions, and other pious works.

6. It seems that the church will be kept cleaner and better adorned, thus moving to greater devotion, and thus also the possibility of rebuilding.

7. The members of the Society will thus be able to give themselves to study and through this be of greater spiritual help to others, and take better care of their own bodies.

8. After two of the Society considered the matter, all the others approved of it. (Ignatius and John Coduri were the two at the time the Society was approved, 1541, *Obras Completas*, p. 318.)

The disadvantages in having a revenue are the advantages in not having any, namely:

1. With a revenue the members would not be so diligent in helping others, nor so ready to go on journeys and endure adversity. Moreover, they could not so well persuade others to true poverty and self-abnegation in all things, as is seen among the advantages of having no revenue, which follow.

The following paragraph was deleted from the original:

The disadvantages of having some revenue (being that they are also the advantages of having no revenue) are as follows:

1. To be a superior of those who have revenues and have management of it and of those who have no revenues and then to take from the same house (revenues) for some necessary things for himself and for the members of the Society, does not look like a good idea.

Advantages and reasons for having no revenue:

1. The Society will have greater spiritual strength and greater devotion by assimmilating and seeing the Son of the Virgin, our Creator and Lord, Who lived so poor and in so many hardships.

2. By not wishing to have a definite income, all worldly greed will the more readily confounded.

2. (*sic*) It seems that the Society is thus united with greater love to the Church, if there is uniformity (among the members) in having nothing and if they look to the poverty of Christ in the Blessed Sacrament.

3. It will be easier to hope for everything from God our Lord if we thus withdraw from everything belonging to the World.

4. It will be greater help in humbling ourselves, and in uniting with Him Who humbled Himself more than all.

4. (*sic*) The Society will live forgetful of worldly consolation.

5. It will live continually in greater divine hope and with greater care in His service.

6. There will be in general greater edification, seeing that we seek nothing belonging to this world.

7. We can speak with greater liberty of spirit and greater effectiveness on all spiritual subjects to the greater profit of souls.

8. It will be a greater help and encouragement to help souls when alms are received daily.

9. It is easier to persuade others to embrace true poverty by following that which Christ our Lord recommended, when He said, "If anyone has left father," etc. (*Matt.* 19:29; *Mark* 10:29)

10. It seems that they shall be more active in helping others and readier to go on journeys and endure hardships.

11. Poverty, without any income, is more perfect than poverty with a partial or total income.

12. In choosing this for Himself, Jesus, Lord of us all, taught it to His apostles and beloved disciples when He sent them to preach.

13. It was this that all ten of us unanimously chose when we took the same Jesus Christ our Creator and Lord as our leader, to go to preach and exhort under His standard, which is our vocation.

14. According to this understanding of poverty the Bull was issued at our petition, and after waiting a year for it to be expedited, while we persevered in the same understanding, it was confirmed by His Holiness.

15. It is an attribute of God our Lord to be unchangeable, and a quality of the enemy to be inconstant and changeable.

The following paragraph was deleted from the original:

16. There are three ways of taking care of the Society: 1) To make sure that everyone has a higher academic degree or near it; 2) for the Jesuit students to care for their clothes, sleep, and traveling expenses some finances could be provided; 3) for furniture and other necessary things for the Society some of those who will eventually join could help.

PART I

Spiritual Diary

February 2, 1544 to March 12, 1544

(First Round: Election And Offering)

[GOING ABOUT "THE ELECTIONS"]

[1][1]

ur Lady.[2]

1. Saturday, February 2nd. Profound devotion during Mass. Tears and increased confidence in Our Lady. Inclined more towards no revenue[3] (this feeling accompanied me) throughout the day.

[2] 2. Sunday,[4] February 3rd. The same (as yesterday) and more inclined to no revenue then (during Mass) and throughout the day.

[3]   Our Lady.

3. Monday, February 4th. The same (as Saturday) and with additional feelings. More inclined to no revenue during the day. By night a turning to Our Lady with deep affection and great confidence.

[4]   Our Lady.

4. Tuesday, February 5th. An ([great]) abundance of devotion before, during and after Mass. Tears ([internal and external]) along with pain in the eyes, being so many, at seeing Mother and Son disposed to intercede with the Father ($\neq$).[5] Felt more inclined to no revenue at the time and through the day. In the evening I knew, or saw as it were, that our Lady was inclined to intercede.

[5]   Our Lady.

5. Wednesday, February 6th. Devotion before and during Mass accompanied by tears. More inclined to no revenue. Later I thought with great clarity, out of the ordinary, that there would be some confusion in having partial revenue, and a scandal[6] in having complete revenue. Little would be made of the poverty which our Lord praises so highly.

[6]   The Most Holy Trinity.

6. Thursday, February 7th. Tears and deep devotion before Mass ([and in it]). Also a notable warmth and devotion all through the day, ([up to night time]) feeling always firm [7] and moved more to no revenue. At the time of Mass, I thought there was a notable impulse with deep devotion and interior movement, to address the Father, as I thought[8] my two mediators[9] had interceded for me, and I had some sign of seeing them.

[OFFERING OF THE OBLATION]

[7]   The Name of Jesus
        7. Friday, February 8th. Beginning with the preparation[10] for Mass[11] I felt notable devotion and tears while at prayer, also during Mass (I felt) deep devotion and tears, and while holding speech *when I could*, feeling inclined to no revenue.
[8]   Soon after Mass, (I felt) devotion and not without tears, going through the elections for an hour and a half or more and putting in front of me what seemed to be better according to reason, and by a stronger inclination of the will, that is, to have no revenue. *Wishing* (then) to *present this to the Father*[12] through the meditation and prayers of the Mother and the Son, I prayed first to Her to help me with Her Son and the Father, and then prayed to the Son to help me with His Father in company with the Mother.[13] I felt (then) within me as if I were going or were being carried away to the Father, and in this movement my hair stood on end, with a most remarkable warmth in my whole body. Following this (I had) tears and the deepest devotion //.
[9]   Reading this later, and thinking it was good to have it in writing, a fresh devotion came upon me, not without water in my eyes, // and later, recalling these graces I had received, (I felt) a fresh devotion.
        In the evening, for an hour and a half or more, *as I was going over the elections in the same way*, and making the election for no revenue *and experiencing devotion*, I found myself with a certain elevation of soul and a deep peace, seeing no inclination to possess anything. I was (then) relieved of the desire of proceeding any further with the election, as I had thought of doing a few days earlier.
[11]   ([The Annunciation of the Blessed Virgin.
        8. Saturday, February 9th. Last night I felt greatly weakened because of bad sleep, but (by) the morning prayer my mind was quiet, with great devotion and a warm spiritual movement and a tendency to tears.
        After getting up, the feeling of weakness left me twice. Later, there was devotion in the prayer while going to Mass, and also in getting ready to vest, together with a desire to weep. During

Mass continuous devotion and weakness, with different spiritual movements and a tendency to weep. The same when Mass was over, *and always with the inclination to no revenue.* The whole day was quiet. Where at the beginning I thought of keeping on with the election, all desire left me, as I thought the matter was clear, that is, to keep no income at all.])

I went through the elections[14] with much peace and devotion, thinking after all that we should have neither partial nor complete revenue, and that it was not a matter *worthy* of further thought. I looked upon it as finished. With much peace of mind, I remained firm in the thought of having no income at all.

[12]   Mass of the Day.

9. Sunday, February 10th. I again repeated the elections and made the offering of having no income with great devotion and not without tears. Likewise earlier, in the customary prayer, and before, during, and after Mass, with much devotion and many tears at the thought of accepting no income. I became at peace when I made the offering, having understood very clearly when reasoning[15] about it. Later (I became aware) of certain clarities ([realizations]) about my mediators not without some form of vision //.

[13]   At night, going over the elections of having complete, partial or no revenue, and making the oblation for no revenue at all, I felt a deep *devotion*, interior peace, and quiet of soul, with a certain security and agreement that it was a good election.

[14]   Of the Holy Spirit.

10. Monday, February 11th. In the midst of my ordinary prayer, with no further thought of the election, offering *or asking* God our Lord that the oblation made be accepted by His Divine Majesty, I felt an abundance of *much* devotion and tears. Later (while) ([offering]) making a colloquy with the Holy Spirit before saying His Mass, (I felt) the same devotion and tears. I thought (that) I saw Him, or felt Him, in a dense[16] brightness, or in the color of a flame of fire, in quite an unusual manner. *With* all this, I *felt satisfied* about the election made //.

[CONFIRMATION OF THE ELECTION IN THE FIRST ROUND]

[15]   Later, considering all aspects of the elections, (and with) my mind made up, and focusing on the reasons I had written down to consider, I prayed to our Lady, and then to the Son and to the Father, to give me their Spirit to consider and discern,[17] although I *was speaking* as of something already agreed upon. I felt great devotion and certain understandings with some clearness of sight. I (then) sat down, considering, as it were in general, whether I should have complete or partial revenue, or nothing at all, *and I lost all*

desire to see any reasons. At this moment other understandings came to me, namely, how the Son first sent the Apostles to preach in poverty, and afterwards, the Holy Spirit, giving His Spirit and *the gift of tongues,* confirmed them, and thus the Father and the Son sending the Holy Spirit, all Three Persons confirmed such a mission.[18]

[NEW OBLATION OR OFFERING]

[16]   At this point (it was with this new insight that) I felt greater devotion, and lost all desire to consider the matter further. *With* tears and sobbing, I made the offering of no revenue, on my knees, to the Father. The tears (were) flowing down my face, sobbing as I made the offering, and following it, so that I could hardly stand up for all the sobs and tears of devotion and the grace I received. Eventually, however, I got up, and even then the devotion and the sobbing followed me, coming upon me because I had made the offering of *having no revenue at all,* holding it as ratified and valid, etc.

[17]   Shortly after this, as I walked and recalled what had taken place, I felt a fresh inner motion to devotion and tears //.

[18]   Not much later, on the way to say Mass and after I said a short prayer, I felt intense devotion and tears at realizing *or beholding in a certain manner* the Holy Spirit.[19] About the election I took it as something finished. Thus I was unable to see or feel either of the other two Divine Persons.

[THANKSGIVING]

[19]   Later in the chapel, before and during Mass I felt much devotion and many tears. Later, great peace and security of soul, (and I felt) like a *tired man* taking too long a rest, neither being able to nor caring to seek anything, considering the matter finished, except to give thanks, out of devotion to the Father, and say the Mass of the Holy Trinity, as I had earlier thought of doing Tuesday morning.

[20]   On the Persons Who Were Hiding: The Trinity.

[21]   11. Tuesday, February 12th. *After* awakening and praying, I could not bring myself to finish giving thanks to God our Lord, with great intensity, understanding, and tears, for so great *a favor and so great* a clarity I had received, just beyond explanation.

[22]   After getting up, the inner warmth and devotion continued, and recalling all the benefits I had received,[20] I *was moved to a fresh and increased devotion* and tears, and the same while I went to D Francisco.[21] While with him and after I did not lose my warmth and intense love.

[(Later on becoming distracted, or because of *a temptation that* came to me[22] (I seemed to lean towards income) only for the church, with great clarity and lights and great devotion. I wanted that point totally closed with great peace and understanding and to be able to give thanks to the Divine Persons with a feeling of great devotion. The occasion (for that temptation was) *when in order to* stop some noise I stood up from prayer, or may be not, [(the noise was in the hall)]. Later on while walking to Mass and during it, it seemed that the inner warmth was fighting with the external wind, and it became clear what was good inside and what bad outside. By the middle of Mass I felt warmth and some devotion, and not cold, but also the restlessness of the noise of the hall and of those attending Mass. After Mass and going over this episode, (I felt) rested, composed, and with inner devotion)].

(Second Round: Election, Oblation, And Thanksgiving)

[THE ELECTIONS AGAIN]

[23]   Our Lady.

12. Wednesday, February 13th—Realizing I had been at fault by leaving *the Divine Persons*[23] at the time of giving thanks on the preceding day, and wishing to abstain from saying the Mass of the Trinity, which I thought of saying, I took the Mother and the Son as my intercessors, in the hope of being forgiven and restored to my former grace. I refrained thus from going to the Divine Persons directly for the graces and former gifts. I resolved not to say their Mass for the whole week, thus doing penance by such absence.

[24]   This brought me much devotion and very many and very *intense* tears, both in prayer and while vesting, accompanied by sobbing. Feeling that the Mother and the Son were my intercessors, I felt *fully* confident that the eternal Father would restore me to my former state.

[25]   Later on, before, during, and after Mass, there was growing devotion and great abundance of tears seeing and feeling my mediators with great confidence of regaining what I had lost, and in all these periods, ([not feeling]), both from Wednesday and Thursday,[24] considering as final the offering made, and found nothing against it.

[26]   The Name of Jesus.

13. Thursday, February 14th—In the customary prayer, thus not seeing my mediators, I had much devotion and elevation of mind and a remarkable tranquillity. Later, while preparing to

leave the room, I was not without tears and inner motions.

[27]   Later, before, during, and after Mass, there was a great abundance of tears, devotion, and heavy sobbing, not being able to speak *many times* without losing my voice, with many spiritual lights, finding free access to the Father when naming Him as He is named in the Mass, together with a great certainty or hope of regaining what I had lost. I felt that the Son was very disposed to intercede, seeing the saints (together) in such a way as cannot be written down, any more than the other things can be explained. There were no doubts about the first offering made, etc.

[28]   Our Lady in the Temple. Simon.

14. Friday, February 15th—At the first prayer, when naming the Eternal Father, etc., a sensible interior sweetness came and continued, not without a motion to tears, and later with great devotion, which became even greater at the end, without revealing any mediators or any other persons.[25]

[29]   Later, on going out to say Mass, when beginning the prayer, I felt or saw a likeness of our Lady, and realized how serious had been my fault of the other day, not without some interior motion and tears. I thought I was putting the Blessed Virgin to shame at praying for me so often after so much failing, to such a degree that our Lady hid herself from me, and I found no devotion either in her or from on high. ([in the others]).

[30]   After a short while, since I did not find our Lady, I sought comfort on high,[26] and there came upon me a great motion of tears and sobbing with some seeing and feeling that the Heavenly Father was showing Himself ([pious]) favorable and sweet, to the extent that He seemed ([to want]) to give a sign that it would be pleasing to Him to be asked through our Lady, whom I could not see.

[31]   While preparing the altar, and after vesting, and during the Mass, (I felt) very intense interior motions, and *many and very intense* tears and sobbing, with frequent loss of speech. Also after the end of Mass, and *for long periods during the Mass*, while preparing and afterwards, a great feeling and seeing of our Lady, very propitious *before the Father*, to such an extent that in the prayers to the Father, to the Son, and at His Consecration, I could not help feeling and seeing Her, as someone who is a part, or the doorway, of *so much grace that I felt in my soul*. ([At the Consecration she showed that her flesh was in that of her Son,]) with such great clarity that I could never write about it. I had no doubt of the first oblation already made.

[32]   Jesus

15. Saturday, February 16th—In the customary prayer I did not feel my mediators, (I felt) no coolness or tepidity, but great devotion, ([and for periods the mind wandering, but not to bad

things, and *towards the end* with a great deep serenity and a certain sweetness as I got up and dressed with nothing to remark one way or another.]) I wanted to get ready for Mass, but doubted to whom and how to commend myself first. In this doubt, I knelt down, and wondering how I should begin, I thought that the Father was revealing Himself more to me and was drawing me *to His mercies*, feeling that He was *more favorable* and *ready to grant*[27] what I desired (*not being able to adapt to my mediators*). This feeling or seeing kept growing, with a great flood of tears on my face, and the greatest confidence in the Father, as though He were removing me from my former exile.

[33]   Later, while on my way to Mass, preparing the altar, vesting, and beginning Mass, *in all these places* with many intense tears which drew me to the Father, Who set in order the affairs of the Son, while I experienced *many lights*, which were incredibly delightful and very spiritual.

[34]   After Mass, while going over *some*[28] [the motives] of the elections for an hour, examining the point[29] and the revenue already given, I thought them to be snares and obstacles of the enemy. But with much tranquillity and peace, I chose and offered to the Father the resolution of having nothing, not even for the church. Recalling the other (the difficulties) elections, I felt the same, not without an interior movement and tears.

[35]   That night I took out some papers to examine and consider the elections, and having failed that day, I was beset by fears to go ahead without delaying the election as before.[30] Finally, I determined to go on as usual, but was in some doubt as to where I should begin to commend myself, feeling a certain shame, or *I have no idea what* before our Mother. (But) at last, I examined first my conscience, covering the entire day, and asked forgiveness, etc. and I felt the Father very favorable, so I did not address my mediators and shed some tears.

[THIRD OBLATION]

[36]   Later, while still warm, I begged Him to give me grace to meditate with his Spirit, and to move me with the same. Before getting up, I thought that I should not examine the elections any more. With this (thought) *I was covered* with such a flood of tears, and so intense a devotion, sobbings, and spiritual gifts, that for a while I felt moved to make my offering of no revenue for the church, and to examine the matter no more, except that perhaps for the next two days, (I would repeat it) to give thanks, and make the same oblation, or make it in better form. This I did with excessive tears, warmth, and inner devotion. Later, while all this lasted,

I did not think I could get up, but desired to remain there with that inner visitation.

[37]   A moment later the thought came ([consolation diminishing]) that during the next two days I could look over the elections, and as I had not determined on the contrary, it bothered and took me away from such intense devotion, although I wanted to repel the thought. Finally, sometimes standing, sometimes sitting down, I placed the matter in some form of election while examining some spiritual reasons. Then I began to weep a little, and thinking it a temptation, I got on my knees and offered to examine the elections in this matter no more, but taking the two days, that is until Monday, to say Mass, to give thanks, and to repeat the offering (already made).

[38]   During this offering and oblation there was again such weeping and tears in such abundance, and so much sobbing and spiritual gifts, that after the oblation made to the Father in the presence of our Lady and the Angels, etc., the same weeping continued, etc., I felt in me the desire not to get up but to remain there, in the experience I was so intensely feeling. And so to the end, with great satisfaction, the same devotion and tears continued. I got up with the determination to keep *the oblation I had made and* everything I had offered.[31]

[SECOND THANKSGIVING]

[39]   16. Sunday, February 17th—While in my customary prayer, without being aware of mediators or any other person, and finished[32] I felt considerable flavor and warmth. From the middle of it on, I had great abundance of tears that were full of warmth and interior flavor, without any intellectual lights, [[(that warmth being moved and lifted]) and I considered the matter (of the election) settled, since it *seemed to me* to be acceptable to God our Lord.

[40]   Getting up and preparing for Mass, I gave thanks to His Divine Majesty, and offered Him the oblation made, *not without devotion and* motion of tears. There were many tears on leaving for Mass, preparing the altar, vesting, and beginning Mass. (They were) *very intense* during Mass and in great abundance with a frequent loss of speech, especially through the whole of the long epistle of St. Paul, which begins: *libenter suffertis insipientes* (Sexagesima Sunday). I had no intellectual lights, nor did I see any distinction of Persons, but I felt an intense love, warmth, and great flavor in divine things, and a growing satisfaction of soul.

[41]   After Mass, both in the chapel and later kneeling in my room, I wanted to thank God for such great graces as I had received, and I *lost* all desire to make further offerings concerning the obla-

tion already made (*[although I always kept making it, and not without devotion]*). I then considered the matter closed. On the other hand, because of the (*[great]*) devotion I felt, I was drawn to remain (*[kneeling]*) in the enjoyment of *what I was feeling.*

[42]   Later, as I considered whether I should go out or not, I decided with great peace on the affirmative. Though I tensed within, when I felt I should delay over my tears and spiritual consolations I got up still weeping and with great satisfaction of soul I left with the resolution of finishing tomorrow, not later than lunch, to give thanks, ask for strength, and repeat the oblation already made out of devotion for the Most Holy Trinity and say Its Mass. The Trinity and End.[33]

[43]   17. Monday, February 18th—*Last* night, *shortly before going to bed, I felt some (*[interior]*) warmth, devotion, and great confidence or grace in finding the Three Persons, as I ended. While in bed I felt a special consolation in thinking of Them embracing me with interior rejoicing[34] in my soul.

[LACK OF CONFIDENCE; DRYNESS, INSTEAD OF CONFIRMATION]

[44]   And then falling to sleep I awoke in the morning a little before daybreak, and later, as a result, I felt heavy and dry in all spiritual things. But I made the customary prayer without any *or very little flavor* until about halfway through, and with this *a loss of confidence of finding the favor*[35] *in the Most Holy Trinity* (followed). I then turned to prayer, and I thought I did it with great devotion, so that towards the end I felt great sweetness and spiritual flavor.

(Third Round: Oblation-Thanksgiving)

[THE ASCENT THROUGH THE MEDIATORS TO THE TRINITY]

[45]   Later, wishing to get up with the thought of fasting,[36] and to take measures that would not distract me until I found what I was looking for, I felt fresh warmth and inclination to tears, and dressed with the thought of fasting for three days until I found what I was seeking. A knowledge came to me that even this thought came from God, and with it came fresh strength and warmth and spiritual devotion, and moved me to *an increase* in tears.

[CONFIRMATION OF THE OBLATION AND FOURTH OBLATION]

[46]   A moment later, considering where to begin, I recalled all the saints. *I commended myself to them,* asking that our Lady and

her Son intercede for me with the Most Blessed Trinity. With much devotion and intensity I found myself covered with tears. This I took as a confirmation of past offerings. (Meanwhile) I began to say many things, beseeching and placing as intercessors the angels, the holy fathers, the apostles and disciples, and all the saints, etc., to intercede with our Lady and her Son. I begged them with long speeches that ([they put me in]) my final confirmation and that my thanks may rise before the throne of the Most Holy Trinity.

[47]   Both at this moment and later I had great flood of tears, interior motions, and sobbing. I thought that the very veins and members of my body made themselves sensibly felt. Then I made the final confirmation to *the Most Holy Trinity, in the presence of the whole heavenly court*, giving thanks with great and intense affection, first to the Divine Persons, then to our Lady and to her Son, then to the angels, the holy fathers, the apostles and disciples, all the saints, and to all persons for the help they had given me in this matter.

[HE ASKS FOR DIVINE ACCEPTANCE — SECOND TIME]

[48]   Later,[37] while preparing the altar and vesting, I felt a strong impulse to say: "Eternal Father, con[firm me]; Eternal Son, con[firm me]; Eternal Holy Spirit, con[firm me]; Holy Trinity, con[firm me]; my only God, con[firm me]!" I said this with great earnestness and with much devotion and tears, very often repeated and deeply felt, saying once, "Eternal Father, will You not confirm me?" understanding it as a sure thing, and the same to the Son and to the Holy Spirit.

[49]   I said Mass without tears, though not the entire Mass without them. Though I felt a warm devotion ([almost new and not as usual]), as it were with much heavy breathing and much devotion, there were some periods when I did not feel these things in *any* abundance. (I had) some thought as why there were no shedding or abundance of tears, which pained me and robbed me of devotion, and moved me in some way or other not to be satisfied with having received a time confirmation (of the elections) in the last Mass of the Trinity.

[50]   After Mass I regained quiet of mind and compared my own size with the greatness and wisdom of God. I (then) continued perambulating for several hours until the thought came not to bother about saying more Masses. I had become impatient with the Trinity and did not want to debate the matter any longer. I felt the past to be true, thought some slight doubt still remained, but (this) did not deprive me of devotion throughout the whole day, though this devotion showed weak in some minor points, and fearful of making any kind of mistake.

[HE DECIDES TO GIVE THANKS]

[51]   The Trinity, 1st.[38] (of six or seven Masses of the Trinity
he decides to say).

18. Tuesday, February 19th—Last night I went to bed with
the thought of examining what I would do in saying Mass or how.
Then on awakening in the morning I began my examination of
conscience and prayer, with a great and abundant flood of tears
down my face. I felt much devotion with many intellectual lights
and spiritual memories of the Most Holy Trinity, which quieted
me and delighted me immensely, even to (the point of) producing a
pressure in my chest, because of the intense love I felt for the Most
Holy Trinity. This gave me confidence, and I determined to say
the Mass of the Most Holy Trinity, to see what I should do later. I
had the same feelings while vesting, with lights about the Trinity.
I got up and made a short meditation with tears, and later I felt
much devotion and spiritual confidence to say successively six or
more Masses of the Most Holy Trinity.

[TRINITARIAN ENLIGHTENMENT WHILE GIVING THANKS]

[52]   On the way to Mass and just before it, I was not without
tears. (I felt)[39] an abundance of them during it, but very peacefully,
with very many lights and spiritual memories concerning the Most
Holy Trinity, which served as a great illumination to my intellect,
so much so that I thought I could never learn so much by hard
study. Later, as I examined the matter more closely, I felt and
understood, I thought, more than if I had studied all my life.

[53]   I finished the Mass and *spent* a short time in vocal prayer:
"Eternal Father, con[firm me]: Son, etc. con[firm me]." I felt a
flood of tears all over my face and a growing determination to go
on with Masses (of the Trinity) (thinking of putting some limit to
their number), with much heavy and intense sobbing. I felt very
near, and became assured in an increased love of His Divine Majesty.

[54]   In general, the intellectual lights of the Mass, and those
preceding it, were with regard to choosing the proper orations of
the Mass when one speaks with God, with the Father or the Son,
etc., or deals with the operations of the Divine Persons, or their
processions more by feeling and seeing than by understanding.

All these experiences corroborated what I had done and
encouraged me to continue.

[55]   Today, even as I walked through the city, with much inner
joy, it appeared to me as if the Most Holy Trinity made itself present to me when I encountered now three rational creatures, now
three animals, now three other things, and so on.[40]

[56]   The Trinity, 2nd.

19. Wednesday, February 20th—Before *beginning* the meditation, I felt a devout eagerness to do so, and, after having begun
it, (I felt) a great devotion that was warm, clear, and sweet, but
without any intellectual lights. It was more like a feeling of security of the soul, not ending in any Divine Person.

[57]   Later, I felt confirmed about the past. (I also) recognized
the evil spirit of the past, namely, the spirit who wished to make
me doubt and caused me to be angry with the Holy Trinity, as I
have said in paragraph 17.

[58]   With this recognition, I felt a fresh interior movement to
tears, and the same later, before Mass and during it with an increased *quiet and tranquil* devotion along with tears, and some
lights.

[59]   Both before and after Mass, I felt, or it seemed, that I was
losing interest in going any further—particularly after (Mass) with
that great quiet or satisfaction of soul. And so I thought there
were no reasons to go on with the Masses of the Holy Trinity,
unless it were to renew thanks and gain favor, but not out of any
need of confirming what has passed.

[60]   The Most Holy Trinity, 3rd.

20. Thursday, February 21st—During the meditation, I
had, on the whole, *very great* and *continuous* devotion, a *warm
clarity* and spiritual flavor, drawing partly to a certain elevation.

[61]   Later, while getting ready in my room, at the altar, and
while vesting, I felt a *few* inner motions and *inclination* to tears.
And thus I finished Mass and remained in great spiritual peace.

[62]   During Mass there were tears in greater abundance than
the day before, and with a loss of speech most of the time. *Once* or
several times I also felt spiritual lights, to such an extent that I
seemed thus to understand that there was *nothing more to learn*
from the Most Holy Trinity in this matter.

[63]   This *took place* because, I had, as formerly, sought to find
devotion in the Trinity in the prayers to the Father (resting there).
I did not wish, nor was I prepared either *to search for* nor to find
it, (the devotion to the Trinity in the Father), as it did not seem to
me that in this way (the Father alone) consolation or illumination
was to come from the Most Holy Trinity. But in this Mass I
recognized, felt or saw, God only *knows*, that in speaking to the
Father, *in seeing that* He was a Person of the Most Holy Trinity, I
was moved to love the whole Trinity all the more since the other
Persons were present in Him essentially. I felt the same in the
prayer to the Son, and the same in the prayer to the Holy Spirit,
rejoicing in any One of Them and feeling consolations, attributing
it to and rejoicing in the fact that it belonged to all Three. Untying

this knot, or something similar, it seemed so great to me, that I kept repeating to myself: "Who are you? Where do you come from? How did you deserve this? Or where does it come from?" etc.

[64]   The Trinity, 4th.

21. Friday, February 22nd—During the customary prayer I felt much assistance in general from a warm grace. (It was) partly illuminating (giving me) much devotion, though for my part I found it easy a few times to become distracted, in spite of the continual presence of grace. Later, while preparing the altar, I felt certain motions to tears repeating over and over again to myself: "I am not worthy of invoking the Name of the Most Holy Trinity." This thought and repetition moved me to greater interior devotion. And on vesting, with this and other considerations, my soul opened wider to tears and sobbing. Beginning Mass and going on to the Gospel, I said it with deep devotion and great assistance from a warming grace, which *later* seemed to struggle with some thoughts, as fire with water, (about salvation and others, at times about (my) death, at times about (my) conservation.[41]

(Fourth Round: Transparent Clarity)

[CONFIRMATION THROUGH JESUS BY A DIFFERENT ROUTE]

[65]   The Trinity, 5th.

22. Saturday, February 23rd—During the customary prayer, *at the beginning, nothing*, but from midway to the end, I found much devotion and satisfaction of soul, with some indication of transparent clarity.

[66]   While preparing the altar, the thought of Jesus came to me. (With it) I felt a *movement* to follow Him, it seemed to me interiorly, since He was the head ([or caudillo]) of the Society, to be a greater argument to proceed in total poverty than all the other reasons, although I thought that all the reasons of the past elections tended towards the same decision. This thought moved me to devotion and tears, and to a conviction, although I had no tears in the Mass, *or Masses*, etc. I thought that this feeling was enough to keep me firm in time of temptation or trail.

[67]   I went along with these thoughts and vested while they increased, and took them as a confirmation. Though I received no consolations on this point, I thought, *in some way*, that the appearance or the felt presence of Jesus was ([the work]) of the Most Holy Trinity. I (then) recalled the day when the Father placed me with His Son.[42]

[68]   As I finished vesting (I only had) this in mind: to carry so deeply the name of Jesus. (I felt) being thus forced and seemingly confirmed for the future. (With this I felt) a fresh attack of tears and sobbing coming upon me, ([and later]) as I began Mass accompanied ([with many and heavy motions]), and with much grace and devotion, I had quiet tears for the most part. But even when I finished, the *one* great devotion and movement to tears lasted until I had unvested.

[69]   Throughout the Mass I had various feelings in confirmation of what had been said, and, as I held the Blessed Sacrament in my hands, speech came to me and an *intense* inner movement never to leave Him for all heaven and earth, etc., while I felt fresh motions of devotion and spiritual joy. For my part I started to improvise, doing as much as I could, and this last step was directed to the companions who had given their signatures. ([The first Constitutions of the Society]).[43]

[70]   Later in the day, as often as I thought of Jesus, or remembered Him, I had a certain feeling, or saw with my understanding (accompanied by) continuous devotion and confirmation.

[DIVINE CONFIRMATION]

[71]   Of the Day.
23. Sunday, February 24th—During the usual prayer, from the beginning to end inclusive, I had the help ([for long]) of a very interior and *gentle* grace, full of warm devotion and very sweet. While preparing the altar and vesting, I saw a representation of the name of Jesus with much love ([much]) confirmation and an *increased* will to follow Him, accompanied by tears and sobs.

[72]   All through the Mass, *for a long* time, (I felt) very great devotion, with many tears, and, many times, the loss of speech. All devotion and feeling was directed to Jesus. I could not apply myself to the other Persons, except to the *First Person* as being the Father of such a Son. On this I would add spiritual dialogues: How He is the Father, How He is the Son!

[73]   Having finished Mass and whole praying (I had) that same feeling towards the Son; (reminding me of) how I had wished the confirmation to come from the Most Holy Trinity.[44] But I felt that it was given to me through Jesus, when He showed Himself to me and gave me such interior strength and certainty of such confirmation, without any fear of the future. The thought came to me to beg Jesus to obtain pardon for me from the Most Holy Trinity. I felt (then) an increased devotion, tears, and sobs, and the hope of obtaining grace. I found myself so vigorous and strengthened for the future.

[HE SEES CLEARLY HIS PAST MISTAKE]

[74]　　Later, by the fire,[45] there was a fresh representation of Jesus along with great devotion and motion to tears. Later, as I walked through the street, I had a vivid representation of Jesus with interior motions and tears. After I had spoke with (Cardinal) Carpi,[46] and was on my way home, equally, *I felt great devotion.* After lunch, especially when I crossed *the door of* the Vicar,[47] in the house of the Cardinal of Trani,[48] I felt or saw Jesus, had many interior motions and many tears, ([all this time I felt so much inner warmth and clarity]) begging and praying Jesus to obtain pardon for me from the Most Holy Trinity, while I felt a great confidence of being heard.

[75]　　At these times, when I sensed or saw Jesus, I felt so great a love within me that I thought that nothing could happen in the future that would separate me from Him, or cause me to doubt about the graces or confirmation I had received.

[76]　　St. Matthias.

24. Monday, February 25th—The first part of the prayer was with much devotion, and thereafter warmth and an accompanying grace. From my part, and because of some obstacles I felt on the part of others, I held back. I neither asked nor sought confirmation, but desired to be reconciled with the Three Divine Persons. Later on, vested for Mass, not knowing to whom to commend myself, or where to begin, a thought came to me at the same time that Jesus was communicating Himself: "I want to go on," and with this I began the confession: "*Confiteor Deo,*" as Jesus said in the Gospel of the day, "Confiteor tibi," etc.

[77]　　With this I began the confession with fresh devotion, and not without motions to tears, entering in the Mass with much devotion, warmth, and tears, with an occasional loss of speech. It appeared to me that Jesus Himself presented the orations that were addressed to the Father, or that he was accompanying those I was saying to the Father; and a feeling and seeing that in no way can be explained.

[78]　　When the Mass was finished I felt a desire to be reconciled with the Most Holy Trinity, and I begged this of Jesus. (I felt) tears and sobbing, reassuring myself and not asking or feeling the need of any confirmation, or of saying Masses for this purpose, but only to be reconciled.

[SUBMISSION TO WHATEVER WAY
IS MOST PLEASING TO THE TRINITY]

[79]　　Of the Trinity, 6th

25. Tuesday, February 26th—The first prayer was without disturbance, nor did I withdraw from it. There was much devotion,

and from the middle on, devotion was much increased, though I felt, especially in the first part, some physical weakness or indisposition.

[80]   After dressing and while still in my room preparing, (I felt) fresh and interior motions to tears as I recalled Jesus. I felt much confidence in Him, and I thought He was ready to intercede for me; yet I did not seek or ask further confirmation concerning the past, remaining quiet and restful in this regard, asking and begging Jesus to make me conform to the will of the Most Holy Trinity, in the way He thought best.

[81]   Later, while vesting, this representation of the love and help of Jesus grew. I began Mass with great, quiet, and restful devotion and with a slight inclination to tears, thinking that even getting less, I would be still more satisfied and contented in allowing myself to be governed by the Divine Majesty who bestows and withdraws His graces as He thinks best. After this I went by the fire, the contentment growing, feeling a fresh interior movement and love for Jesus. I found myself not being disturbed by that former distraction regarding the Most Holy Trinity. During Mass I continued with great devotion towards the Trinity.

[82]   The Beginning of Lent.

26. Wednesday, February 27th—During the customary prayer I felt quite well, as it was customary, but towards the middle and then on to the end (I felt) great devotion, spiritual quiet, and sweetness, followed by a continuous devotion which *remained*. As I got ready in my room, I asked Jesus, not in any way for a confirmation, but that He do His best service in the presence of the Most Holy Trinity, etc., and by the most suitable manner, provided I find myself in His Grace. In this I received some light and strength.

[VISIONS THAT CONFIRM HIM IN THIS NEW PHASE]

[83]   While going into the chapel and while praying, I felt or more properly saw, beyond my natural strength, the Most Holy Trinity and Jesus, presenting me, or placing me, or being the means of union with the Most Holy Trinity and Jesus, presenting me, or placing me, or being the means of union with the Most Holy Trinity, in order that this intellectual vision be communicated to me. With this feeling and seeing, I was covered with tears and love, ending in Jesus; and to the Most Holy Trinity (I felt) a respectful surrender (*acatamiento*: see *Spiritual Exercises* no 38.) which was *more* on the side of a reverential love than anything else.

[84]   Later, I thought of Jesus doing the same duty as I was thinking of praying to the Father. And it seemed to me and I felt inside

that He was doing everything with the Father and the Most Holy Trinity.

[85]   I began Mass with many tears, great devotion and tears continuing all through it. Thus all of a sudden, I clearly saw the same vision of the Most Holy Trinity as before, with an ever increasing love for His Divine Majesty, and several' times losing the power of speech.

[86]   After Mass, in my prayer and later by the fire, several times I felt great and intense devotion, terminating in Jesus, and *not* without special motions to tears later.

[87]   Even while writing this, I feel a drawing of my understanding to behold the Most Holy Trinity, as if seeing, although not as distinctly as formerly, Three Persons; and at the time of Mass at the prayer "Domine Jesu Christe, Filii Dei vivi," etc., I thought in spirit that I had just seen Jesus, that is, white; i.e., His humanity, and at this other time[49] I felt it in my soul in another way, namely, not His humanity alone, but being all my God, etc.,[50] with a fresh flood of tears and great devotion, etc.

[88]   Of the Trinity, 7th.

27. Thursday, February 28th—Through the whole of the customary prayer, much devotion and *much grace, helpful,* warm, bright and loving. Entering the chapel, fresh devotion, and as I knelt a revelation of a vision of Jesus at the feet of the Most Holy Trinity, and with this, motions and tears. This vision did not last as long, nor was it as clear as that of Wednesday, although it seemed to have taken place in the same way. Later, at Mass, tears with much devotion and profitable thoughts, and some also after Mass and not without tears.

[89]   Of the Wounds.

28. Friday, February 29th—During the customary prayer, from beginning to end inclusive (I felt) very great and very lucid devotion covering my sins and not allowing me *to think* of them. Outside the house, in the church, before Mass, a vision of the heavenly fatherland, or of its Lord, after the manner of understanding the Three Persons, and in the Father the Second and the Third. At times during Mass great devotion, ([after) without any lights *or* motions to tears.

[90]   After it was over, a vision likewise of the fatherland, or of its Lord, indistinctly but clearly, as frequently happens at other times, sometimes more, sometimes less, and the whole day with special devotion.

[91]   Of the Day. (Saturday after Ash Wednesday)

29. Saturday, March 1st—During the accustomed prayer (I felt) great assistance and devotion; and while saying mass outside (I felt) great peace and devotion with some motions to crying

(lasting till) after midday with great satisfaction of soul; from there on I (was busy) somewhere else.

[92]   Of the Day

30. Sunday, March 2nd—(I felt) much help from grace, devotion, and a certain clearness mingled with warmth during the customary prayer.

[93]   Later, while going out (of my room) because of the noise, and also upon my return, I was somewhat torn apart, either struggling with the thoughts about the noise, or being disturbed to such a point that *even after* vesting for Mass, I thought not to say it. However, this *was* overcome, and not wanting to give cause to the others for talking *to anyone*, (I was) encouraged by the thought of Christ being tempted. Thus I began Mass with much devotion.

[94]   This (devotion) continued with the help of much grace and with tears at various times and almost continually, which I felt from the middle of Mass on. I finished without any understandings. But towards the end, during the prayer to the Most Holy Trinity, (I was filled) *with a certain motion to devotion and tears*, and felt a *certain* love which drew me to the Trinity, without any remaining bitterness for what had happened, only peace and quiet.

[95]   Later, during my prayer after Mass, (I felt) some fresh interior movements, sobs, and tears, all for my love of Jesus, *telling Him and wishing to die with Him rather than live with another, feeling* no fear, and receiving a certain confidence and love for the Most Holy Trinity. I (then) wished to commend myself to It as two distinct Persons, but could not find what I sought. I felt something towards the Father, as though feeling the other Persons in Him.

[96]   At this time, Mass being over, and the Masses of the Most Holy Trinity being all finished, I thought that I should end this part at once, or at the very first time that I had any divine visitation—but thought that it was not up to me to decide the time for finishing. But then I will find the visitation at the end (of the Masses); *then*, or when His Divine Majesty found it convenient to *bestow on me such visitation*.

[97]   Of the Trinity, 8th.

31. Monday, March 3rd—During the customary prayer at four-thirty in the morning[51] (I felt) great devotion, without any motions or disturbances, and with some heaviness of the head; so

much so that I did not venture to get up for Mass, but went back to sleep.

[98]   Getting up later at eight-thirty in the morning I felt very dull, but neither ill nor well and had no one to commend myself to. Afterwards, inclining more to Jesus at the Preparatory prayer in my room, I felt there a slight movement to devotion, and a desire to weep, with satisfaction of soul and such confidence in Jesus, and was drawn to hope in the Most Holy Trinity.

[99]   Entering *thus* in the chapel I was overwhelmed with a great devotion to the Most Holy Trinity. I felt very increased love and intense tears, though I did not see the Persons distinctly, as in the past days, but perceived in one luminous clarity a single Essence. It drew me entirely into Its love.

[100]   [(Thus)], later while preparing the altar and vesting I felt *great devotion* and tears, (sometimes more, some less) as well as grace assisting all the while with much satisfaction of soul.

[101]   Due to such great devotion at the start of Mass, I was not able to begin. I found great difficulty to pronounce the words, "*In Nomine Patris,*" etc. Throughout all of the Mass (I felt) much love and (much) devotion and a great abundance of tears, and all the devotion and love ended in the Most Holy Trinity. I had no knowledge or distinct vision of the Three Persons, but a simple advertence to or representation of the Most Holy Trinity. Likewise, at times, I felt the same, ending in Jesus, as though finding myself in His shadow, *as though He were guide, but without lessening the grace from the Holy Trinity. Rather, I thought I was more closely joined to His Divine Majesty.*

[102]   In the prayers to the Father I was not able to (adapt) or wished to find devotion, except for a few times when the other Persons were represented in Him, so that mediately or immediately, everything turned upon the Most Holy Trinity.

[GOD WISHES FOR MASS TO CONTINUE
OFFERING HIS ELECTION]

[103]   After Mass ([in front of the altar while praying]) I unvested, and in the prayer at the altar I found intense love, sobbing, and tears ending in Jesus. Subsequently they all ended in the Most Holy Trinity. (I felt) a certain reverent surrender (*acatamiento*). It seemed to me that if it were not for the devotion of the Masses to be said, I was (much) satisfied. With this I had every confidence of finding an increased grace, love, and *greater satisfaction* in His Divine Majesty.

[104]   Of the Trinity, 9th

32. Tuesday, March 4th—During the customary prayer (I

felt) much assistance of grace and devotion; *even* more lucid than clear with an infusion of some warmth. For my part I found it easy to go into any occurring thoughts; thus, I got up with that assistance. After dressing, (coming) I looked over the *Introitum* of the Mass. It stirred me to (terminal) devotion and love, ending in the Most Holy Trinity.

[105]   Later, when I went to the preparatory prayer for Mass, I did not know with whom to begin. I *first* noticed Jesus, *thinking that He did (not) allow Himself to be seen or perceived clearly, but in some manner obscure to the sight.* Noticing this, I thought that the Most Blessed Trinity did allow Itself to be perceived or seen more clearly or lucidly. I began, *and later, (while) thinking about i* in the presence of His Divine Majesty, a flood of tears overwhelmed me, with sobbing, and (I felt) a love so intense that it seemed to join me most closely to His Love, which was always so clear and sweet. I thought this intense visitation and love *to be* outstanding or excellent among all other visitations.

[106]   Thus later, when I entered the chapel, I felt fresh devotion and tears, always ending in the Most Holy Trinity. Also at the altar, after having vested, I was *overcome* with a much greater flood of tears, sobs, and most intense love for the love of the Most Holy Trinity.

[107]   As I was to begin Mass, I felt very deep (inner) touches and intense devotion to the Most Holy Trinity. After I began Mass, I felt great *devotion* and tears, which continued through the Mass. Because of the very considerable pain I felt in one eye, on account of so much weeping, the thought came to me that I would lose my eyes by continuing these masses, and that it would be better to preserve my eyes, etc. The tears stopped, though *with* the presence of much grace. Later, during the greater part of the Mass, the help grew less, mostly because of the noise of talking in the room, etc.

[108]   Later on, almost at the end, I turned to Jesus, and recovered something of what was lost at the prayer, *Placeat tibi, Sancta Trinitas*, etc., *ending in His Divine Majesty.* A great and excessive love covered me with intense tears, so that all the time, before and throughout the Mass, I had *special* spiritual visitations. They all ended in the Most Holy Trinity, carrying me on and drawing me to Its Love.

[109]   After Mass and unvesting, and at the prayer at the altar, there was so much sobbing and such profusion of tears, all ending in the love of the Most Holy Trinity, that I thought I did not want to rise, as I was feeling so much love and so much spiritual sweetness.

[110]   Later, at various times and by the fire, I felt interior love for the Trinity and motions to tears. Later on in the (Cardinal of)

Burgos'⁵² home, and in the streets *until three-thirty* in the after-noon, I recalled the Most Holy Trinity with intense love, some-times with motions to tears. All these visitations ended in the Name and Essence of the Most Holy Trinity. I did not *feel* or see *clearly* distinct Persons, as I did on other occasions, as I said before. All of these drew me to great security, and not with the purpose of saying more Masses or seeking greater reconciliation. I wanted *to* fulfill them (the Masses), *hoping to rejoice* in His Divine Majesty.

(Fifth Round: Clear And Warm Devotion: Reconciliation And Submission)

[COMPLETE RECONCILIATION]

[111]   Of the Trinity, 10th.
        33. Wednesday, March 5th—During the customary prayer I felt much assisting grace from beginning to end, without my effort to seek it. I felt much lucid devotion and very clear, and felt help-ing warmth.
[112]   Even while dressing I thought of the grace, assistance, and devotion to the Most Holy Trinity I experienced the day before and which was still with me. Then, as I began the prayer in prepa-ration for Mass, and wishing for *help* and *humility*, I addressed Jesus. The Most Holy Trinity presented Itself to me a little more clearly, and as I turned to His Divine Majesty to commend myself, etc., I felt a flood of tears, sobs, and intense love for the Trinity, so much so that I thought I did not want to, or that I could not look at myself or recall the past in order to reconcile myself with the Most Holy Trinity, ([and so once or several times]).
[113]   Later on, in the chapel, I had a ([very]) sweet and quiet prayer. It seemed to me that my devotion was leading me to termi-nate in the Most Holy Trinity. But it also led me in another direction, like to the Father. Thus I felt as if It wished to communi-cate to me in various ways, so much so that, as I readied the altar, I felt *and said*: "Where do you wish to take me, Lord?" And repeat-ing it *frequently*, ([I felt I was guided]) my devotion increased, bringing tears to my eyes. Later, at prayer, while vesting, I felt many motions and tears. I offered myself to be guided and led, etc., but He being more powerful than I in these steps, where would He take me? After vesting, not knowing just where to begin, and after taking Jesus for guide, and addressing the orations to each One, I went on to the third part of the Mass with a *great* assistance of grace and warm devotion, and *great* satisfaction of soul, without

tears, and without, *I think*, an inordinate desire of having them. I felt satisfied with the Lord's will. Turning, however, to Jesus, I said, "Lord, where *I go*," "or where," etc., "following You, my Lord, I shall never be lost."

[115]   From here on, I *continued the Mass* with many tears, courage, and spiritual vigor, terminating those greater consolations in the Most Holy Trinity, less in Jesus, and much less in the Father. On the one hand, I felt always (that I was) increasing in confidence regarding reconciliation with the Most Holy Trinity, so that when Mass ended, I felt in the oration tranquillity and repose. I wished to examine in some way (the past), but I could not, or did not conform myself to seeing or perceiving any discord or worry *in the past*. I was like someone who rests *after* weariness, with his mind at peace, devout and consoled.

[116]   Later, by the fire, also and on other occasions, I recalled this repose. At night I did not find in the prayer to the Father any revelation to fresh devotion and motions, so I terminated everything with the Most Holy Trinity.

[REST AFTER WORK]

[117]   Of the Trinity, 11th.

34. Thursday, March 6th—During the customary prayer I made no effort to seek devotion, but had plenty of it. Further on, devotion increased greatly with much sweetness and light mingled with color (bright light). After dressing I felt some fresh devotion and summons to it. I ended in the Most Holy Trinity.

[118]   During the preparatory prayer I felt closer to the Most Holy Trinity. I felt greater spiritual calm and serenity. I was moved to greater devotion, and to tears, *wishing but not seeing anything of the past regarding my reconciliation*.

[119]   In the chapel I felt much quiet devotion. On making ready the altar I felt an increase of certain feelings or fresh movements, as to tears. Thereafter, while vesting, considerations of some parts of the past came to me, like thoughts and reflections as to what (God) the Most Blessed Trinity wished to do with me, that is, the path by which to lead me. As I reflected on how and where He might take me, I *thought* with myself and *conjectured* that perhaps They wished to make me content without the consolation of tears and without being too eager or inordinate about them.

[120]   Beginning the Mass I felt an interior humble satisfaction. As I continued as far as the *Te igitur* I felt great interior and sweet devotion which overcame me several times with an *interior sweetness as* conducive to tears.

[LUCID CLARITY OF THE DIVINE ESSENCE]

[121]   It was at the *Te igitur* that I felt and saw, not obscurely, but clearly and *very clearly*, the very Being or Essence of God, under the figure of a sphere, slightly larger than the appearance of the sun, and from this Essence the Father seemed to go forth or derive, in such a way that on saying "*Te*," that is, "*Pater*," the Divine Essence was represented to me before the Father. In this vision, I saw represented the Being of the Most Holy Trinity without distinction *or sight* of the other Persons, and I felt an intense devotion to what was represented to me, feeling many movements and *shedding* of tears. Thus I went through the Mass, considering, remembering, and again seeing the same (vision), accompanied by a great flood of tears and an increase of intense love for the Being of the Most Holy Trinity, without seeing or distinguishing the Persons, except that they proceed from the Father, as I said.

[122]   At the completion of the Mass and after so many ([satisfactions and devotions]) tears and spiritual visitations, I could not see anything against my reconciliation. I became aware with great certainty, and beyond all possibility of doubt, of *what I had seen represented*. And as I examined and considered it again, I felt new interior movements, leading me wholly to the love of the vision I had seen; to the point that it was obvious to me that I saw with greater clarity what lay beyond the heavens than what I sought to consider here ([or see united]) with my understanding. It was (better) exemplified there, as I said.

[123]   After unvesting, and while in the prayer at the altar, the same *Being* and spherical vision appeared again to me ([it seemed to me]). I saw in some way, the Three Divine Persons, in the manner of the First; that is, the Father on the one hand, the Son on the other, and the Holy Spirit on the other, proceeded or exited from the Divine Essence without leaving the frame of the vision of the sphere. With what I felt and saw there were fresh motions and tears.

[124]   Later, when I went to the Basilica of St. Peter and began my prayer at "*Corpus Domini*", the same Divine Being presented Itself to me *in the same lucid color*, so that I could not help seeing it. Also, later as the Mass of (Cardinal) Santa Cruz[53] began, I saw the representation in the same manner, with fresh interior movements. Two hours later I came down to the same place of the *Blessed* Sacrament, wishing to find again the vision and seeking it, without success.

[125]   When night came, sometime after I wrote this, I saw the same representation and had some understanding of the intellect, although to a great extent it was not so clear or so distinct, nor of

such great size, but like a fairly large spark, *appearing to the under-standing*, or drawing it to itself, and appeared as being the same.
[126]   Of the Trinity, 12th.

25. (bis);. ("Repet."). Friday, March 7th—I began the customary prayer with much devotion, and wished (to see some-thing of the past day). I did not find increasing devotion as I kept looking up. From the middle (of the prayer) on, I felt very great and continued devotion, with much lucid clarity. It was warm and very sweet, lasting even beyond the time of the prayer.

[THIS DIVINE ESSENCE AS PRESENT BELOW IN ALL CREATURES]

[127]   My mind settled into a state of calmness while doing the preparation prayer. Also while in the chapel. Later, while vesting, there were fresh movements to tears and to conformation with the Divine Will, praying that It be my guidance, etc. *Ego sum puer*, etc. Beginning Mass I felt great devotion and interior reverence, and movements to tears and to say *Beata sit Sancta Trinitas*. Dur-ing all this I had a new feeling, a new and greater devotion and tears, not by elevating my attention to the Divine Persons, as far as they are distinct, nor by distinguishing Them, nor by lowering it to the words (in the Missal), but by an interior consolation which seemed to me to come from between a place on high and the words (of the Missal).

[128]   Continuing thus with many copious tears, I did not feel that I had the right to gaze higher. Thus by not looking up but (only) mid-way my devotion increased sharply with intense tears. It kept increasing my surrender (*acatamiento*) and reverence for the visions above, and I felt a certain confidence that permission would be granted me, or that (the high vision) would be made known to me at the proper time, ([without effort on my part]).

[129]   At these times I felt these consolations in a detached way. They terminated now in the *Most Holy Trinity, now* in the Father, now in the Son, now in our Lady, now in particular saints.[54] I felt many tears. Later, I paused at *the middle* or *after the middle of Mass, that is about* the *Hanc igitur oblationem*, and at times *con-trasting* a large fire with water, *at not finding the Sacrament*.

[130]   *As I wished to end the matter*, I sat by the fire[55] after Mass, undecided for a good space of time, as to whether to bring the Masses to an end now, or when to do so. Later, the thought occurred to me that tomorrow I should say the Mass of the Most Holy Trinity, ([and in it or after it]) to determine what was to be done, or to end it altogether. I felt *movements* come upon me and

tears. From moment to moment over some space of time, I felt great motions, sobs, and floods of tears, drawing me entirely to the love of the Most Holy Trinity.

[131] Making many colloquies and ([*giving reasons*]), I felt a disposition in me for greater and greater enjoyment of these very intense visitations, *if I cared to wait* and humble myself. I thought that I should not place a limit for finishing the matter, but that (I should do it) where it revealed itself to me. Thus I would place everything (in that event) and *bring it to an end*, then be glad when I find this occasion.

[132] Another thought occured to me at this time: If God were to send me to hell, then two choices appeared to me: the first, the pain I should suffer there; the second, how His name would be blasphemed there. As to the first, I was not able to feel or see the pain, and so it seemed to me that it would be more painful to hear His holy Name blasphemed.

[133] Later, as I sat down to eat, my tears ceased. For the rest of the day I felt a very interior and warm devotion.

[CONFIRMATION OF THIS NEW ATTITUDE
WITH MANY THANKS]

[134] 26. (bis). Saturday, March 18th—During the customary prayer I felt a great help of grace from beginning to end. I felt it increasing with a very clear, lucid, warm devotion, and a *great satisfaction* while doing the preparatory prayer and while in the chapel.

[135] *While vesting*, I had fresh motions, lasting to the end and increasing with many tears. I felt a very great humility in not looking even to the heavens, and the less I wished to look above, and humbled and lowered myself, the more I felt spiritual flavor and consolation.

[136] All through Mass I felt great interior devotion and spiritual warmth, with tears, and with a continuation of devotion and a disposition to weep. *During these intervals since I did not intend to lift up the eyes of my understanding up above, in an effort to be content with everything, nay, even praying that, it being equal glory to God, I be not visited with tears*, it sometimes happened that my understanding unwittingly did go up, and I seemed to see something of the Divine Essence, which on other occasions when I want it is not within my power.

[137] Of the Day.

27. (*bis*.) Sunday, March 9th—The customary prayer as

in the past. After dressing during the preparatory prayer I felt fresh devotion and movement to tears, terminating principally in the Most Holy Trinity and in Jesus.

[138]   Entering the chapel, I had greater movements and tears, all terminating in the Most Holy Trinity, and other times in Jesus, or sometimes together or nearly so, in such a way that the termination in *Jesus did not lessen the devotion* to the Most Holy Trinity, nor the opposite. This devotion lasted until I vested, accompanied at times with tears.

[139]   Later, in the Mass, I had an exterior warmth as reason for devotion and felt cheerfulness of mind. I had few movements or inclination to tears, and even none at all but felt more satisfied than having them, and then I had them in good measure. It seemed to me that in some way, even without lights, visions, and tears, God our Lord wanted to show me some other way or method of acting.

[140]   The whole day passed with great contentment of soul. At night I felt I was prepared for devotion, terminating in the Most Holy Trinity and Jesus. They somehow appeared to the understanding, letting themselves be seen in a certain way. Wishing to apply myself to the Father, the Holy Spirit, and our Lady, I found neither devotion nor any vision. The understanding or vision of the Most Holy Trinity and *of* Jesus remained for some time.

[141]   Of the Name of Jesus.

28. (bis.) Monday, March 10th. I experienced great devotion in the customary prayer, especially from the middle of it on. I had new devotion before the preparatory prayer, with the thought or judgment that I ought to live or be like an angel for the privilege of saying Mass. With this thought gentle waters came into my eyes.

[142]   Later, in the chapel and at Mass, I had devotion to the same, and conformed myself to what our Lord ordered, thinking that His Divine Majesty would provide, taking always the good, etc. In these intervals sometimes I saw in a certain way the Being of the Father, that is, *first* the Being and then the Father—my devotion terminating first in the Essence and then in the Father, and sometimes in another way, lacking of much distinction.

[143]   Of Our Lady

29. (bis.) Tuesday, March 11th—The whole of the customary prayer passed with much devotion, clear, lucid, and warm. In the chapel, at the altar, and afterwards, I had tears. I directed my devotion to our Lady, but without seeing her. I felt devotion through all of the Mass. Sometimes I felt movements to tears. *Later much devotion.* During these intervals I often partly saw the Divine Being, sometimes ([later]) terminating in the Father, that is, first

the Essence and then the Father. *In the chapel, before Mass*, I felt as if I had permission to look above. The thought came to me that looking above would be a remedy for my being disturbed by low things. With this thought motions and tears came. Later on, I tried to look above; at times I saw, and at times I did not see. I found *devotion* and a remedy to help me not to remove my attention from what I had to do throughout Mass.

[144]   The Holy Spirit.

30. (bis.) Wednesday, March 12th—I felt great devotion in the customary prayer, and from midway on there was much of it, clear, lucid and as it were warm. In the chapel, because I looked down hurriedly and did not prepare myself for the Mass, I returned to the room to ready myself and compose myself. I had tears, I went back to the chapel, and later said Mass, feeling great devotion and tears in parts of it. On the other hand, I felt a struggle, which *happened at the end*, because I did not come upon what I was looking for. During these intervals there were no signs of visions or lights.

[HE SURRENDERS TO "THE PLEASURE OF GOD"
DURING DESOLATION]

[145]   After Mass, in my room, I found myself alone and without help of any kind. I had no power *to savor any of my mediators*, or any of the Divine Persons. I felt so remote and separated, as if I never felt anything of Them, or would never feel anything again. Instead thoughts came to me at times against Jesus, at times against another.[56] I was being so confused with different thoughts that I wanted to leave the house and hire a room[57] to get away from the noise, and go without eating. I thought of starting the Masses all over and put the altar on a higher floor. I found peace where I wished to finish up at a time when my soul was consoled and completely at rest.

[146]   Examining, however, whether I should proceed, it occurred to me I wanted to find too many signs, both in time and during the Masses already ended for my own satisfaction. The matter was so clear in itself that it needed no further seeking of certainty. Putting a stop to it would be much to my liking. On the other hand, I thought that if I gave up altogether while being in such distress, I would not be satisfied later on, etc.

[147].   Finally, I thought that since there was no difficulty in the matter itself, it would be more pleasing to God our Lord to end it. Not waiting or looking for further proof, or saying more Masses for it, I placed it thus in an election. I ([*judged and felt*]) that it would be more pleasing to God our Lord to bring it to an end, and

I felt in myself *the wish* that the Lord would condescend to my desire, that is to finish at the time when I had a special visitation. As soon as I realized what was my inclination, and on the other hand, the will of God our Lord, I began at once to take notice and to wish to succeed in pleasing God our Lord.

[148]   With this, the darkness began to leave me gradually, the tears came back, and they increased. I lost all desire to say more Masses for this purpose. The thought of saying three Masses of the Holy Trinity in thanksgiving came to me. I dismissed it as coming from the evil spirit. I decided that I would say none. I grew much in divine love, and had such tears and sobs and strength that I knelt for a long time, and walked about, and knelt again, with *many different reasonings*, and with so much interior *satisfaction*. Though I had such great a consolation as this (which caused great pain in my eyes), it lasted for the space of an hour, more or less. The tears stopped at last, and with them doubting whether I *should finish* by night with a similar flood of tears (*if I found them*) or now.

[149]   The flood stopped, so it seemed better to end now. To keep on seeking, or to wait for the evening, would still be wishing to seek, there being no reason to. So I made my resolution in the presence of God our Lord, and *all* His court, etc., to put an end to this point and not to proceed any further in this matter—although while making this last proposal I experienced interior movements, sobbing, and tears. Even at the time when they were most abundant, I considered everything concluded. I sought no further, nor would say more Masses, nor attend to more consolation of any kind. This day would see the end.

[CONCLUSION: COMPLETE DIVINE CONFIRMATION]

[150]   Finished.[58]

[151]   After the stroke of one-thirty, as I sat down to eat, and for a good space of time, I felt that the tempter did nothing, though he sought to have me make some sign of hesitating. I answered at once, without any disturbance, rather as in the event of victory. "Down, to your place!" I felt confirmation with tears and every security concerning all that had been determined.

[152]   A quarter of an hour after this, I awoke to a knowledge or clear understanding of how at the time that the tempter was suggesting thoughts against the Divine Persons and my mediators, he caused, or wanted to cause, some hesitation in the matter, and, on the other hand, (I understood the process by which) I felt the consolations and visions of the Divine Persons and mediators as bringing every firmness and confirmation of the matter. This was

followed by a feeling of spiritual flavor, and my eyes filled with tears with great security of soul.

[153]   On saying grace at table a partial revelation of the Being of the Father came upon me, and likewise of the Being of the Most Holy Trinity, with a certain spiritual movement to tears, something which all day I had not felt or seen, though I looked for it often. The great consolations of this day did not terminate distinctly in any Person in particular, but they did terminate, in a general way, in the Giver of graces.

Spiritual Diary
March 13, 1544 to February 27, 1545

(Sixth Round: Walking The New Path)
["CONTENTMENT AND JOY OF SOUL"]

[154]

URING THESE FOUR DAYS, I determined to examine nothing concerning the Constitutions.
[155]   Of the day.
1. Thursday, March 13th—(Before Mass) During the Mass I felt a conformity with the Divine Will in not having tears, ([and it would be some relief for me to say Mass without tears or looking for them]). It was as though this was to *relieve me of some labor*, or give me rest in not seeking, or (relieve me of) examining whether to have an income, or not to have it. Later throughout the day I felt ([much]) contentment and peace of soul.

[ACCEPTANCE AND REVERENCE]

[156]   Of the Holy Spirit.
2. Friday, March 14th—Before Mass,[59] all through it, and after it, I had many tears, sometimes ending in the Father, sometimes in the Son, sometimes, etc., and also in the saints. I had no vision, except in so far as devotion went, at intervals; ending now in one and now in another. During all these times before, during and after Mass, I had a thought penetrate my soul of the deep reverence and surrender (*acatamiento*. See note in *Spiritual Exercises* no. 38) with which, going to say Mass, I ought to pronounce the name of God our Lord, etc., and not look for tears, but instead look for this surrender (*acatamiento*) and acceptance.
[157]   (This surrender was) to such a degree that I exercised myself often in this surrender in my *room* before Mass, *in the chapel*, and during Mass. If tears came, I at once repressed them and turned my mind to surrender. This did not seem to be any-

219

thing of my own or coming from me. This surrender came by itself to me, and always increased my devotion and tears. As a result, I persuaded myself that this was the way our Lord wished to show me. I kept thinking for the past two days that He wanted to show me something; thus, while saying Mass, I was *persuaded* that a higher value was placed on this grace and *knowledge* or the spiritual advantage of my soul, than on all those that went before.

[158]   Of Our Lady.

3. Saturday, March 15th—During a part of the Mass I felt a certain interior surrender and reverence. But for the most part I felt no possibility of feeling this interior surrender and reverence.

[159]   Of the day.

4. Sunday, March 16th—I had tears before Mass and throughout it. The devotion and tears terminated now in one Person, now in another, without any clear or distinct visions. I made my prayer in my room before Mass and asked that surrender, reverence, and humility be given me, and that visitations or tears not occur if it were for the equal service of His Divine Majesty, so that I could enjoy His graces and visitations purely and unselfishly.

[160]   And so, from that time on, all these spiritual consolations came to represent for me surrender, not only in naming or recalling the Divine Persons, but even in reverence for the altar and other things having to do with the Sacrifice (of the Mass). I resisted tears or visitations when I thought to notice or desire them and turning my attention first to surrender, visitations would follow. On the other hand, i.e., to pay attention to visitations rather than surrender seemed to me to be wrong, which was a confirmation of what I thought the previous Friday, ([and that it was by this way that I was to go directly to the service of God our Lord, valuing this more than anything else.])

[MAKING ELECTION BY THE NEW WAY OF SURRENDER]

[161]   Here I began to prepare the first examination concerning missions. (i.e., pontifical missions).

[162]   Our Lady.

1. Monday, March 17th—I had tears before Mass, and many of them during it, to such an extent that *several times* I lost the power of speech. This whole visitation ended ([indifferent to all]), now in one *Person, now in Another*, in the same manner as on the preceding day, and in the same way, that is, concerning surrender and reverence as a confirmation of all the past, and of having found a way of actions that was to be shown me, which I think to be the best of all and the one I should always take.

[163]   For certain periods before saying Mass, as I was recollecting myself *in my room*, I found no surrender or reverence with any interior grace or flavor. In fact, I was completely unable to find it, and yet I desired to have it or find it.

[164]   A little after this, in the chapel, I thought that it was God's will that I make an effort to look for and find it. But even if I did not find it, I thought to search for it was good. As there was no possibility of my finding it by myself, the Giver of all graces provided such an abundance of knowledge, consolation, and spiritual flavor, as I said, with ([so many tears]) tears, and they were so continuous that I lost my speech. I thought that every time I named God, Lord, etc., I was penetrated through and through with a wonderful and reverential surrender and humility, which seems impossible to explain.

[165]   Of Jesus.

2. Tuesday, March 18th—Before, during, and after Mass I had tears terminating in surrender and reverence.

[166]   Trinity.

3. Wednesday, March 19th—During Mass, for the most part, I had great abundance of tears, and after it also. During it, I often lost the power of speech, ending in surrender and reverence and many interior feelings.

[167]   Lady.

4. Thursday, March 20th—I was not without tears *before Mass* and during it, and with different interior movements, ending in surrender.

[168]   Of Jesus.

5. Friday, March 21st—I was not without some tears before and during Mass, terminating in surrender and some interior motions.

[169]   Holy Spirit.

6. Saturday, March 22nd—In the Mass, as a rule, I had many soft tears, and after it also. Before it I had some movement to tears, feeling or seeing the Holy Spirit Himself, all surrender.

[170]   Of the day.

7. Sunday, March 23rd—Before and during Mass many and intense tears, all ending in surrender.

[171]   Trinity

8. Monday, March 24th—During Mass, tears at different times, ending in surrender.

[VISIONS AND DARKNESS IN THIS NEW PATH]

[172]   Lady.

9. Tuesday, March 25th—Tears before and after Mass. I had many tears during it, with a vision of the Divine Essence sev-

eral times, *ending* in the Father, in a circular figure, and all leading to surrender.

[173]   Of Jesus.

10. Wednesday, March 26th—I had tears at various times before and during Mass and movements to them. Until the *Memento for the Living* in the Mass I was not only unable to feel any interior surrender, but not even able to find a disposition for helping me. From this I inferred and saw that I could do nothing to find surrender. From the *Memento of the Living* on, I felt spiritual consolation ending in surrender.

[174]   Holy Spirit.

11. Thursday, March 27th—I had tears before Mass, and many during it, all terminating in surrender, with a vision of the Divine Essence in spherical form, as on past occasions.

[175]   Trinity.

12. Friday, March 28th—Tears before and during Mass.

[176]   Lady.

13. Saturday, March 29th—I had no tears or any sign of them before or during Mass. But I found in the customary prayer special or very special grace. During Mass, the greater part of it, I felt much sweet devotion. I thought that it was greater perfection to find interior devotion and love, as do the angels, without tears. At times I had more rather than less satisfaction than yesterday.

[177]   Day.

14. Sunday, March 31st—I had many tears before Mass, in my room, in the chapel during preparation, and great abundance of them in the Mass, continuing all through it. After Mass I had many intense tears. *Vision*.

[LOVING HUMILITY AND REVERENCE]

[178]   In this interval of time, I thought that humility, reverence, and surrender should not be fearful but loving, and this was so firmly established in my soul that I said confidently: "Give me a loving humility, and thus reverence and surrender." I received fresh visitations in these words. I also resisted tears to turn my attention to this loving humility, etc.

[179]   Later in the day, I had much joy in remembering this. I also thought that I should not stop *there*, but that the same loving humility should be directed later to all creatures, for this is to the honor of God our Lord, as it is said in today's Gospel, "I will be like to you, a liar."

[180]   During these intervals, several times I had the vision of the Divine Essence in circular form as before.

[181]   Day.

15. Monday, March 31st—I had tears during and after Mass terminating in *loving reverence*, etc. At times I thought that neither love nor reverence was in my power.

[182]   Day.

16. Tuesday, April 1st—Many tears at Mass, terminating in loving humility, etc. I thought that in order to find this in the Sacrifice (of the Man) it was necessary for me to use it throughout the day without distraction.

[COMPLETE DETACHMENT FROM THE NEW GRACES]

[183]   Day.

17. Wednesday, April 2nd—There were tears in the customary prayer, later in my room, in the chapel, while vesting, and very abundantly at Mass (Vision). I also had a vision at different times of the Divine Essence, sometimes terminating in the Father in the form of a circle, with much intellectual light and interior knowledge.

[184]   At times, when the knowledge or the consolations were greater, I thought I ought to be just as content as when I was not visited with tears. I thought it was better that our Lord do as He pleases to console me or not. At other times, *when I was not* visited with tears, I thought that this was such great perfection. I *had* little hope and feared I would be unable to receive this grace.

[185]   At a later time when I was much consoled, I thought I was satisfied. I thought it better that I should not be consoled on the part of God our Lord, either, because I was without the visit, or by not disposing myself or helping myself throughout the whole day, or in giving place to some thoughts that distracted me from His words in the Sacrifice and from His Divine Majesty. Thus I thought it would be better not to be consoled in the time of my faults, and that this was God our Lord's order (Who loves me more than I love myself), for my greater spiritual benefit. It is better for me to walk straight not only in the Sacrifice (of the Mass), but throughout the whole day, in order to be visited. This corresponds to what dawned on me the other day about these and similar great and delicate intellectual lights, for which I have neither memory nor understanding competent to explain or describe.

[186]   Day.

18. Thursday, April 3rd—I had no tears either before, during, or after Mass. I was more content without them, and I affectionately felt that God our Lord did this for my greater good.

[187]   Day.

19. Friday, April 4th—I had tears before Mass, and an abundance of them during it. I had many interior lights and feelings, also before Mass. Not finding loving reverence or surrender, I must seek fearful surrender by examining my own faults so as to reach Him who is love.

[188]   Day.

20. Saturday, April 5th—I had tears before Mass and many during it.

[FULL AND MYSTIC CONFIRMATION ON THE DIVINE WILL]

[189]   21. Sunday, April 6th—I had tears before and during Mass. I had more after the Passion (the Gospel), many and continued, ending with a conforming of my will to the Divine Will and likewise tears after Mass.

[190]   Day.

22. Monday, April 7th—Many tears for the most part during Mass, leading to conformity with God's will.

[191]   Day.

23. Tuesday, April 8th—I had tears at Mass.

[192]   Day.

24. Wednesday, April 9th—I had tears at Mass.

[193]   Day.

25. Thursday, April 10th—I had no tears.

[194]   26. April 11th—No masses are celebrated on Holy Friday and Saturday. These two days appear

[195]   27. April 12th. separated thus in the original.

[196]   Day.

28. Easter Sunday, April 13th—I had many tears at Mass, and tears after it.

[197]   Day.

29. Monday, April 14th—I felt much interior and exterior warmth, apparently ([all restful]) more supernatural. I had no tears.

[198]   30. Tuesday, April 15th—No notable ([extreme]) consolation or desolation. No tears.

[199]   Day.

31. Wednesday, April 16th—I had many tears during and after Mass.

[200]   Day.

32. Thursday, April 17th—I had tears before and after Mass and many during it.

[201]   Day.

33. Friday, April 18th—I had tears at Mass.

[202]   Day.

34. Saturday, April 19th—I had tears before and during Mass.

[203]   35. Sunday, April 20th—I had tears before and during Mass.

   Preparing.
[204]   Lady.

36. Monday, April 21st—I had tears before and during Mass.

   Beginning, because I dropped it a few days ago.
[205]   Saints.

37. Tuesday, April 22nd—I had tears before and after Mass, and during it I had many and continuous tears.

[206]   38. Wednesday, April 23rd—No tears. Here it was put aside.

(The phrases underscored here in these lines seem to be connected. Some project not carried through.)

[207]   39. Thursday, April 24th—I had no tears.

[208]   St. Mark.

30. Friday, April 25th—Tears before and during Mass.

[209]   Holy Spirit.

31. Saturday, April 26th—No tears.

[210]   Day.

32. Sunday, April 27th—I had tears before and during Mass.

[211]   Trinity.

33. Monday, April 28th—Tears before and during Mass.

[212]   34. Tuesday, April 29th—With tears.

[213]   35. Wednesday, April 30th—With tears.

[214]   36. Thursday, May 1st—With tears.

[215]   37. Friday, May 2nd—No tears.

[216]   38. Saturday, May 3rd—Tears.

[217]   39. Sunday, May 4th—With tears.

[218]   40. Monday, May 5th.—Tears, I think.

41. Tuesday, May 6th.—Tears, I think.

[219]   42. Wednesday, May 7th.—No tears, I think.

43. Thursday, May 8th—No tears, I think.

44. Friday, May 9th—No tears, I think.

[220]   45. Saturday, May 10th—Many tears at Mass.

[FINAL THANKS AND *LOQUELA:* INNER VOICES]

[221]   46. Sunday, May 11th—Tears before and during Mass. An abundance of them, and continued, together with the interior *loquela* (voices) during Mass. It seems to me it was a divine gift, as

I had asked for it that same day, for during the whole week, I sometimes found the external *loquela*, and sometimes I did not. I found the interior less, although last Saturday I was a little more clear.

[222]   In the same way, in all the Masses of the week, although I was not granted tears, I felt greater *peace* and contentment throughout *the whole* Mass because of the relish of the *loquelas*, together with *inner* devotion. *I felt* more than at other times when I shed tears in parts *of the Mass*. Those of today seemed to be much, much different from *those* of former days, as they came more slowly, more interiorly, gently, without noise[60] or notable movements, coming apparently from so deep within, my not knowing how to explain them. During the interior and exterior *loquela* everything moved me to divine love and to the gift of the *loquela* divinely bestowed. I felt so much interior harmony in the interior *loquela* that I cannot explain it.

[223]   This Sunday before Mass I began to think of taking up the Constitutions.

[224]   Of all the Saints.

47. Monday, May 12th—I had many tears at Mass, and tears after it. All these were similar to those of the preceding day, and with great relish of the interior *loquela*. It was like remembering the heavenly *loquela* or music, which increased my devotion with tears at the thought that I felt or apprehended it miraculously.

[225]   St. Sebastian.

48. Tuesday, May 13th—I had *tears before and after Mass, and a great abundance of them* during it, and had a wonderful interior *loquela*, greater than at other times.

[226]   Conception of our Lady.

49. Wednesday, May 14th—I had tears before Mass, and many after it, the same interior *loquela* following.

[227]   Jesus.

50. Thursday, May 15th—No tears but with some *loquela*, and disturbance of hearing some whistling, but I was not so disturbed.

[228]   Holy Spirit.

51. Friday, May 16th—I had tears before Mass, and many during it, with *loquela*.

[229]   Trinity.

52. Saturday, May 17th—I had tears before Mass, and many and continuous during it, with a wonderful interior *loquela*.

[230]   Day.

54. Sunday, May 18th—I had no tears, but some *loquela*. I felt no bodily strength, or any disturbances.

[231]   Litanies.

    54. Monday, May 19th—Tears and *loquela*.

[232]   All Saints.

    55. Tuesday, May 20th—No tears or disturbance. Some *loquela*.

[233]   Lady.

    56. Wednesday, May 21—. No tears and much *loquela*.

[234]   Ascension.

    57. Thursday, May 22nd—I had many tears before Mass in my room and in the chapel. During the greater part of the Mass, no tears, but much *loquela*. I felt some doubt about the relish and sweetness of the *loquela* for fear it might be from the evil spirit, thus causing the ceasing of the spiritual consolation of tears. Going on a little further, I thought that I took too much delight in the tone of the *loquela*, attending to the sound, without paying so much attention to the meaning of the words and of the *loquela*. I then felt many tears, thinking that I was being taught how to proceed, with the hope of always finding further instruction as time went on.

[235]   Ascension.

    58. Friday, May 23rd—Tears.

[236]   Holy Spirit.

    59. Saturday, May 24th—No tears.

[237]   40. Sunday, May 25th—I had many tears before Mass, in my room, and tears in the chapel, and at Mass a great abundance of them continuing with wonderful *loquelas*.

[238]   Ascension.

    41. Monday, May 26th—Tears at Mass and interior *loquela*.

[239]   42. Tuesday, May 27th—Tears before Mass, and I had many during it, together with an increasing interior *loquela*.

[240]   Ascension.

    43. Wednesday, May 28th—I had tears before and after Mass; during it, I had many tears with a wonderful interior *loquela*.

[LAST NOTE ON TEARS]

[241]   Ascension.

    44. Thursday, May 29th—I had tears before, during, and after Mass.

[242]   45. Friday, May 30th—No tears.

[243]   46. Saturday, May 31—. Tears.

[244]   47. Sunday, June 1st—Tears.

[245]   48. Monday, June 2nd—No tears.

[246]　　49. Tuesday, June 3rd—No tears.

[247]　　50. Wednesday, June 4th—I had many and continued tears.

[248]　　51. Thursday, June 5th—No tears.

[249]　　52. Friday, June 6th—No tears.

[250]　　53. Saturday, June 7th—No tears.

[251]　　Trinity.

54. Sunday, June 8th—I had ([many]) tears in my room and in the chapel before Mass, and I had many and continued during Mass.

[252]　　Trinity.

Monday, June 9th—Continued tears during Mass, and tears after it.

[253]　　Trinity.

56. Tuesday, June 10th—The same.

[254]　　Trinity.

57. Wednesday, June 11th—No tears.

[255]　　Corpus Christi.

58. Thursday, June 12th—No tears.

[256]　　Corpus Christi.

59. Friday, June 13th—No tears.

[257]　　Corpus Domini.

60. Saturday, June 14th—Tears during mass.

[258]　　Of the day.

61. Sunday, June 15th—No tears.

[259]　　Corpus Christi.

62. Monday, June 16th—I had many and continued tears during mass.

[260]　　63. Tuesday, June 17th—I had tears before Mass in my room and in the chapel, and during Mass many and continued.

[261]　　Corpus Christi.

64. Wednesday, June 18th—Tears during mass.

[262]　　Corpus Christi.

65. Thursday, June 19th—Tears before Mass in my room and in the chapel, but none during Mass.

[263]　　66. Friday, June 20th—No tears.

[264]　　67. Saturday, June 21st—Tears during mass.

[265]　　68. Sunday, June 22nd—Tears during mass.

[266]　　69. Monday, June 23rd—I had many and *continued* tears at Mass, and tears before it in my room and in the chapel.

[267]　　The Baptist.

70. Tuesday, June 24th—I had many tears before Mass *in my room* and in the chapel, and during Mass I had a great abundance of continued tears.

[268]　　The Baptist.

71. Wednesday, June 25th—Many and continued tears during and after Mass.

[269]   The Baptist.

72. Thursday, June 26th—Tears during mass.

[270]   73. Friday, June 27th—Tears *before Mass*, and *during it scarcely any.*

[271]   74. Saturday, June 28th—Tears before Mass, and during it scarcely any.

[272]   75. Sunday, June 29th—Tears before Mass, and none during it.

[273]   Trinity.

76. Monday, June 30th—I had many tears before, during and after Mass.

[274]   Trinity.

77. Tuesday, July 1st—I had many tears before and during Mass.

[275]   Visitation Our Lady.

78. Wednesday, July 2nd—I had many tears before, during and after Mass.

[276]   Five Wounds.

79. Thursday, July 3rd—I had many tears before Mass in my room and in the chapel, and none during Mass.

[277]   Trinity.

40. Friday, July 4th—I had great abundance of tears before Mass in my room and in the chapel, and also during and after Mass.

[278]   41. Saturday, July 5th—Tears during mass.

[279]   42. Sunday, July 6th—No tears.

[280]   43. Monday, July 7th—No tears.

[281]   44. Tuesday, July 8th—I had many tears before and during Mass.

[282]   45. Wednesday, July 9th—No tears.

[283]   46. Thursday, July 10th—I do not know.

[284]   47. Friday, July 11th—A great abundance of tears before, during, and after Mass, leading to taking pleasure only in the Lord Himself.

[285]   48. Saturday, July 12th—I had great abundance of tears *before* and *during Mass*, remaining in our Lord.

[286]   49. Sunday, July 13th—No tears.

[287]   50. Monday, July 14th. Tears before and during mass.

[288]   51. Tuesday, July 15th—Tears during mass.

[289]   52. Wednesday, July 16th—

[290]   53. Thursday, July 17th—No tears.

[291]   54. Friday, July 18th—Tears during mass.

[292]   56. Saturday, July 19th—I had many and continuous tears before and during Mass.

[293]   57. Sunday, July 20th—I had many tears before and during Mass.

[294]   58. Monday, July 21st—*Almost* without tears.

[295]   59. Tuesday, July 22nd—I had tears before Mass, but scarcely any during it.

[296]   60. Wednesday, July 23rd—I had great abundance of tears before and during Mass, and tears after it.

[297]   61. Thursday, July 24th—I had many tears before Mass, and none during it.

[298]   62. Friday, July 25th—I had many tears before Mass, and none during it.

[299]   63. Saturday, July 26th—*Many tears during Mass* and some after it.

[300]   64. Sunday, July 27th—I had many tears before, during, and after Mass.

[301]   65. Monday, July 28th—I had great abundance of tears before and during Mass.

[302]   66. Tuesday, July 29th—I had many tears before, during, and after Mass.

[303]   67. Wednesday, July 30th—*Tears before Mass*, and none *during it*.

[304]   68. Thursday, July 31st—I had great abundance of tears before, during, and after Mass.

[305]   69. Friday, August 1st—I had tears before Mass, none during it.

[306]   70. Saturday, August 2nd—I had many tears before and during Mass.

[307]   71. Sunday, August 3rd—I had many tears during Mass.

[308]   72. Monday, August 4th—Tears before Mass. They became very abundant and continuous during Mass, with *frequent* loss of speech.

[309]   73. Tuesday, August 5th—I had many tears before Mass and several times during it.

[310]   74. Wednesday, August 6th—No tears.

[311]   75. Thursday, August 7th—I had tears before Mass and none during it.

[312]   76. Friday, August 8th—Tears before Mass, none during it.

[313]   77. Saturday, August 9th—Many tears during Mass.

[314]   78. Sunday, August 10th—*I do not remember.*

[315]   79. Monday, August 11th—Many tears during Mass, and tears before and after it.

[316]   80. Tuesday, August 12th—Many tears during Mass, and tears before it.

[317]   81. Wednesday, August 13th—No tears.

[318]   82. Thursday, August 14th—No tears.

[319]   83. Friday, August 15th—No tears.

[320]   84. Saturday, August 16th—Tears during Mass.

[321]   85. Sunday, August 17th—Many tears before and during Mass.

[322]   89. Monday, August 18th—No tears.

[323]   90. Tuesday, August 19th—Tears during Mass.

[324]   91. Wednesday, August 20th—Tears before Mass and many during it.

[325]   92. Thursday, August 21st—Before Mass, in my room and out of it, I had a great abundance of tears, which were also continuous during Mass.

[326]   93. Friday, August 22nd—I had many tears before and during Mass.

[327]   94. Saturday, August 23rd—Many tears before Mass, but none during it.

[328]   95. During this interval I was ill and did not say Mass. (5 days.)

[329]   100. Friday, August 29th—Many tears before and during Mass.

[330]   101. Saturday, August 30th—Many tears before, after, and during Mass.

[331]   102. Sunday, August 31st—The same, continuous and very abundant.

[332]   103. Monday, September 1st—Many tears before Mass, but none during it.

[333]   104. Tuesday, September 2nd—Many tears before Mass and a few during it.

[334]   105. Wednesday, September 3rd—Many tears during Mass, and some after.

[335]   106. Thursday, September 4th—Great abundance of tears before, during, and after Mass.

[336]   107. Friday, September 5th—No tears.

[337]   108. Saturday, September 6th—Many tears before and during Mass.

[338]   109.Sunday, September 7th—No tears.

[339]   110. Monday, September 8th—Many tears before and during Mass.

[340]   111. Tuesday, September 9th—A few tears during mass.

[341]   112. Wednesday, September 10th—Many tears before, during, and after Mass.

[342]   113. Thursday, September 11th—Many tears before, during, and after Mass.

[343]   114. Friday, September 12th—The same.

[344]   115. Saturday, September 13th—Many tears before and during Mass.

[345]   116. Sunday, September 14th—The same.

[346]   117. Monday, September 15th—The same.

[347]   118. Tuesday, September 16th—The same.

[348]   119. Wednesday, September 17th—Many tears during and after Mass.

[349]   120. Thursday, September 18th—Many tears before and during Mass.

[350]   121. Friday, September 19th—Many tears before, during, and after Mass.

[351]   122. Saturday, September 20th—Many tears before and during Mass.

[352]   123. Sunday, September 21st—Many tears before Mass.

[353]   124. Monday, September 22nd—Great abundance of tears before Mass.

[354]   125. Tuesday, September 23rd—Great abundance of tears and tears several times during it.

[355]   126. Wednesday, September 24th—Late tears after Mass.

[356]   127. *Thursday*, September 25th—Great abundance of tears before Mass.

[357]   128. Friday, September 26th—Many tears before and during and after Mass.

[358]   128. Saturday, September 27th—Many tears before and during Mass.

[359]   129. Sunday, September 28th—Many tears before and during Mass.

[360]   130. Monday, September 29th—Many tears before and some during Mass.

[361]   131. Tuesday, September 30th—Many tears before and during Mass.

[362]   1. Wednesday, First of October. Many tears before and during Mass.

[363]   2. Thursday. Many tears before and during Mass.

[364]   3. Friday. Many tears before and during Mass.

[365]   Here we start the dots but not using them as before.

[366]   4. Saturday. Before the three prayers (1st prayer, in the room, in church) and in Mass great abundance of tears, and tears after it.

[367]   5. Sunday. Before the three prayers and a great super-abundance of tears at Mass, with frequent loss of speech, continuous tears, and fear of losing my sight, and tears following.

[368]   6. Monday. Before the three prayers with a great abundance of tears at Mass, with fear of losing my sight, and tears later.

[369]   7. Tuesday. Before the three prayers, and a great abundance of continuance of tears in the Mass, together with a feeling of danger concerning my eyesight.

[370]   8. Wednesday. Before 1st prayer and during Mass, and after it with *great abundance* and continuance of tears, through all (the day).

[371]   9. Thursday. An abundance of tears before Mass and the three prayers.

[372]   10. Friday. Many tears before 1st prayer and a few during Mass.

[373]   11. Saturday. Tears before 1st prayer, during Mass, and many afterwards.

[374]   12. Sunday. Tears before room and church prayer, many during Mass, and many later in the afternoon.

[375]   13. Monday. Many tears at Mass.

[376]   14. Tuesday. Many tears (before) room and church prayer.

[377]   15. Wednesday. Up to the middle of Mass warmth and a desire for tears; afterwards, as a consequence to the thought and light that God was protecting me in those desires, I began to weep and continued to do so through the Mass.

[378]   16. Thursday. Tears before church prayer, and in it, and later in abundance.

[379]   17. Friday. Tears before room prayer, and in it, and many afterwards.

[380]   18. Saturday. Tears before room prayer and a few at Mass.

[381]   19. Sunday. Before room and church prayer and many at Mass.

[382]   20. Monday. Tears before room and church prayer at Mass, and a great abundance of them after it.

[383]   21. Tuesday. Tears (before) room and church prayer, a great abundance and continuance of them in Mass, and some after, with fear for my eyes. I asked for contentment when tears did not come, without contrary thoughts, etc.

[384]   22. Wednesday. Tears (before) the three prayers, and a great abundance and continuance of them at Mass, and some afterwards.

[385]   23. Thursday. Tears before three prayers, and a great abundance and continuance at Mass, and tears afterwards.

[386]   24. Friday. Tears before 1st prayer, and many at Mass.

[387]   25. Saturday. Tears *before* 3 prayers, and a few at Mass.

[388]   26. Sunday. Tears before 3 prayers, and many at Mass.

[389]   27. Monday. Tears before room and church prayers, and many at Mass.

[390]   28. Tuesday. Tears before church prayer, and many at

Mass, and afterwards.

[391]   29. Wednesday. Tears before three prayers, many continuous at Mass and after it.

[392]   30. Thursday. Tears before three prayers, a great abundance and continuance of them at Mass.

[393]   31. Friday. Tears before three prayers, and a great abundance and continuance of them during Mass, and afterward.

[394]   1. Saturday—First of November. Tears at three prayers, and a great superabundance and continuance of them during Mass.

[395]   2. Sunday. Tears before three prayers, and a great abundance and continuance of them during Mass.

[396]   3. Monday. Tears before three prayers, and a great abundance and continuance of them during Mass, and afterwards.

[397]   4. Tuesday. Tears before 1st and room prayers, and many during Mass.

[398]   5. Wednesday. Tears before room and church prayers, and during Mass.

[399]   6. Thursday. Tears before 1st prayer, at Mass, and many after.

[400]   7. Friday. Tears before 1st and church prayers, and many and continuous tears during Mass.

[401]   8. Saturday. Tears before three prayers, during Mass many and continued, and some afterwards.

[402]   9. Sunday. Tears before room and church prayer, and many during Mass.

[403]   10. Monday. Tears before three prayers, and a great abundance during Mass and after.

[404]   11. Tuesday. Tears (before) three prayers, and a great abundance and continuance of them during Mass.

[405]   12. Wednesday. Tears (before) room and church prayer, and some during Mass.

[406]   13. Thursday. Tears before 1st and room prayer.

[407]   14. Friday. Tears before 1st and room and many during Mass, and after it.

[408]   15. Saturday. Tears before room and church prayer, and a great abundance and continuance of them during Mass, and after it.

[409]   16. Sunday. Tears before three prayers, and a great abundance and continuance of them during Mass, and after it.

[410]   17. Monday. Tears before 1st and church prayers, and during Mass a great abundance and continuance of them.

[411]   18. Tuesday. Tears before 1st prayer.

[412]   19. Wednesday. Tears before 1st prayer, and many during Mass.

[413]   20. Thursday. Tears before room prayer, and many during and after Mass.

[414]   21. Friday. Tears before three prayers, and during Mass, with loss of speech.

[415]   22. Saturday. Tears before three prayers, many during Mass and after it.

[416]   23. Sunday. Tears before three prayers, and a super-abundance of them during Mass, with frequent loss of speech, and tears after Mass.

[417]   24. Monday. Tears before three prayers, and many during Mass.

[418]   25. Tuesday. Many tears during Mass, and after some.

[419]   26. Wednesday. I did not say (Mass).

[420]   27. Thursday. Tears before room and church prayer, many during Mass, and some after it.

[421]   28. Friday. Tears before three prayers, and an abundance of them during Mass and afterward.

[422]   29. Saturday. Tears before three prayers, and a great abundance of them during Mass and also afterward.

[423]   30. Sunday. Tears before 1st and room prayer during Mass, and late afterward.

[424]   1. Monday, First of December. Tears before three prayers, and many during Mass, and late afterward.

[425]   2. Tuesday. Tears before 1st and church prayer, and a great abundance of them during Mass and also afterward.

[426]   3. Wednesday. Tears ([without them]) before 1st prayer.

[427]   4. Thursday. Tears before 1st and church prayer, and some during Mass, and afterward.

[428]   5. Friday. Tears before 1st and church prayer, some during Mass, and after it.

[429]   6. Saturday. Tears before three prayers during Mass, and many later in the afternoon.

[430]   7. Sunday. Tears before 1st prayer and many during Mass.

[431]   8. Monday. Tears (before) 1st and room prayer, during Mass a great abundance, and afterward.

[432]   9. Tuesday. Tears (before) room and church prayer, many during Mass, and later.

[433]   10. Wednesday. Tears (before) three prayers, a great abundance during Mass.

[434]   11. Thursday. Tears (before) three prayers, a great abundance during Mass and afterwards in the afternoon.

[435]   12. Friday. Tears (before) three prayers, a great abundance during Mass, and later.

[436]   13. Saturday. Tears (before) three prayers, a great abundance during Mass, and later.

[437]   14. Sunday. Tears (before) three prayers, a great abundance during Mass, and later.

[438]   15. Monday. Tears (before) room and church prayer, many during Mass.

[439]   16. Tuesday. Tears (before) room and church prayer, and during Mass.

[440]   17. Wednesday. Tears (before) three prayers, and during Mass.

[441]   18. Thursday. Tears (before) room and church prayer, many during Mass, later.

[442]   19. Friday. Tears (before) room prayer, a great abundance during Mass.

[443]   20. Saturday. Tears (before) room and church prayer, a great abundance during Mass, and later.

[444]   21. Sunday. Tears (before) room and church prayer, many during Mass and later.

[445]   (22.) Monday.
         (23.) Tuesday.   Room prayer. I did not say Mass.
         (24.) Wednesday.

[446]   25. Thursday. (Before) room and church prayer, tears during Mass; many during Mass; and some in the third (part of the Mass) and afterwards tears in my room.

[447]   26. Friday. Tears (before) room and church prayer.

[448]   27. Saturday. Tears (before) three prayers, a great abundance and continuance during Mass, and later.

[449]   28. Sunday. Tears (before) room and church prayer. Many during Mass, and afterwards.

[450]   29. Monday. Tears (before) three prayers, a great abundance and continuance during Mass, and later.

[451]   30.Tuesday. Tears (before) three prayers, a great abundance and continuance during Mass, and afterward.

[452]   31. Wednesday. Tears (before) three prayers, a great abundance and continuance during Mass, and afterward.

([Thursday 1st and church prayers, tears during Mass.])

[453]   1. Thursday, First of January (1545). Tears before 1st and room prayers and tears during Mass.

In this interval I did not say Mass, and except for one day, there were tears every day.

[454]   11. Sunday. Tears before three prayers, a great abundance during Mass, and later.

[455]   12. Monday. Tears before three prayers, a great abundance during Mass, and later.

[456]   I did not say Mass.

[457]   20. Tuesday. Tears before three prayers and a great abundance during Mass.

[458]   21. Wednesday. Tears before room and church prayer, and tears during Mass.

[459]   22. Thursday. Tears before room and church prayer, and a great abundance and continuance during Mass, and afterward.

[460]   23. Friday. A great abundance during Mass.

[461]   24. Saturday. Tears before three prayers, a great abundance during Mass, and later.

[462]   25. Sunday. Tears before room and church prayer, a great abundance during Mass.

[463]   I did not say Mass in this interval.

[464]   1. Sunday, First of February. Tears before three prayers, a great abundance and continuance during Mass, and later.

[465]   2. Monday. Tears before three prayers, a great abundance and continuance during Mass, and afterward.

[466]   3. Tuesday. Tears before 1st prayer, a great abundance during Mass, and afterward.

[467]   4. Wednesday. Tears before three prayers, a great abundance during Mass and afterward.

[468]   5. Thursday. Tears before three prayers, a great abundance and continuance during Mass, and afterward.

[469]   6. Friday. Tears before three prayers, many during Mass, and afterward.

[470]   7. Saturday. Tears before three prayers, a great abundance during Mass, and afterward.

[471]   8. Sunday. Tears before room and church prayer, many during Mass and afterward.

[472]   9. Monday. Tears before church prayer, many during Mass, and afterward.

[473]   10. Tuesday. Tears before 1st and room prayer, many during Mass, and afterward.

[474]   11.Wednesday. Tears before three prayers, a great abundance during Mass, and afterward.

[475]   12. Thursday. Tears before three prayers, a great abundance during Mass, later afterward.

[476]   13. Friday. Tears before three prayers, in the afternoon and later.

[477]   14. Saturday. Tears (before) room and church prayer, many during Mass.

[478]   15. Sunday. Tears (before) room and church prayer, during Mass, and afterward.

[479]   16. Monday. Tears before three prayers, a great abundance and continuance during Mass, and afterward.

[480]   17. Tuesday. Tears (before) room and church prayer, a great abundance and continuance during Mass, and later.

[481]   18. Wednesday of Lent. Tears at three prayers, a great abundance and continuance during Mass and afterward.

[482]   19. Thursday. Tears at three prayers, a great abundance

and continuance during Mass and afterward.

[483]   20. Friday. Tears at three prayers, a great abundance and continuance during Mass and afterward.

[484]   21. Saturday. Tears (before) three prayers, a great abundance during Mass and afterward.

[485]   22. Sunday. Tears (before) three prayers, a great abundance and continuance during Mass and afterward.

[486]   23. Monday. Tears (before) three prayers, during Mass and afterward.

[487]   24. Tuesday. Tears (before) three prayers, many during Mass and afterward.

[488]   25. Wednesday. Tears (before) three prayers, during Mass and afterward.

[489]   26. Thursday. Tears (before) three prayers, a great abundance and continuance during Mass and afterward.

[490]   27. Friday. Tears (before) three prayers, a great abundance and continuance during Mass and afterward.

AUTO-
BIOGRAPHY

≈≈≈≈≈≈≈≈≈≈≈

Also known as
Diary of a Pilgrim
(1521-1538)

Contents

Ignatius de Loyola, in the last years of his life, between 1553 and 1555, consented to narrate the story of his inner life. This *Autobiography* does not include the whole of Ignatius' life. It starts with his youth in 1521 and concludes in 1538, eighteen years before his death. The composition of this document was done by Ignatius after long hesitation and only at the insistence of several of his Jesuits, as may be seen from the two introductions of Nadal and da Camara accompanying this translation. These two introductions explain the manner in which this document was composed: by dictating it to Father da Camara, who in turn dictated it to his secretaries. For this reason half of the *Autobiography* was originally composed in Spanish and half in Italian.

The *Autobiography* spread originally in manuscript form, the most famous being the one carried by Father Nadal and the Latin translations by du Coudray and Juan Veseto. We do not have the original manuscript and notes dictated by da Camara to his secretaries. The first publication to appear in the *Monumenta Historica Societatis Jesu* did not happen until 1904 in the first volume of the *Scripta de Sancto Ignatio* and the second in 1943 in the first volume of the *Fontes Narrativi de S. Ignatio de Loyola*. In 1731 the Bollandists published a Latin version by du Coudray in their *Acta Sanctorum*. The reason why this document was not made public until the eighteenth century in Latin and the twentieth in its original Spanish is due to the attitudes, tribulations, and fears of the early Jesuits. St. Francis de Borja, the Jesuit General, asked Father Ribadeneira in 1566 to write the official life of St. Ignatius. At the same time he ordered the collecting of all the standing manuscripts of the *Autobiography*, and he even forbade the Jesuits from reading or propagating it. The same behavior was followed by the next General of the Jesuits, Father Claudius Aquaviva.

This translation is based on the 1943 edition of the *Fontes Narrativi de S. Ignatio de Loyola* as it appears in *Obras Completas* (Biblioteca de Autores Cristianos, Madrid, 1963). I have tried to avoid all inconclusive and speculative footnotes. Those notes I considered necessary to the reading of the text I have included in the text within parentheses or as footnotes.

Since I have already discussed in the hermeneutic text of this volume the place of the *Autobiography* within the spiritual writings of Ignatius de Loyola, I need only add at this time the same warning that Father da Camara writes at the conclusion of the *Autobiography*. In paragraph 100 of the *Autobiography*, Father da Camara points out how the visions Ignatius had were part of a process of meditation in relation to some decision he had to make. In fact he refers the reader, in the same paragraph, to the *Spiritual Diary* as the model from which to read the inner life of Ignatius de Loyola.

ANTONIO T. DE NICOLÁS

Autobiography

PREFACE OF FATHER NADAL[1]

He asks St. Ignatius to tell his children the manner in which God guided him from the beginning of his conversion. After much insistence on Fr. Nadal's part, he succeeds.

 1.
E HAD HEARD FROM OUR FATHERS, and I from our Father Ignatius, that he wished God would grant him three wishes before he died: the first, that the Institute of the Society be confirmed by the Holy See; the second, that the *Spiritual Exercises* be equally approved; the third, that he could finish writing the *Constitutions*.

2. I remembered this, and seeing that he had achieved everything,[2] I was afraid that he would soon be called from amongst us to a better life; and, knowing that the holy founding saints of several monastic institutes had left to their descendents, by way of a will, those councils that would help them to their perfection, I was looking for the opportunity to ask the same of Fr. Ignatius. And so one day in the year 1551[3] when we were together Fr. Ignatius told me, "I was just now higher than the heavens." I took it that he had just experienced some ecstasy or rapture, as it used to happen to him frequently. With full respect I asked him, "What do you mean, Father?" He changed the conversation, so that his story would serve as his will and paternal teaching. And then I added, "For, since God has granted you the three wishes that you wanted to see fulfilled before your death, we are afraid you might be called to His glory."

3. Our Father made excuses, pointing out how busy he was and saying that he could not dedicate his attention and time to this task. And then he added, "Celebrate three masses to this intention, yourself, Polanco and Pontius,[4] and then tell me what you think about it."

"Father, we will think the same we are thinking now," I replied. And he added with great softness, "Do as I tell you." We celebrated the masses and after telling him what we thought, he promised to do what we asked him. The following year,[5] after my return from Sicily and about to be sent to Spain, I asked our Father if he had done anything. "Nothing," he told me. When I returned from Spain in the year 1554, I asked him again, but he had done nothing.[6] But then, moved by I do not know which impulse, I insisted again, "It is now over four years that I keep asking you, Father, not only in my name, but in the name of the others, that you tell us the way the Lord guided you from the beginning of your conversion, for we are sure that to know this will be extremely useful for us and the Society; but, since I see you are not doing it, I wish to assure you of one thing: if you grant us what we so much desire, we will profit very much by this gift; but if you do not, we will not lose our spirit, but we will continue with such confidence in the Lord as if you had written down everything."

4. Our Father did not answer, but I believe that the same day he called Fr. Luis Conçalves (da Camara) and began to tell him all those things that he later, with his excellent memory, put down in writing. These are the *Deeds of Fr. Ignatius* that go from hand to hand. Fr. Luis had a vote in the first General Congregation,[7] and he was then chosen assistant to the General Fr. Laínez. Later he was teacher and director of the King of Portugal, D. Sebastián; he was a Father of high virtue. Fr. Gonçalves wrote part in Spanish and part in Italian, depending on the secretaries he could find. Translation was made by Fr. Aníbal du Coudret,[8] a very learned and pious man. Writer and translator are still alive.

PREFACE OF FATHER LUIS GONÇALVES da CAMARA

1-2. St. Ignatius decides to tell his life. 3-5. How and when the *Autobiography* was written.

1. ONE FRIDAY MORNING, THE FOURTH of August of the year 1553, the eve of Our Lady of the Snows, while Our Father was in the orchard by the house or residence known as the Duke's,[9] I began telling him of some particulars of my soul, and amongst other things I told him of my vanity. Our Father offered me as a remedy to make God, many times, the source of all my actions, working towards making Him a continuous offering of any good I found in me, acknowledging it as His and thanking Him for it. In this manner he spoke to me, causing great consolation in me, so much so that I could not restrain my tears. This led to Our Father telling

me how for two years he had been bothered by this vice, so much so that when he was about to embark from Barcelona for Jerusalem, he did not dare tell anyone that he was sailing for Jerusalem, and the same in other particular instances. He then added how much peace he had felt ever since in his soul regarding this matter. An hour or two later we went to lunch, where Father Polanco[10] joined us. While eating, Our Father said that Master Nadal and others of the Company had asked many times one thing of him, but he was never able to make up his mind about it; but that after he spoke with me he had collected himself in his chambers and felt a great devotion and inclination to do it; then, speaking as showing that God had given him great clarity in having to do so, he said he was fully determined to carry it out. The thing he was referring to was to reveal everything that had happened in his soul up to now; and that he had also determined that I would be the one to whom he would reveal these things.

2. Our Father was then very ill, never able to promise himself one single day of life; just the contrary, whenever anyone would say, "I'll do this in fifteen or in eight days," Our Father, as if amazed, would say, "What, do you expect to live that long?" But on that occasion, he asserted, he expected to live three or four months in order to conclude this business. A few days later I asked him when would he like to start; he answered that I should remind him of it every day (I do not remember during how many days) until he felt inclined to do so; thus, being unable to find the time because of his obligations, he then asked me to remind him every Sunday. Finally, in September (I cannot remember the exact date) Our Father called me and began to tell me about his whole life, clearly and distinctly, starting with his youthful escapades with all their circumstances (this part is missing in the *Autobiography*. Trans.). That same month he called me again three or four times and carried his story to his stay at Manresa a few days, as may be seen by the change in handwriting.

3. The way Our Father has of narration is the same he has in everything else: it is so clear that he seems to make present everything of the past to the listener; thus, it was not necessary to question him about anything, for whatever was necessary to make the listener able to understand, Our Father would remember to tell. I would then hurry to write it down immediately, without consulting with Our Father, first in notes by my own hand and then at greater length as it is now written down. I have not tried to add a single word I have not heard from Our Father, and in those things I am afraid I might have failed; the reason is that in order not to depart from Our Father's words, I have not been able to explain well the power of some of them. Thus, I wrote this, as it is said above, until

September 1553. From then on, until Fr. Nadal arrived on October 18, 1554, Our Father kept on finding excuses through illnesses and different works that kept cropping up, saying, "As soon as this business is over, remind me." I would do so as soon as the business was over, but then he would say, "We are now into this other one; as soon as it is over remind me."

4. When Fr. Nadal returned, he was very pleased with what had already been accomplished and requested me to urge Our Father, telling me many times that Our Father could do nothing of greater benefit for the Society than this and that this was truly to found the Society. He himself spoke to Our Father many times in this way. Our Father told me to remind him of it as soon as the business of endowing the College[11] was finished; but after it was over he postponed it until the affair of Preste John[12] and then until after the mail had gone. We picked up the story, again, on the 9th of March. But then Pope Julius III became ill and died on the 23rd. Our Father delayed the writing until a new Pope was elected. But as soon as he was elected, he also became ill and died (this was Pope Marcellus II). Our Father delayed until the coronation of Pope Paul IV[13] and even later because of the heavy heat and many obligations. On the 21st of September the decision of sending me to Spain came up, and for this reason I pressed Our Father very hard to finish what he had promised me. Thus, he decided to do so the morning of the twenty-second in the Red Tower. When I finished Mass,[14] I went to him to ask if it was time.

5. He answered by sending me to the Red Tower so that when he arrived I would be there waiting. I realized I would have to wait for him there for a long time, so I delayed in a porch talking to a Brother who had asked me about something. Our Father caught me and reprimanded me for not waiting for him at the Red Tower, having thus failed in obedience. He thus refused to do anything that whole day. We, then, became very insistent with him. And so he returned to the Red Tower and started to dictate, pacing up and down, as he had always done his dictation before. I, in order to see his face, would always try to come closer to him, but Our Father would say, "Keep the rule." At times, when forgetting his advice, I would come closer to him (and I did this two or three times), Our Father repeated the same warning and left. Finally he returned later to the same Red Tower to finish dictating what now is already written down. But since I was for some time about to start my journey (the eve of my departure was the last day on which Our Father spoke to me on this matter), I could not dictate everything down in full at Rome. In Genoa, not having a Spanish secretary, I dictated in Italian what I had brought from Rome in summary and finished this dictation in Genoa, December 1555.

1

Convalescence and Conversion

(MAY 1521 - FEBRUARY 1522)

1. A soldier's wound. 2-5. Return to his home. Convalescence and readings. 6-12. The birth of the spirits.

1. UP TO THE AGE OF TWENTY-SIX[15] the man gave himself over to the world and its vanities with a great and vain desire, delighting mainly in the exercise of arms and in winning fame. Thus while defending a fortress[16] which was under attack by the French, and the others saw clearly that they could not defend themselves, desiring only to lay down their arms in surrender, if only to spare their own lives, he gave so many reasons that at last persuaded the commander (Miguel de Herrera. Trans.) to defend the fortress against all voices of the knights; and thus his valor and energy gave them courage. When the day came when the attack was expected, he made his confession to one of his companions in arms.[17] Late and long into the attack, a shot hit him in the leg, breaking it completely, and as the ball axed through both legs, the other limb, too, was badly spoiled.

2. When he fell, the defenders of the fortress surrendered at once to the French, who, after taking possession of the fortress, treated the wounded very well man in courteous and friendly tones. After he had spent twelve or fifteen days in Pamplona, they carried him upon a litter to his own country. There he was very ill, and he summoned up doctors and surgeons from many places. They decided that the leg ought to be severed again and the bones set one more time since they had been poorly set at first or had been broken on the road, and being put out of place could not heal. This butchery was done again, and still he stayed as in all the sufferings before, never speaking a word nor showing sign of pain except the clench of fists very hard.

3. Yet he continued to worsen; he could not eat and showed the other colorings that in their course foreshadow death. When the Feast of Saint John came, because the doctors had no confi-

dence in his recovery, he was advised to confess; he received the sacraments on the vigil of Sts. Peter and Paul. The doctors said that if he did not improve by midnight, he could consider himself dead. The sick man was very devoted to St. Peter, and so Our Lord wished that he should begin to improve that very midnight. His improvement made way so quickly that some days later it was thought that he had escaped from danger of death.

4. As his bones came together, one bone below the knee remained on top of another, shortening his leg. The bone stuck out so much that it was an ugly sight. He could not bear it, for he was bent on following the world, and he thought it would deform him; he asked the surgeons if it could be cut away. They said that indeed it could be done, but that the pain would be greater than all he had suffered, because it was quite healed and cutting it required time. Yet he was bound to martyr himself out of his own decision. His older brother[18] was horrified and said that he himself would not have courage to bear such pain, but the wounded man suffered it with customary patience.

5. After the flesh and excess bone were cut away, the leg was stretched continually with instruments and rubbed with many ointments so that it would not be so short; he suffered martyrdom for many days. But Our Lord was restoring his health, and he was getting well. In all else he was healthy, except that he could not stand easily on his leg and had to stay in bed. As he was much given to reading false and worldly books, usually called books of chivalry, when he sensed himself better, he asked to be given some of them to pass the time. But in that house none that he usually read could be found, so they gave him a Life of Christ (*Vita Christi.* Trans.) and a book of the lives of the saints in Spanish.[19]

6. As he read them over many times, he became rather fond of what he found written there. Sometimes putting his reading aside, he stopped and thought about the things he read and sometimes about the things of the world he thought about before. Of the many vain things that came to his mind, one bound his heart so that he was as in a trance in thinking on it for two or three or four hours without even knowing it. He imagined how he would serve a (certain) lady, how he would go to the place where she lived, the graceful speeches and words he would bring her, the deeds of arms he would serve her with. He grew so conceited with this that he did not consider how impossible it would be to achieve it, for the lady was not of the lower nobility, not a countess nor a duchess, but her standing was higher than even these.[20]

7. Nevertheless, Our Lord assisted him, causing other thoughts that arose from the things he read to follow these. While reading the life of Our Lord and of the saints, he stopped to think, reasoning within himself: "What if I should do what St. Francis did,

what St. Dominic did?" So he pondered over many things that he found to be good, always proposing to himself what was difficult and important, and as he proposed them, they seemed light and easily done. But all this thought was to say to himself: "St. Dominic did this; therefore, I have to do it." These thoughts all lasted a good long while, but when other matters intervened, the worldly thoughts mentioned above wooed him back, and he spent more time upon them. This chain of such diverse thoughts, either of the worldly deeds he wished to do or of the deeds of God that came to his fantasy lasted for a long time. He always dwelt at length on the thought before him, until, tiring of it, he put it aside and turned to other matters.

8. Yet there was this difference: When he thought about the things of the world, he enjoyed them, but afterwards, when he tired of them and put them aside, he found that he was dry and unhappy. But when he thought of going to Jerusalem, barefoot, eating nothing but herbs and savoring all the other rigors that the saints had savored, not only did he find consolation while he thought these thoughts, but even after putting them aside, he stayed content and happy. However, he did not stop to think about or ponder this difference, until one day his eyes were opened a bit, and he began to marvel at this difference and reflect upon it, establishing from experience that some thoughts left him sad and others left him happy. Little by little he came to unveil the difference between the spirits that bewildered him from within, one from the demon, the other one from God.[21] This was the first thought he had of the things of God; later, when he made the *Exercises*, he took light from this to understand the diversity of spirits.

9. From this lesson he obtained not a little light, and he began to think more ruminatively about his past life and about the great need he had to do penance for it. At this point the desire to imitate the saints came to him, and he had no thought for the particulars, promising only, with God's grace, to do as they had done. All he wanted to do was to go to Jerusalem as soon as he had healed, as mentioned above, performing all the disciplines and abstinences which a generous soul, inflamed by God, wants to do in its course.

10. And so, through these holy desires he began to forget the thoughts of the past, and they were confirmed by a vision in the following manner: One night while he was awake, he saw clearly an image of Our Lady with the holy child Jesus. From this sight he was heartened for a considerable time, and he was left with so much loathing for his whole past life and especially the things of the flesh that it seemed that all the images that were previously imprinted in his mind were removed from it. Thus from that hour until August 1553, when this was written, he never had the slightest inclination to the things of the flesh. For this reason the effect

may be considered the work of God, although he did not dare to claim this or to say more than to affirm the above. But his brother and the rest of the household knew from his exterior that a change had taken place inwardly in his soul.

11. Without caring for anything else he persevered in his reading and his good intentions, and he spent all his time in conversation with members of the household, speaking about the things of God, and in so doing he benefitted their souls. Taking great pleasure in those books, the idea came to him to excerpt in brief some of the more essential things from the life of Christ and the saints; so with great diligence—because he was now beginning to be up and about the house a bit—he set himself to write a book in a good hand, because he was a very fine penman, using red ink for the words of Christ, blue ink for those of Our Lady, and polished and lined paper. Part of his time was spent in writing and part in prayer. The greatest consolation he received was to look at the sky and the stars, which he did often for a long time, because as a result he felt within himself a very great desire to serve Our Lord. He often thought about his intention and wished to be healed completely now so he could take to the road.

12. Considering what he would do after he returned from Jerusalem, he thought to ask to enter the Carthusian house in Seville[22] so he could always live forever as a penitent; he would not say who he was so they would hold him in less esteem, and there he would eat nothing but herbs. But when he thought again of the penances he wished to do as he went about the world, the desire to enter the Carthusians cooled; he feared that he would not be able to give vent to the hatred that he had conceived against himself. Still he ordered one of the household servants who was going to Burgos to get information about the rule of the Carthusians,[23] and the news he obtained about it seemed good. But for the reason mentioned above, and because he was wholly absorbed in the journey he was soon planning to make, and because that matter did not have to be dealt with until his return, he stopped thinking about it so much. Finding now that he had some strength, it seemed to him that the time to depart had come, and he said to his brother, "Sir, the Duke of Nájera,[24] as you know, is aware that I am well. It will be good for me to go to Navarrete."[25] (The duke was there at that time. Trans.) His brother took him from one room to another and with many protestations begged him not to throw his life away and to consider what hopes others had placed in him and what he could become, and he advanced other similar arguments all with the purpose of dissuading him from his good intention. But he answered in such a way that, without departing from the truth, for he was now very scrupulous about that, he was able to soothe his brother.

2

The Pilgrim
(MARCH 1522)

13. Leaves Loyola. 14-15. The encounter with the Moor. 16-18.
Montserrat and journey to Manresa.

13. And thus he set out, riding on a mule. On the road he
persuaded his other brother (a priest, Pero López de Loyola. Trans.),
who wanted to accompany him as far as Oñate, to keep vigil with
him at Our Lady of Aránzazu. That night he prayed there for
renewed strength for the journey; he left his brother at Oñate at
the home of a sister he was going to visit (probably Magdalena, at
Anzoula. Trans.) and went on to Navarrete. There he remembered
a few ducats owed him at the Duke's household, and he thought it
would be a good idea to collect them; for this purpose he wrote a
bill to the treasurer. The treasurer said he had no money, but when
the Duke learned of it, he said they could be short of money for
everything else but that this should not be lacking for Loyola, whom
he wanted to give a position, if he wanted to take it, due to the
credit earned in the past. He collected the money and ordered it to
be distributed among certain persons to whom he felt certain obligations and a certain sum to be given for a statue of Our Lady that
was in poor condition, so that it would be restored and very well
adorned. And then saying goodbye to the two servants who had
come along with him from Navarrete, he set out alone on his mule
for Montserrat.

14. On this road something happened to him which it will be
good to write down, to understand how Our Lord dealt with this
soul, still so blind, though highly desirous of serving Him in every
way he knew. He felt such rejection for his past sins and such vivid
desire to carry out great things for the love of God, that, not even
considering if those sins had been forgiven, he would forget them,
blinded by the thought of the penances he was going to undertake.

Thus, no longer so interested in paying for his sins, but rather in pleasing and placating God, he decided to do great penances. When he remembered some penance that the saints had done, he determined to do the same and even more. From these thoughts he took all his consolation, not paying attention to interior matters, nor knowing what humility, charity, or patience were, nor the discernment to guide and measure these virtues, but all his attention was directed at doing these other great external works, for those were the works the saints had done for the glory of God, without consideration for any other particular circumstance.

15. Then, as he went on his way, a gentleman on a mule, a Moor, came up to him. As they went on talking together, they began to talk about Our Lady, and the Moor said it seemed all right to him that the Virgin had indeed conceived without a man, but he could not believe that she remained a virgin after giving birth, offering in support of this, the natural reasons that suggested themselves to him. The pilgrim, in spite of the many reasons he gave the Moor, could not dissuade him from this opinion. The Moor then went on ahead so rapidly that he lost sight of him, and he was left to think about what had happened with the Moor. Suddenly, various emotions came over him that caused discontent in his soul, as it seemed to him that he had not done his duty. This also aroused his indignation against the Moor, for he thought that he had done wrong in allowing a Moor to say such things about Our Lady and that he was obliged to defend her honor. And thus a desire came over him to go after the Moor and stab him with his dagger for what he had said. He struggled with his conflict of desires for a long time, doubtful as to what he must do. The Moor, who had gone on ahead, had told him that he was going to a place on the same road a little farther on, very near the highway, though the highway did not pass through the place.

16. Tired of examining what would be best to do and not finding any certainty as to what to do, he decided as follows: to let the mule go with the reins slack as far as the place where the road separated; if the mule took the town road, he would seek out the Moor and strike him; if the mule did not go toward the town but kept on the highway, he would let him be. So he did as he proposed. Although the town was little more than thirty or forty paces away, and the road to it was very broad and very good, Our Lord wished that the mule take the highway and not the town road. Coming to a large town before Montserrat, he wanted to buy there the clothing he had decided to wear when he went to Jerusalem. He bought cloth from which sacks were usually sewn, loosely woven and very prickly. Then he ordered a long garment reaching to his feet to be made from it. He bought a pilgram's staff and a small gourd and

put everything up front on the mule's saddle. He also bought a pair of coarse sandals, though he only wore one; this he did not do out of ceremony but because one leg was all bandaged up and sore; so much so that though he rode on horseback he found the leg all swollen at night; he thought this foot should wear a shoe.

17. He went on his way to Montserrat, thinking as he always did of the deeds he would do for the love of God. His mind was filled with ideas from books such as *Amadis of Gaul* and others like that; images and things alike came to his mind. Thus, he began a night watch before the altar of Our Lady of Montserrat, a vigil kept without sitting or going to bed; over his arms he sometimes stood and sometimes knelt. There and then he resolved to leave his clothing and dress himself in the armor of Christ. Leaving this place he walked on, thinking as usual of his intentions. When he reached Montserrat, he said a prayer and arranged for a confessor.[26] He made his general confession in writing, and this lasted three days. He arranged with the confessor to see that his mule was given away and that his sword and dagger were hung on the altar of Our Lady in the church.[27] This was the first man to whom he uncovered his intentions, for until then, he had not told any confessor.

18. In March of the year 1522, on the Eve of the Feast of Our Lady, he went at night secretly as could be, to strip himself of his garments, which he gave to a beggar; dressing himself in his desired clothing, he went to kneel before the altar of Our Lady. At times in this way, at other times standing, with his pilgrim's staff in hand, he spent the whole night. At daybreak he left, so as not to be recognized. He did not take the road that would lead him straight to Barcelona, where many would have recognized and honored him in meeting, but went off instead to the town called Manresa. For a few days he stayed in a hospital to note down some things in his book that he carefully carried with him, for it consoled him greatly.[28] Later, a league away from Montserrat, a man who had been hurrying after him caught up and asked him if he had given clothing to a beggar, as the beggar claimed. Answering that he had, tears ran from his eyes in sympathy and compassion for the beggar to whom he had given his clothes; he felt compassion, for he understood they were harassing him, thinking he had stolen the clothes. Even if he shunned public esteem, he had not been long in Manresa before people started to say great things about him because of what happened at Montserrat. Eventually the story was greater than the actual happening, telling of the wealth he had surrendered, and so on.

3

Manresa

(MARCH 1522 - EARLY 1523)

19-21. The diversity of Spirits. 22-25. Scruples. 26-33. The Trinity. 34. Illness. 35-37. Barcelona, where he prepares his journey to Italy.

19. At Manresa he would be begging alms every day. He did not eat meat nor drink wine, even if given to him. On Sundays he did not fast, and if they offered him some wine he would drink it. Since he had been very vain in taking care of his hair, as it was the fashion in those days, and he had a fine head of hair, he decided to let it grow without care, without combing or cutting or covering it with anything by night or day. For the same reason he let the nails of his toes and fingers grow, for he had been very vain in this matter too. While he lived at this hospital, it happened on many occasions on bright days that he would see something in the air near him, and this gave him great consolation, for it was very beautiful in a great way. He could not distinguish very clearly the kind of thing it was, but in some way it appeared to him to be shaped like a serpent, with many things shining like eyes, though they were not. He would take great pleasure and consolation on seeing this thing; the more he would see it, the more the consolation would grow; and when it would disappear, it would displease him.[29]

20. Up to this time he had remained always in an even inner state, with a great evenness of joy, not having any knowledge of inner spiritual matters. During the days that that vision lasted, or even just before it began (for it lasted many days), a powerful thought came to him that bothered him; it would vividly present to him the difficulty of his life, as if someone were writing on his soul: "How can you endure this life for the seventy years you have yet to live?" (In the belief that this came from the enemy) he answered inwardly with great strength to this: "O miserable creature! Can you promise me one single hour of life?" In this manner he over-

256

came the temptation and remained calm. This was the first temptation he experienced after what was said above. It happened as he was entering a church where he would go daily to hear Solemn Mass, Vespers, and Compline, all chanted, giving him great consolation; he would regularly read the Passion during Mass, following always an even spirit.

21. Soon after the said temptation he started to experience great changes in his soul. At times he felt so depressed he found no joy in prayer, nor Mass, nor in any other form of prayer he would try. But at other times he so experienced the opposite of this and to such high degree, that all sadness and desolation would seem to have disappeared, as one snatches a cape from another's shoulders. This began to frighten him, for he had never tasted such varieties before, and he began to talk to himself: "What new life is this that we are now beginning?" At this time he still conversed occasionally with spiritual people who had faith in him and wanted to talk to him, because, though he had no knowledge of spiritual matters, still, when he talked, he showed great fervor and a great will to forge ahead in the service of God. At that time there was at Manresa a woman,[30] gone in years, very old also in being God's servant, and known as such in many parts of Spain, so much so that the Catholic King had summoned her once to confide in her certain things. This woman speaking one day to the new soldier of Christ said, "O! May my Lord Jesus Christ wish to appear to you someday!" But he was frightened by this, taking the statement literally, and said, "How would Jesus Christ appear to me?" He kept persevering in his usual confession and communion each Sunday.

22. But then he began to experience many difficulties from scruples. For though the general confession he had made at Montserrat had been made with great care and all in writing, as has already been said, still at times it seemed to him that he had not confessed certain things, and this caused him great distress. He would then confess that, but he was never satisfied. He then began to search for some spiritual men who would cure him of these scruples, but to no avail. At last a very spiritual man, a Doctor of the Cathedral (Seo) who used to preach there, asked him one day in confession to write down everything he could remember. The pilgrim did so, but after confession the scruples still came back and each time in more fine detail, so that he was very troubled. Though he almost realized those scruples caused him much harm, that it would be good to remove them, he could not do that himself. Sometimes he thought it might cure him if his confessor would order him in the name of Christ never to confess any of the things of the past again, and he wished his confessor would direct him thus, but he dared not say so to his confessor.

23. His confessor ordered him not to confess anything from the past, without his saying so, unless it were something very clear. But since the pilgrim saw all those things as very clear, this command was of no use to him, and so he was always in trouble. At this time the pilgrim lodged in a small chamber that the Dominicans had given him in their monastery. There he kept a routine of seven hours daily of prayer on his knees, getting up always at midnight and following all the other exercises already mentioned. But he found no cure for his scruples in any of the above; many months had now passed since they had begun to trouble him. Once when he was very upset by them, he began to pray with such fervor that he began to shout out loud to God: "Help me, Lord, for I find no remedy in men, nor in any creature. If I thought I could find it, no labor would seem great. Show me, Lord, where to find it, for even if I had to follow a little dog to find the remedy, I would do it."

24. While lost in these thoughts, he often felt very strong temptations to throw himself through a large hole that was there in his room, next to the place where he was praying. But, knowing it was a sin to kill oneself, he would turn to shouting: "Lord, I will do nothing that will offend you," repeating these words many times, as well as the other ones. Then the story of a saint came to his mind, who, in order to get from God something he wanted very much, went without eating many days, till it was granted. While thinking about this a long time, he decided at last to do the same, telling himself that he would not eat or drink until God took care of him or he saw that death was indeed near; for if he saw he would reach that point of being near death if he did not eat, then he thought he would ask for bread and food (as if at that point he were able, indeed, to ask for it or eat it).

25. All this happened one Sunday after he had received Communion. He spent a whole week not putting anything in his mouth nor ceasing to do his usual exercises, even attending divine office and saying his prayers on his knees, even at midnight and so on. On the following Sunday he had to go to confession, and since he used to tell his confessor, in the smallest details, all he had done, he also told him how he had eaten nothing the whole week. The confessor ordered him to break off his fast; though he still felt strong, he obeyed the confessor, and for the duration of that day and the following one he felt free from scruples. But on the third day, a Tuesday, while at prayer, he began to remember his sins one by one, and like something unravelling he began to think out one sin after another in his past and felt he was required to confess them again. At the tail end of these thoughts disgust for the life he was leading and a desire to give it up came over him. At this time the Lord wished that he awake as if from a dream. From the les-

sons given him by God he had by now some experience of the diversity of spirits, and he began to look for the means by which that spirit had come to him. Thus he decided with great clarity not to confess anything from the past any more; and from that day on he became thus free from those scruples, feeling certain God had wanted to free him out of His mercy.

26. Besides his seven hours of prayer, he would engage in helping certain souls, who came there looking for him, in spiritual matters. Whatever of the day was left free, he would use it by thinking things about God, from what he had meditated upon or read that day. But as soon as he went to bed great enlightenment and spiritual consolation would come over him often, so that he lost much of the time meant for sleeping, which was not much. Wondering about these happenings at times, he thought to himself that he had assigned so much time for conversing with God plus he had the whole day, and so he began to doubt that this enlightenment came from the good spirit; he came to the conclusion that it would be better to ignore it and to sleep for the appointed time; and so he did.

27. He continued to abstain from eating meat and was so firm about this that he could not see giving it up for any reasons. One morning, after rising from bed, meat to be eaten appeared to him, as if he were seeing it with his own corporeal eyes, though he had felt no previous desire for it. He felt, at the same time, a firm assent of the will to eat it in the future. Though he remembered his earlier promise, he now had no doubt that he had to decide to eat meat. When, later on, he told his confessor, the confessor asked him to consider whether that was, perhaps, a temptation; but he, after careful examination, could never doubt about it.

God treated him at this time just as a teacher treats a child, by teaching him. Whether this was due to his dense and thick intelligence, or because he had no one else to teach him, or because of the strong determination God himself had given him to serve Him, he clearly believed, and he has always believed, that God treated him in this manner; and if he doubted this, he would be afraid he might offend His Divine Majesty. Some of this may be seen from the five following points:

28. *First*. He had a great devotion to the Most Holy Trinity;[31] thus, everyday he said a prayer to the three persons individually. He would then add one more to the Most Holy Trinity and so the thought came to him: Why did he say four prayers to the Trinity (when there were only Three Persons)? This thought, however, appeared to him to be a matter of little importance and gave him no difficulty. One day, while reciting the Hours of Our Lady on the steps of the same monastery, his understanding began to be

lifted up as if he were seeing the Most Holy Trinity in the shape of three musical keys. This was accompanied with so many tears and sobbings that he could not control himself. While going on a procession that set out from there that morning he could not control his tears up to the time of having lunch; after lunch he could not stop talking about the Most Holy Trinity, using many and diverse comparisons and with great consolation and joy; as a result, and for the rest of his life, he had this impressed in him: to feel great devotion while praying to the Most Holy Trinity.

29. *Second.* At another time it was made present to his understanding, with great spiritual joy, the manner in which God had created the world. It seemed that he saw something white, out of which some rays were coming, and that from this God was making light. But he did not know how to explain these things, nor did he remember well the spiritual illuminations which God impressed on his soul at that time.

Third. While at Manresa, where he stayed almost one year, after God began to comfort him and saw the fruit he brought out in helping souls, he gave up those extremes he formerly observed; he now cut his nails and hair. One day, in this town, when he was hearing Mass in the church of the monastery already mentioned, while the Body of the Lord was being raised, he saw with his inner eyes something like white rays coming down from above. Although he cannot explain this after so long a time, yet what he clearly perceived with his understanding was to see how Jesus Christ Our Lord was present in that Holy Sacrament.

Fourth. When he was at prayer, he often saw for a long time with his inner eyes the humanity of Christ. The shape that appeared to him was like a white body, not very large or very small, but he did not make out any distinction of members. He saw this many times at Manresa. If he said twenty or forty, he would not dare say it was a lie. He saw it another time at Jerusalem and again while on the road near Padua. He also saw Our Lady in similar form, without distinguishing the members. These things which he saw confirmed him then, and gave him thereafter such great confirmation of his faith that he often thought to himself: Even if there were no Scriptures to teach us these matters of faith, he would be determined to die for them merely because of what he saw.

30. *Fifth.* One time he went, following his devotion, to a church a little more than a mile from Manresa, which I believe was called St. Paul's.[32] The road ran next to the river. As he went along occupied with his devotions, he sat down for a while with his face toward the river, which there ran deep. As he sat, the eyes of his understanding began to open; not that he saw a vision, but (he came) to understand and know many things, matters spiritual and those

pertaining to faith and learning. This took place with such great clarity that everything appeared to him to be something new. And it happened to enlighten his understanding in such a manner that he thought of himself as if he were another man and that he had an intellect different from the one he had before. Though there were many, he could not set down the details of all he understood then, except by saying that he experienced a great clarity in his understanding; so much so that in the whole course of his life, through sixty-two years,[33] even if he put together all of the many gifts he had had from God and all of the many things he knew and added them all together, he does not think they would amount to as much as he had received on that one single occasion.

31. After this had lasted for a good while, he went to kneel before a nearby cross to give thanks to God. There the vision that so many times had appeared and that he had never been able to understand, namely, that thing mentioned above that appeared to him to be so beautiful, with many eyes (n. 19. Trans.), appeared again. But while kneeling before the cross he saw clearly that that thing did not have its usual beautiful color; then he had a very clear understanding and great confirmation of the will that that was the devil; later, often and for a long period of time it used to appear to him, but he, as a sign of contempt, would drive it away with a staff he used to carry in his hand.

32. Once, while he was ill at Manresa, a very severe fever brought him near death, and he wholly believed that his soul was about to leave him soon. At this time a thought kept coming to him telling him that he was a saint, but this caused him so much pain that he would try to reject it by placing before him all his past sins. He suffered more on account of this thought than of the fever itself; but could not completely reject such thought regardless of how much effort he put into it. But slightly relieved of the fever, he did not feel so close to death, and started to shout loudly to some ladies who had come to visit him that, for the love of God, the next time they saw him about to die, they should shout to him as loudly as possible, calling him a sinner and reminding him of the offenses he had committed against God.

33. Another time, while going from Valencia to Italy by sea, the rudder of his ship was broken in a terrible storm, and the situation reached such a point that in his judgment and that of many others who sailed on the ship, they could not by natural means escape death.[34] At this time, examining himself carefully and preparing to die, he was unable to be frightened by his sins or of being condemned, but he felt greatly humbled and sorrowful, as he believed he had not used well the gifts and graces which God our Lord had given him.

Another time, in the year 1550, he was very ill with a severe sickness which, in his opinion and that of many others, would be his last. At this time, thinking about death, he felt such joy and such spiritual consolation at having to die that he dissolved entirely with tears. This happened so often that he stopped thinking many times about death so as not to feel so much of that kind of consolation.

34. When winter (1522) came, he fell ill with a very severe sickness, and for his care the town put him in a house belonging to the father of one Ferrara, who was latter in the service of Baltasar de Faria. There he was treated with great attention, and many prominent ladies, out of devotion to him, came to watch over him by night. Though he recovered from this illness, he was still very weak and frequently suffered stomach pains. For these reasons and because the winter was very cold, they made him dress better and wear shoes and cover his head; they made him wear two brown doublets of very coarse cloth and a hat of the same stuff, a kind of beret. At this time there were many days when he was anxious to talk about spiritual matters and to find persons able to do so. Meanwhile, the time when he planned to set out for Jerusalem was approaching.[35]

35. Thus, at the beginning of the year 1523, he set out for Barcelona to take ship. Although various people offered to accompany him, he wanted to go alone, for his whole purpose was to have only God as his refuge. One day when some people were insisting that he ought to have a companion since he did not know either Italian or Latin, telling him how much this would help him and strongly praising the idea, he said that he would not go even in the company of the son or the brother of the Duke of Cardona,[36] because he wanted to practice three virtues: charity, faith, and hope. If he took a companion, he would expect help from him when he was hungry; if he fell down, he would expect to be helped to get up; and he would also trust him and would feel affection for him on this account; but he wanted to place that confidence, affection, and hope in God alone. What he said in this way, he felt in his heart. With these thoughts, he not only had the desire to set out alone but also to go without any provisions. When he began to bargain for his passage, he persuaded the master of the ship to carry him free, as he had no money, but on the condition that he brought to the ship some food to sustain himself; in no other way in the world would they take him aboard.

36. Great scruples came over him trying to negotiate his obtaining food. "Is this the hope and faith you have in God who would not fail you?" and so on. At last, not knowing what to do because he saw probable reasons on both sides, he decided to place himself in the hands of his confessor. He told him how much he

wanted to seek perfection and to do whatever would be more to the glory of God and the reasons that had caused him to question whether he ought to take with him any sustenance. The confessor decided that he should beg for what was necessary and take it with him. When he begged from a lady, she asked where he was sailing. He hesitated a bit whether he would tell her, but at last he resolved to say no more than that he was going to Italy and to Rome. Frightened, she said: "Do you want to go to Rome? Well, I don't know in what shape those who go there come back." (By this she meant that in Rome they profited little from the things of the spirit.) The reason why he didn't dare say that he was going to Jerusalem was for fear of vanity. This fear disturbed him so much that he never dared to say from what country he came or to what family he belonged. At last, having obtained some food, he went on board. Standing on the shore he found that he had five or six coins given him when he was begging from door to door (for he used to provide for his living that way); he left them on a bench that he found near the beach.

37. After being in Barcelona a little more than twenty days, he embarked. While still in Barcelona before setting sail, he sought out spiritual persons, as was his custom, for conversation, even though they lived in hermitages far from the city. But neither in Barcelona nor in Manresa during the whole time he was there did he find persons who could help him as much as he wished; only in Manresa that woman alone, mentioned above, who told him to ask God that Jesus Christ might appear to him, seemed to him to enter more deeply into spiritual matters. And so, after leaving Barcelona, he completely lost his eagerness to seek out spiritual persons.

4

Journey to Jerusalem

(MARCH-SEPTEMBER 1523)

38-39. Rome. 40-41. Journey to Venice. 42-43. Obtains free trip to Holy Land. 44-48. Visit to Jerusalem and return to Europe.

38. They had such a strong wind astern that they reached Gaeta from Barcelona in five days and nights, even though very frightened on account of the great storm. Through all that region there was fear of pestilence, but as soon as he disembarked, he set out on foot for Rome. From among those that had come on the ship, a mother and her daughter, who wore boy's clothes, and another young man joined him. These people joined him because they were also begging. When they arrived at a farm house, they found a large fire and many soldiers around it. These soldiers fed them with plenty of wine, urging them on as if they only wanted for them to warm up. Later they separated them, the mother and daughter being lodged in an upper room and the pilgrim and the young man in the stable. But at midnight he heard loud cries coming from upstairs; getting up to find out what was the matter, he found mother and daughter full of tears in the courtyard below, complaining that the soldiers had attempted to rape them. At hearing this, such a strong feeling came over the pilgrim that he began to shout: "Does this have to be tolerated?" and similar protests. He said this with such conviction that all those in the house were frightened, so much so that no one lay a hand on him. The young man had already fled; and though it was still night, all three continued their journey.

39. When they arrived at a nearby city, they found it closed. Unable to enter, the three of them spent the night in a damp church there. In the morning they were refused entrance to the city, and they found no alms outside, even though they went to a castle

which was nearby. There the pilgrim felt weak because of the hardship of the sea voyage as well as of the other trials and so on. Unable to travel farther, he stayed there. The mother and her daughter went on to Rome. That day many people came out of the city; learning that the lady who owned the land had also come out, he stood in front of her and told her that he was ill only from weakness and asked her to let him enter the city to seek some remedy. She readily granted it, and he began to beg in the city and obtained many *quatrini* (small coins). After resting there two days, he set out on his journey again and arrived at Rome on Palm Sunday.

40. There all who spoke to him, on discovering that he did not carry any money for the trip to Jerusalem, dissuaded him from making the trip, reasoning that it was impossible to find passage without money. But he was secure within his soul—which he couldn't doubt—that he would find a way to go to Jerusalem. After receiving the blessing of Pope Adrian VI, he then set out for Venice eight or nine days after Easter. He had six or seven ducats given to him for the passage from Venice to Jerusalem; he had accepted them somewhat overcome by the fears they had aroused that he would not be able to go in any other way. But two days after leaving Rome he began to realize that this was a lack of trust on his part, and it bothered him a good deal that he had accepted the ducats, so he thought it would be good to get rid of them. He finally decided to spend them generously on those whom he encountered, who usually were poor. He did so, and when he arrived at Venice, he had no more than a few *quatrini*, which he needed that night.

41. While on the journey to Venice he slept in doorways because of the preventions set against the pestilence. It happened once that when he got up in the morning, he collided with a man who, seeing what he saw, fled in great fear because he must have seemed very pale to him. Traveling in this way, he came to Chioggia with some companions who had joined him; he learned that they would not be allowed to enter Venice. As his companions decided to go to Padua to obtain a certificate of health there, he set out with them. But he could not travel very well, and they went on very rapidly, leaving him at nightfall in a large field. While he was there, Christ appeared to him in the manner in which He usually appeared to him, as we have mentioned above; this comforted him very much. Consoled in this way, the next morning, without forging a certificate as (I believe) his companions had done, he came to the gates of Padua and entered without the guards asking him for anything. The same thing happened when he left. This greatly astonished his companions who just came back from obtaining a certificate so they could go to Venice, but he did not care about it.

42. When they arrived at Venice, the guards came to the boat to examine everyone, one by one, as many as there were, but he was the only one they left alone. He sustained himself in Venice by begging, and he slept in St. Mark's Square. He never wanted to go to the house of the Emperor's Ambassador, nor did he take any special steps to seek what was needed for his passage. He had a great certainty in his soul that God would give him the means to go to Jerusalem; this strengthened him so much that no arguments or fears could cause him to doubt.

One day he met a rich Spaniard who asked him what he was doing and where he wanted to go. Learning his purpose, he took him home to lunch and kept him there a few days until his departure was arranged. Ever since Manresa the pilgrim had the habit when he ate with anyone not to speak at the table except to answer briefly; but he listened to what was said and noted some things which he took as an occasion to speak about God; and when the meal was finished, he did so.

43. For this reason the good man and all his household were so fond of him that they wanted him to stay and tried to keep him there. The host himself took him to meet the duke of Venice so he could speak to him—that is, he obtained entrance and an audience for him. When the duke heard the pilgrim, he ordered that he be given passage on the ship of the governors who were going to Cyprus.

Many pilgrims had come that year to go to Jerusalem, but most of them had returned to their own countries because of a recent event which had occurred: the fall of Rhodes. Even so, there were thirteen in the pilgrim ship which sailed first, and eight or nine remained for the governors' ship. As the ship was about to sail, a high fever came over our pilgrim, but, after treating him badly for a few days, it left him. The ship sailed on the day he took a laxative. The people of the house asked the doctor if he could embark for Jerusalem, and the doctor said that indeed he could embark, if he wanted to be buried there. He embarked and sailed that day. He vomited so much that he felt very relieved and began to recover completely. He severely condemned some public obscenities and indecencies that were done on the ship.

44. The Spaniards who were there warned him not to do so, because the ship's crew were planning to abandon him on some island. But Our Lord made it so that they should arrive quickly at Cyprus. Leaving the ship there (Famagusta), they went overland to another port called Las Salinas (Larnaca), ten leagues from there. They boarded the pilgrim ship, but he brought no more for his sustenance than his hope in God, as he had done on the other ship. During all this time our Lord appeared to him many times, giving

him great consolation and strength. It seemed to him that he saw something round and large, as though it were of gold, and this appeared to him after they left Cyprus before arriving at Jaffa. As they were journeying to Jerusalem on little donkeys, as was the custom, a Spaniard, a noble it would seem, named Diego Manes, two miles before reaching Jerusalem suggested with great devotion to all the pilgrims that since in a little while they would reach the place from which they could see the Holy City, it would be good for all to prepare their consciences and go in silence.

45. This seemed good to them all, and each one began to recollect himself. A short way before coming to the place from where they would see the city, they dismounted because they saw the friars with a cross waiting for them. Upon seeing the city the pilgrim felt within a warm wonder, which was common to them, as they later said, a joy which did not seem natural. He always felt this same devotion on his visits to the holy places.

His firm intent was to stay in Jerusalem to continue visiting the holy places, and in addition, to help souls. This is why he brought letters of recommendation for the guardian and gave them to him. He also told him of his intent to stay there where his calling was, but not the second part about wanting to help souls, because he had not spelled this out to anyone, though he had often spoken about the first part. The guardian answered that he did not see how he could stay there since his house was so poor it could not even support the friars; this was why some were to be sent back to (Europe) with the pilgrims. The pilgrim replied that he wanted nothing from the house, except only to confess at times and to be heard when he came to confess. The guardian of the house told him that that could be done except that he would have to wait until the provincial (the head, I think, of the order in that area) who was at Bethlehem, returned.

46. Assured with this promise, the pilgrim began to write letters to the spiritual people of Barcelona. Having already written one and while writing yet another on the eve of the departure of the pilgrims, he was summoned by the provincial, who had returned, and the guardian. The provincial told him with good manners that he knew of his good intent to remain in the holy places, that he had thought much on the matter, but because of his experience with others, it was his judgment that this would not be convenient. Many had had that desire, but some had been made prisoners, others killed, and the order was later coerced into ransoming the captives. Therefore, he should prepare to leave on the following day with the pilgrims. He replied that he was very firm in his resolve and could not imagine anything that would stop him from carrying it out. He let the provincial know that, even though he might not

approve, he would not abandon his intention out of any fear, unless it were a matter on which he could be forced under pain of sin. To this the provincial replied that they had authority from the Apostolic See to compel anyone whom they wished to leave or to remain there and to excommunicate anyone who did not wish to obey them and that in this matter they were determined that he should not remain, and so forth.

47. He wanted to show him the bulls giving them power to excommunicate, but he said he didn't need to see them, for he believed their reverences; inasmuch as they had decided with the authority they had, he would obey them. When this was over, he returned to where he was before. Since it was not Our Lord's will that he stay in those holy places, he felt a strong desire to visit Mount Olive again before leaving. There was a stone on Mount Olive from which Our Lord rose up to heaven, and His footprints were still seen there intact; this was what he wanted to see again. So without saying anything or taking a guide—for those who go without a Turk as guide invited trouble—he stole away from the others and went alone to Mount Olive. But the guards did not want to let him enter. He gave them a desk knife that he carried in a sack, and after saying his prayer with deep consolation, he felt the desire to go to Bethphage. While there, he remembered that he had not clearly noticed on Mount Olive in which direction the right foot was pointed, nor in what direction the left faced. Returning there, I believe he gave his scissors to the guards so they would let him enter.

48. When it was learned in the monastery that he had gone out without a guide, the friars took steps to find him. So, as he descended from Mount Olive, he met a "Christian of the belt" (that is, a Syrian Christian), who served in the monastery. He held a large staff and with a great show of annoyance made signs of striking him. When he came near him, he grabbed him firmly by the arm, but the pilgrim let himself be led easily. The good man, however, never let go. As he went along the road, held in such way by the "Christian of the belt," he felt greatly consoled by our Lord, and it seemed to him that he saw Christ as if hovering above him continually. This consolation lasted in great abundance all the way until they reached the monastery.

5

Return to Spain

(SEPTEMBER 1523 - EARLY 1524)

49. Venice. 50-53. Decides to return to Barcelona to study. At Ferrara he is imprisoned as a spy. He boards a ship for Barcelona.

49. They set out on the following day, and after coming to Cyprus, the pilgrims went off in different ships. There were in the port three or four ships bound for Venice. One was a Turkish ship, another was a very small boat, the third was a very rich and powerful ship belonging to a rich Venetian. Some pilgrims asked the master of this ship if he would please take the pilgrim; but on learning that he had no money, he refused, even though many pleaded, praising the pilgrim, and so on. The master of the ship answered that if the pilgrim were a saint, he could travel the way Saint James did, or something to that effect. These same begging friends were granted their request by the master of the small ship. They set out one day in the morning, but in the afternoon they came upon a storm, and the ships were scattered. The large ship was lost near the islands of Cyprus, and only the people were saved. The Turkish ship and all the people in it were lost in the same storm. The small ship went through great difficulties, but finally they landed in Apulia. This happened in the middle of winter, and it was very cold and snowing. The pilgrim had no other clothes than some breeches of coarse cloth that reached to the knee; his legs were left bare; he wore shoes and a long blouse of black cloth, opened by many slashes at the back, and a short doublet of thin hair.

50. He arrived in Venice in the middle of January of 1524, having been at sea from Cyprus the whole of November and December and part of January. In Venice one of the two men who had received him in his house before he set out for Jerusalem met him

and gave to him as alms fifteen or sixteen *giulii* (a little more than one and a half ducats) and a piece of cloth, which he folded over many times and wrapped about his stomach because of the great cold.

When the pilgrim realized that it was not God's will that he stay in Jerusalem, he continually thought to himself what path he ought to take. At last he leaned toward study for some time more, so he would be able to help souls, and he decided to turn to Barcelona. So he set out from Venice for Genoa. One day in Ferrara in the principal church, while at his devotions, a poor man asked him for alms, and he handed him a *marchetto*, which is a coin worth five or six *quatrini*. After that another man came, and he gave him another small coin that he had, somewhat of greater worth, and a third man he gave a *giulio*, as he had nothing but *giulii*. The poor people, seeing him giving alms, kept on coming until everything he had was gone. Finally, many poor people came together to beg for alms. He asked them for their forgiveness, as he had nothing left.

51. Thus he left Ferrara for Genoa. On the road he met with Spanish soldiers who treated him well that night, though they were much amazed that he walked that road, because it required passing through almost the middle of both armies, the French and the Imperial (Spanish).[37] They asked him to leave the main road and take safely to the one they pointed out to him. But he did not follow their advice. Instead, walking on the main road, he came upon a burned and destroyed village, and until nighttime he found no one to give him anything to eat. But when the sun went down, he came to a walled place where the guards immediately seized him, taking him for a spy. They put him in a small house beside the gate and began to question him, as is the way when a person is suspected; but he replied to all their questions that he knew nothing. They stripped him and search him down to his shoes and every part of his body to see if he was carrying any letters. Unable to learn a thing by any means, they bound him in order to take him to the captain, for he would make him talk. The pilgrim asked them to take him clothed in his doublet, but they refused to give it to him and took him in his breeches and long shirt (mentioned above).

52. On the way the pilgrim saw a kind of representation of Christ being led away, but this was not a vision like the others. He was taken though three main streets, and he went with joy and contentment instead of sadness. It was his way to speak to any person, regardless of who he might be, using the devotional *vos*, instead of the familiar *tu*, holding to the devotion that Christ and his apostles had spoken in this way and so forth. As he walked through the streets, the thought came to his mind, put there by the fear of tortures that would be inflicted on him, that it would be

wise to give up that custom in this situation and to speak in more formal ways to the captain. But he realized this thought was a temptation. "Since it is such," he said, "I will not speak formally to him, nor will I show him reverence, nor will I take off my cap."

53. They reached the captain's palace and left him in one of the lower rooms. Much later the captain spoke to him. Without showing any shade of courtesy, he answered in a few words with an exaggerated pause between one word and the next. The captain took him for a madman and said this to those who had brought him: "This man has no brains. Give him his things and throw him out." Leaving the palace, he soon met a Spaniard who lived there; he took him to his house and gave him something for breakfast, and all he needed was taken care of for that night. Setting out in the morning, he traveled until evening, when two soldiers in a tower saw him and climbed down to seize him. They took him to their captain, who was French; the captain asked him, among other things, from what country he came, and learning that he was from Guipúzcoa, he answered him, "I come from near there," apparently from near Bayonne. Then he said, "Take him and give him something to eat and treat him well." On the road from Ferrara to Genoa many other small things happened. At last he reached Genoa, where a Vizcayan named Portundo, who had spoken with him on other occasions when he served in the court of the Catholic king, recognized him. This man got him passage on a ship sailing for Barcelona, which ran great danger of being captured by Andrea Doria,[38] who was then in the French service, and who gave the ship pursuit.

6

Studies at Barcelona and Alcalá

(LENT 1524 - JUNE 1527)

54-55. Studies at Barcelona. 56-57. Studies at Alcalá. 58-59.
Gives the Exercises. First difficulties with the Inquisition. 60-62.
Jail. 63. Leaves Alcalá for Valladolid and Salamanca.

54. On arrival at Barcelona he made known his wish to study
to Isabel Roser and to Master Ardevol, who was a teacher of grammar. Both agreed this was a good idea; he (Ardevol) agreed to
teach for free, and she offered whatever was necessary for his
support. The pilgrim had known a friar at Manresa, of the Order
of Saint Bernard, I think, who was a very spiritual man and with
whom he wanted to stay in order to learn, to be able to dedicate
himself to the things of the spirit, and even to help other souls.
Thus he answered (both friends) that he would accept the offer if
he did not find at Manresa the comfort he hoped for. But when he
want there (Manresa), he found out the friar had died, and so,
upon returning to Barcelona, he set himself to study with great
diligence. One thing, though, became a great impediment: this was
that as soon as he would start to recite aloud, as it is necessary at
the beginnings of grammar, new understandings and flavors of spiritual matters would come to him, and this would happen with such
abundance that he was not able to recite or dismiss those spiritual
pleasures, as hard as he tried.

55. So as he thought about this, he would say to himself, "Not
even when I pray nor when I am at mass do such vivid lights come."
Thus, slowly he came to realize this to be a temptation. After
finishing his prayer, he went to Santa María del Mar,[39] near the
master's house, since he had asked him please to listen to him for a
while in that church. So, when they were seated, he told him faithfully everything that passed through his soul and what little prog-

272

ress he had made so far on account of it; but he made a promise to his master saying, "I promise never to fail to hear your lessons for the next two years, so long as I can find bread and water in Barcelona to support myself." And since he spoke this promise with great strength, he never again had those temptations. The stomach pain which he had suffered at Manresa, for which reason he wore shoes, left him, and his stomach felt well since he set out for Jerusalem. For this reason, while he was studying at Barcelona, he felt the desire to resume his former penances; and so he began by making a hole in the soles of his shoes. He went on widening it little by little so that when the cold of winter came, he had only the upper piece of his shoes left.

56. After two years of study, during which he was told he had made great progress, his master informed him he could now study arts and should go to Alcalá. Still, he had a doctor of theology examine him, and he gave him similar advice. So he set out all alone for Alcalá, although as I believe, he already had some companions. When he arrived at Alcalá, he began to beg and to live on alms. After he lived in this fashion for ten or twelve days, a cleric and others who accompanied him, seeing him beg alms, began to laugh at him and insult him, as one usually does to those who, being healthy, go about begging. At this moment the man who had charge of the new hospital of Antezana passed them by and apologized for the others. He called him and took him to the hospital, where he gave him a room with all he needed.

57. As he arrived at Barcelona during Lent in 1524 and studied there two years, he thus arrived at Alcalá in the year 1526, and he studied there almost a year and a half. He studied the logic of Soto, the physics of Albert, and the Master of the Sentences.[40] While at Alcalá he was busy giving spiritual exercises and teaching Christian doctrine and in so doing did some good to others for the glory of God. There were many persons who came to a great knowledge and delight in spiritual things; but others had a variety of temptations, such as the one who wanted to scourge himself but could not do so, as if someone were holding back his hand, and other similar cases. (I remember the fear he himself felt one night.) This gave rise to gossip among the people, especially because of the great crowd that gathered wherever he was instructing. Soon after he arrived at Alcalá, he became acquainted with Don Diego de Eguía[41] who lived in the house of his brother, who had a printing shop in Alcalá and was well-to-do. They helped him with alms to feed the poor and kept the pilgrim's three companions in his house. Once, when he came to ask alms for some necessities, Don Diego told him that he had no money, but he opened a chest in which he held various objects and gave him bed coverings of differ-

ent colors and candlesticks and other similar things, all wrapped inside a sheet. The pilgrim put them on his shoulders and went off to help the poor.

58. As mentioned above, there was much gossip throughout the entire region about the things happening at Alcalá: one person spoke one thing, another something else. The rumor reached the inquisitors at Toledo. When they came to Alcalá, the pilgrim was warned by their host, who told him that his companions were being called "sack wearers" and, I believe, "illumined ones" (*alumbrados*), and that they would make mincemeat of them. So the inquisitors began then to carry out their investigation and inquiry into their life; but at last they went back to Toledo without summoning them, though they had come for that reason alone. They left the trial to the vicar Figueroa (he is now with the Emperor). A few days later he summoned them and told them of how an investigation and inquiry into their life had been made by the inquisitors and that no error had been found in their teaching nor in their life, and therefore, they could do as they had been doing without any impediment. But since they were not of any religious order, it did not seem right for them all to wear the same habit. He commanded them that it would be better if two of them, the pilgrim and Arteaga, were to dye their clothing black, and if the other two, Calixto and Cáceres, were to dye their clothing brown; Juanico, a young Frenchman, could remain as he was.[42]

59. The pilgrim said that they would do as they were ordered. "But," he said, "I do not know what benefit these inquisitions provide; the other day a priest did not want to give the Sacrament to one of us because we take communion every eight days, and they have caused me difficulty too. We would like to know if they have found any heresy in us." "No," said Figueroa, "for if they had, they would have burned you." "They would also burn you," said the pilgrim, "if they found heresy in you." They dyed their clothes, as they had been ordered, and fifteen or twenty days later, Figueroa ordered the pilgrim not to go barefoot but to wear shoes. He did so quietly, as he did all other matters of this sort when ordered.

Four months after, Figueroa himself again began an investigation of them. Besides the usual reasons, I believe, as Bustamante told me, there was also the instance of a married woman of quality who had a special devotion for the pilgrim. In order not to be seen, she came to the hospital in the morning twilight, wearing a veil, as is the custom in Alcalá de Henares. On entering she removed her veil and went to the pilgrim's room. But they did nothing to them this time, nor did they summon them after the investigation had been ended, nor did they say a thing to them.[43]

60. Four months after that, when he was living in a small hut outside the hospital, a policeman came to his door one day and

called him, saying, "Come with me a while." He put him in jail
and said to him: "You may not leave here till you are ordered to do
otherwise." This was in the summer, and as he was not caged,
many people came to visit him. He did the same things as when he
was free, teaching Christian doctrine and giving the exercises.
Although many offered their services, he did not want to have an
advocate or an attorney. He well remembered Doña Teresa de
Cárdenas, who sent somebody to visit him and frequently offered
him a way out of jail, but he accepted nothing, always answering,
"He, for whose love I entered here, will get me out, if he so pleases."

61. He was in prison for seventeen days without being examined or told why he was there. At the end of that time Figueroa
came to the jail and examined him on many things, even asking
him if he observed the sabbath, and whether he knew two particular women, a mother and her daughter. To this he answered yes.
(Figueroa then asked) whether he had known of their departure
before they had set out. By the oath he had sworn, he replied no.
The vicar then placed his hand on his shoulder with a show of
pleasure and said to him: "This was the reason why you were
brought here." Among the many people who followed the pilgrim
there were a mother and her daughter, both widowed. The daughter was very young and very attractive. They had entered deeply
into the spirit, especially the daughter. Although they were noble
women, they had gone to the Verónica of Jaen alone and on foot,
although I do not know if they went begging. This caused considerable gossip in Alcalá, and Doctor Ciruelo, who had some responsibility for them, though that the prisoner had persuaded them, and for
this reason, had him arrested. Having heard what the vicar said,
the prisoner said to him: "Would you like me to speak a little more
about this affair?" He said, "Yes." "Then you should know," said
the prisoner, "that these two women have often repeated to me
their desire to go about the world serving the poor from one hospital to another. I have always dissuaded them from this idea, because
the daughter is so young and attractive and so forth, and I have
told them that when they wanted to visit the poor, they could do so
in Alcalá and could accompany the most Holy Sacrament." When
this conversation was finished, Figueroa left with his notary, who
had taken all this down in writing.

62. At this time Calixto was in Segovia; learning of the pilgrim's imprisonment, he came at once, though he had recently
recovered from a grave illness, and he went into the jail with him.
But the pilgrim told him it would be better to present himself to
the vicar, who treated him kindly and told him he was going to
order him put in jail. He would have to stay there until those women
returned to see whether their story agreed with his. Calixto stayed
in jail a few days, but when the pilgrim saw that this was hampering

his health, because he was still not wholly recovered, he had him let go through the help of a doctor, a very good friend of his.

From the day the pilgrim entered jail until the day they let him out, forty-two days passed. At the end of that time, as the two devout women returned, the notary came to the jail to read the sentence: he was to be set free, but they all should dress just like the other students and should not speak of matters of faith until studying four more years, because they had no learning. For in truth, the pilgrim was the one who knew the most, though his learning had no formal training. This was the first thing he used to say whenever they examined him.

63. This sentence left him somewhat doubtful of what he should do, since it seemed they were closing the door through which he could help souls, without any reason being given except that he had not studied. At last he decided to go to Fonseca, the archbishop of Toledo, and put the case into his hands.

He set out from Alcalá and found the archbishop in Valladolid. Faithfully recounting the affair, he said that even though he was not in his jurisdiction now nor obliged to abide by the sentence, he would still heed whatever was asked him; (he used the reverential pronoun in speaking to him, as he did with everyone else). The archbishop received him very well, and understanding that he wanted to go to Salamanca, he told him that he also had friends and a college in Salamanca[44] and offered him everything, and then, as he was leaving, he handed him four *escudos*.

7

Difficulties at Salamanca

(JULY - LATE 1527)

64-66. Arrives at Salamanca and is at once questioned by the Dominican Fathers. 67-70. Goes to jail and is left free on certain conditions. 71-72. Decides to leave for Paris.

64. After arriving at Salamanca, and as he was praying in a church, he was recognized by a devout woman who belonged to the group, for his four companions had already been there several days. She asked him his name and then took him over to the lodgings of his companions. When at Alcalá they passed sentence that they should all wear the dress of students, the pilgrim had said, "When you ordered us to dye our clothes, we did so; but now we cannot do it, for we have no money to buy our clothes." So the vicar himself provided them with clothes and caps and everything else the students wear. Dressed in this manner, they had left Alcalá.

At Salamanca he had as a confessor a Dominican friar at Saint Esteban. Ten or twelve days after his arrival the confessor told him, "The fathers of the house would like to speak with you." The pilgrim answered, "In the name of God." "Then," the confessor continued, "it would be good if you would come here to eat on Sunday; but I warn you of one thing: they will want to know many things about you." Thus on Sunday he arrived with Calixto. After lunch the subprior, in the absence of the prior, with his confessor who was present and, I believe, another friar, took them to the chapel. With great kindness the subprior began to speak of the good reports they had heard of their life and customs—that they went about preaching in an apostolic manner—and that they would be pleased to learn of these things with greater detail. So he began to ask them what they had studied. The pilgrim replied, "Of all of us, I am the one who has studied the most," and he gave a clear account of the little he had studied and of the poor foundation of those studies.

65. "Well, then, what do you preach?" they were asked.

"We do not preach," said the pilgrim, "but we do speak privately with some people about the things of God; for example, after eating with some people who may invite us."

"But," said the friar, "what things of God do you talk about? That is what we would like to know."

"We speak," said the pilgrim, "at times about one virtue, others about another, and this we praise; at times about one vice, others about another, and this we condemn."

"You are not educated men," said the friar, "and you speak about virtues and vices; no one can speak about these except in one of two ways: either through education or through the Holy Spirit. If not through education, then through the Holy Spirit. And we wanted to know that what you do is from the Holy Spirit." Here the pilgrim was a bit beside himself because that kind of argument did not seem correct to him. After staying silent a while, he said it was not necessary to speak further of these things. The friar insisted: "Well, now that there are so many errors of Erasmus and of so many others who have deceived the world, don't you wish to explain what you say?"[45]

66. The pilgrim said, "Father, I will say no more than I have said except before my superiors who can oblige me to do so." Before this the friar had asked why Calixto came dressed as he was; he wore a short sack and a large hat upon his head, with a staff in his hand and boots almost halfway up his leg. As he was very big, he seemed even more deformed. The pilgrim related how they had been imprisoned in Alcalá and had been ordered to dress like students and that his companion, because of the great heat, had given his long gown to a poor cleric. Here the friar, speaking through his teeth, giving signs that he was displeased, said, "Charity begins at home."

Now returning to the story, the subprior, unable to draw any other word out of the pilgrim, said, "Well, then, remain here, for we will easily make you tell all." Then all the friars left with some haste. The pilgrim first asked if they wanted them to stay in that chapel, or where it was they wanted them to stay. The subprior answered that they should remain in the chapel. The friars then ordered all the doors closed and, it seems, negotiated the affair with the judges. Still the two of them were there in the monastery for three days, eating in the refectory with the friars, though nothing was heard from the court. Their room was almost always full of friars who came to see them. The pilgrim always spoke of his favorite subject; as a result, there was already some division among the friars, for many of them showed that they had been interiorly touched.

67. At the end of three days a notary came and took them to jail. They did not put them down below with the criminals but in an upper room, which, because it was so old and unused, was very dirty. They were both bound with the same chain, each by his foot. The chain was hooked to a post in the center of the room and was ten or thirteen palms long. Each time that one wanted to do something, the other had to keep him company. All that night they kept vigil. The next day, when their imprisonment became known in the town, people sent them something on which to sleep in jail and, in abundance, most of what they needed. Many people came again and again to visit them, and the pilgrim continued his exercises, speaking about God and so on.

Bachelor Frías[46] came to examine each of them separately, and the pilgrim gave him all his papers, which were the *Exercises*, so they could examine them. Asked if they had companions, they said they did and told him where they were. On the bachelor's orders they went looking for them and brought Cáceres and Arteaga to jail, but they left Juanico, who later became a friar. But they were not put above with the other two, rather down below where the common prisoners were housed. Here, too, he did not want to have an advocate or attorney.

68. A few days later he was summoned before four judges, the three doctors: Sanctisidoro, Paravinhas, and Frías, and the fourth was bachelor Frías. All of them now had seen the *Exercises*. Here they asked him many things not only concerning the *Exercises*, but also theology; for example, about the Trinity and the Sacrament and how he understood these articles. First he made his speech and yet, commanded by the judges, he spoke further in such a manner that they had no reason to condemn him. Bachelor Frias, who had always intervened in these matters more than the others, also asked him about a case in canon law. He was required to answer everything, but he always said first that he did not know what scholars said about those matters. Then they commanded him to explain the first commandment the way he usually explained it. He started to do so and said so many things for so long about the first commandment that they had no desire to ask him more. Before this, when they spoke about the *Exercises*, they insisted a good deal about one point only, which was at the beginning: when a thought is a venial sin, and when it is mortal. The reason was that he, though uneducated, was deciding upon this. He answered, "If this is true or not, resolve it now; and if it is not true, condemn it." But in the end they left without condemning anything.

69. Among the many who came to talk to him in jail, Don Francisco de Mendoza, who is now Cardinal of Burgos, came one time with bachelor Frías. In a concerned manner he asked him

how he was doing in prison and if it bothered him to be a prisoner. He replied, "I will answer what I answered today to a lady who, upon seeing me in prison, spoke words of compassion. I said to her, 'By this you show you do not wish to be imprisoned for the love of God. Does imprisonment seem to be such a great evil to you? Well, I will tell you that there are not enough grills and chains in Salamanca that I would not wish for more, for the love of God.'"

At this time it happened that all the prisoners in the jail fled, but the two companions who were with them did not. In the morning when they were found there alone without anyone, with the doors open, everyone was deeply edified, and there was much talk in the city; so they were then given an entire palace nearby as their prison.

70. After twenty-two days of imprisonment, they were summoned to hear the sentence, which was that no error was found in either their life or teaching. Thus, they could do as they had been doing before, teaching Christian doctrine and speaking about the things of God, so long as they never defined that "this is a mortal sin or this is a venial sin," until they had studied four more years. After the sentence was read, the judges displayed great kindness, as they wanted it to be accepted. The pilgrim said he would do everything the sentence ordered, but that he could not accept it, because, without condemning him for anything, they shut his mouth so he could not help others insofar as he was able. Despite Doctor Frías' insistence, and showing himself to be very touched, the pilgrim said only that as long as he were in the jurisdiction of Salamanca, he would do what had been ordered. Then they were set free from jail, and he began to commend himself to God and to think of what he ought to do. He found great difficulty in remaining in Salamanca, for in the matter of helping souls, it seemed to him that the door had been closed by this prohibition not to define mortal and venial sin.

71. So he decided to go to Paris to study.

When the pilgrim, at Barcelona, was considering whether he should study and how much, his entire concern was whether after those studies he should enter religion or go thus about the world. When thoughts of entering religion came to him, then he also had the desire to enter a decadent and poorly reformed order so that he would enter religion in order to suffer more. He also thought that perhaps God would help those around him. God gave him, then, great confidence that he would suffer easily all the insults and injuries they could do him.

Now at the time of his imprisonment in Salamanca the same desire that he held, to help souls, and for which he should first study and gather others together in one and the same goal and keep those he had, did not fail him. Determined as he was to go to Paris, he arranged with his companions to wait there while he went to see if he could find some means by which they could all study.

72. Many important persons strongly insisted that he should not leave, but they could never dissuade him from going. Fifteen or twenty days after he got out of prison, he set out alone, taking some books, on a small donkey. When he arrived at Barcelona all those who knew him tried to dissuade him from the journey to France because of the great wars there, recounting many specific examples, even telling him that they put Spaniards on roasting spits, but he never felt the least sense of fear.

8

The University of Paris
(FEBRUARY 1528 - MARCH 1535)

73-75. Studies Humanities at Salamanca. 76. Goes to England. 77-78. Disciples. 79-80. First companions of Ignatius. 81. He is denounced to the Inquisition. 82-84. Higher Studies. More companions. 85. The vow at Montmartre. 86. Before leaving for Spain to recover he visits the Inquisitor General and on his request he gives him a copy of the *Exercises.*

73. And so he set out for Paris, alone and on foot. He reached Paris in or about the month of February, and as he said to me, this happened in the year 1528 or 1527.[47] (When he was in jail, at Alcalá, the Prince of Spain was born [Felipe II, Valladolid, May 21, 1527. Trans.] From this it is easy to set the dates, including the past.) He lodged in a house with several Spaniards and attended humanities at Montaigu.[48] The reason for doing this was that since they had made him advance in his studies too quickly, he was found to be too weak in the fundamentals. He sat with the children for his studies following the order and manner of Paris.

As soon as he arrived in Paris, a merchant gave him twenty-five *escudos* for a bill of exchange from Barcelona; this sum he gave to one of the Spaniards in his lodgings for safe keeping, but in a short time the Spaniard spent the money and had nothing to pay him with. So, after Lent, the pilgrim had no money left, either because he had spent his own or because of the above-mentioned reason. Thus he was forced to beg for alms and even leave the house where he was lodging.

74. He was received into the hospital of Saint Jacques, far beyond the church of the Innocents. This made it very inconvenient

for his studies, since the hospital was a long distance from the College of Montaigu, and it was required to arrive at the sound of the "Ave Maria" in order to find the door open and leave with daylight; in this manner he could not attend his classes very regularly. Another difficulty came from the fact that he had to beg for alms to feed himself. For almost four or five years now, he had had no stomach pains, and so he started to subject himself to greater penances and abstinences. Having spent some time in this way of life at the hospital and begging and noticing he made little progress in his studies, he began to wonder what he should do. He discovered that some students served professors at the Colleges and thus made time to study, and so he decided to find a master.

75. He would make this consideration and determination within himself and would find consolation in it. He would imagine that the master would be Christ, one of the students he would name Saint Peter, another Saint John, and so with each one of the Apostles; "When the master would command me I will think Christ commands me; when someone else, I will think Saint Peter commands me." He tried very hard to find a master; he spoke first to Bachellor Castro,[49] then to a Carthusian friar who knew many professors and to several others, but they never succeeded in finding him a master.

76. Finally, having found no solution, a Spanish friar one day suggested to him it would be better for him to spend two months, or even less, and go to Flanders every year so he could bring back enough to feed himself the whole year round; this suggestion, after commending it to God, appeared to him to be a good one. Once he went to England and brought back more alms than he used to in the previous years.[50]

77. The first time he returned from Flanders he began to dedicate himself more intensely to spiritual conversations and would give the *Exercises* almost simultaneously to three different people, namely: Peralta, Bachellor Castro, who was at the Sorbonne, and Amador, a Basque from the Province of Vizcay who was at Saint-Barbe. These people underwent great changes; they gave all they had to the poor, even their books; they went about seeking alms through Paris and went to lodge at the hospital of Saint Jacques, where the pilgrim had stayed before but had now left for the reasons mentioned above. This created annoyance at the University, for the first two people were very distinguished and very well-known. The Spaniards, besides, started to attack the two masters, but not being able to claim victory over them through many reasons and arguments so that they would return to the University, many of them, one day, went with weapons and took the masters away from the hospital.

78. Upon being forced back to the University the two masters came to the following decision: They would carry out their plans as soon as they had finished their studies. Bachellor Castro returned later to Spain and preached for a while at Burgos; then he became a Carthusian friar at Valencia. Peralta left for Jerusalem on foot as a pilgrim. In this manner he was taken in by a relative of his, a captain, who had the means to take him to the Pope and have him order Peralta to return to Spain. These things did not happen immediately but several years later.

Great gossip arose in Paris, especially among the Spaniards, against the pilgrim. Even our Master Govea said that he had caused Amador, who attended his College, to go mad. He decided and so he promised that the first time the pilgrim would show his face at Saint-Barbe he would order the pilgrim to be caned as a seducer of students.

79. A Spaniard, who had spent (the pilgrim's) money and not paid it back and with whom he stayed at the beginning, left for Spain by way of Rouan, and while waiting to board at Rouan, he fell ill. The pilgrim found out about his sickness through a letter he wrote, and felt the desire to visit him and help him. He thought also that under such conditions he could win him over to leave the world and surrender completely to the service of God.

(The original text of the *Autobiography* continues in Italian.)

To gain this end he felt the desire to walk the twenty-eight leagues from Paris to Rouan on bare feet, not eating or drinking. As he prayed over all this, he felt very fearful. Finally he went to St. Dominic's Church, and there he resolved to walk as described above, for he had overcome that great fear he felt of tempting God.

On the morning he had to leave he got up early, but as he started to dress he felt so fearful that he almost thought he could not finish getting dressed. In spite of that fear he left the house and the city even before dawn. In spite of this the fear always remained and stayed with him as far as Argenteuil, a town three leagues from Paris on the way to Rouan, where, it is said, the garments of Our Lord are being kept. He left the town with that spiritual fear, but as he climbed up a small hill, the fear left him, and he felt instead a great consolation and spiritual vigor. He felt such intense joy that he started shouting through those fields and speaking with God and so on. He walked that day fourteen leagues and shared the night with a poor beggar in a hospital. The next day he spent the night in a barn and on the third day he arrived at Rouan. All this time he had remained without eating or drinking and barefoot, as he had resolved. In Rouan he consoled the sick man and was of help in finding him a passage on a ship for Spain. He gave him letters recommending him to his companions who were then at Salamanca, i.e., Calixto, Cáceres and Arteaga.

80. So as not to speak further of his companions this was their end: While the pilgrim was in Paris he used to write to them frequently, as they had agreed, explaining to them how few were the facilities to make them come to Paris to study. This notwithstanding, he ingeniously found a way to write to Dona Leonor Mascarenhas, asking her to help Calixto by giving him letters of introduction to the Court of the King of Portugal, so he could obtain one of the scholarships the King of Portugal gave to study in Paris. Dona Leonor gave Calixto the letters of introduction and a mule for the journey plus some money for expenses. Calixto went to the Court of Portugal, but in the end he did not go to Paris. Upon returning to Spain he left for the India of the Emperor with a certain spiritual woman. He returned to Spain later on, but again he took off for the same India and then returned to Spain a rich man to the astonishment of all those who had known him earlier on in Salamanca.

Cáceres returned to Segovia, his native place, but there he began to live in such manner that he seemed to have forgotten his original intention.

Arteaga was named *Comendador*. Later on, when the Society was already in Rome, he was given a bishopric in the Indies. He wrote the pilgrim, asking him that it be given to someone in the Company. He was answered negatively and left for the India of the Emperor a bishop. There he died in a strange accident. While he was ill, he had by his bedside two glasses to refresh him, one with water prescribed by the doctor, the other with *soliman* water, a poison. They gave him the latter by mistake, and it killed him.

81. The pilgrim returned from Rouan to Paris. He found out that on account of what had happened with Castro and Peralta, people were talking greatly against him and that the Inquisitor had summoned him. He did not want to wait and went to the Inquisitor directly, saying he had heard he was looking for him, and that he was ready for anything he wanted, only that would he, please, hurry it all up for he had intention to enter the art's course on St. Remy's day of that year (October 1, 1529. Trans.), and would like all this to be over before that so that he could devote himself to his studies better. (The Inquisitor was named Our Master Orí, a Dominican friar.) But the Inquisitor did not call him back, but only confirmed the truth that others had spoken to him about his doings and so on.

82. A short time after this the feast of St. Remy came, at the beginning of October. He started the course on arts under Master Juan Pena, and started with the resolution to keep those who had decided to serve the Lord but avoid searching for new ones, so that he could study more easily.

As he began to listen to the lectures of the course, those same temptations he had experienced when studying grammar at Barcelona[51] started to come to him. Every time he would listen to the lecture, he could not pay attention on account of the many spiritual things that came to him. Seeing that in this manner he was making little progress in his studies, he went to his teacher and promised him he would not fail to hear the whole course as long as he were able to find bread and water to sustain himself. As soon as he made this promise, all those devotions that would come to him at the wrong time left him, and he was able to continue his studies peacefully. At this time he was holding conversations with Masters Peter Favre and Francis Xavier, whom he later won for the service of God through the *Exercises*.

While following this course, he was not persecuted as before. On this point Doctor Frago once told him he was amazed they left him alone, without anyone giving him trouble. And he answered, "The reason is that I do not speak to anyone about the things of God, but on finishing the course, we will go back to the usual."

83. While the two were speaking together, a friar joined them, asking Dr. Frago to find him a home, for where he was staying at present many had died, and he thought they had died of the plague, which was then spreading through Paris. Dr. Frago and the pilgrim wanted to see the house and took along a woman who understood much about this. When she entered the house, she confirmed it was the plague. The pilgrim wanted to enter too, and finding a sick person, he consoled him by touching the sore on his hand. After consoling and lifting his spirits, the pilgrim left alone, and his hand began to hurt, and he thought he had caught the plague. This imagination was so strong he could not overcome it. Finally, with great impetus he thrust his hand in his mouth, moving it about inside many times, saying: "If you have the plague in the hand, have it also in the mouth." This done, the imagination, as well as the pain in the hand, left him.

84. On returning to the College of Saint-Barbe where he then lodged and attended the course, those in the College who knew that he had entered the house with the plague fled from him and would not let him enter. Thus he was forced to live outside for a few days.

It is a Paris custom for those who study arts that on the third year in order to receive the Bachelor's Degree, they must take a stone (an examination. Trans.), as they call it, but since this would cost one *escudo*, some very poor students could not take it. The pilgrim began to doubt whether it would be good for him to take it. Finding himself full of doubts and unresolved, he decided to place the whole matter in the hands of his teacher. He advised him to take it, which he did. This notwithstanding, some critics appeared; at least one Spaniard mentioned it.

During this time, while at Paris, he was very sick in his stomach, with pains every fifteen days, lasting as long as an hour and causing fever. Once the pain lasted sixteen or seventeen hours. This illness continued getting worse; he was unable to find any remedy for it even when many were tried, but at this time he passed his course on arts, studied theology for several years, and gathered his companions.[52]

85. The doctors agreed that there was no remedy left but to try his native air. His companions, besides, advised him to do the same and insisted upon it. At this time, they all had decided what it was they had to do, namely: go to Venice and Jerusalem and spend their lives in the service of souls. Were they not given permission to stay in Jerusalem, they would return to Rome and make themselves available to the Vicar of Christ, so that he could make use of them to the greater glory of God and salvation of souls. They had resolved, also, to wait for one year at Venice for passage, and if this passage to the East were not available that year, they would be free from their vow to go to Jerusalem and would then go to the Pope and so on.[53]

At last the pilgrim let himself be persuaded by his companions and also because some of the Spaniards amongst them had some businesses which he could take care of, they agreed then that as soon as he felt well, he would take care of the businesses of the companions; then he would proceed for Venice, where he would wait for the companions.

86. This was the year of 1535. The companions were to set out, according to their agreement, in the year 1537 on the day of St. Paul's conversion (January 25. Trans.); although later, due to the wars that broke out, they left in November, 1536 (November 15, 1536. Trans.). As the pilgrim was ready to leave, he heard he had been accused to the Inquisitor and that an action had been started against him. On hearing this, and on seeing no one summoned him, he went to the Inquisitor and told him what he had heard, and that since he was about to leave for Spain and had companions, would he, please, pass sentence. The Inquisitor said it was true he had been accused, but he did not see it to be any mat-

ter of importance. He just wanted to see his book of the *Exercises*.
On seeing them, he praised them very highly and asked the pilgrim
to let him have a copy, which he did. In spite of all this he insisted
again, asking the Inquisitor to carry on with the action until sentence was passed. The Inquisitor gave him only some excuses, and
so the pilgrim brought a notary public and witnesses to his house
and took down a record of all this matter.

9

Return to Spain
(APRIL - LATE 1535)

87. Leaves for Spain. 88-89. Lives in a hospital. 90. Visits Pamplona, Almazán, Sigüenza, Toledo, Valencia. 91. Leaves for Genoa, then Bologna and Venice.

87. This being over with, he mounted a small horse his companions had bought for him and left for his home land. On the road he felt much better. When he arrived at the province (so Guipuzcoa was then called. Trans.), he left the main road and took the mountain road, which was more solitary. After riding on it for a while, he met two armed men advancing towards him (that road was notorious for assassins). These men, having gone a little ahead of him, turned around, following him very fast. He was a little scared. Yet, he talked to them and found out they were the servants of his brother[54] (his older brother, Martín García de Oñaz, lord of Loyola. Trans.), who had sent them in order to find him. It seems the pilgrim was recognized at Bayonne, in France, and so his brother had received news of his coming. Thus the servants went ahead, and he followed the same road. Just before reaching his home town, he again came across the said servants, who came to meet him again, entreating him to let them take him to his brother's home, but they could not force him to do so. And so he went to the hospital, and later, at a convenient hour, he went begging through the village.

88. In the hospital he began to speak of the things of God with many people who came to visit him, and much fruit was gathered through His grace. As soon as he arrived, he decided to teach Christian doctrine every day to the children. His brother opposed this idea very strongly, saying no one would attend. He answered that one would be enough. But as soon as he started doing it, many came continually to listen to him, including his own brother.

289

Besides teaching Christian doctrine, he would preach on Sundays and holidays with great usefulness and profit to those souls that from many miles around came to listen to him. He tried to suppress certain abuses also, and with the grace of God some order was put into some. For example, he was able to make gambling forbidden by law by persuading the man in charge of justice. There was also another abuse and it was this: in that part of the country young women went about with their heads uncovered, and they did not cover them until they got married. But there were many women who became the concubines of priests and other men and were faithful to them, as if they were their wives. And this was so common that the concubines were in no way ashamed of admitting that they had covered their heads for someone, and they were known as belonging to him.

89. Great harm arose from such custom. The pilgrim convinced the Governor to issue a law by which those women covering their heads for someone, not being their wives, would be punished by law. This way the abuse began to subside. He also saw to it that an order be given so that the poor be provided for publicly and regularly; also, that bells should sound three times daily, at the "Ave Maria" time, namely, in the morning, noon, and evening, so that people would pray, as they do in Rome. Though on arrival he felt well, later on he became gravely ill. As soon as he recovered, he decided to leave to take care of the businesses entrusted to him by his companions. He was leaving without money, and this very much angered his brother who was ashamed he would want to leave on foot. But by the afternoon the pilgrim had already compromised with his brother that he would go to the end of the province on horseback with his brother and relatives.

90. As soon as he crossed the line of his province, he left the horse, took no provisions, and went towards Pamplona. From there he went to Almazán, Fr. Laínez's hometown, and then to Sigüenza and Toledo, and from Toledo to Valencia. At all these native places of his companions, he did not want to take anything, though they made him many offerings with great insistence.

In Valencia he spoke with Castro, who was then a Carthusian monk. He wanted then to sail for Genoa, but his Valencian friends begged him not to do so, for, they said, Barbarossa was at sea with many ships and so on. In spite of the many things they told him, enough to bring fear into him, it was not enough to make him hesitate.

91. He sailed on a large ship, went through a storm, which was mentioned earlier, when it was said he was about to die three times.

When he arrived at Genoa, he took the road to Bologna, on which he suffered much; mostly on one occasion when he lost his way and started to walk along a riverbank. The river was down below, while the road followed higher. The further he went on this road, the narrower it became, and it became so narrow that he could not proceed nor turn back; so he went down on all fours and thus advanced a long distance with great fear, for everytime he moved, he thought he would fall in the river. This was the hardest fatigue and corporal punishment he had ever had, but in the end he got out of this predicament. As he was about to enter Bologna, he had to cross a small wooden bridge, and he fell under it; as he was getting up, covered with mud and water, he made many of those present laugh.

On entering Bologna, he began to beg for alms and found not even a *quatrino*, though he covered the whole city.

He was ill for some time in Bologna; then he left for Venice in the same manner as always.

10

Venice and Vicenza

(LATE 1535 - LATE 1537)

92. Gives the *Exercises*. 93. Difficulties. The companions from Paris join him. Those who were not priests are ordained. 94-95. They wait to visit Holy Land. 96-97. Return to Rome. On the way Ignatius has his famous vision.

92. During that time, while in Venice, he busied himself giving the *Exercises* and in other spiritual conversations. The most distinguished people he gave them to were Masters: Pietro Contarini and Gasparo de Doctis and a Spaniard by the name of Rozas. There was also there another Spaniard, Bachelor Hoces,[55] who became very close to the pilgrim, and the Bishop of Chieti, and though he wanted to make the *Exercises*, he never managed to do so. Finally he decided to make them. Three or four days after he had started them, he opened his soul to the pilgrim, saying he was afraid he might be teaching him, through the exercises, some wrong doctrine, as some one had warned him. For this reason he had taken with him certain books so he could consult them if he tried to deceive him. He was very much helped by the exercises and finally decided to follow the path of the pilgrim. He was also the first one to die.

93. In Venice, the pilgrim again had to endure another persecution, for many were saying his effigy had been burned in Spain and Paris. This went as far as to go to trial, and sentence was passed in favor of the pilgrim.

The nine companions arrived in Venice at the beginnings of 1537. There they divided into groups to serve several hospitals. After two or three months they left for Rome to receive the blessing for the journey to Jerusalem. The pilgrim did not go on account of Dr. Ortiz and also because of the new Theatine Cardinal. The companions returned from Rome with notes for 200 or 300 *escudos*, which were given to them as alms for the journey to Jerusalem. But they refused to take that money except in promissory notes. These monies were later returned to those who provided them when they were unable to leave for Jerusalem.

The companions returned to Venice the same way they left it, namely, on foot and begging; they were divided into three groups in such a way that they were always from different nations. In Venice those who had not been ordained were ordained priests. The Nuncio, who was then in Venice and later on became Cardinal Verallo, granted them priestly faculties. They were ordained under title of poverty; all of them also took vows of chastity and poverty.[56]

94. In that year there were no ships sailing for the East since the Venetians had broken relations with the Turks. Thus, seeing that their hope for sailing for Jerusalem was becoming more remote, they spread through Venice to wait out the year they had agreed upon; if after it was over there would still be no passage, then they would return to Rome.

It fell to the pilgrim to go to Venice with Favre and Lainez. There they found a certain house outside of the city which had no doors nor windows; they slept in it on a bit of straw they had brought along. Two of them would go daily to the city to beg for alms twice a day, but they received so little that they could hardly sustain themselves. They would normally eat some boiled bread, when they had it; the one who stayed home was in charge of boiling it. In this manner they survived forty days, not attending to anything else but prayer.

95. Master Jean Cordure joined them after those forty days, and the four decided to start preaching. The four would find four different public squares; the same day, at the same time, they would start their sermons, first shouting very loudly and calling the people with their hats. These sermons became the talk of the town, and many people were moved to devotion; as a result, they had the things they needed for their lives in greater abundance.

While he was in Venice, he had many spiritual visions, and many, almost routine, consolations, just the opposite of what happened to him in Paris. Particularly, as he was getting ready to become a priest at Venice, while preparing to say Mass, and during all that journeying, he had great supernatural visitations, as those he used to have while at Manresa. Also, while at Venice, and while ill with fever, he came to know that one of his companions who was at Bassano (Simón Rodríguez. Trans.) was ill and about to die. Nonetheless he set out on the road, walking so fast that Favre, his companion, could not keep up with him. While on this journey, he became assured by God, and so he told Favre, that the companion would not die of that illness. On arriving at Bassano, the sick companion was deeply consoled and soon recovered.

After this they all returned to Venice, and the ten stayed there for a while; some would go to the nearby villages begging for alms.

96. When the year was over, having found no passage, they decided to return to Rome. The pilgrim wanted to go with them this time, for the previous time when the companions had gone to Rome, the two people he doubted had shown great benevolence.

They left for Rome divided into three or four groups; the pilgrim went with Favre and Laínez. In this journey he was very especially visited by the Lord.

He had decided that once he became a priest he would remain for a whole year without saying Mass, preparing himself and begging the Virgin Mary that she would place him with her Son. One day, a few miles before reaching Rome, while in a church praying, he felt such mutation in his soul and saw so clearly that God the Father placed him with His Son, Christ, that he could never have the nerve to doubt that God the Father placed him with His Son.

And I, who am writing these things, said to the pilgrim as soon as I heard the above, that Laínez was telling these things in more detail, as I myself had heard. He told me that what Laínez was saying was all true, but he did not remember them in such detail; but that as he was recounting it, he knew he only spoke the truth. He told me the same about other things.

97. Later on, coming upon Rome, he told his companions that he saw all the windows closed there, meaning that they would have many obstacles. And he also said: "We must be on guard over ourselves and not engage in conversation with women, unless they are of high rank." And by the way, later on while in Rome, Master Francis[57] heard the confession of a woman and visited her some times to talk spiritual matters with her; this woman was later on found pregnant. The Lord wished that whoever committed the wrong would be found out. Something similar happened to Jean Cordure and a spiritual daughter of his who was found with a man.

11

Rome

(1538)

98. The pilgrim went from Rome to Monte Cassino to give the exercises to Dr. Ortiz. He stayed there forty days, during which time he once saw bachelor Hoces entering into heaven (n. 92. Trans.). This caused him many tears and great spiritual consolation, and he saw this so clearly that if he said the contrary, it would seem to him to be lying. From Monte Cassino he brought back Francisco Estrada.[58]   When he returned to Rome, he busied himself helping souls. They were still living at the vineyard,[59] and he would give the *Spiritual Exercises* to several people at the same time; one of them lived by Santa Maria Maggiore, the other by Ponte Sesto.

Then the persecutions began. Miguel[60] started annoying and speaking badly about the pilgrim. The pilgrim made him to be summoned before the Governor. He first had shown him a letter by Miguel in which he praised the pilgrim very highly. The Governor examined Miguel, and the outcome was to banish him from Rome.

Mudarra and Barreda[61] then began their persecutions, saying that the pilgrim and his companions were fugitives from Spain, Paris, and Venice. Finally the two of them confessed, in the presence of the Governor and of the one who was then the legate of Rome (Cardinal Vincenzo Carafa. Trans.), that they had nothing bad to say against them, nor about their behavior nor their teaching. The legate ordered silence to be imposed on the whole affair, but the pilgrim refused, saying he wanted a final sentence. Neither the

Governor nor the Legate was pleased by this, nor were those who earlier favored the pilgrim; but at last, after a few months, the Pope returned to Rome. The pilgrim went to Frascata to speak with him and presented him several reasons. The Pope took over and ordered sentence to be given, and it was in his favor, and so on.

Several pious works were accomplished in Rome with the help of the pilgrim and his companions, such as the Instructions to new Christians (Catechumens. Trans.), Saint Martha (house for women. Trans.), and the orphanage. Master Nadal may recount the rest.

99. After all these things had been told, I asked the pilgrim on October 20 about the *Exercises* and the *Constitutions*, eager to know how he had drafted them. He told me he had not drafted the *Exercises* all at once, but that when he discovered certain things in his soul he found useful, he thought they might also be helpful to others, and so he would put them down in writing; for example, to examine one's conscience with that form of the lines, etc. (Exer.n. 30. Trans.). In particular, he had drawn he elections, he told me, from the variety of spirits and thoughts he had when he was at Loyola, while still suffering with one of his legs (no. 7-9. Trans.). He told me he would talk to me about the *Constitutions* in the evening.

That same day, before supper, he called me with the air of a person more collected than usual and made me a sort of protestation. Its substance was to make clear to me the intention and simplicity with which he had related these things, saying he was very sure he had not exaggerated anything; that he had committed many offenses against Our Lord after his conversion, but that never had he consented to mortal sin; but on the contrary, he kept on growing in devotion, namely, in an ease to find God, more so now than at any other time in his whole life. He could find God always, and at any time he wanted to find Him. And even now he had visions many times, especially those mentioned above, in which he could see Christ as the sun and so on (n. 29. Trans.). This happened to him frequently while dealing with important matters, and it would become as a confirmation and so on.

100. He also had many visions while saying Mass, and while writing the *Constitutions* he would have them very frequently. Now he could affirm this more easily, for he would write down each day what went on in his soul, and he had it now in writing.

He then showed me a very large bundle of writings from which he read some to me. Most of them related to visions he saw as confirmation of some part of the *Constitutions*; sometimes he saw God the Father, other times the three persons of the Trinity, others the Virgin, at times interceding, other times confirming.

He talked to me in particular about decisions over which he spent forty days saying Mass every day with daily tears. It had to do with the church having some income and whether the Society could make use of it.

101. Our Father used to keep the following habit while drafting the *Constitutions*: he would say Mass daily and present the subject he was dealing with to God; then he would pray about it. He would always say prayer and Mass with tears.

I wanted to see all those papers on the *Constitutions*, and begged him to let me have them for a while, but he refused.

LETTERS

Letters of
St. Ignatius de Loyola

Introduction

 GNATIUS DE LOYOLA, DIRECTLY OR through his secretaries, wrote over seven thousand letters. Any edition of these letters can only be a short selection. The letters presented here are only samples of and concrete decisions made by the saint in the regular routine of running the Society of Jesus. It is, therefore, very important to separate the *spirit* of the *Exercises* or the *Constitutions* and the concrete guidelines given in these letters written for a time and circumstance different from ours. In other words it would be a great mistake, and one propagated too often, to take the text of the letters literally and cancel thereby the freedom of the spirit. This warning applies to all letters of Ignatius' correspondence, including the Letter on Obedience.

A remarkable feature of Ignatius' correspondence, one that this selection cannot bring out, is the abundance of extraordinary people with whom Ignatius corresponded. Kings, Emperors, Popes, Cardinals, and a long procession of future saints make a list of names that reads like the *Who's Who* of the sixteenth century.

The present selection focuses mainly on spiritual matters. A much larger selection of Ignatius' letters is available in English: *Letters of St. Ignatius of Loyola*, Selected and Translated by William J. Young, s.j. Loyola University Press (Chicago, 1959). The present translation of these letters adds only few changes to the translated letters found in this volume.

TRANSLATOR'S NOTE TO THE LETTER ON OBEDIENCE

Ignatius wrote several letters on obedience, but the letter we include here is considered the classical expression of his thought on the subject. This letter he dictated to his assistant Fr. Polanco, but it is signed and no doubt revised and edited by him. Ignatius' reason for writing this letter appears to come from the alarming news he had received from Portugal that young Jesuits under the guidance of Fr. Francisco Rodríguez were leaving the society in large numbers. The news that arrived in Rome spoke of 127 Jesuits, when in fact only about 30 left the society. But Rome was under the impression of the large numbers, and Ignatius decided to write his statement on obedience.

There were many reasons for the insubordinations of the Portuguese Jesuits, Fr. Rodríguez being one of them. The superiors were so condescending with their subjects that the subjects had become superiors. At stake was the spirit of the society and the fact that the young Jesuits were using meditation as an excuse for studying less and subverting the Ignatian spirituality.

Letter On Obedience

TO THE FATHERS AND BROTHERS AT COIMBRA

Rome, March 26, 1553

IHS. May the grace and intimate love of Christ our Lord ever salute and visit you with His most holy gifts and spiritual graces.

It gives me great consolation, my most dear breathren in Christ our Lord, to know of the deep and positive desires that He, who called you to this Institute, gives you of your perfection and of His divine service and glory, as well as how He keeps you in this Institute and leads you to the blessed end where He guides His chosen ones.

And though I wish for you all perfection in every virtue and spiritual grace, it is also true (as you must have heard from me on other occasions) that it is in obedience more than in any other that God our Lord gives me the desire to see you become outstanding, not only for the particular good to be found in it, as the Holy Scripture so praised with examples and words in the Old and the New Testament, but because (as St. Gregory says) (*Moralium*, c. 14 no. 28 PL 76,765B) "Obedience is a virtue that by itself imprints in the soul all the other virtues, and once printed, it keeps them there." For as long as obedience blooms, all other virtues will also be seen to be blooming and bear the fruit that I wish for your souls, which is the same desired by Him. He redeemed, out of obedience, a world lost for lack of it: "Made obedient unto death and death in the cross" (Phil. 2:8).

We may tolerate that other Religious Orders surpass us in fastings, vigils, and other hardships they religiously observe according to their Institute; but it is my true desire, dearest Brethren, that in the purity and perfection of obedience, with a true submission of our wills and abnegation of our judgments, those that serve God our Lord in this Society become outstanding and that in this the true children of the Society be known; they should never see the person that they obey, but in that person see Christ our Lord for whom they obey.

(Fundamental Origin of Obedience)

For the Superior should not be obeyed because he is very prudent or very good, or because he is very qualified in any other of the gifts of God our Lord, but because he takes His place and authority, repeating the eternal truth: "Who hears you, hears Me; who despises you, despises Me" (Luke 10:16). One should not, on the other hand, stop obeying a Superior because he is less prudent, for he represents the person of infallible wisdom, and He will complement what is lacking in his minister; nor should one stop obeying because a Superior lacks goodness and other good qualities; for Christ our Lord expressly said: "In the chair of Moses scribes and pharisees sat and read", and adds: "Keep, therefore and do the things they tell you but do not do as they do".(Matt. 23:2-3).

Thus I wish you all to practice recognizing in any of your Superiors Christ our Lord and pay reverence and obedience to His divine Majesty in him with full devotion. This should not sound new to you because remember that St. Paul orders that temporal and ethnic superiors be obeyed as (they would to) Christ Himself from whom all ordered power descends, as He writes to the Ephesians: "Those of you who are slaves obey your temporal lords and masters with fear and trembling and with simple heart, as you would Christ Himself; do not serve them only when they are present, as someone wanting to please only men, but as slaves of Christ fulfilling in this the will of God with desire and good will, as serving the Lord, not only men" (Eph. 6:5).

You may infer from this that when a religious person takes someone not only as his Superior but expressly in the place of Christ our Lord, so that he may lead and govern him in His divine service, at which level he must carry him in his soul and whether he should look at him as a man or rather as the vicar of Christ our Lord.

(Degrees of Obedience)

I also want to imprint deeply in your soul the following, that the first degree of obedience which consists in the execution of what one is ordered to do is very low; this hardly deserves the name of obedience, for it does not carry the value of this virtue; one must rise to the second degree, which consists in making one's own the will of the Superior, in such a way that there is not only execution in the effect but conformity of the affect, sharing the same willing and not willing. This is the reason why the Scripture says that "Obedience is better than sacrifices" (1 *Sam* 15:22); for, as St. Gregory says: "Through other sacrifices someone else's flesh is killed, but through obedience our own will is killed" (St. Greg., *Moralium*, 1.35 c.14 n. 28: PL 76,765B).

Now, because this will in men is of so much value, so also is the sacrifice of it, when by obedience it is offered to his Creator and Lord. How deceptive and how dangerous it is for those who think it lawful to withdraw from the will of their superior, I do not say only in those things pertaining to flesh and blood, but even in those which of their nature are spiritual and holy, such as fasts, prayers, and other pious works! Let them hear Cassian's remarks in the Commentary of Daniel the Abbot: "It is one and the same kind of disobedience, to break the command of the superior out of the desire to work or to be idle; and it is as damaging to break the statutes of the monastery for reason of sleep as it is for reason of vigil; and finally it is as bad to stop doing what the abbot commands for reason of going to read as it would be for going to sleep." (*Collationes*, 4. c.20: PL 49, col. 608-09). Holy was the action of Martha, holy the contemplation of Magdalene, holy the penance and tears with which the feet of Christ our Lord were washed, but all this had to be done in Bethany, which is interpreted as the house of obedience; which as St. Bernard notes, appears to be what Christ our Lord wants us to understand: "Neither the occupation of the good act, nor the leisure of contemplation, nor the cries of penance could be pleasant to Him outside of Bethany" (St. Bernard, *Ad milites templi* c. 3: PL 182,939).

Therefore, my dearest Brethren, try to make your wills entirely submissive; offer with liberality your freedom, as given by Him, to your Creator and Lord in the person of His representatives. And do not consider a small outcome of your free will that you may return it entirely through obedience to Him who gave it to you: thus you do not lose it but improve it by entirely conforming your will with the most sure rule of all rectitude, which is the Divine Will, whose interpretor is the Superior who rules in His place. But then you must never try to bring the will of the Superior (which we must always think as that of God) to your will, for this would not be to measure your will by the Divine Will but the Divine Will by yours, thus perverting the order of Wisdom. It is a great deception, and one that belongs to minds blinded with self-love, to think that one is obedient when the inferior tries to lead the Superior to what he wants. Listen to St. Bernard, well-versed in this matter: "Whoever, openly or underhandedly, negotiates so that his spiritual Father orders him what he wants, he deceives himself if he praises and considers himself, with vain glory, to be obedient, for in that he does not obey his spiritual Father, but his spiritual Father obeys him" (St. Bernard, *Sermo de diversis* 35 n.4: PL 183, 636A-B).

Therefore, and I conclude, it is necessary to climb to the second degree of obedience for whoever wishes to climb to the virtue of obedience; and this consists (besides its execution) in making one's own the will of the Superior, by disrobing oneself of one's will and putting on the Divine Will as interpreted by the Superior.

But for anyone who intends to make complete and perfect oblation of one's self, it is necessary that he offers, *besides* his will, his understanding (and this is another level and the highest of obedience); he must not only have one will, but be of one mind with his Superior, by subjecting his judgment to his, in so far as the devout will may sway the understanding.

Even if the understanding does not have the same freedom as the will and naturally assents to what is represented to it as true, it is the case that in many instances where the power of evidence of the known truths does not coerce it, it can, by means of the will, sway more to one side or another. In such cases, every true obedient person must lean to see things the way the Superior sees them. And this is true, for obedience is a holocaust in which the whole man, without denying anything of himself, offers himself in the fire of charity to his Creator and Lord by the hand of his ministers; this is a total surrender of oneself by which he dispossesses himself of his whole self, so that he may be possessed and governed by Divine Providence through the Superior. We cannot say, therefore, that obedience embraces only the execution to carry out the command, and a will to feel good about it, but that it also carries the judgment to see things the way the Superior orders them, in so far (as I said earlier) as one's understanding may be swayed by the will.

God our Lord would wish that this obedience of judgment were as understood and practiced as it is necessary for whoever lives in the religious community, and it is also most agreeable to God our Lord. I call it necessary, because, just as in the celestial bodies in order for the inferior to receive movement and effect from the superior it is necessary that it be subject and subordinate to the convenience and order of one body to the other, in the same manner the movement of one rational creature by another (as it happens through obedience) makes it necessary that the creature that is moved be subject and subordinate, so that he may receive the virtue and influence of the one that moves. This subjection and subordination is not possible without conformity of the understanding and will of the inferior to the superior's.

If we look at the goal of obedience, our will may go wrong and so can our understanding in those things that are for our convenience; but if we look at the cause, it is always expedient, to avoid twisting it with our will, to make it conform to that of the Superior, in the same manner; not to twist the understanding, we must conform it with that of the Superior. "Do not trust your own prudence," says the Scripture (Prov 3:5).

In the same manner it is commonly accepted by wise people, even in ordinary human affairs, that it is true prudence not to trust one's own prudence, and especially in those things that are our own, where people are not usually good judges due to passion.

Being the case, therefore, that men should follow another's opinion (even though he may not be his Superior) rather than one's own judgments when it comes to deciding on one's affairs, how much more should he follow the judgment of the Superior, whom he has taken in the place of God to be guided by him as interpreter of the Divine Will?

Furthermore, this advice is even more necessary in spiritual things and persons, for the dangers of the spiritual life are great when one runs through it without the brakes of discretion. This is the reason why Casianus, commenting on the sermon of the Abbot Moisen, says, "With no other vice does the devil bring the monk to see him in his damnation than when he persuades him that, by despising the advice of the elders, he may trust his own judgment, decision, and knowledge" (Casianus, *Collationes*, PL 49, 541B).

On the other hand, if there is no obedience of judgment, it is impossible for the obedience of the will and execution to be as they should. For the appetitive powers of our soul naturally follow prehension; and thus it would be a violent thing to obey with the will against one's own judgment in the long run; and even if one could obey in this manner for some time, due to the general idea that one must obey even when something is not properly ordered, this is not going to last, and thus one will end losing perseverance; and if one does not, then one loses the perfection of obedience which consists in obeying with love and joy, for whoever goes against what he feels cannot obey with love and joy while this lasts. Spontaniety and quickness are lost, for they are not possible where there is a divided judgment, doubting whether it be good to do or not to do what one is ordered. The simplicity of blind obedience, so much praised, is also lost, disputing if the order is good or bad, and one may even condemn the Superior for ordering what is not to one's pleasure. Humility is lost, for on the one hand we chose ourselves, even when on the other we subject ourselves to the Superior. Fortitude in difficult things is lost; in short, all the perfections of this virtue are lost.

Furthermore, if our judgment is not controlled, one finds in obedience unhappiness, pain, slowness, laziness, grumbling, excuses, and other great imperfections and inconveniences that remove from obedience its value and merit. For St. Bernard, with good reason, says of those people that feel depressed by doing the orders of the

Superior against their own wish: "If you start by (obeying) with a heavy heart, to judge your Prelate, to grumble in your heart, even though exteriorly you do as he commands, this is not virtue of true patience but a cover of malice" (St. Bernard *Serm. 3 de Circumcisione* n.8: PL 183,140C.).

If one looks at the present tranquility of the truly obedient, neither truth nor tranquility will be present in the soul that carries the cause of agitation and doubt, and that is one's own judgment against what obedience orders.

It is for this reason and for the unity with which the being of a whole congregation is held together that St. Paul preaches for "all to feel and say the same thing" (Rom 15:5) so that it may be preserved with the union of judgments and wills. For if the feeling of the head and the members must be one, it is easy to see if it is reasonable for the head to feel with the members or for the members with the head. On account of all these things above said, it is obvious how necessary is the obedience of judgment.

If one were to see how perfect in itself and agreeable to God our Lord (this offering is), he will see it by the worth of the most noble oblation that one makes of this most worthy part of man; in this manner the obedient person becomes a living and acceptable host to his Divine Majesty, holding nothing of himself; also the difficulty involved in conquering oneself for His love by going against the natural inclination men have to follow their own judgment. Thus obedience, though properly a perfection of the will (by making it ready to fulfill the will of the Superior), must, as I said before, extend it to cover the understanding, by swaying it to see things the way the Superior sees them; in this manner one proceeds with the whole power of the soul, of the will, and of the understanding, to a quick and perfect execution.

(General Means to Achieve Obedience)

I seem to hear you say, my dearest Brethren, that you see how important this virtue is but that you would like to see how you could become perfect in it. To which I answer with the Pope St. Leo: "Nothing is difficult to the humble, nor hard to the meek" (St. Leo *Serm. 5 de Epiphaniae* c.3: PL 54,252A). Let there be humility in you, let there be meekness; God our Lord will provide the grace for you to maintain with softness and love the oblation you have already made of yourselves.

(Particular Means)

Were humility and weakness to fail, I give you three particular means which will help you very much to attain perfection in the obedience of the understanding.

The first one is that (as I said at the beginning) you do not consider the person of the Superior as subject to errors and miseries but be sure to see in the man you obey Christ Himself, highest wisdom, immense goodness, infinite charity, who, as you know, neither can deceive Himself nor wants to deceive you. And being the case that you have put yourself under his obedience out of His love, subjecting yourselves to the will of the Superior to be more in conformity with the Divine Will of God, His most faithful charity will not fail in leading you by the means given by Him. Therefore, do not take the voice of the Superior, when he orders you, but as that of Christ, in the manner that St. Paul, addressing the Colossians exhorting the subjects to obey the Superior, said, "And whatever you do, do it with joy, as doing it to serve the Lord and not men; and knowing that you are going to receive as payment the eternal inheritance of God, serve Christ our Lord" (*Col* 3.23-24). And St. Bernard adds, "Whether it be God or man, his vicar, who orders you whatever, he must be obeyed with equal care and respected with equal reverence, as long as man does not command things against God." (St. Bernard *De praecepto et dispensatione* c.9 n.19: PL182,871D). In this manner, if you look not for the man with your external eyes, but for God, with your interior ones, you will find no difficulty in conforming your will and judgment with the rule you have taken for your actions.

The second means is that you should be quick in searching for reasons to defend what the Superior orders, or to that to which he leans, and not to attack it; it will help for that to love what obedience orders; this will give rise to obedience with joy and without any disturbance, for as St. Leo said, "One does not serve with forced servitude when one loves and wants what one is ordered." (St. Leo, *De ieiunio septimi mensis serm.*89 c.1: PL 54,444B).

The third means to subject the understanding is even easier, more secure, and used by the holy Fathers, and it is this: presuppose and believe (in a manner similar to things pertaining to the faith) that everything that the Superior orders is a command from God our Lord and His most Holy Will; thus, blindly, without any thought, proceed, with the strength and quickness of a will ready to obey, to the execution of what it is ordered. This, it is believed, was the way Abraham followed in his obedience when he was ordered to sacrifice his son Isaac (Gen 22:2,3); in the same manner we find in the New Testament the example of some holy Fathers, as narrated by Casianus, as the Abbot John, who would not consider if what he was ordered was useful or not, like watering for a year, with great labor, a dry stick; nor would he consider if it was possible or impossible, like trying to move, as ordered, a stone which a large number of people could not move (Casianus, *De coenob. instit.* 1.4 c.24: PL 49,183D-184B; Ib., 1.4 c.26: PL 49,186A).

We know that God our Lord, in order to confirm such obedience, would sometimes contribute some miracles, as in the case of the disciple of St. Benedict, Maurus, who entered the water by command of the Superior and would not sink in it (Cf. St. Gregory, *Dialog.* 1.2 c.7: PL 66,146A-B); and in another case, when ordered to bring the lioness, he took her in his arms and brought her to the Superior (*De vitis Patrum* 1.3 n.27: PL73,755D-756A-B) and other similar cases you already know. What I mean to say is, therefore, that this manner of subjecting your own judgment, by presupposing that what is ordered is holy and in conformity with the Divine Will without further inquiry, is used by the Saints, and it must be imitated by whoever wants to obey with perfection in everything, except in sinful matters.

(The Representation)

This, of course, does not change the fact that, if you saw something different from the Superior, and after having prayed, it would seem to you to be convenient, under the Divine Will, that you should represent it to the Superior, that you could. If you wish to proceed, however, without any suspicion of self-love and judgment, you must remain indifferent before and after making the representation, not only in relation to the execution of doing or not doing the thing in question, but also so that you may feel more happy and consider better whatever the Superior orders.

(Final Observations)

What I have said about obedience is to be understood to apply to inferiors in relation with their immediate Superiors, as in the case of Rectors and local Superiors with their Provincials, and to these in relation to the General, and for this in relation to the Superior given to him by God our Lord, who is his Vicar on earth (the Pope), so that in this manner a total subordination may be maintained and as a consequence union and charity, without which the good being of the Society cannot be maintained, nor of any other congregation.

This is the way the Divine Providence softly disposes all things: by subordinating the lower things to the middle ones, and the middle ones to the highest, towards His ends. Thus there is subordination from one hierarchy to another in the angels, in the heavens, and in all corporal movements there is a subordination of the inferiors to the superiors and of the superiors, according to their level, towards a supreme movement.

The same can be seen on earth in every well-ordered secular army, and in the ecclesiastical hierarchy, which leads to a universal Vicar of Christ our Lord. And as this subordination is better kept, the government becomes better, and because of the lack of it, we see such important faults in every congregation.

In this Society, of which God our Lord has given me some charge, I so wish this virtue to be improved as if all the good of the Society depended upon it.

(Final Exhortation)

I wish to conclude as I started, dealing only with this matter and without leaving it: I pray to you, for the love of Christ our Lord, that not only ordered obedience, but preceded with His example of obedience, that you all try to achieve this virtue with a glorious victory over yourselves, by conquering yourselves in what is highest and most difficult, which is your will and judgment; in this manner the knowledge and true love of God our Lord may entirely possess and guide your soul through this pilgrimage to lead you, with many others through your means, to the ultimate and most happy end of His eternal happiness.

I commend myself, very much, to your prayer.
Rome, March 26, 1553.
In Domino,

Ignatius

―――――――――――――――

TO INÉS PASCUAL

(MI, I 71-73)

This was the first woman Ignatius encountered on his way from Montserrat to Manresa. She became one of Ignatius' benefactresses. She was feeling depressed on account of the death of one of her friends, and this is the reason Ignatius wrote to her offering consolation.

I thought I should write you this on account of the great desire I know you have of serving the Lord. I believe that now you feel fatigued, not only because of the absence of that blessed servant whom God has pleased to take to Himself, but also because of the many enemies and inconveniences you meet with in God's service there, and also because of the enemy of human nature who never ceases with temptations. But for the love of God our Lord try always to go forward and avoid all obstacles, for if you do so, temptation will have no power against you. You should always act thus, preferring God's praise to everything else. More so, since our Lord does not bid you do anything that is labor or dangerous to your person, but He would rather have you live in His joy, giving the body all that is necessary. Let all your words, thoughts, and conversations be in Him, and direct to this end whatever care you have to give your body, always giving priority to the observance of God's commandments. It is this He wishes and this He bids us. And whoever gives thought to this will discover that there is more trouble and pain in his life . . . (a few words missing).

A pilgrim by the name of Calixto is now in that place (Barcelona), and I would very much like to see you communicate with him your affairs. It is more than likely that you will discover in him more than might appear.

For the love of our Lord let us make every effort in Him, seeing that we are so much in His debt. (Ignatius' quotations in his letters are mostly by heart. He changes phrases and places many times. Trans.) For we will sooner tire of receiving His gifts than He of giving them.

May it please our Lady to intercede with her Son for us poor sinners and obtain grace that, with our own labor and effort, she may convert our weak and sad spirits and make them strong and joyful to praise God.

Barcelona, St. Nicolás, 1525
The poor pilgrim,

Iñigo

TO INÉS PASCUAL

(MI I, 74-75)

Ignatius wrote to Inés as a member of the family informing her of his arrival in Paris. He includes some advice for Juan, her son, who later became Ignatius' good friend and testified when Ignatius' process of canonization was started.

One may also see how Ignatius was taken care of by these benefactresses who raised money and helped him in his studies.

May the true peace of Christ our Lord visit and protect our souls.

In view of the good will and love which you have always had for me in God our Lord and proved to me by deeds, I have decided to write you this letter to let you know of my travels since leaving you. With favorable weather, and in perfect health by the grace and goodness of God our Lord, I arrived here in the city of Paris on the second of February. I will study here until our Lord ordains otherwise.

I should like very much to hear from you and inform me if and what Fonseca answered to the letter you wrote to him, and whether you spoke with him.

Remember me sincerely to Juan, and tell him to be obedient to his parents always and to keep the feast days; for if he does so, he will fare well in this life and also in heaven above.

Remember me to your neighbor. Tell her that the jewels have arrived. And that her love for and good will for God our Lord are ever present to me. May the Lord of the world repay her, and ever remain by His goodness in our souls, so that His will and desires may be always fulfilled in us.

Paris, March 3, 1528

Poor in goodness,

Iñigo

TO ISABEL ROSER

(MI I 83-88)

A well known noble lady of Barcelona, Isabel Roser was one of Ignatius' benefactresses. Ignatius answers three of her letters and consoles her in a moment of her life made difficult because of the death of a friend and her inability to help Ignatius financially.

May the grace and love of Christ our Lord be with us.

I received from Dr. Benet your three letters and the twenty ducats. May God our Lord be pleased to count them credit for you on the day of judgment and repay you for me, as I hope He in His divine goodness will do in new and sound coins. I hope that He will not have to consider me ungrateful, if in some way He makes me worthy of giving some praise and service to His Divine Majesty. You speak in your letter of God's will being fulfilled in the banishment and withdrawal of Canillas from this life. In truth, I cannot feel any pain for her, but only for ourselves, who are still in this place of endless weariness, pains, and calamities. I knew that in this life she was dearly loved by her Creator and Lord, and I can easily believe that she will be well-received and housed, with little desire for the palaces, the pomps, the riches, and the vanities of this world.

You also mention the excuses of our sisters in Christ our Lord (his benefactresses at Barcelona). They owe me nothing, and it is I who am eternally indebted to them. If they see fit to employ their means somewhere else for the service of God our Lord, we should rejoice. But if they do not or are unable, I wish really to have something to give them so that they could do much for the service and glory of God our Lord. For as long as I live I cannot but be their debtor, and I am thinking that, after I leave this life, they will be well repaid by me.

In your second letter you tell me of the long-drawn-out illness you have undergone and of the great stomach pains that still remain. Indeed I cannot help feeling with you in your present sufferings, seeing that I desire every imaginable happiness and prosperity for you, provided it will help you to glorify God our Lord. And yet when we reflect, these infirmities and other temporal privations are often seen to be from God's hand to help us to a better self-knowledge and to rid ourselves of the love of created things. They help us moreover to focus our thought on the brevity of this life, so as to prepare for the other, which has no end. When I think that with these afflictions He visits those whom He loves, I can feel no sadness or pain, because I realize that a servant of God, through an illness, turns out to be almost a doctor for the direction and ordering of his life to God's glory and service.

You also speak of my forgiving you if you can no longer help me, since you have many obligations to meet and your resources are not sufficient for all. There is no reason for you to speak of forgiveness from me. It is I who should fear; for when I think of failing to do what God wishes me to do for all of my benefactors, I begin to fear that His Divine Justice will not forgive me, and all the more so, that I have received so much from you. Finally, since I am quite unable to fulfill my duties in this respect, my only refuge is to consider the merits I shall gain before the Divine Majesty— that is, with the help of His grace, which the same Lord will distribute to those to whom I am indebted, to each one according as he has helped me in His service, and especially to you, to whom I owe more than to anyone else I know in this world. As I recognize this debt, I hope that our Lord will help me to repay it, and I will profit through acknowledging it. Be sure that your solid and sincere affection for me will bring me as much pleasure and spiritual joy as if you sent me all the money you could. Our Lord insists that we look to the giver, and love him more than his gift, and thus keep him ever before our eyes and in the most intimate thoughts of our heart.

You also suggest that I write, if I think it good, to our other sisters and benefactresses in Christ to ask help for the future. I would rather be guided in this by your judgment than by my own. Even though Cepilla offered help in her letter and shows a desire to help me, I do not think for the present that I will write her for help in my studies. There is no certainty of my remaining here for a whole year. And if I do, God, I hope, will give me the light and judgment to do all for His greater service and always carry out His will and desire.

In the third letter you speak of the enmities, the intrigues, and the untruths which have surrounded you. I am not at all surprised at this, not even if it were worse than it is. For just as soon as you determined to bend every effort to procure the praise, honor, and service of God our Lord, you declared war against the world and raised your standard in its face, and got ready to reject what is lofty by embracing what is lowly, taking as in a thread what is high or low: that is, honor and dishonor, riches and poverty, affection and hatred, welcome and repulse, in a word, the glory of the world or all the wrongs it could inflict upon you. We cannot be much afraid of the reproaches of this life when they are confined to words, for all the words in the world will never hurt a hair of our heads. As to words of insult, ugly or hurtful, even they will give neither pain nor satisfaction except insofar as they are willfully admitted. But if we wish absolutely to live in honor and to be held in esteem by our neighbors, we can never be solidly rooted in God our Lord, and it will be impossible for us to remain unscathed when we meet with affronts. Thus, the satisfaction I once took in the thought of the insults the world offered you was balanced by the pain I felt at the thought of your having to seek a medical remedy against this pain and suffering. May it please the Mother of God to hear my prayer for you, which is that you may meet with even greater affronts so that you may have the occasion of greater merit, provided that you can accept them with patience and constancy and without sin on the part of others, remembering the greater insults which Christ our Lord suffered for us. If we find that we are without this patience, we have all the more reason to complain, not so much of those who hurt us as of our own flesh and sensuality and not being yet fully dead to the world as we should. For these people make it possible for us to gain a more precious treasure than anyone can win in this life and greater riches than anyone can put together in this world. . . .

May the most holy Trinity grant you all in all your trials and in everything else in which you can serve God all the grace that I desire for myself, and may no more be given to me than I desire for you.

Please remember me most sincerely to Rev. Roser, and to any who you think will be pleased to hear from me.

Paris, November 10, 1532

Poor in goodness,

Iñigo

TO SISTER TERESA RAJADELL

(MI I 99-107)

This letter is perhaps the most famous from the pen of Ignatius on spiritual guidance and commentary on the Rules for the Discernment of Spirits and on Scruples as he wrote them in the *Spiritual Exercises*.

Sister Teresa Rajadell was a nun in the monastery of Santa Clara, Barcelona.

May the grace and love of Christ our Lord be always with us to protect and help us.

When I received your letter a few days ago, it gave me such joy in the Lord whom you serve and desire to serve better, to whom we ought to attribute all the good we find in creatures. As you said he would in your letter, Caceres has informed me at length about your affairs, and not only about them, but also about the suggestions or guidance he gave you for each particular case. On reading what he says to me, I find nothing else he need have written, although I should have preferred to have the information in a letter from you, for no one can describe sufferings so well as the one who actually experiences them.

You ask me to take charge of you for the love of God our Lord. It is true that, for many years now, His divine Majesty has given me the desire, without any merit on my part, to do everything I possibly can for all men and women who walk in the path of His good will and pleasure, and, in addition, to serve those who work in His holy service. Since I do not doubt that you are one of these, I am pleased to find myself in the position of being able to put what I say into practice.

You also beg me to write to you what the Lord says to me and that I should say freely what I think. What I feel in the Lord I will tell you frankly with a right good will, and if I should appear to be harsh in anything, I shall be more so against him who is trying to upset you than against you. The enemy is troubling you in two ways, but not so as to make you fall into the guilt of sin which would separate you from your God and Lord. He does, however, draw and separate you from God's greater service and your own greater peace of soul. The first thing is that he sets before you and persuades you to cultivate a false humility, the second that he strives to instill into you an excessive fear of God with which you are too much taken up and occupied.

(1) As to the first point, the general course which the enemy follows with those who love and begin to serve God our Lord is to set hindrances and obstacles in their way. This is the first weapon with which he tries to wound them—by suggesting, "How will you be able to live in such penance all your life without the enjoyment of parents, friends, and possessions and in so solitary a life, without even some slight relief? In another way of life you could save yourself without such great dangers." He thus gives us to understand that we have to live a life which is longer, on account of the trials which he sets before us, than that of any man who ever lived, whereas he hides from us the many and great comforts and consolations which the Lord is wont to give to such souls, if the man who has newly embraced the Lord's service breaks through all these difficulties, choosing to want to suffer with his Creator and Lord.

Then the enemy tries his second weapon, namely, boasting or vainglory, giving the soul to understand that there is much goodness or holiness in it and setting it in a higher place than it deserves. If the servant of the Lord resists these darts with humility and lowers himself, not consenting to be what the enemy would persuade him to be, he brings out the third weapon, which is that of false humility. That is, when he sees the servant of the Lord so good and humble that, when he does what the Lord commands, he thinks it all valueless and looks at his own shortcomings, not at any glory for himself, the enemy puts it into his mind that if he discovers any particular blessing given him by God our Lord, any good deed done, or good intention or desire, he is sinning by another kind of vainglory, because he speaks in his own favor. Thus the enemy strives that he should not speak of the blessings received from his Lord, so that there shall be no fruit either in others or in the person himself, for the recognition of what one has received is always a stimulus to greater things, although such speaking must be practiced with restraint and motivated by the greater profit both of others and of the man himself, as opportunity provides and when others are likely to believe what we say and profit by it. When, however, we make ourselves humble, he tries to draw us into false humility, that is, into humility which is exaggerated and corrupt. Of this your words are clear evidence, for after you relate certain weaknesses and fears which are true of you, you say, "I am a poor nun, desirous, it seems to me, of serving Christ our Lord"—but you still do not dare to say: "I am desirous of serving Christ our

Lord," or: "The Lord gives me desires to serve him," but you say, "I seem to be desirous." If you look closely, you will easily see that those desires of serving Christ our Lord do not come from you, but are given you by our Lord. Thus when you say, "The Lord has given me increased desires to serve him," you praise him, because you make his gift known and you glory in him, not in yourself, since you do not attribute that grace to yourself.

(2) Thus we ought to be very circumspect, and if the enemy lifts us up, humble ourselves, going over our sins and wretchedness. If he casts us down and dejects us, we ought to look upwards with true faith and hope in the Lord, going over the benefits we have received and considering with how much love and kindness he waits for us to be saved, whereas the enemy does not care whether he speaks the truth or lies, but only that he may overcome us. Ponder well how the martyrs, standing before their idolatrous judges, declared themselves Christ's servants. So you, standing before the enemy of the whole human race and tempted in this way by him, when he wants to deprive you of the strength the Lord gives you and wants to make you weak and full of fear with his snares and deceits, do not merely say that you are desirous of serving our Lord—rather you have to say and confess without fear that you are his servant and that you would rather die than separate yourself from his service. If he represents God's justice to me, I bring up his mercy; if he puts God's mercy before me, I reply with his justice. If we would avoid trouble, this is the way wherein we should walk, that the deceiver may in turn be deceived, applying to ourselves the teaching of Holy Scripture which says, "Beware that thou be not so humble that in excessive humility thou be led into folly" (cf. Eccles. 13:11).

(3) Coming to the second point, as the enemy has placed in us a certain fear under the cloak of a humility which is false, and so suggests that we should not speak even of good, holy, and profitable things, so he brings in its train another, much worse fear, namely whether we may not be separated and cut off from our Lord as outcasts—in great measure on account of our past lives. For just as through the first fear the enemy attained victory, so he finds it easy to tempt us with this other. To explain this in some measure, I will bring up another device the enemy has. If he finds a person with a lax conscience who passes over sins without noticing them, he does his best to make venial sin seem nothing, mortal sin venial and very grave mortal sin of small account—so that he turns the defect he finds in us, that of too lax a conscience, to account. If he finds some other person with an overtender conscience—a tender conscience is no fault—and sees that such a person casts far from him mortal sin and as far as possible venial sin—for it is not

in us to avoid all—and even tries to cast away from himself every semblance even of small sin, imperfection, or defect, then the enemy tries to throw that good conscience into confusion, suggesting sin where there is no sin and defect where there is perfection, so that he may disturb and trouble us. In many instances where he cannot induce a soul to sin and has no hope of ever bringing that about, at least he tries to trouble it.

(4) In order to explain more clearly how fear is caused, I shall speak, although briefly, of two lessons which the Lord usually gives or permits. The one he grants, the other he permits. That which he gives is interior consolation, which casts out all trouble and brings one to the full love of our Lord. To such souls as he enlightens with this consolation, he reveals many secrets, both at the time and later. In short, with this divine consolation, all trials are a pleasure, and all weariness rest. In the case of him who walks in this fervor, warmth, and interior consolation, there is no burden so great that it does not seem light to him, no penance or other trial so severe that it does not seem sweet. This shows and lays open to us the way we ought to follow, fleeing from the contrary. This consolation does not always remain with us—it follows its due seasons according to the divine ordinance. All this is to our profit, for when we are left without this divine consolation, then comes the other lesson, which is this: our old enemy now puts before us all possible obstacles to turn us aside from what we have begun, and he harasses us unceasingly, everything being the contrary of the first lesson. He often makes us sad, without our knowing why we are sad; we cannot pray with any devotion, contemplate, or even speak of or listen to the things of God our Lord with relish or any interior delight. Not only this, but if he finds us to be weak and much dejected by these harmful thoughts, he suggests that we are entirely forgotten by God our Lord, and we come to imagine that we are separated from God in everything and that however much we have done and however much we want to do, it is of no value whatsoever. Thus he strives to bring us into distrust of everything, and we shall see that our great fear and weakness is caused in this way, for we then make too much of our miseries and are too passive in the face of his false arguments. It is necessary, therefore, that he who fights should look to what condition he is in. If it is consolation, we should be humble and lowly and think that afterwards the test of temptation will come. If temptation, darkness, or sadness comes, we must withstand it without any irritation and wait with patience for the Lord's consolation, which will scatter all troubles and darkness coming from without.

(5) It now remains for me to say something of what we feel when we belong to God our Lord, how we must understand it and,

when it is understood, learn to profit by it. It often happens that our Lord moves and impels our soul to one particular course or another by laying it open—that is, speaking within it without the sound of any voice, raising it all to his divine love, without our being able to resist what he suggests, even if we wanted to do so. In accepting such suggestions, we must of necessity be in conformity with the Commandments, the precepts of the church, obedient to our superiors, and full of complete humility, for the same divine Spirit is in all. Where we can frequently deceive ourselves is that after this consolation or inspiration, while the soul remains in bliss, the enemy creeps in under cover of joy and an appearance that is good, to make us exaggerate what we have felt from God our Lord, so as to make us disturbed and upset in everything.

At other times he makes us undervalue the lesson received, making us disturbed and ill at ease, because we cannot perfectly carry out all that has been shown to us. More prudence is necessary here than in any other matter. Many times we must restrain our great desire to speak of the things of God our Lord. At other times we must speak more than the desire or movement we have in us prompted—for in this it is necessary to think more of the good of others than of our own desires. When the enemy thus strives to increase or diminish the good impression received, we must go forward trying to help others, like someone crossing a river. If he finds good footing, that is, if he confidently hopes that some good will follow, he goes forward. If the river is muddy, that is, if others would take scandal at his good words, then he always draws rain, seeking a more suitable time and hour to speak.

Matters have been mentioned into which it is impossible to enter further without writing at great length. Even then, there would be much which is easier to feel than to explain, above all in writing. If it thus pleases our Lord, I hope we shall meet soon and then we shall be able to go into these matters more deeply. In the meantime, since you have Castro nearer to you, I think it would be good for you to write to him, for, whereas harm cannot follow, some good may result. Since you tell me to write all I feel in the Lord, I will say that you will be fortunate if you know how to keep all you possess.

I conclude, praying the most holy Trinity through God's infinite and supreme goodness to give us full grace to know and follow out perfectly his most holy will.

From Venice, June 18th, in the year 1536

Poor in goodness,

Ignatius

(MI I 107-109)

In this letter Ignatius continues the spiritual directions given in the previous letter. Ignatius makes a distinction between two kinds of meditations: one that tires the body and the other that gives rest to both body and soul. Ignatius advocates the need of a healthy body for any kind of prayer or meditation.

May the grace and love of Christ our Lord be always our help and support.

I have received two letters from you at different times. The first I think I answered at some length, and as I understand, you have receive it by now. In your second letter you add only a few words to what you had to say in the first, and I will now answer these briefly.

You say that you find in yourself great ignorance and great shortcomings, and so forth. To know this alone is to know much. But you go on to add that this condition is produced by the many and vague directions you have received. I agree with you that, who decides little, little does he understand, and helps less. But the Lord, who sees this need, will Himself come to your aid.

Every kind of meditation in which the understanding is engaged tires the body. There are other kinds of meditation, orderly and restful, which are pleasant to the understanding and offer no difficulty to the interior faculties of the soul, and which can be made without interior or exterior waste of effort. These methods do not tire the body but rather help to rest it, except in the two following instances. The first is when you withdraw the natural nourishment and recreation which you should give to the body. By nourishment I mean when one is so taken up by such meditations that he forgets to give the body its proper nourishment at the proper hours. By recreation I mean to allow the understanding to roam at will, provided only that the subjects it deals with be good or indifferent, or at least not bad.

The second instance is this, and it is of frequent occurrence in those who are much given to prayer or contemplation. They find trouble getting to sleep because just before bedtime they exercise their minds on the matter of their meditation and keep thinking about it, and consequently find it difficult to fall asleep. It is the enemy who chooses this moment to present good thoughts to the mind. He has but one purpose, to make the body suffer by robbing it of its sleep. This must be avoided entirely. With a healthy body you will be able to do much. I don't know what you can do with one that is infirm. A healthy body is a great help either for good or evil: evil for those whose wills are depraved by evil habits, but good in those whose will is entirely given to God and trained to habits of virtue.

If, however, I do not know what meditations and exercises you make and the amount of time you give to them, I cannot say more than what I have written, unless Caceres has told you otherwise. And here once more I insist especially that you think of God as loving you, as I have no doubt He does, and that you correspond with this love and pay no attention whatever to the evil thoughts, even if they are obscene or sensual when they are not deliberate, or of trivialities or tepidity. For even St. Peter and St. Paul did not succeed in escaping all or some of these thoughts. Even when we do not succeed fully, we gain much by paying no attention to them. I am not going to save myself by the good works of the good angels, and I am not going to be condemned because of the evil thoughts and the weaknesses which the bad angels, the flesh, and the world bring before my mind. God asks only one thing of me, that my soul seek to be conformed with His Divine Majesty. And the soul so conformed makes the body conformed, whether it wish it or not, to the divine will. In this is our greatest battle, and here the good pleasure of the eternal and sovereign Goodness. May our Lord by His infinite kindness and grace hold us always in His hand.

Venice, September 11, 1536

Poor in goodness,

Iñigo

TO MANUEL MIONA

(MI I 111-113)

Father Miona was a priest and professor when Ignatius arrived in Alcalá. Ignatius made him his confessor. In this letter Ignatius exhorts him to make the exercises. He did and joined the Society of Jesus in Rome in 1545. He died in Rome on March 4, 1567.

The grace and love of Christ be our protection and help.

I am very eager to have some news of you; and no wonder, seeing how much I am indebted to you as your spiritual son. It is only right that I make some return for the great love and affection which you have always felt for me and shown me in your actions. But in this life I do not know of any other way of paying even the smallest part of this debt than by having you make the Spiritual Exercises under the man I shall name. You have already offered to make them, and I beg of you by the service of God our Lord that if you have tried and liked them, you write me and let me know. If you have not, I beg of you, by the love and the bitter death He suffered for us, to begin them. If you, however, turn back from your intention, besides the pain you will cause me, which I accept, you may look upon me as making fun of the spiritual persons to whom I owe everything.

I have not written to you before this because I felt that in writing to one, I was writing to all. If you read the letter I am addressing to Faber, you can find in it any news you may wish to have of me. Once again, and again, and as often as I can, I beg of you by the service of God our Lord, take my advice for fear that some day the Divine Majesty reprove me for not having exerted myself to the utmost, knowing as I do that the Spiritual Exercises are the best means I can think of in this life both to help a man to benefit himself and to bring help, profit, and advantage to many others. Even though you might feel no need in yourself for the first, you will see how they will help you for the second.

I have nothing else to add, and so close, begging of the divine mercy of God our Lord the grace to know His most holy will and perfectly to fulfill it, according to the talent entrusted to each of us, lest some day He apply to us the words: "Thou wicked servant, thou knewest, etc."

Venice, November 16, 1536
All yours in the Lord,

Iñigo

TO FATHERS SALERMÓN AND BRÖET

(MI I 179-181)

Fathers Salmerón and Bröet, two Jesuits, were sent by Pope Paul III to Ireland. Ignatius gave them written instructions of which the following extract is only one part. The instructions are entitled "How to negotiate and deal with others in our Lord."

In your dealings with all be slow to speak and say little, especially with your equals and those lower in dignity and authority than yourselves. Be ready to listen for long periods and enjoying it, until each has finished talking. Answer the questions put to you, come to an end, and take your leave. If a rejoinder is offered, let your reply be as brief as possible, and take leave promptly and politely.

In dealing with men of position or influence, if you are to win their affection for the greater glory of God our Lord, look first to their disposition and accommodate yourselves to them. If they are of a lively temper, quick and merry of speech, follow their lead in your dealings with them when you talk of good and holy things, and do not be too serious, glum, and melancholic. If they are shy, slow to speak, serious and weighty in their talk, use the same manner with them, because such ways will be gratifying to them. "I became all things to all men."

Do not forget that, if one is of a lively disposition and deals with another who is like him, there is very great danger of their failing to come to an agreement if they are not of one spirit. And therefore, if one knows that one is of such a lively disposition, he ought to approach another of similar traits well prepared by self-examination and determined to be patient and not to get out of sorts with him, especially if he knows him to be in poor health. If he is dealing with one of slower temper, there is not so much danger of a disagreement arising from words hastily spoken.

Whenever we wish to win someone over and engage him in the greater service of God our Lord, we should use the same strategy for good which the enemy employs to draw a good soul to evil. He enters through the other's door and comes out his own. He enters with the other by not opposing his ways but by praising them. He gains familiarity with the soul, suggesting good and holy thoughts which bring peace to the good soul. Later he tries, little by little, to come out his own door, always suggesting some error or illusion under the appearance of good, but which will always be evil. So we with a good purpose can praise or agree with another concerning some particular good thing, overlooking whatever else may be wrong. After thus gaining his confidence, we shall have better success. In this sense we go in with him his way but come out our own.

We should ingratiate ourselves with those who are sad or tempted, speak at length and show great satisfaction and cheerfulness, both interior and exterior, so as to draw them to the opposite of what they feel, for their greater edification and consolation.

In everything you say, especially when you are trying to restore peace and in spiritual exhortations, be much on your guard and remember that everything you say may or will become public.

In business matters be generous with your time; that is, if you can, do today what you promise for tomorrow.

On the supposition that you hold office, it would be better if Master Francis took charge of contributions or offerings. You will thus be better able to accept or decline obligations in respect of all if none of the three of you touch money but rather sent it by another to the person in charge of it. Or it would be better that the person seeking a dispensation give the fee to the person in charge and take a receipt for it to show that the dispensation was given. If any other way be more convenient, use it, but see to it that none of the three of you even touches any of the money connected with the mission.

September, 1541

TO FATHER NICOLÁS BOBADILLA

(MI I 277-282)

Father Bobadilla was one of Ignatius' first companions. He had worked in Germany and Italy with great success. He was a man of great virtue but his external behavior was at times exasperating.

This letter is a perfect example of the clarity and humility with which the first Jesuits dealt with one another. In few other letters does the human and clever side of Ignatius appear as in this one.

May the perfect grace and love of Christ our Lord be always in our continuous help and favor.

As I find myself by His infinite grace more disposed to humble myself on all points rather than defend myself on a few, and as I think it will be to His greater glory, I have decided to make the most of both.

1. Concerning the fraternal correction between us which I have had a mind to make for God's greater glory, you say that you understand my mind, but that all will not accept it with your understanding and sincerity. I have all in mind—that is, all the members of the Society-because it is for them alone that I have written. If, however, you should feel that some of them on receiving word on this point will not take what I have to say with your sincerity and simplicity of mind, I hope in our Lord that I will agree completely with each of them, to your and their complete satisfaction.

2. You say that it is one thing to put something in writing and another to say it by word of mouth, and you insist that it would be impossible to make my stomach the standard of taste for all. I remember having written that the principal letter should be gone over twice; that is, written once and corrected, then rewriting it or having it copied to avoid the untidiness of hurried writing, a fault into which I think some of us have fallen. If all of us were to do this—and myself the first, as I think I have greater need—we should be a greater help to one another in the Lord. I did not want to say, nor do I say now, that, if one has used a certain expression, he should change it to another, nor that he should try to write with

greater ability than he has. If I cannot add to my own low, natural level of understanding, I could ill afford to try to raise that of others, seeing that it belongs to our Creator and Lord to give much or little. But I mean that each one should write the principal letter once, correct it and rewrite it or have it rewritten, and thus each one of us will be aided by the other. For neither I myself nor any other can give to another more than we have ourselves. But with this attentiveness and care each one gives in a better way what he has received from His Creator and Lord. It does not seem from this that I am aiming at exercising so widespread and detailed an authority.

3. You think it good enough to draw up a brief summary of your letter and have copies made of this, but not to send us a full account as we desire. You are well aware that I wrote to you, and that there is a general agreement among us, that in the principal letter there will be news of some edification, according to what God our Lord works in each for the spiritual good of souls; but if one wishes to give other information, such as bits of news, illnesses, or needs, he may write it at as great length as he wishes, but on separate sheets or in another letter.

4. You observe that in the copy of my letter to you I had said *"Procuro de expedir mi tiempo"* when I should have said *"expender mi tiempo."* If you will look well at that letter, you will see in my own hand "expender" and not "expedir." That may be explained by the fact that the one who transcribed my letter here wrote "expedir" in place of "expender," which I, relying on another, did not correct, as it was not a principal letter which could be shown to others. I am willing to acknowledge myself as guilty as you judge me to be in our Lord.

5. With regard to the fault you find in the address on the letter I wrote you, which runs, *"En el palacio del rey de los romanos,"* I admit writing that, thinking that you would be better known in the palace where you are a frequent caller than in the court at large, since that is coextensive with the city or town. But if there was a fault in writing *"de los romanos,"* I will say hereafter, *"En la corte del rey de romanos."* If everybody laughed at that, as you say they did, I think that, when you saw that some laughed, you would not have shown it to everybody. I will be very grateful to you in our Lord if you show them this letter also, for if I correct the one, I can also correct the other. This will be my lifelong desire, to be directed and corrected for my faults in the hope that the correction extend to all of them and be given with brotherly affection. I recall that I made this earnest request of all the Society from the time you made your profession; thus, after prayer to God our Lord and, conferring with His Divine Majesty, inform me of my faults and thus help me to correct them in our Lord.

6. You think that I should not be losing time in correcting details of so little importance, and that some who do not know me might think that I have nothing to do with my time. Do not lose sight of the fact that this matter of correspondence has been agreed upon among us after long discussion. Recall too that I have already written you at length, begging to rewrite your principal letters twice in the manner I have described and to avoid the inconveniences I have already enumerated, and that, if you did not do so, I should be compelled, although much against my inclination, in view of the spiritual profit in general and the obligations of my conscience, to command you in virtue of holy obedience. You received my letters and answered with sufficient edification and contentment; but later, after the first few letters, you disregarded entirely the requests I had made so earnestly in our Lord and included in your principal letter much that was merely local news, all of which, coming in another letter or on separate sheets, would have given us all much gratification as being news of you. But the fact that you were suffering from a touch of skin irritation which was tormenting you should have been put on a sheet by itself, as we had often agreed, so that we could give to each a morsel according to his taste, and everything be for the good. Many friends and acquaintances who know that we have letters from some of the Society wish to see them and find a great delight in them. If we don't show the letters when they ask, we estrange them; if we show them a disorderly letter, they are disedified. I am not so eager to correct the wording of your letters as I am for your perfection in general, and some part of that consists in humbling yourself and in obeying Him in whose hands you made your vow of obedience, especially in things that are in themselves good, or indifferent, or without sin. Hence I am of the opinion up till now that giving a part of my time to this would be to the greater glory of God our Lord, and to the greater spiritual benefit of the Society. If you think otherwise, I will be able to conform to what you judge to be better in our Lord, because I do not think that I should be less the gainer in your company, in the eyes of His Divine Majesty, than I would be with anyone else in the Society.

7. You say, "You think that everybody is edified with these copies of yours. I don't show many of them, nor do I read many of them. I haven't the time. Two letters could be made out of the superfluous matter in your principal letter." Indeed, I never thought that you would show them to everybody or that everybody would be edified. But I did think that you would show them to a few and that they for the most part would get some good from them, as up to this all those to whom I have written this same principal letter think that they have benefitted, unless I deceive myself from what

they say in their letters. This holds true even of Dr. Ortiz and his brother Francis and Dr. Picard at Paris. As to you thinking my letters not worth reading for lack of time, I have by God's grace time to spare and the inclination to read and reread all of yours. If it will make you read mine, I will make a real effort to follow your advice as best I can in the Lord and remove from my letters everything you think superfluous. This I will do also for the others to whom I have written who share your disapproval, if only you will let me know. For it would be a great mistake on my part to spend so much time and labor and succeed only in displeasing, without advantage to anyone.

Therefore, I beg of you by the love and reverence of God our Lord to let me know the best way of writing you, whether I do it myself or with the help of a secretary, so that I may be sure to please you in every respect. In the meantime, as I do not know what course to take, I will await your letter, or I will have someone else write who will know better how to meet with your requirements.

Moreover, since you know my earnest desire, I beseech you by the same love and reverence of His Divine Majesty to do your very best in your letters to me, as I have so often asked you and do now once more beseech you in our Lord. If I cannot obtain what I so earnestly ask of you, it will be because I am wholly unworthy, or for any other reason you may entertain.

On condition that the Society, or the half of it, approves, I give you my vote, whatever it may be worth, and gladly and sincerely offer to turn over to you the office I now hold. Not only do I choose you, but if you think otherwise, I am perfectly willing to choose anyone you or any of the others may name. I am convinced that whatever would be thus decided would be for the greater praise, reverence, and service of God our Lord and to my own greater peace of soul in His Divine Majesty. For it is the very truth that, absolutely speaking, my desire is to have a lowly station and be without this weight of responsibility as long as I live. Thus always and in everything I wish to set aside my own poor judgment. I hold now, and hope that I shall always hold, as much better whatever you or the Society, or a part of it, shall determine. And this determination I here and now with my own hand approve and confirm. In the meantime I return to the subject of your own personal needs. You know that it is our profession to offer ourselves to be sent wherever the vicar of Christ shall think good as he shall decide, without asking even for any provision for the journey. In speaking for others, I did not see anything wrong in calling attention to your needs there, so that in providing, or not, for your needs, they might do as seemed to them more for God's glory. Guided therefore by the contents of your letter to me, I spoke to Cardinal Santa Cruz and also to Cardinal Morone. If I were in your place, I would be quite satisfied with this, and accept relief for my needs from any who offered as coming from God's hand. If occasionally I was left in want, I would think that God was pleased to try me, to give me an opportunity for more merit in His greater service, praise, and glory. But I don't see why I should enlarge on this point, as I think I have long known your spirit in our Lord.

If I have delayed in writing you, it is because I did not know where you could be found. You spoke to me of taking the baths, and I did not know where you were going to stay.

May it please God our Lord that this letter find you in perfect health, wherever you may serve Him best, and praise His most holy name.

Rome, 1543.

TO THE FATHERS AND SCHOLASTICS AT COIMBRA

(MI I 495-510)

Ignatius wrote this letter to the fathers and scholastics teaching and studying at Coimbra in Portugal. This was a community of about 80 people and growing in numbers and good name. Ignatius wrote to them this letter, known also as the "Letter of Perfection," in order to a) encourage them to continue on their good path; b) warn them against indiscreet fervor; c) tell them how to use their spiritual zeal during their times of study. In this letter Ignatius makes also a strong appeal to obedience.

May the grace and everlasting love of Christ our Lord be ever our protection and help. Amen.

Master Simón's letter and those of Santa Cruz bring me continued news about you, and God, from whom all good things descend, knows what comfort and joy it gives me to see that He so helps you, not only in your studies but in your pursuit of virtue as well. Indeed, the good odor of these virtues has carried to very distant lands, to the encouragement and edification of many. And if every Christian should rejoice because of the common obligation we all have of seeking God's honor and the good of His image, which has been redeemed by the blood and death of Jesus Christ, I have an especial reason for rejoicing in our Lord, seeing that I have a distinct obligation of keeping you in my heart with a special affection. May our Creator and Redeemer be ever blessed and praised for all, since it is from His liberality that every blessing and grace flows, and may it please Him to open more and more every day the fountain of His mercy to increase and advance what He has already begun in your souls. I have no doubt concerning that Supreme Goodness, who is so eager to share His blessings, or of that everlasting love which makes Him more eager to bestow perfection on us than we are to receive it. If this were not so, our Lord Jesus Christ would never encourage us to hope for what we can have only from His generous hand. For He tells us, "Be you therefore perfect, as also your heavenly Father is perfect" (Matt. 5:48). It is certain then that for His part He is ready, on condition that we have a container of humility and desire to receive His graces, and that He sees that we make good use of the gifts we have received and cooperate diligently and earnestly with His grace.

1. On this point I will not fail to put the spurs even to those of you who are running so willingly. For I can tell you that you must be persistent both in your studies and in the practice of virtue if you are to come up to the expectations which so many entertain of you, not only in this kingdom (of Portugal) but in many other countries, who, considering the helps and advantages of every kind, both interior and exterior, that God gives you, rightly hope for more than ordinary results in you. No commonplace achievement will satisfy the great obligations you have of excelling. If you consider the nature of your vocation, you will see that what would not be slight in others would be slight in you. For not only has God called you "out of darkness into His marvelous light" (1 Pet. 2:9), and "moved you into the kingdom of His beloved Son" (1 Col. 1:13), as He has done with the rest of the faithful, but because you have better preserved your purity and are more united in His service in the love of spiritual things, he thought it good to withdraw you from the perilous sea of this world to preserve your consciences from the dangers of the storms which the gusts of passion are wont to raise— the desire now of possessions, now of honors, now of pleasures—and on the other hand from the fear of losing all such things. Another reason over and above this is that, if these earthly concerns have no place in your thoughts or affections, you will be preserved from distraction and dissipation, with the result that you will be able to direct your thoughts and affections and employ them in attaining the end for which God created you; that is, His own honor and glory, your own salvation, and the help of your neighbor.

It is true that all the orders in the Christian life (of the Church) are directed to this end. And yet God has called you to this, in which His glory and the salvation of the neighbor are set before you, not as a general end but one toward which all your life and its various activities must be made by you into a continuous sacrifice. This requires a cooperation from you that should not stop with example and earnest prayer, but includes all the exterior means which His divine providence has provided for the mutual help we should give one another. From this you can understand how noble and royal is the manner of life you have chosen. For not merely among men, but not even among the angels, is there a nobler work than glorifying the Creator and bringing His creatures to Him as far as they are able.

2. Therefore, take serious thought of your vocation, so that on the one hand you can give many thanks to God for so great a favor, and on the other ask Him for that special help which is needed if you are properly to correspond with it with the courage and diligence you must have in large measure if you are to attain such ends. Sloth, tepidity, weariness in study and in the other exercises which you have undertaken for the love of our Lord you must recognize as the sworn enemies of your end.

For his encouragement each one should keep before his eyes, not those who he thinks will accomplish less, but rather those who are active and energetic. Do not ever permit the children of this world to show greater care and solicitude for the things of this world than you show for those of eternity. It should bring a blush to your cheek to see them run to death more unhesitatingly than you to life. Hold yourselves as little worth if a courtier serve with greater care merely to have the favor of an earthly prince than you do for the favor of the King of Heaven, and if a soldier for the honor and glory of a victory and a little booty gets himself ready and battles more bravely than you do for the victory and triumph over the world, the devil, and yourselves, with the kingdom of heaven and everlasting glory as your prize.

For the love of God, therefore, be not slow or tepid. For if "tautness breaketh the bow, idleness breaketh the soul", while on the contrary, according to Solomon, "the soul of them that work shall be made strong" (Prov. 13:4). Try to maintain a holy and discreet ardor in work and in the pursuit of learning as well as of virtue. With one as with the other, one energetic act is worth a thousand that are listless, and what a lazy man cannot accomplish in many years a diligent man usually achieves in a short time.

In the matter of learning, the difference between the diligent and the negligent student stands out clearly. And the same holds true in the mastering of passion and the weaknesses to which our nature is subject, as in the acquiring of virtue. It is certain that the negligent, because they do not struggle against themselves, never win peace of soul, or do so tardily, and never possess any virtue in its fullness, while the energetic and diligent make notable advances on both.

Experience proves that in this life peace and satisfaction are had, not by the listless but by those who are fervent in God's service.

And rightly so. For in the effort they make to overcome themselves and to rid themselves of self-love, they rid themselves of the roots of all passion and unrest. And with the acquirement of habits of virtue they naturally succeed in acting easily and cheerfully in accordance with these virtues.

By this means they dispose themselves to receive His holy consolations from God, our faithful consoler, for "to him that overcometh I will give the hidden manna" (Apoc. 2,17). On the other hand, tepidity is the cause of a lifetime of uneasiness, for we never get rid of its cause, which is self-love, not do we deserve God's help. For this reason you should animate yourselves to work earnestly at your commendable tasks, since even in this life you will see the advantages of holy fervor, not only in the growth of perfection in your souls but even in the peace of mind it gives you in this present life.

But if you look to the eternal reward, as you should do often, St. Paul will easily convince you that "the sufferings of this time are not worthy to be compared with the glory to come that shall be revealed in us (Rom 8:18), because "that which is at present momentary and light of our tribulation worketh for us above measure exceedingly an eternal weight of glory" (2 Cor. 4:17).

If this is true of every Christian who serves and honors God, you can understand what your crown will be if you correspond with our Institute, which is not only to serve God for your own sakes but to draw many others to His honor and service. Of them Holy Scripture says that "they that instruct many to justice (shall shine) as stars for all eternity" (Dan. 12:3). And this is to be understood of those who employ themselves in the discharge of their duty, not only later in the exercise of arms but even before that, while they are getting themselves ready. If this were not so, we certainly could not apply to works that are in themselves good the words of Jeremias, "Cursed be he that doeth the work of the Lord carelessly" (Jer. 48:10) and of St. Paul, "Know you not that they that run in the race, all run indeed, but one receiveth the prize" (1 Cor. 9:24) and, "For he also that striveth for the mastery is not crowned except he strive lawfully" (2 Tim, 2:5), and that means any one that is a good worker.

3. But more than anything else I should wish to awaken in you the pure love of Jesus Christ, the desire for His honor and for the salvation of souls whom He has redeemed. For you are His soldiers in this Society with a special title and a special wage. I say special because there are many motives of general import which likewise oblige you to work for His honor and service. His wage is everything you are and have in the natural order, for He bestows and preserves your being and life, and all the perfections of body and

soul, as well as blessings that are eternal. His wage is also the spiritual gifts of His grace, with which He has so generously and lovingly anticipated you and continues to offer even when you oppose Him and rebel against Him. His wage is also those incomparable blessings of His glory which, without any advantage to Himself, he has promised you and holds in readiness for you, actually sharing with you all the treasures of His happiness, so that you may be, by a remarkable participation in His divine perfection, what He is by His essence and nature. Finally, His wages are the whole universe and everything material and spiritual it contains. For He has placed under our ministry, not only all that is under heaven but even the whole of His sublime court, not excepting even any of the heavenly hierarchy: "Are they not all ministering spirits, sent to minister for them who shall receive the inheritance of salvation" (Heb. 1:14)? As though this wage were not enough, He has made Himself our wage, becoming a brother in our own flesh, as the price of our salvation on the cross and in the Eucharist to be with us as support and company. Oh, what an unworthy soldier he would be whom such a wage would not induce to labor for the honor of such a prince! We know indeed that, to oblige us to desire and labor for this glory, His Majesty has anticipated us with these inestimable and priceless favors, in a sense stripping Himself of His own possessions to give us a share in them; taking upon Himself all our miseries to deliver us from them; wishing to be sold as our redemption, to be dishonored to glorify us, to be poor to enrich us; accepting a humiliating and painful death to give us a blessed and immortal life. How extremely ungrateful and hardhearted is he who after all this does not recognize his obligation to serve our Lord Jesus Christ diligently and to seek His honor!

4. If, therefore, you recognize this obligation and wish to employ yourselves in promoting God's honor, the times you are living in make it incumbent indeed on you to make your desire known by deeds. Can you find a place where the Divine Majesty is in honor today, or where His infinite greatness is worshipped, where His wisdom and infinite goodness are known, or His most holy will obeyed? Behold rather, with deep grief, how His holy name is everywhere ignored, despised, blasphemed. The teaching of Jesus Christ is cast off, His example forgotten, and the price of His blood lost in a certain sense as far as we are concerned because there are so few to profit by it. Behold likewise your neighbors, images of the most holy Trinity and capable of enjoying His glory whom all the world serves, members of Christ, redeemed by so much pain, opprobrium, and blood. Behold, I say, the miseries that surround them, the darkness of ignorance that envelops them, and the whirlwind of desires, empty fears, and other passions that torment them,

set upon by so many visible and invisible enemies, with the peril of losing, I do not say their property or their earthly lives, but an eternal kingdom and its happiness by falling into the insufferable misfortune of everlasting fire.

To sum up briefly, if you were to examine carefully the great obligation you have of seeking the honor of Jesus Christ and the salvation of your neighbor, you would see how fitting it is for you to get ready by diligently striving to make yourselves fit instruments of God's grace, especially since in these days there are so few real laborers who do not seek the things that are their own, but the things that are Jesus Christ's. And the more that others fall short, the more you ought to endeavor to make up for them, since God bestows so especial a grace on you and one so proper to your vocation and goal.

5. What I have said up to this for the purpose of awakening the drowsy and spurring on those who may be loitering on the way should not be taken as a justification for going to the other extreme of fervor. Spiritual infirmities such as tepidity are caused not only by colds but even by over-warmth, such as excessive fervor. "Let your service be a reasonable service" (Rom. 12:1), says St. Paul, because he knew the truth of the words of the Psalmist, "and the king's honor loveth judgment" (Ps. 98:4), that is, *discretion*; and what was prefigured in Leviticus: "Whatsoever sacrifice thou offerest, thou shalt season it with salt" (Lev. 2:13). It is thus, as St. Bernard says, that the enemy has no more successful trick for depriving the heart of real charity than to get her to act rashly and not in keeping with spiritual reasonableness. "Nothing in excess," said the philosopher. And this principle should be our guide even in a matter pertaining to justice itself, as we read in Ecclesiastes, "Be not over just" (Eccles. 7:17). If one fails to observe this moderation, he will find that good is turned into evil and virtue into vice. He will also learn that many inconveniences follow which are quite contrary to the purpose of the one who so acts.

The first is that God is not really served in the long run, as the horse worn out in the first day does not as a rule finish the journey, and thus it happens that someone must be found to care for it.

Second, gains that are made with this excessive eagerness are not usually kept, as Scripture says, "Substance got in haste shall be diminished" (Prov. 13:11). Not only diminished, but it may be the cause of a fall: "And he that is hasty with his feet shall stumble" (Prov. 19:2); and if he stumbles, the higher he falls, the greater the danger, for he will not stop until he has reached the bottom of the ladder.

Third, there is the danger of being careless about overloading the boat. There is danger, of course, in sailing it empty, as it can then be tossed about on the waves of temptation. But there is also danger of so overloading it as to cause it to sink.

Fourth, it can happen that, in crucifying the old man, the new man is also crucified and thus made unable through weakness to practice virtue. St. Bernard tells us that because of this excess we lose four things: "The body loses the effects of the good work, the soul its devotion, our neighbor good example, and God His honor" (*Ad fratres de Monte Dei*, I, c. II, n.32 *PL* 184,328). From this we infer that whosoever thus mistreats the living temple of God is guilty of sacrilege. St. Bernard says that the neighbor is deprived of good example, because the fall of one and the ensuing scandal are a source of scandal to others; he calls them, in cause at least, disturbers of unity and enemies of peace. The example of such a fall frightens many and makes them tepid in their spiritual progress. In the fallen there is danger of pride and vainglory, since they prefer their own judgment to the judgment of everyone else, usurping what is not their own by setting themselves up as judges in their own cause when the rightful judge is their superior.

Besides these, there are also other disadvantages, such as overloading themselves with weapons which they cannot use, like David with the armor of Saul. They apply the spurs to a spirited horse rather than the rein. Therefore, there is need of discretion on this point to keep the practice of virtue between both extremes. St. Bernard gives this advice: "Good will is not always to be trusted, but it must be bridled, regulated, especially in beginners" (*Ibid.* 1.1 C.9: *PL* 184,324), if one wishes to benefit others without disadvantages to himself, for "he that is evil to himself, to whom will he be good?" (Eccles. 14:5)

6. If discretion seems to you to be some rare bird and hard to come by, make up for it with obedience, whose counsel is certain. Hear what St. Bernard says of those who wish to follow their own opinion: "Whatever is done without the approval or against the wish of the spiritual father should be set down as vainglory, and not as something worthy of reward. (*Cantica* serm. 19.7: *PL* 183, 866B). We should remember that "it is like the sin of witchcraft to rebel, and like the crime of idolatry to refuse to obey" (1 Sam. 15:23), as is said in Holy Scripture. Thus, if you wish to hold the middle way between the extreme of tepidity and indiscreet fervor, discuss your affairs with the superior and keep within the limits set down by obedience. If you have a great desire of mortification, use it rather in breaking your wills and bringing your judgments under the yoke of obedience rather than in weakening your bodies and afflicting them beyond due measure, especially in these years of your studies.

7. I should not wish you to think from what I have here writ-

ten that I do not approve of what I have learned of some of your mortifications. I know that these and other holy follies have been profitably used by the saints and that they are useful to obtain self-mastery and bring down richer graces on us, especially in the beginning. But for one who has acquired some mastery over his self-love, what I have said about reducing to a discreet moderation I consider best, provided one does not withdraw from obedience. It is thus obedience that I recommend very earnestly to you, joined with that virtue which is a compendium of all the others and which Jesus Christ so earnestly recommends when He calls it his especial commandment: "This is my commandment, that you love one another as I have loved you" (John 15:12). And I wish that you preserve this union and lasting love, not only among yourselves, but that you extend it to all, and endeavor to enkindle in your souls the lively desire for the salvation of your neighbor, appraising the value of each soul from the price our Lord paid of His life's blood. This you do on the one hand by acquiring learning and on the other by increasing fraternal charity, making yourselves perfect instruments of God's grace and co-laborers in the sublime work of leading God's creatures back to Him as their last end.

Do not imagine that in this interval given to your studies you are of no use to your neighbor; because, besides the profit to yourself which well-ordered charity requires—"Have pity on thy own soul, pleasing God (Eccles. 30:24)—you are serving God's honor and glory in many ways.

First, by your present labor and the intention with which you undertake and regulate everything for your neighbor's edification, just as soldiers waiting to get supplies of arms and munitions for the operation about to be launched cannot say that their labor is not in the service of their king. Even if death should overtake one before he begins to work exteriorly for his neighbor, he shall not for that reason have failed in the service of his neighbor, having helped him by the mere fact of his preparation. But besides the intention for the future, he should each day offer himself to God for his neighbor. As God is willing to accept the offering, he can serve as an instrument for the help of his neighbor no less than he would have done by preaching or hearing confessions.

8. The second way is to attain a high degree of virtue, because you will thus be able to make your neighbor such as you are yourselves. For it is God's will that the process of generation observed in material things be observed in due proportion in things spiritual. Philosophy and experience teach us that in the generation of man or animals, besides the general causes such as the heavens, another cause or agent of the same species is required which possesses the same form as that which is to be transmitted, and for this reason

the form of humility, patience, charity, and so forth, to others, God wills that the immediate cause which He uses as instrument, such as the preacher or confessor, be humble, charitable, patient. With the result, as I said, that, when you benefit yourselves with a growth in virtue, you are also of great service to the neighbor. You are preparing an instrument that is not less, but better fitted to confer grace by leading a virtuous life than by leading a learned one, although both learning and virtue are required if the instrument is to be perfect.

9. The third way of helping the neighbor is by the example of a good life. In this respect, as I have told you, the good scent of your lives has spread abroad and exerts a good influence even beyond the limits of this Kingdom (Portugal). I trust that the author of all good will continue His gifts and increase them in you, so that, as you daily grow in perfection, the fragrance of your virtues and the resulting edification will likewise grow, even without your seeking it.

10. The fourth way of helping your neighbor is very far-reaching indeed, and consists in holy desires and prayers. The demands of your life of study do not permit you to devote much time to prayer, yet you can make up for this by desires, since the time you devote to your various exercises is a continuous prayer, seeing that you are engaged in them only for God's service. But in this and other matters you have close at hand those who can advise you as to details. Indeed, for the same reason part of what I have written might have been omitted, but it is so seldom that I write you that I thought I could give myself the consolation of writing at some length.

11. This is all for the present, except to beg God our Creator and Redeemer that, as it has pleased Him to bestow so great a grace on you as to call you and give you the firm desire of being employed entirely in His service, so He would be pleased to continue and increase His gifts in all, so that you will persevere unwaveringly and grow in His service to His greater honor and glory and the help of His Church.

Rome

Yours in Our Lord,

Ignatius

TO THE MEMBERS OF THE SOCIETY IN PADUA

(MI I 572-577)

This letter was written by Ignatius' secretary Father Polanco at the request of the saint expressing the feelings of the early Society about poverty.

The founder of the College of Padua, Andrés Lippomani, was not coming up with the income promised to the college. With this excuse Ignatius not only consoles his Jesuits but expands on the virtue of poverty.

May the grace and true love of Jesus Christ our Lord be ever in our hearts and increase from day to day to the very end of our lives. Amen.

Dearly beloved Fathers and Brothers in Christ.

A letter addressed to Father Master Laínez in Florence has come to us through the hands of our and your friend Peter Santini. In it we learn, among other things, of the love of poverty, of that poverty which you have chosen for the love of the poor Christ, and the opportunity you sometimes have of suffering some lack of necessities owing to the inadequacy of the help offered you by the kind and charitable Prior of the Trinidad.

It is not necessary to exhort to patience those who are mindful of the state they have embraced and who keep before their eyes the naked Christ upon His cross. And this is especially true since it is clear from the aforementioned letter what a welcome this poverty is given by all of you when you experience its effects. And yet since our Father Ignatius, who has a true father's affection for you, has entrusted me with the task of writing you, I will console myself, while consoling all of you, with this grace which His Infinite Goodness allows both you and us of feeling the effects of that holy poverty. I have no means of knowing how high a degree of this grace is yours, but with us it is in a very high degree, quite in keeping with our profession.

I call poverty a grace because it is a very special gift from God; as Scripture says, "Poverty and riches are from God" (Eccles. 11:14). How much God loved it His only-begotten Son has shown us, who, coming down from the kingdom of heaven, chose to be born in poverty and grow up in it. He loved it, not only in life, suffering hunger and thirst, "without any place to lay His head" (Matt. 8:20: Luke 9:58), but even in death, wishing to be despoiled of everything, even His clothing, and to be in want of everything, even of water in His thirst.

Wisdom which cannot err wishes to show the world, according to St. Bernard, how precious a jewel is poverty, the value of which the world did not know. He chose it for Himself, so that His teaching, "Blessed are they that hunger and thirst, blessed are the poor, etc." (Matt. 5:3: Luke 6:20) should not be out of harmony with His life.

Christ likewise showed us the high esteem He had of poverty in the choice and employment of His friends, who lived in poverty, especially in the New Testament, beginning with His most holy Mother and His apostles, and continuing on with so many Christians through the course of the centuries right up to the present, vassals imitating their king, soldiers their captain, and members their head, Jesus Christ.

So great are the poor in the sight of God that it was especially for them that Jesus Christ was sent into the world: "By reason of the misery of the needy and the groans of the poor, now will I arise, saith the Lord" (Ps. 11:6). And elsewhere, "He hath anointed me to preach the gospel to the poor. (Luke 4:18), words which our Lord recalls when He tells them to give an answer to St. John, "The poor have the gospel preached to them" (Matt. 11:5). Our Lord so preferred the poor to the rich that He chose the entire college of His apostles from among the poor, to live and associate with them, to make them princes of His Church, and to set them up as judges of the twelve tribes of Israel—that is, of all the faithful—and the poor will be His counselors. To such a degree has He exalted the state of poverty!

Friendship with the poor makes us friends of the eternal King. Love of poverty makes kings even on earth, kings not of earth but of heaven. And this can be seen from the fact that the kingdom of heaven is promised in the future to others. To the poor and to those who suffer persecution for justice' sake the Immutable Truth promises it for the present: "Blessed are the poor in spirit, for theirs is the kingdom of heaven" (Matt. 5:3; Luke 6:20). Even in this world they have a right to the kingdom.

And not only are they kings, but they share their kingdom with others, as our Lord teaches us in St. Luke, "Make unto you friends of the mammon of iniquity, that when you shall fail they may receive you into everlasting dwellings" (Luke 16:9). These friends are the poor, particularly the voluntary poor, through whose merits they who help them enter into the tabernacles of glory. For they, according to St. Augustine, are the least of all, of whom our Lord says, "As long as you did it to one of these my least brethren, you did it to me" (Matt. 24:40).

In this, therefore, we see the excellence of poverty which does not stoop to make a treasure of the dunghill or of worthless earth, but with all the resources of its love buys that precious treasure in the field of the Church, whether it be our Lord Himself or His spiritual gifts, from which He Himself is never separated.

But if you consider the genuine advantages which are properly to be found in those means that are suited to help us attain our last end, you will see that holy poverty preserves us from many sins, ridding us as it does of the occasion of sin, for poverty has not wherewith to feed its love, *non habet unde suum paupertas pascat amorem* (Ovid, *De remedio amoris*, 749). It kills the worm of riches, which is pride; cuts off the infernal leeches of lust and gluttony, and many other sins as well. And if one should fall through weakness, it helps him to rise at once. For it has none of that attachment which, like glue, binds the heart to earth and to earthly things and deprives us of that ease in rising and turning once more to God. It enables us to hear better in all things the voice—that is, the inspiration—of the Holy Spirit by removing the obstructions that hinder it. It gives greater efficacy to our prayers in the sight of God because "the Lord hath heard the desire of the poor" (Ps. 9:17). It speeds us on our way along the path of virtue, like a traveler who has been relieved of all his burdens. It frees us from that slavery common to so many of the world's great ones, in which everything obeys or serves money (Eccles. 10:19). The soul is filled with every virtue if poverty is in the spirit, for the soul that is swept free of the love of earthly things shall in the same proportion be full of God, having received His gifts. And it is certain that it must be very rich, for God's promise is at the rate of a hundred to one, even in this life. The promise is fulfilled even in a temporal sense, when that is for our good. But in the spiritual sense it cannot fail of fulfillment. Thus it is inescapable that they who freely make themselves poor in earthly possessions shall be rich in the gifts of God.

This same poverty is that land fertile in strong men *fecunda virorum paupertas* (Lucan, *Pharsalia*, I, 165), as the poet said in words which are truer of Christian poverty than Roman. This poverty is the furnace which tests the progress of fortitude and other virtues and the touchstone which distinguishes genuine gold from counterfeit. It is also the moat which renders secure the camp of our conscience in the religious life; it is the foundation upon which the edifice of perfection should rise, according to the words of our Lord, "If thou wilt be perfect, go, sell what thou hast, and give to the poor . . . and come, follow me" (Matt. 19:21). It is the mother, the nurse, the guardian of religion, since it conceives, nourishes, and preserves it; while on the other hand an abundance of temporal possessions weakens, corrupts, and ruins it. Thus we can easily see the great advantage and the excellence of holy poverty, especially since it is poverty that wins salvation from Him who "will save the poor and the humble" (2 Kings 22:28; Ps. 17:28) and obtains for us the eternal kingdom from the same Lord, who says that the kingdom of heaven belongs to the poor, an advantage that is beyond all comparison. So, no matter how hard it may happen to be, holy poverty should be accepted voluntarily.

But really it is not hard; rather, it is the cause of great delight in him who embraces it willingly. Even Seneca (*Epistola* 80 *ad Lucillum*) says that the poor man laughs with greater ease because he has no cares to upset him, a truth which daily experience shows us in the instance of the wayside beggar. If you were to observe the satisfaction in his life, you would see that he is more cheerful than the great merchants, magistrates, princes, and other persons of distinction. If this is true of people who are not poor by choice, what shall we say of those who are poor because they choose to be? For, neither possessing nor loving anything earthly which they could lose, they enjoy a peace that is imperturbable and a tranquillity that is supreme. On the other hand, riches are for those who possess them like the sea that is tossed by the storm. Moreover, these voluntary poor, because of the peace and security of their conscience, enjoy an uninterrupted cheerfulness which is like a banquet without end. They prepare themselves in a very special way by means of this very poverty for heavenly consolations, which are wont to abound in the servants of God in proportion as they lack an abundance of the goods and the comforts of earth, if only they know how to fill themselves with Christ, so that He will make up for everything and occupy in their hearts the vacancy left by all else.

But I must not pursue this further. Let what I have said suffice for your consolation and mine to encourage us to love holy poverty, remembering that the excellence, advantage, and joy I have mentioned belong only to that poverty which is loved and willingly embraced, not to the poverty that is accepted because it cannot be avoided. I will add only this, that those who love poverty should as occasion offers love her retinue, which consists of poor meals, poor clothes, poor sleeping accommodations, and to be held of little account. Whoever loves poverty and is unwilling to feel want, or any of its effects, would be a very delicate poor man and would give the impression of one who loved the name rather than the reality, of one who loved rather in words than in the depth of his heart.

That is all for the present, except to ask our Lord, our Master and true model of spiritual poverty, to grant all of us the gift of this precious heritage, which He bestows on His brothers and coheirs, to the end that the spiritual riches of His grace abound in us, and at the end, the ineffable riches of His glory. Amen.

Rome
August 6, 1547

TO ST. JUAN DE AVILA

(MI II, 316-320)

Ignatius had an extensive correspondence with St. Juan de Avila. At one time it had been considered to join forces together and form a single order out of the two communities. The idea was abandoned by Ignatius, though their friendship continued. In this letter Ignatius thanks Juan de Avila for his support to the Society and advises him how to avoid and counterattack the accusations raised by the inquisitor Melchor Cano.

Very reverend Sir in our Lord.

May the sovereign grace and everlasting love of Christ our Lord greet you and visit you with His most holy gifts and spiritual graces.

I have heard on different occasions and from several of Ours of the unfailing support and ardent charity which your reverence has always given to this least Society, and I made up my mind to write you for two reasons. The first is to give some sign of recognition and gratitude by way of the warmest thanks to God, and to your reverence in His most holy name, for all that you have done for the glory of the Divine Majesty in behalf of us, your reverence's devoted servants, to secure an increase in our numbers and our devotion, I offer myself to your reverence as one of your associates or spiritual sons in our Lord, who am willing to comply with the utmost of the strength His Divine Majesty will give me with whatever the Lord of all may command. By so acting I am persuaded I shall be much the gainer in the Divine Goodness, both because of the return I can make for my great obligations and the service I can be to the servants of my Lord, in serving whom I feel that I am serving the same Lord of all.

My second reason is that, as your reverence will have heard reports that are favorable to us, it seems to me to be only just in the Divine Majesty that you also hear other reports that are not. It is my firm hope that this great spiritual trial of theirs will result in greater glory to God. The fact is, as one of Ours writes from Salamanca, they have suffered and still are suffering considerable opposition from certain Dominican fathers who are moved, I think, more by a pardonable zeal than by trustworthy information. This opposition must have been going on for the last ten months. But now again from letters dated November 25 and December 2 last, it would seem that the opposition has increased and gone beyond all limits, so that we have been driven to adopt measures recommended by St. Augustine and many other holy doctors. In his treatise *De viduitate (De bono viduitatis, epistula ad Julianam viduam, cap. 27)* St. Augustine says, "Our life is necessary for ourselves, our reputation for others." And St. Chrysostom, "Let us learn from His example to bear our wrongs magnanimously, but wrongs against God we should not bear even to listen to" (*Homilia quinta super Matthaeum*, op. imperf., post medium).

St. Jerome in his letter against Rufinus says, "I would not have any one put up with the accusation of heresy" (*Ad Pammachium adversus errores Ioannis Hierosolymitani episcopi Opera*, edit. Basileae, 1565, II. 162). And St. Thomas: "We must be ready to undergo insults, should it be expedient. Sometimes, however, we should repel the insult offered, for two reasons particularly: (1) because of the good of him who offers the insult, that his boldness may be held in check, and he not repeat his attempt in the future, according to the proverb, 'Answer a fool according to his folly, lest he imagine himself to be wise', (Prov. 26:5); and (2) because of the good of others, whose progress might be impeded by the insults offered us. Whence Gregory, in the ninth homily on Ezekiel, says, "They who are a model for others in life should, when they can, repress the words of detractors, lest those who hear their preaching heed them not and, remaining in their bad habits, condemn virtue" (II, II, q. 72, a.3).

St. Bonaventure in his *Apologeticum* says, "Although you ought patiently to put up with wrongs done you and make no complaint against them, why is it that you not only fail to do that but, not satisfied with the judgments of the bishops, you obtain judges and protectors from the Holy See and at great cost and expense summon before them whoever are a source of annoyance to you, even though it be slight, until they have given you full satisfaction? This is in open contradiction to the Apostle, who says in his Epistle to the Corinthians, 'There is plainly a fault among you, that you have lawsuits one with another.' (I Cor. 6:7). I answer, 'Religious should patiently endure wrongs and annoyances from which no other evil ensues, except what is felt for the moment, as is the case with offensive words, or loss of property, or blows, and the like, since they cause no further harm. But when greater damage can result, such as serious harm to souls, patience is no longer expedient' " (*Libellus apologeticus in eos qui fratrum minorum adversantur*, quaest. 12). Cajetan says in the *Summula*, "It is a sin to disregard one's own good name which has been falsely besmirched, when such neglect can result in harm or the fear of harm to others, since reputation is necessary to us for the benefit of others. And, as St. Augustine says in such a case, 'He who, confident of his innocence, disregards his reputation, is cruel, because he kills the souls of others' " (Cajetan, *Summa*, Pars I).

This, we think, should be our course for God's glory. First, with all politeness and kindness send them a letter from one of the cardinals, one who seems to have some influence with them. (Juan Alvarez de Toledo, O.P.). Second, present them with a patent from their general. Third, if we get no results from either of these attempts, in order to live up to our obligations to God our Lord and charity toward our neighbor and, moreover, to squelch the power of the enemy of our human nature, who in this manner prevails on people of learning and even religious created for God's greater glory, we shall proceed to a formal process with all fulminations of a papal brief. Your reverence will see, after being thus informed, that you will have greater reason for earnestly recommending to God in your holy sacrifices and prayers our petition that His Divine Majesty may deign to bestow His favor and aid on the side which will redound more to His praise and glory. With the help of His grace we neither seek nor desire aught else.

May this and all things else tend always to His glory, and may He deign in His infinite and sovereign goodness to give us all His bountiful grace so that we may always know His most holy will and perfectly fulfill it.

January 24, 1549

TO FATHER DIEGO LAÍNEZ

(MI IV, 498-500)
This letter was dictated by Father Ignatius to Father Polanco, and it is most remarkable for its hard tone against Father La[4]inez, one of Ignatius' first companions and the next general of the Society of Jesus.

My dear Father.

Let this letter be understood not as coming from a son of your reverence, as I, Polanco, really am, who owe you all respect and reverence, but from the pen of our father, who has bidden me write what is here contained. I have wanted to write for some days, but as you have had a quartan fever, I have waited to give you a chance to improve.

Our father is not a little displeased with your reverence, and the more so, that the faults of those who are loved are always more serious to those who love them. How much more reason we have to bewail these faults when they are committed by one we least thought would be guilty! He has charged me to write you concerning a few of these faults, so that, once they are called to your attention, you will avoid repeating them in the future. This will be easy for one to whom God has given so much good will as He has to your reverence.

First of all, then, the Prior of La Trinidad wrote about Master Andrew, urging that he (Ignatius) send Master Jerome Otello in his place. To quote his own words, "For many reasons, my dear son in Christ, Master Jerome Otello would be quite acceptable, according to what Father Laínez has told me." This was no slight mistake, even though it was done with a good intention; for there is no reason why you should have encouraged or counseled the Prior to ask our father for what he did not have to give. At least, you might have learned the mind of our father before giving such advice to the Prior. I wanted to give the reasons for this, and for what follows, but our father thought otherwise; that is, that none should be given, since the submission of your own judgment, which you owe to your superior in all that pertains to his office, should be reason enough for you. Besides, it is expressly forbidden to suggest to persons of position to write to our father and ask for certain individuals without first consulting him. Otherwise many inconveniences may follow, especially when the request has to be refused.

The second mistake was the cause of the first; more than a merely personal fault, it was your disagreeing with your superior over the removal of Father Frusius from Venice. You not only disagreed, but you showed Frusius himself and Father Salmerón and Father Olave that you disagreed, or that you did not approve of our father's order. Of course, your reverence sees how becoming it is to let newcomers, who should find in him a mirror of perfection, see that he thinks bad what the superior thinks good. Later Master Andrew wrote a few reasons which to himself and Fathers Salmeron and Olave seemed sufficient to warrant his removal from Venice to Rome. Neither did he like some of the observations made by your reverence in your answer, such as the remark about the bad feeling that spread through the towns, and so forth, as indicating a disagreeing of your own judgment with the judgment of the superior. Advice or representation is good if it is reasonable, but a difference of opinion is not.

The third mistake which has caused our father no little pain is that you sent Gaspar here, without first giving some notice of his condition, merely contenting yourself with saying, "because they were from Padua," and so forth. It is not right for your reverence to act so secretly when sending a person like him to our house here. Every kind of secrecy and pretense like this with the superior, who ought to be helped with one's knowledge and not impeded, is looked upon as quite out of place in this Society, or in any other order. Our father has also been displeased because, after having sent him to you to be dismissed by you, you approved of his wish to return here, saying that you thought he was worthy of mercy, among other things, which our father calls "decrees." It does not at all please him to see you act in this way, as though you were issuing decrees, seeing that it is so unbecoming in writing to a superior. What is more, he has told me to write to you and tell you to attend to your own office, which if you do well, you will be doing more than a little. You are not to trouble yourself in giving your view of his affairs, as he does not want anything of the kind from you unless he asks for it; and much less now than before you took office, since your administration of your own province has not done much to increase your credit in his eyes. Examine these mistakes in the presence of God our Lord, and for three days take some time for prayer to this end. Then write, if you admit that they are mistakes and faults. Choose also the penance you think you deserve; write it out and send it to him. But do not do penance in this matter before you receive the answer of our father.

This is all for the present, except that I pray God our Lord to grant all, and especially to this scribe as the most needy, much light to know ourselves and abase ourselves, and grace to know and do His holy will in all things.

Rome
November 2, 1552

TO THE EMPEROR CHARLES V

(MI VI, 421-422)

Ignatius was trying to gain the favor of the emperor to introduce the Society of Jesus into Flanders and endowing the college of Louvain with a fixed income. Ignatius asks the Emperor to interest his sister, Mary, then regent of the Low Countries, in this enterprise.

This letter is interesting for several reasons. The emperor was not favorable to the Jesuits, and yet his own daughter, Princess Juana, was soon to become a Jesuit. The Jesuits used a code name of Mateo Sánchez to refer to the Princess and the "father of Mateo Sánchez" to refer to the Emperor. This letter was never sent to the Emperor, but we include it here to better understand the admission of the princess into the Society.

The sovereign grace and eternal love of Christ our Lord be with your Majesty, with his most holy gifts and spiritual graces.

Since the Providence of God, our Creator and Lord, has placed Your Majesty in such a position and office, and given you so much zeal that you regard matters of universal good and of God's glory as your own, and since His glory has raised up in Your Majesty's time, this humble Society of ours by whose ministry He is served and I hope will be served increasingly in your realms and in other parts of Christendom and beyond the bounds thereof—it seemed to me in our

Lord that, since a great obstacle to this work has arisen, it was fitting to have recourse to Your Majesty, whose every thought, I am persuaded, goes straight to God's service. I therefore humbly beseech Your Majesty that you would deign to listen to certain details which will be submitted to you by us, and that you would make provision as should seem to you to be for God's greater glory.

We all hold ourselves as a thing very much your own, as we are in our Lord, yours and the King of England's, as we are likewise at the disposal of the most serene Princesses, your daughters, of the King of the Romans and the Queen of Portugal, Your Majesty's brother and sister, not only as your vassals which we are for the most part, certain of us coming from families well known to Your Majesty, but as under a deep obligation for the kindness and goodwill which God our Lord and the author of all good inspired you with for the furthering of this Society in its early days.

May it please Him to give us all His abundant grace that we may know His most holy will and fulfill it perfectly.

Rome
March 3, 1554

TO FATHER FRANCIS BORGIA

(MI I,viii,198-219 *et.seq.*)

The following letter, though in appearance merely indicating the procedure to admit new members into the Society, was forced on Ignatius by one of the most bizarre incidents of the early Society.

Princess Juana, daughter of the Emperor Charles V, and also the Regent of Spain, had become a widow at the age of nineteen. It is probable that at this time she made a vow to enter the Franciscan Order. While she was a regent, there was, of course, no question of this happening. Suddenly, in the summer of 1554, under the influence of Borgia and Araoz, she decided to enter the Society of Jesus instead. Father Araoz, contrary to Ignatius, considered a female branch of the Society desirable. To that end he had encouraged several women with hopes of establishing one. Father Francis Borgia informed Ignatius in Rome of the regent's decision. A lively correspondence began between Borgia and Ignatius in which the Infanta always appeared under the pseudonym of Mateo Sánchez. In October 1554 Ignatius summoned the Jesuits named in the letter to find the solution to the problem. A refusal of the obviously very definite request of Her Highness was simply impossible. On the other hand, the nineteen-year-old widow was naturally still so much a possible subject for the Hapsburg matrimonial policy that no irremovable obstacle to marriage, such as the taking of religious vows, could be considered. So Ignatius decided to give Mateo Sánchez permission to take the vows of a scholastic in the Society of Jesus. Though these vows of poverty, chastity, and obedience bind the individual, the Society re-serves to itself the freedom to release from them when the case arises. In this manner both parties were satisfied.

Information about the acceptance of a person into the Society and of the manner of procedure.

Dr. Nadal, Dr. Olave, Dr. Madrid, P. Luis Goncalves, and Master Polanco have taken counsel together by order of our Father Master Ignatius, to treat of the manner of admitting Mateo Sánchez into the Society by virtue of a bull from the apostolic Penitentiary which commutes the simple vow of the religion of St. Francis into ours. If, on the one hand, we regard our constitutions which forbid such an admission, and the privileges of our foundation bulls, we cannot be forced to accept such a charge. On the other hand, understanding that three persons of like condition were admitted in the early days of the Society, and in view of the terms of the above-mentioned bull, we have resolved on the following:

That this person be admitted, and that the admission might be fittingly made in the way in which the scholars of the Society are received, on probation, it being made clear to the said person that for two years (and longer if it seem good to the superior), it is usual to be on probation, and that until this period has elapsed our constitutions do not impose any obligation to take a vow of any kind. If anyone, however, makes a vow of his own free will before this time has elapsed, in conformity with the Society's constitutions he should make it in this form:

My God and my creator, eternal Father and Lord of all things, I, N., although in all things I find myself most unworthy to appear and present myself before your divine Majesty, yet looking to your infinite mercies and with the desire of serving you (through the help of your most holy grace) always and without end, I hereby make a vow and promise to your most sacred and divine Majesty, in the presence of the most glorious Virgin Mary and of the whole court of heaven, to enter the congregation of the Society of Jesus and to live and die therein. In this order I promise perpetual poverty, chastity, and obedience, interpreted according to the constitutions of the said Society. I beseech your divine mercy to accept me as a pleasing sacrifice through the blood of Christ our Lord, and to vouchsafe to grant me the grace to accomplish what you have deigned to make me desire and offer.

In such a place, on such a day, month and year.

Whoever makes such a vow is a religious of the Society, as may be seen from the sixth part of the constitutions.

It further seemed that it should be explained to this person that such vows have full force and vigor just so long as the superior wants to keep in the Society the person making them, and no longer. If this person is admitted in this form, on probation for two years, during which where is no obligation to make a vow, if, nevertheless, a private vow is made, after the probation of two years, the obligation of the initial vow must be fulfilled by entering the Society in the ordinary way.

Similarly the above-mentioned fathers were of opinion that whosoever the person may be, since they are admitted to the Society with such a special privilege and on that alone, they should keep the admission under the seal of secrecy and as in confession, because, if it came to be known, it might be taken as a precedent, so that some other person of like condition would trouble the Society for a similar admission.

As to the rest, this person shall not have to change their dress, or residence, nor to give any demonstration whatever of what it is sufficient should be kept between themselves and God our Lord. The Society or someone from it, shall have the obligation of the care of this person's soul, in so far as it is demanded by God's service and the comfort of that soul, to the glory of God our Lord.

Rome, October 26, 1554

TO THE PRINCESS JUANA, REGENT OF SPAIN

(MI I, 8 235)

Thus it came about that the daughter of that Emperor Charles V became a true member of the Society of Jesus. The immediate preparation still took a few months. In November 1554, Ignatius had to ask the pope for commutation of the regent's previous vow to join the Franciscans, without, of course, mentioning her real name. At the same time he hastened to write once more to Spain, saying that although Mateo Sánchez could be accepted, this must remain an absolute exception.

When all the formalities were completed, Ignatius could send in a formal letter to the Regent at Salamanca the actual permission to enter the society. With perfect tact and diplomatic skill, the Princess was informed of everything necessary, without the uninitiated reader being able to learn the real nature of the letter's contents.

My Lady in our Lord,

The sovereign grace and eternal love of Christ our Lord be always with us, to our continual help and favor.

From a letter from Father Francis Borgia I have understood what a great service it would be to you that we should comply with the pious and holy desires of a certain person. Although there was no small difficulty in the matter, we put such difficulty second to the will we all have and should have to serve Your Highness in our Lord.

Because Father Francis will speak of the details of which Your Highness will wish to be informed, since I have confidence in whatever he will say on my behalf, I shall say no more, but humbly beg Your Highness to consider us all as a thing very much yours, since we are so in our Lord.

I beseech the divine and sovereign goodness that He gave us all His abundant grace that we may always know His holy will and accomplish it perfectly.

Rome
January 3, 1555

THE WAY OF DEALING WITH SUPERIORS

(MI IX, 90-92)

These instructions were drawn by Ignatius on December 1, 1554. They were sent to the colleges and houses of the Society in Spain and Sicily.

1. He who has business with a superior should have the matter well in hand, arranged in order, and thought out by himself or others, in keeping with the greater or lesser importance of the matter. In smaller matters, however, or when there is need of hurry and no time is available for study or conferring, it is left to his own judgment as to whether he should represent the matter to the superior or not, if he has not been able to confer with others or study the matter himself.

2. After he has examined and studied his proposals, he should place them before the superior, and tell him that this point has been examined by himself or with others, as the case may be. He should give the superior the results of his examination and study, but he should never say to a superior in discussing a point with him, "This or that is right, or this or that will be," but he should speak conditionally and with a certain amount of reserve.

3. Once he has proposed the matter to the superior, it will be the superior's duty to make a decision, or wait for further study, or refer the proposals back to those who submitted them, or name others to examine them, or make the decision then and there, according to the nature of the difficulty involved.

4. If I point out some drawback in the decision of the superior, and the superior reaffirms his decision, there should be no answer or discussion for the time being.

5. But if, after the decision of the superior, he who is dealing with him sees that something else would be better, let him call the

superior's attention to it, adding his reason. And even if the superior had withheld judgment, this may be done after three or four hours, or a day. He could then represent to the superior what he thinks would be good, preserving, however, a manner of speaking and using such words that there would neither be nor appear to be any dissension or altercation. He should then accept in silence what is then and there decided.

6. But even supposing that a decisive answer was given the first time, or even the second, he might, a month or more later, re-present his view in the manner already indicated. For time and experience uncover many things, and the superior himself may change his mind.

7. He who deals with a superior should accommodate himself to the character and abilities of the superior. He should speak distinctly and so that he can be heard, clearly, and whenever possible at an hour that is suited to the superior's convenience.

8. As far as possible, they should not wait until the day or the evening before to write what is supposed to be written by Saturday, nor at other ordinary or extraordinary times should they wait until the post is ready to leave for places beyond Italy, and then write in a hurry. But they should try to arrange that what should be written by Saturday be begun the Sunday previous, and continue until the end of Wednes-day, leaving as little as possible unwritten of the answers to letters received before that date. In this way Thursday, Friday, and Saturday will be free to deal with and answer matters of importance which may turn up and need an immediate answer.

9. Ordinarily do not write to different parts of Italy oftener than every month, informing the rectors of this order which is given, unless there be cases which do not admit of greater delay.

10. Write every three months to places that are more distant, unless there is an occurrence of some importance, or the posts are more convenient than usual.

11. With regard to the reception of candidates for the Society in Italy, the following points are sent to the colleges, which deal with the qualities required of those who are to be admitted to the Society. And they should not receive anyone, or send anyone here, until we have been informed about them, point by point.

12. However, if there are some who very strikingly and beyond the possibility of any doubt fulfill the conditions set forth in the points, they may be received, or even sent to Rome, if they are of such high standing or if there be danger in delay, in which case superiors will have to use their own judgment. But it would be much better to advise the general in Rome and wait for an answer. There might be no difficulty about the candidates, but there might well be difficulty for the house in Rome.

13. We are sending the same points and directions everywhere,

which have been made out for Italy and Sicily (which is always to be understood when we speak of Italy). It will be of advantage to know in other places what goes on in Italy, as this will be of the greatest possible help to them. True it is that in places far distant from Rome, such as in other kingdoms, there is no need of consulting with the general about admissions, or sending men to Rome. But the charity and discretion of the commissary or provincial with whom lower superiors such as rectors will consult, will take the place of the general's consultation. There could well be cases which would not admit of the delay in consulting the general.

14. Provision has been made that a copy of this notice be sent to all places where there are any of the Society, and in the book in which this is entered in Rome a note has been made at the foot of the page that it has been sent everywhere, and that it has been received. Let a reminder be made of this notice each time that a letter is written until such time that a notice comes of its receipt.

15. The same instructions will be sent to India, and the provincial should send the same to the remote parts of his jurisdiction. The same dispatch can be sent from Portugal to Brazil and the Congo, although in such remote places, especially among infidels and recently converted Christians, even though they should be helped by what is written, it is left to the discretion of superiors, who, taking into consideration the condition of the region and other circumstances, will act according to their judgment of what is best for the greater glory of God and the greater spiritual progress of souls.

Notes

FOREWORD

1. See, for example, Frank Manuel, *A Portrait of Newton* (Cambridge, Mass.: Harvard University Press, 1968), Frances A. Yates. *Giordano Bruno and the Hermetic Tradition* (Chicago: Chicago University Press, 1964), Alexandre Koyré *Mystiques, spirituels, et alchemistes* (Paris, 1955), and P.M. Rattansi, "The Social Interpretation of Science in the Seventeenth Century," in P. Mathias (ed.), *Science and Society, 1600-1900* (Cambridge: Cambridge University Press, 1972), pp. 1-31.

2. See Rattansi, "Social Interpretation of Science in the Seventeenth Century."

3. See, for example, the excellent study of medieval and early renaissance mnemonic art, *The Art of Memory*, by Frances A. Yates (London: Penguin. 1969).

4. See Jonathan D. Spence. *The Memory Place of Matteo Ricci* (New York: Viking, 1984) chapter one.

5. See Hugo Rahner, *Ignatius the Theologian* (London: Chapman, 1968).

6. This article has been published in English as a separate monograph entitled, *Discernments of Spirits* by Jacques Guillet, Gustave Bardy, Francois Vandenbroucke, Joseph Pegon, and Henri Martin (Collegeville, Minn.: Liturgical Press, 1970).

NATIVE GENERAL BACKGROUND
OF IGNATIUS DE LOYOLA

1. Bataillon, Marcel (1950) *Erasmo y España*. Mexico: Fondo de Cultura Económica, pp. 1-71.
This is the most complete and scholarly book about the spirituality of XVIth century Spain. It completes and at times corrects the Jesuit sources of the same

period. Unfortunately, it is not available in English, though besides the Spanish translation it may be found in the original French.

2. Byron, William (1978) *Cervantes, A Biography*. New York: Doubleday & Co., pp. 3-69.

Technologies may be better described, as we do in this study, than defined. One should, however, remember that the origins of discussion on technology go as far back in our culture as Plato. One should read in this respect Plato's *Gorgias* and Aristotle's *Rhetoric* and *Poetics*. A very good summary of these works may be found in a little-known book: de Romilly, J., *Magic and Rhetoric in Ancient Greece* (1975) Cambridge, MA and London: Harvard University Press).

3. Williams, Charles (1959) *Witchcraft, A History of Black Magic in Christian Times*. New York: Meridian Books, The World Publishing Co., p. 14.

4. "Autobiografía", San Ignatius de Loyola (1977) *Obras Completas* Abrr. O.C. Madrid: Biblioteca de Autores Cristianos. A translation may be found in this volume. This is also known as the *Diary of a Pilgrim*, and it is written in the third person singular.

5. de Osuna, Francisco (1981) *The Third Spiritual Alphabet*. trans. by Mary E. Giles New York: Paulist Press.

6. Brenan, Gerald (1973) *St. John of the Cross* Cambridge, London: Cambridge University Press, pp. 91-98.

7. The term *audial* I started using while working with Eastern cultures. I used the term to signify this connection between musical criteria and text, what I call a reading technology. I knew of no other term that denoted this epistemological connection.

8. Tuning theory, as used in audial cultures, establishes the genesis of a musical composition in these four steps: 1) an original blank string fixed at both ends; 2) the string plucked, that is, divided (dismembered) into halves (octave), fourths, fifths, etc.; 3) the sacrifice of tone for new ones to come into being; 4) the embodied identity of singer and song by sharing the same dimensions.

On this model the four weeks of Ignatius follow not only the same pattern, but the pattern is the exercises: 1) Dismemberment of the initial unity the retreatent brings to the exercises; 2) Embodiment of different images and sensitization to them; 3) death to any fixity in image or stage; 4) embodied resurrection and gain of love.

9. Boethius (1967) *The Principles of Music*. trans. Calvin Martin Bower Ann Arbor, Michigan: University Microfilms, Inc. See in particular the classical division of the string, as Plato does in the *Republic*, by the proportions 6:8:9:12. Pp. 61 and 129-143.

10. Spitzer, Leo (1963) *Classical and Christian Ideas of World Harmony*. Baltimore: The John Hopkins Press, p. 8.

This little book is the most comprehensive and insightful reading of early Christianity. I follow it very closely, to the point of paraphrasing Spitzer in parts and correcting him in others. The reader should go directly to this book to put together much material I had to leave out.

11. Turchetto, Gerald (1983). *Plato's Musical Imagination*. Doctoral Thesis, at Stony Brook. Ann Arbor, Michigan: University Microfilms, Inc.

12. Rivers, Elias (1982). "Language and Reality in Quevedo's Sonnet," in *Quevedo in Perspective*, ed. James Iffland (Juan de la Cuesta), Newark, N.J., pp. 17-32.

IMAGINING
PRIMARY TEXT, PRIMARY TECHNOLOGY

1.   Ortega y Gasset met Nietzsche's sister in South America and asked her what her brother thought of the Spaniards. This quotation is her reply, as quoted in Ortega's *Obras Completas* Vol. 8, p. 58.
2.   Williams, Ch. (1941) *Witchcraft*. London: Faber and Faber. (1939) *Descent of the Dove*. Michigan: William B. Eerdmans Publishing Co.
3.   Teresa de Avila only a few years later than Ignatius writes in the same sense that "God is not the product of the imagination: but it is through the imagination that God becomes present" (*Life*,28,10). She also reminds us, with her Castilian irony: "The toad does not fly" (*Life*,23,13). Santa Teresa de Jesus (1982) *Obras Completas*, Bibliotecca de Autores Cristianos. Madrid.
4.   We need only remember the complaints of Teresa de Avila: "And very often, for many years, I was more anxious for the hour I had determined to spend in prayer to be over than I was to remain there...and so unbearable was the misery I felt on entering the oratory, that I had to master all my courage" (*Life*,8,7).
5.   Teresa de Avila describes for us, with her usual clarity, this trans- formation: "The soul undergoes a change; it is always absorbed...the intellectual vision is represented to the imagination so that in conformity to our weakness this presence may last in the memory and keep the thought well-occupied" (*Life*,28,9).
6.   The same sense of reading is in Teresa's works: "At one time I took advantage for my soul in seeing fields, water, flowers; in those things I used to find memory of the Creator; that is they would wake me up and recollect myself; they were as a book" (*Life*,9).
7.   I have in mind books like: Masters, Robert and Jean Houston (19723) *Mind Games: The Guide to Inner Space*. New York: Dell Publishing Co.
8.   This is Carl Gustav Jung's position in (1975) *Grundlagen der analyti- schen Psychologie*. Hamburg: Fischer Taschenbuch Verlag, pp. 106-107.
9.   The image of dismemberment is as old as the *Ṛg Veda*, 2500 B.C. The Dragon Vtra, which never dies, is dismembered again and again so that creation may take place. See: de Nicolás, Antonio (1976) *Meditations through the Ṛg Veda*. Maine. Nicolas Hays. York. Fontenrose, Joseph (1959) *Python: A Study in Delphic Myth and its Origins*. Berkeley, Los Angeles, London: University of California Press.
10. Teresa de Avila is always a challenge in her descriptions. She summarizes the process here described in this manner: "The faculties are like wild horses, they run in all directions; meditation proper begins with the technologies that gather them within" (*Life*,14,2); "There the faculties are not lost, nor do they sleep" (Ibid.); "Only the will is occupied" (Ibid.): "Without knowing how, it becomes captive; it merely consents to God allowing Him to imprison it as one who well knows how to be captive of its lover" (Ibid.). When the soul reaches total death, Teresa describes it: "The water of grace rises up to the throat of this soul" (*Life*,16,2); "This experience does not seem to be anything else than the almost total death to all earthly things" (Ibid.) and she continues: "It seems to me that the soul is crucified since no consolations come to it from heaven, nor visit heaven; neither does it desire any from earth, nor is it on earth...it is as though

crucified between heaven and earth...the intense pain takes away sensory consciousness...and this experience resembles the death agony with the difference that the suffering bears along with it great happiness...it is arduous, delightful martyrdom" (*Life*,20,11).

IMAGINING AND THE PUBLIC DOMAIN

1.   Laureano Albán (1983) *Viaje Interminable*. Madrid: Ediciones Cultura Hispánica. Translated into English by Frederick Fornoff (1983) *The Endless Voyage*. Pittsburgh: International Poetry Forum.
2.   As quoted by James W. Reites, S.J. in "St. Ignatius de Loyola and the Jews," in *Studies in the Spirituality of the Jesuits*, vol. XIII, Sept. '81, n.4, p. 17.
3.   San Ignacio de Loyola (1977) *Obras Completas*. Madrid: Biblioteca de Autores Cristianos, p. 169.
4.   The translations are my own. Teresa's life may be seen in St. Teresa de Avila (1976) *The Collected Works*, trans. Kieran Kavanaugh and Otilio Rodríguez. 2 vols. Washington, D.C.: ICS Publications.
5.   Roland Barthes (1976) *Sade, Fourier, Loyola*. Trans. by Richard Miller. New York: Hill & Wang, pp. 39-75.
6.   Émilie Zum Brunn (1969) *Le Dilemme de L'etre et du Néant chez Saint Augustin*. Paris: Centre National de la Recherche Scientifique. (1978) "L'exégèse augustinienne de 'Ego sum qui sum' et la métaphysique de l'Exode" in *Dieu et l'Etre*, Paris: Centre National de la Recherche Scientifique, p. 155.
7.   Émilie Zum Brunn (1969) Ibid., p. 19ff.
8.   Émilie Zum Brunn (1978) Ibid., p. 3.
9.   Martin Heidegger (1958) "La Question de la Technique," in *Essais et Conférences*, trans. André Préaud. Paris: Gallimard.
10.   See in this respect the inspiring article of Frederick Turner (1983) "The Neural Lyre: Poetic Meter, the Brain, and Time," in *Journal of Social and Biological Structures*, 8, pp. 277-307. The Bibliography in this article is excellent to follow up on some of the suggestions made here.

CONSEQUENCES OF HERMENEUTICS

1.   John Bremer's *On Plato's Polity* (1984, Institute of Philosophy, Houston) deals, in the most pertinent way for this study, on these points. This little monograph and Ernest McClain's *The Pythagorean Plato* are the most insightful studies to come out recently on Plato. Both studies complement each other and also verify each other's insights. From both I use several themes and verifications. I recommend the reader to study both authors diligently. See on the first words of the Republic *On Plato's Polity* pages 18-32.
2.   *On Plato's Polity* p.20
3.   Ortega y Gasset (1971) *Obras Completas,* abbr. *O.C.* 7th Edition. 11 volumes. Madrid: Revista de Occidente, Vol. 8, pp.269-270. (All the translations from the Spanish are my own.)
4.   *Spiritual Exercises* (47): "...on a visible object, for example, contemplating Christ Our Lord during his life time, for He is visible..." It is easy to see the coincidences with Plato's world of Er and its visibility.

5. *O.C.*, vol.5, p.540.
6. *O.C.*, vol.4, p.314. Only the sense. The actual quotation is found in *Mission of the University*, Noatrans, trans. N.Y.: Norton, p.23.
7. *O.C.*, vol. 3, p.500.
8. *O.C.*, vol. 9, p.361.
9. *O.C.*, vol. 5, pp.532-533.

SPIRITUAL EXERCISES

1. This well-known prayer is recommended by Ignatius in the second and third Method of Prayer and whenever he orders the three colloquia. It is already found in some codices of the sixteenth century and in the Book of Hours of the fifteenth. There are differences in the last verses, and therefore it is not easy to know which version Ignatius used. This prayer is not found in the Autograph of the Exercises nor in the Prayers nor editions of the *Exercises* previous to 1576. (See *Obras Completas*, p. 206.)

2. These "Annotations" are a concise directory to the one giving the *Exercises*. In them Ignatius explains the form and goal of the *Exercises* (1); the general way of procedure (2,3); the division and duration (4); the fundamental disposition required of the exercitant (5); behavior of the director towards the exercitant in vital points and main obstacles the exercitant might encounter (6-17); different ways to adapt the *Exercises* and the different types of exercitants (18-20). (MANR 19 [1947], pp. 275-339. *Obras Completas*, p. 207, n.)

3. To reorganize all kinds of love according to the "Origin and Foundation," Calveras (1956) MANR. 28, p. 155; *Práctica de los Ejercicios espirituales* (1964) Barcelona: Balmes, p. 37.

4. This is a classical summary of a method of interiority. A. Cayuela (1930-1931) MANR. 6:137-150 and 7:133-144. Also Codina (1925) MANR. 1:291-292.

5. The "Additions" found at the end of the First Week (73-90) are to be changed in the following weeks (130-131, 206, 229) as Ignatius suggests.

6. This is the only time the classical division of the three ways appears in the *Exercises*. Ignatius does not call them "*vías*" (ways) but "*vidas*" (lives). Fr. La Palma in his *Camino espiritual* is the best exponent of this tendency to include Ignatius' *Exercises* within the classical division.

7. A *benefice* is an ecclesiastical position that includes monetary endowments, or fixed income.

8. The last three annotations are very important to understand how the *Exercises* may be adapted to different circumstances when one is unable to make them for a month within close quarters. Here one may read the matter, goal, and ways proper to each one of those adaptations. Codina (1950) MANR. 6:314-319; Nicolau (1954) MANR. 26:23-29, Asselin, D.T. (1969) "Notes on Adapting the Exercises of St. Ignatius." *Review for Religious*, 28:410-420.

Burke, Thomas A. (1966) "Formation through the Spiritual Exercises." *The Christian Formation of High School Students*, Los Angeles: Loyola University, pp. 103-116. Futrell, John Carroll (1974) "An eight day communitarian retreat, based on the Spiritual Exercises of St. Ignatius de Loyola." *CIS* 1:15-40.

Hillier, F.L. (1957) "The Flexibility of the Ignatian Exercises." *The Church Quarterly Review*, 158:333-338.

Iparraguirre Ignacio and González, Luis. *Ejercicios Espirituales Cómentario Pastoral*. Madrid: BAC (1965).

Laplace, Jean A. (1977) *An Experience of Life in the Spirit. Ten Days in the Tradition of the Spiritual Exercises*. Trans. John R. Mooney. Chicago: Franciscan Herald Press. Rondet, Henri (1967) *Retraite de dix jours, sur le plan des Exercices de Saint Ignace*. Paris: Lethielleux.

Ruiz Jurado, Manuel (1978) *Práctica Abreviada de los Ejercicios Espirituales de San Ignacio*. Barcelona: Editorial Balmes.

9.   J. Cusson (1973) *Conduis-moi sur le chemin d'éternité*. Les Editions Bellarmin. Montreal-Rome. In this book guidance is given to making the *Exercises* according to Annotation 19.

10.   On the Annotation 20: A.Oraá (1935) MANR. 11:46-60.

11.   In the days of Ignatius Mass would be chanted most of the time, especially in convents and monasteries. (*Obras Completas*, p. 212. n.)

12.   This is a short definition of the end of the Exercises. Other places where Ignatius returns to the end of the Exercises are 1:87, 189,233. In n.87 Ignatius explains what it means "to conquer oneself." On these points see the following: Jiménez, J.L. (1951) *La definición de los Ejercicios*. MANR. 23:243-246.

On the end of the Exercises see: Rovira, J. (1933) MANR. 9: 23-29, 107,112,209-217,311-317. Orlandis, R. (1936) MANR. 12: 3-35, and 97-125. Peeters, L. (1926) MANR. 2:306-329. Calveras, J. (1936) MANR. 12:224-245 and 13:26-37. Puiggrós, L. (1927) MANR. 3:3-11; Fernández, J.M. (1948) MANR. 20:25-46 and 111-124, also 21:225-256. Gómez Nogales, S. (1952) *Cristocentrismo en la teología de los Ejercicios*. MANR. 24: 33-52.

There seems to be a triple interpretation of the end of the *Exercises*. Some (Casanovas, Calveras) see it as a preparation of the soul to right itself up to serve and love in all His Divine Majesty. Others (Peeters) see it more as a school of prayer and union with God. Others (Iglesias, Grandmaison) see it as a means to make decisions.

13.   Originally the Exercises were not written down; they were given orally. Due to the curiosities of the time and the fears of heresy and prayer of recollection there were many who were present at the Exercises only out of curiosity or to find something wrong with them (much as I expect will happen with this study). For this reason Ignatius wrote this "Presupposition." See *Obras Completas*, pp. 213-214; also E.D. (1935) "El Presupuesto" MANR. 11:327-342.

In my own translation I have chosen as the referent of save "the proposition of the other," rather than "to save the other." MI, *Exer.* pp. 164-165.

14.   "Origin and Foundation" is key to understanding the method at work in the Exercises. In the main body of this study I explain why I have chosen *Origin* instead of *Principle*. I explain it more fully in the Introduction to the *Exercises*. General works of the subject: Segarra, J.A. (1933) MANR. 9: 3-11,193-208, 289-300. Defrennes, P. (1939) *Revue d'Ascetique et de Mystique*, Toulouse, pp. 113-135. Iglesias, E. (1930) MANR. 6:289-302. Torres, A. (1944) MANR. 16:58-65. Granero, J.M. (1962) *Sal Terrae* 40:629-636. Bouvier, Pierre (1943) *The Authentic Interpretation of the Foundation*. West Baden: West Baden. Bracken, J.A. (1969) "The Double 'Principle and Foundation' in the Spiritual Exercises." *Woodstock Letters* 98:319-353. Coyne, John. (1957) "The Fundamentum in the Exercises." *Our Colloquium* 31-39. Harriot, John. (1972) "The Mood of the Principle and Foundation." *The Way, Supplement* 16:17-27. Levie,

Jean (1955) "The Meditation on the 'Foundation' in the light of Saint Paul." Trans. Louis Mountéer. *Woodstock Letters* 84:18-33. Lyonnet, Stanislas. (1973) "A Scriptural presentation of the Principle and Foundation." *Ignis*. 6:24-32. Moran, James. (1968) *A Study of the Principle and Foundation, Spiritual Exercises, St. Ignatius de Loyola*. Manila: Mission Band La Ignaciana. Santiago, Juan (1964) "Three notes on the Principle and Foundation." *Woodstock Letters* 193-206.

Particular studies: Bover, J.M. (1919) *El Principio y Fundamento a la luz de las Epístolas de San Pablo. Razón y Fe* 54: 343-355. Calveras, J. (1931) "Cómo se ha de Proponer el Principio y Fundamento." MANR. 7:97-106. Bover, J.M. (1925) "El Principio y Fundamento, por razón o por Fe? MANR. 1:321-326. Rovira, J. (1931) "El fin del hombre, la gloria de Dios." MANR. 7:107-115. Brunet, L. (1933) "Que relación guardan entre sí el Principio y Fundamento y los Ejercicios?" MANR. 9:301-310. Royon, E. (1967) MANR. 39:349-354. Días T. (1972) MANR. 53-68.

On the sources of the "Principio y Fundamento" see: Watrigant, H. (1907) "La Méditation Fondamentale avant S. Ignace." *CBE* 9. On the dependance of Ignatius on Erasmus see: García-Villoslada, R. (1942) *Estudios Eclesiásticos*. 16:244-248. MI, *Exer*. (1969) pp. 56-57. O'Reilly Terence (1974) *St. Ignatius and Spanish Erasmism*. MHSI 43:301-32.

15. On the "end of man" Ignatius repeats the same idea in numbers: 169,179,189. See Calveras (1929) MANR. 5:226-228. Rovira, J. (1931) MANR. 7:107-115. Also St. Thomas Aquinas 1-2,q.69,a.1.

16. Ignatius proposes not just the salvation of the soul but its health, its perfection. See: Rovira, J. (1932) MANR. 8:236-244; Calveras. (1930) MANR. 5:226.

17. "All other things on the face of the earth." Rovira, J. (1932) MANR. 8:236-244.

18. The rule *tanto..cuanto* ("as much..as") Calveras, J. (1931) MANR. 7:193-205.

19. On "indifference" see: Rovira, J. (1932) MANR. 8:327-332. Calveras, J. (1930) MANR. 6:195-205,303-313. March, J. (1936) MANR. 6:190,254-258 and 12:82-83. Brunet, L. (1935) MANR. 11:31-45. Cantin, R. (1950) *Sciences Ecclesiastiques*. Montreal 3:114-145. Dirk, G. Nouv (1951) *Rev. Theol*. 75:740-743. Ribas, I. and Wandenfels, H. *Shingaku Kenkyu* (1961) 11:34-44 and 45-62. Bottereau, G. (1969) *Revue d'Ascetique et de Mystique*. Toulouse 45:395-408.

20. The examination of conscience has been misunderstood by some as a damaging and egocentric spiritual accountability. It was practiced by the Fathers of the Desert and even by Stoic and Pythagorean philosophers. Ignatius gives these rules to the Director of the Exercises so that he gives them to the exercitant according to his/her needs and abilities. The primary purpose is the training of the will. See *Obras Completas*. p.215 n. and Watrigant, H. (1909) CBE 23. La Palma (1903) *Tratado del Examen de Conciencia*. Barcelona. Méndez, A. (1949) *La educación de la voluntad y el examen particular*. Mexico. Pujadas, L. (1934) MANR. 10:32-39. Codina, A. (1940) MANR. 13:38-49. Espinosa, M. (1945) MANR. 17:116-124,18:269-282. Ledrus, M. (1959) *Rev.Asc.Mist*. 4:435-457. Araoz, D. (1964) "Positive Examination of Conscience" *Review for Religious* 23:621-624. (1972) Aochenbrenner, George A. (1972) "Consciousness

Examen." *Review for Religious.* 31:14-21; also (1980) "A check on Our Availability. The Examen." *Review for Religious.* 39:321-324. Brosnahan, T. (1943) "Some notes on the particular Examen." *Review for Religious.* 2:85-90. Campbell, Mary Hugh. (1971) "The Particular Examen—Touchstone of a Genuinely Apostolic Spirituality." *Review for Religious* 30:775-781. Keefe, Gerald E. (1978) "The Companion Examen." *Review for Religious* 37:59-68. Kleist, James (1945) "The Daily Examination of Conscience." *Review for Religious* 4:36-47. Pasquier, Jean. (1971) "Examination of conscience and Revision de Vie." *The Way* 11:305-312. Savary, Louis M. (1980) "The Thanksgiving Examen." *Review for Religious* 39:238-246.

21. "After lunch" in Ignatius' time would take place in mid-morning. Today we would say "before" lunch. (*Obras Completas.* p.215.n.)

22. "Letter g=" has had several interpretations. In Basque this is the first letter of the word *guar* meaning today. (*Obras Completas*, p.216 n) and *Boletín de la Real Sociedad Vascongada de Amigos del País*, (1948) 4:111-120.

23. In the days of Ignatius confession was generally a long, once a year ordeal. The penitent would revise the whole catechism—prayers, morals and imperfections. Circumstances and all sorts of details would be examined so that a confession could take several days. Ignatius summarizes the whole procedure with more method and brevity than was usual. (*Obras Completas*, p. 217.n.) See Calveras (1948) *Los Confesionales.* AHSI 17:57-61, 65-66. MI, Epp., XII, 666-673.

24. On "sins of thought" see Mantilla, S. (1933) MANR. 9:244-257.

25. On "General Confession" see Pujadas, L. (1933) MANR. 9:45-53. Calveras, J. (1951) MANR. 23:211-217.

26. The First Exercise or first meditation, see Pérez, A. (1933) MANR. 9:30-44, Teixidor, L. (1928) MANR. 4:3-21, Peypoch, M. (1931) MANR. 7:314-325, Dannefel, O. *Studien* I:98-108, Fiorito, M. (1972) *Boletín de Espiritualidad.* Buenos Aires. 21-32.

27. The "preparatory prayer" is nothing more than the "Origin and Foundation" applied to the meditation. This prayer is repeated identically through the whole of the *Exercises.* (*Obras Completas.* p.221.n). Sierp, W. (1931) *Zeitschrift für Aszese und Mystik.* 6:266-275.

28. The "composition seeing the place" is Ignatius' way of using imagining. See Barrera, T. (1935) MANR. 11:158-168, Heredia, C. (1941) *Composicion de lugar.* Mexico. Brou, A. *S. Ignace, maitre d'oraison.* p.2,c4. p.113-129. (O.C. p.222.n.)

29. The sense of "prayer of petition" in: Teixidor, L. (1929) MANR. 5:101-123; 6:25-45, 202-217, Codina, A. (1927) MANR. 3:103-111, Sierp, W. (1931) *Petere id quod volo. Zeitschrift für Aszese und Mystik.* 6:173-174.

30. This is Ignatius' use of the three faculties in meditation, as seen in nos. 48 and 49. Roothan, J. (1946) *Método para la Meditación.* Trans. into Spanish by P. Toni. Bilbao. pp. 425-487. de Maumigny *Práctica de la oración mental* tr.1,p.6th.c.1.pp.251-255. de Glassen (1956) *Ignatius von Loyola.* Wurrzburg pp.263-300. (O.C. page 222.n.)

31. The "Colloquy" is fundamental to Ignatian meditation. Though it is here placed at the end of the meditation, it may be used anywhere within the meditation. This is expressly pointed out by Ignatius in the Directory c. 15.n.5. *Obras Completas*, p.223n.

32. On "tears" see: Navatell, J.J. (1920) *La devotion sensible, les larmes et les exercices de S.Ignace.* CBE (*Collection de la Bibliotêque des Exercices*, Enghien-Paris) 64.

33. The "Repetitions" are not meant to be just repetitions of the same meditation. On the contrary, they are a different way of meditating, as he explains: "He wants that supernatural ideas and principles become joined to our emotional life." In this manner "they will easily flow, just like natural ideas and desires, together with the natural sensible tendencies," so that they "become flesh, as the psychologists say." (Hand-written notes E. Hernández). Arnaiz, J. (1956) *Misc. Comillas* 26:20-21. O'Leary, Brian (1976) "Repetition and Review." *The Way Supplement* 27:46-58.

34. This third exercise is in the form of three colloquies. These three colloquies summarize what Ignatius understood to be the fruits of the first week (*Obras Completas*. p.225n.).

35. Here again Ignatius repeats the same formula of repetition in order to imprint more deeply in the exercitant the sensations accompanying the meditations. This is an exclusive Ignatian formulation in line with other mystics. Hernández, E. (1950) MANR. 22:30b-42b and *Misc. Comillas* (1956) 26:21-22.

36. On "hell" see Rovira J. (1927) MANR. 3:211-216, Dalmau, J.M. (1927) MANR. 3:320-325.

The *Vulgate* adds that before or after the exercises on hell other meditations may be "added" like death, individual and final judgment. Contemporaries of Ignatius used to do so, like Dr. Ortiz and Polanco. MI *Exercitia* pp.606,623-624, 718-720. de Santa Ana A.L. (1932) MANR. 8:333-338. Morrell F. (1940) MANR. 13:50-62. Batllori, M. (1952) MANR. 24:133-141.

37. The "Additions" are complementary norms to make the Exercises better. They direct the faculties and rule the senses, imagination, and body. They apply not only during meditation but the whole day. They keep the exercitant "in shape," and create the inner willful context of the exercises. They presuppose an individual retreatant.

Espinosa, Cl. (1960) *Misc. Comillas* 33:173-195. *Psicología de las Adiciones. Persevera* 98. Madrid (1966).

Grogan, Brian (1976) "To Make the Exercises better. The Additional Directions." *The Way Supplement* 27:15-26.

38. Additional reading for the first week: Santiago, Juan (n.d.) *The Ignatian composition of place.* Jersey City: PASE.

Torfs, Louis (1956) "The Application of the Senses" *Ignatiana* 7:137-139. Walsh, James. (1976) "Application of the Senses." *The Way Supplement* 27:59-68. Connolly, William (1974) "Experience of Darkness in Directed Retreats." *Review for Religious.* 33:609-615. Barry, William A. (1973) "Silence and the Directed Retreat." *Review for Religious* 32:347-351; also (1978) with Mary C. Guy "The Practice and Supervision in Spiritual Direction." *Review for Religious* 37:834-843. Connolly, Wiliam (1973) "Freedom and Prayer in Directed Retreats." *Review for Religious* 32:1358-1364. Orsy, Ladislas M. (1966) "Directed vs. Preached Retreats." *Review for Religious* 25:781-796. Sudbrack, Josef (1967) "The Role of the Retreat Master. *Woodstock Letters* 96:239-240.

Beirnaert, Louis (n.d.) *Awareness of God and Sin in the Spiritual Exercises. Jersey City: PASE. Broucker, W. de The First Week of the Exercises*. Jersey City: PASE.n.d. Hanrahan, Thomas (1969/70) "Sin, the 'Celestina' and Iñigo

López de Loyola." *Romance Notes* 11:385-391. Hitter, Joseph (1978) "The First Week and the Love of God." *The Way Supplement* 34:26-34. Ong, Walter (1954) "St. Ignatius' Prison-Cage and the Existentialist Situation." *Theological Studies* 15:34-51. Osiek, Carolyn. (1977) "The First Week of the Spiritual Exercises and the Conversion of St. Paul." *Review for Religious* 36:657-665.

39. In this classical and fundamental meditation Ignatius presents Jesus as the embodiment of the "Origin and Foundation." The exercitant need only identify with Jesus in order to fulfill the norm of the "Origin and Foundation." This is the program of perfection for man/woman to enter history. See: Bover, J.M. (1914) *Razón y Fe* 39:433-442. Rovira, J. (1934) MANR. 10:140-145, 318-326. (1935) 11:127-136. (1936) 12:126-135. Iglesias, E. (1931) MANR. 7:206-210. Cayuela, A. (1933) MANR. 9:54-68. Bracken, J.A. (1969) "The Double 'Principle and Foundation' in the Spiritual Exercises." *Woodstock Letters* 98:319-353. Alfaro, J. (1975) *Teología de los misterios de la Vida de Cristo.* Bilbao. Ashton, John (1973) "The Kingdom of Christ: The Scriptural Background." *The Way Supplement* 18:38-51. (This whole *Supplement* is dedicated to the Kingdom.) Ashton, John (1972) "The Imitation of Christ." *The Way Supplement* 16:28,45. Butterworth, Robert. (1973) "The Kingdom of Christ: Theological Dimensions." *The Way Supplement* 18:38-51. Cahill, E. "The Kingdom of Christ." *Our Colloquium,* 40-49. Connolly, W. (1973) "Story of the Pilgrim King and the Dynamics of Prayer." *Review for Religious* 32:268-272. Coventry, J. (1965) "The Call of the King." *The Way Supplement* 1:5-13. Croft, George. (1973) "Psychological Reflections on the Kingdom." *The Way Supplement* 18:76-83. Hebblethwaite, Peter. (1973) "The Kingdom and the Way." *The Way Supplement* 18:64-75. Lewis, Daniel. (1979) "The Exercise on the Kingdom in the Spiritual Exercises of St. Ignatius." *Review for Religious* 38:566-570. Molinari, Paul. (1973) "The Place of the Kingdom in Apostolic Spirituality." *The Way Supplement* 18:52-63. Peters, W. (1973) "The Text of the Exercise." *The Way Supplement* 18:6-16; and 17-27. Walsh, James. (1975) "The Christ of the Kingdom and the Company." *The Way Supplement* 24:83-91. Whelan, Joseph (1970) "Contemplating Christ." *The Way.* 10:197-198.

40. "Synagogues" was added at the margin by Ignatius after removing the word "temples" (*Obras Completas*, p.231n.).

41. "Castles" refers to those built by the Crusaders which he saw while in the Holy Land (*Obras Completas* p.231n).

42. This sentence refers to *Matt.* 9:35.

43. "unworthy knight" evokes all the ideals of chivalry of the times. See: Clemence, J. (1956) *Rev. Asc. Myst.* 32:145-173, also 148 for the above point. Danielou. (1950) *Rev. Asc. Myst.* 26:8.

44. The sentence "Eternal Lord of all things, I make this offering" it has been suggested should read: Eternal Lord, I make this offering of all things. See: Valle, F. (1928) MANR. 4:162-164. Others disagree. Frías, L. (1928) MANR. 4:210-218 and Calveras, J. (1929) MANR. 5:8-18. On the actual punctuation of this line see MI. *Exer.* pp.97-98.

45. Readings for the second week and thereafter, see: Toni, T. (1929) MANR. 5:56-65. MANR. 20:295-310 (1948)

46. "First Day and First Contemplation," is a new way of meditation different from using the three powers of the soul. It is a softer and more adaptable way of meditation according to de Guibert (1923) *Rev.Asc.Myst.*

4:79. See also Bover, J.M. (1930) "De la Meditación a la contemplatión según San Ignacio." MANR. 6:104-122. Hernández, E. (1952) MANR. 24:441-475. Stanley, David. (1968) "Contemplation of the Gospels." *Theological Studies* 29:417-443; and *Para entender mejor los Ejercicios.México* (1972) 41-74.

47.   See Petty, Michael (1908) "The Infancy Narratives and the Spiritual Exercises." *Woodstock Letters* 97:241-251. Holstein, Henri. "Contemplation of the Mysteries of Christ." *Finding*, 90-103. Teixidor, L. (1933) "Un punto de vista para contemplar la Encarnación." MANR. 9:222-232. Labarriere, Jean-Pierre (1979) "The Christology that is at work in the Second Week." *CIS*. 10/3:55-71.

48.   Ignatius' way of applying the senses to the scenes imagined. Marechal, J. (1920) CBE3,n.61; *Dict.Spir.*I,col.810-828; *Etudes sur la psychologie des mystiques.*t.2,pp.365-382. Ruiz, M. (1946) MANR. 18:257-268. Calveras, J. (1948) "Los cinco sentidos de la imaginación de los Ejercicios." MANR. 20:47-70,125-136. Torfs, Louis. (1956) "The Application of the senses." *Ignatiana* 137-139. Walsh, James. (1976) "Application of the Senses." *The Way Supplement* 27:59-68.

49.   This meditation is the foundation and orientation to make a good election. It has been considered by many Ignatius' masterpiece. Errandonea, I. (1928) MANR. 5:19-25. Rovira, L. (1931) MANR. 4:329-333. L. Brunet. (1929) MANR 5:19-25. Iglesias, E. (1931) MANR. 7:304-313. Clark, Thomas (1977) "The Spiritual Exercises as a Paradigm of Christian Decision." *Loyola Papers* 2:38-51. Dhotel, Jean-Claude. (1979) "The Place of the Election." *CIS* 10/3:72-82. Dulles, Avery. "Finding God's Will." *Schroth*, 9-22. Herbst, C.A. (1955) "The Third Mode of Humility." *Review for Religious* 14:150-155. Hughes, Lachlan M. (1975) "Affectivity, Conscience and Christian Choice." *The Way Supplement* 24:36-45.

50.   The three classes of men is the contemporary usage for what Ignatius calls "binarios." This term was used in the XV and XVI centuries in the resolution of moral cases to designate, in an indeterminate manner, some one. (*Obras Completas*, p.240n.)

51.   This meditation is a test of the will to find out if it is ready to make the best decision. Calveras. J. (1925) MANR. 1:31-42. Iglesias, E. (1932) MANR. 8:97-109. Codina, A. (1931) MANR. 7:229-235. Pydynkowsky, H. (1919) *CBE* 57.

52.   "Three forms of humility" are Ignatius' way of showing the exercitant the inner dispositions of the soul. Humility in this sense equals the degree of love for God and his will. Dr. Ortíz, who made the Exercises with Ignatius, notes instead of the word *humility* "manner and degree of love for God" *Miscelánea Comillas* 25:41 (1956). MI. *Exer.* p.635.

53.   "Discernment of diverse spirits" is Ignatius' practiced way in the *Spiritual Diary*, enclosed in this volume. It needs a great expert in reading.

54.   "The first method" implies, on the one hand, that one has become indifferent to the moves of one's will. Secondly, that the three faculties of the soul have been completely impregnated by the sensitizations of imagining. Thirdly, that now all of them—intelligence, memory, will—should be ready to move in accordance with God's will only. This method of election is a test for intelligence.

55.   "The second method" is considered of less spiritual perfection or for

those with less spiritual perfection. Imagine yourself in someone else's shoes or at the moment of death or in the final judgment. Nadal, J. *Instrucciones et Acta.* MHSI. *Nadal* IV p.847.

56.   On the third and fourth weeks see the following: Althafegoity, Jean (1979) "Confirmation: The Third and Fourth Weeks." *CIS* 10/3:87-95. Ambruzzi, Luigi (1921) "The Third Week of the Exercises and the Unitive Way." *Woodstock Letters* 50:161-168. Fennessy, Peter J. (1978) "The Third Week of the Spiritual Exercises." *The Way Supplement* 34:45-60. Iparraguirre, I. (1966) "The Paschal Mystery and the Exercises of St. Ignatius." *Woodstock Letters* 95:239-240. McNamara, B. (1976) "Jesus' Prayer in Gethsemane: Interpretation and Identification." *The Way Supplement* 27:79-87. Buckley, Michael J. (1975) "The Contemplation to attain love." *The Way Supplement* 24:92-104. Kelly, Hugh. "The Contemplatio ad Amorem." *Our Colloquium.* 61-67. Little, Arthur. (1950) "The Problem of the 'Contemplation for Obtaining Love' " *The Irish Ecclesiastical Record.* 73:13-25. Granero, J.M. (1974) MANR. 46:231-246.

57.   "de los dos binarios": according to *Obras Completas*, p.250 note 121 there is a mistake in the autograph. Some say it should be "tres binarios" (three classes of men); others that it should say "dos banderas" (two standards). We have kept the two versions in the translation since both use the same colloquies (n.147,156).

58.   These rules refer to self-control in eating. See: P Suárez, F. *De Religione Soci. Iesu* 1.9 c.7 n.1-2. Bover, J.M. (1933) MANR. 9:128-133. Hernández, E. (1934) MANR. 10:242-252. Serrat, L. (1933) MANR. 9:345-348.

59.   The "Contemplation to attain love", is Ignatius' summary of the return of love in everything to the Creator of everything. Iglesias, E. (1932) MANR. 8:301-311. Ubillos, G. (1934) MANR. 10:146-147. Díez Alegría, J.M. (1951) MANR. 23:171-193. Merk, A. (1932) ZAM 7:117-134. Días, T. (1973) MANR. 45:289-308. González Quevedo, J. (1964) MANR. 36:317-336.

60.   These three ways of prayer are very useful for the proficient, as a break from harder exercises, and for the not so proficient as a way to be introduced into the harder exercises. Calveras, J. (1925) MANR. 3:193-202,310-319. Also 4:22-33,133-152,193-209. Also MANR. 16:158-172,249-260,333-341.(1944) and 17:125-144. (1945). By the same author: *Los tres modos de orar en los Ejercicios Espirituales de S. Ignacio.* (1951) Barcelona: Librería Religiosa.

61.   The mysteries of the Life of Christ are presented by Ignatius in an order different from the Gospels. He indicates the quotes with parentheses and introduces them with a letter since the numbers now in use were not introduced until 1551. Apparently (*Obras Completas*, p.262n) Ignatius translated from the Vulgate directly, instead of using any of the translations available. MI. *Exer.* pp.33-55; Ibid. p.114.

62.   These rules establish a methodical reading of the signs of meditation. They are based on Ignatius' own experience, as he indicates in *Autobiography* (8). In the same *Autobiography* one may read also numbers: 8-9,20,22,25-26, 54-55,99-101. See also the letters addressed to Teresa Rejadella, June 18 and September 11,1545 (included in this volume).

The classical commentary to the Discernment of Spirits is that of Gagliardi, A. (1851) *De Discretione Spirituum* (Naples). Suárez, *De Religione* 1.9 c.5 n.30-45; c.6n.9-11. Pujadas, L. (1933) *Discreción de Espíritus.* Zaragoza. p.264. Albrecht, Barbara (1979) "Discernment of Spirits." *Review for Religious* 38:382-398.

Asselin, D. (1968) "Christian Maturity and Spiritual Discernment." *Review for Religious* 27:581-595. Ayerra, J. (1956) *Función electiva de la consolación, en el segundo tiempo de elección.* San Sebastián: Facultad de Teologia. Ayésteran, Jose C. (1975) *La Experiencia de la divina consolación: Un estudio filosófico-teológico de las anotaciones sobre los Ejercicios de los hermanos Pedro y Francisco Ortiz.* Rome: Gregorian University. Bacht, H. (1962) "Good and Evil Spirits." *The Way* 2:188-195. Buckley, Michael (1973) "The Structure of the Rules for Discernment of Spirits." *The Way Supplement* 20:19-37. Charmot, Francois, "Discernment of Spirits and Spiritual Direction." *Finding,* 183-190. Dubay, T. (1977) *Authenticity: A Biblical Theology of Discernment.* Denville, New Jersey: Dimension Books. Dunne, Tad (1974) "Models of Discernment." *The Way Supplement* 23:18-26. Futrell, John C. (1970) "Ignatian Discernment." *Studies in the Spirituality of the Jesuits* II/2. Futrell, John C. (1975) "Ignatian Attitude for Discernment." *Communal Discernment.* Rome: *CIS*:34-43. Gil, Daniel (1971) *La Consolación sin causa precedente.* Rome: *CIS.* Giuliani, Maurice "Movements of the Spirits." *Finding* 191-202. Gonzalez Hernandez, Luis (1956) *El Primer tiempo de la Elección según San Ignacio.* Madrid/Buenos Aires: Ediciones Studium. Guillet, Jacques and others. (1970) *Discernment of Spirits.* Colleville, Minnesota: The Liturgical Press. Hagemann, E. (1959) "Ignatian Discretio." *Woodstock Letters* 88:131-138. Hansen, Faith. (1973) "Discernment of Spirits." *Encounter* 1-9. Hurley, Neil. (1974) "Institutional Discernment of Spirits." *The Way Supplement* 23:27-36. Kelsey, Morton (1978) *A Study in Ecstasy and Evil.* N.J. Paulist Press; Kyne, M. (1974) "Difficulties in Discernment." *The Way* 14:103-109. Laplace, Jean. (1956) "Experience of the Discernment of Spirits in the Spirit. Exerc. of St. Ignatius." *Ignatiana* 6:117-121. Murphy, L. (1976) "Consolation." *The Way Supplement* 7:35-47. O'Leary, Brian (1975) "Good and Evil Spirits." *The Way* 15:174-182. O'Leary, Brian (1979) *The Discernment of Spirits in the Memorial of Blessed Peter Favre.* O.Mahoney, Gerald (1978) "What only God can do." *The Way Supplement* 34:61-69. Penning de Vries, Piet (1973) *Discernment of Spirits According to the Life and Teaching of St. Ignatius de Loyola.* New York: Exposition Press. Peters, W. (1973) "Discernment: Doubts." *Review for Religious* 32:814-817. Rahner, Hugo (1965) "The Discernment of Spirits." *Ignatius the Theologian.* 136-180. Roy, L. (1956) "Faut-il chercher la consolation dans la vie spirituelle? Saint Ignace et Saint Jean de la Croix." *Sciences Ecclèsiastiques* 8:109-170. Rulla, Luigi. (1978) "The Discernment of Spirits and Christian Anthropology." *Gregorianum* 59:229-235. Sheeran, Michael (1969) "Discernment as a Political Problem: The Ignatian Art of Government." *Woodstock Letters* 98:446-464. Sheets, J.R. (1971) "Profile of the Spirit: A Theology of Discernment of Spirits." *Review for Religious* 30:363-376. Walsh, James (1972) "The Discernment of Spirits." *The Way Supplement* 16:54-66.

63. The original states *sindérese* of reason. St. Thomas defines *sindérese* as "the law of our understanding, in so far as it is a habit which contains the rules of natural law, that is, the first principles of human action." (i-2 q.94 a.1 ad2.) In today's language we call this a judgment, a habit of reason.

64. Note that in this section Ignatius does not give rules but simple notes. Numbers 1 and 2, for example, are simple observations, while 5 and 6 are true rules or norms. Cruz Moliner, J.M. de la (1956) MANR. 28:213-230. Gil Calvo J. (1961) MANR. 53:143-152.

65. With these rules Ignatius intends to give a practical manual of action

for real life for the exercitant to follow after the Exercises. These rules are known in English as the rules to "think" with the Church. Ignatius' word *sentir* means much more. It has a broader meaning than thinking and feeling. It is more like having found a home, feeling at home, having established a place at home, so that one does not have to think any more. It is, in fact, a habit of always being able to "make home" in the Church that shares a common origin even if the sounds are many. On this point I refer the reader to chapter two of this volume. In any case, *sentir* is something one does with others; therefore, I have chosen as more appropriate the translation "Rules for *conforming with* the Church," embracing a much wider activity than thinking or simply feeling. It does not mean to *conform to*, but rather, *with* the Church, implying a readjustment within the normal mutation of doctrines, styles, and institutional pronouncements.

See also: López de Santa Ana (1931) MANR. 7:27-31. Texidor, L. (1934) MANR. 10:234-241. Granero. (1956) "Sentir con la Iglesia" *Miscelánea Comillas* 25:203-233. Broutin, Paul. (1962) "Perspectives of the Church in the Spiritual Exercises." *Woodstock Letters* 91:337-357. Dinechin, Olivier de (1979) "The Rules for Thinking with the Church." *CIS* 10/3:96-110. Ganss, George E. (1973) "Thinking with the Church. The Spirit of St. Ignatius." *The Way Supplement* 20:72-82. Maciá, Juan (1967) "Modern Rules for Thinking with the Church." *Woodstock Letters* 96:81-83. Rahner, Hugo. "The Spirit and the Church." *Ignatius the Theologian* 214-238. Wright, Ganss, Orsy, Ladislas. (1975) "On Thinking with the Church Today." *Studies in the Spirituality of the Jesuits.* vol.VII/1.

66.   "White is black and black is white," is found in Erasmus in his *Supputationes*, 1527:" Neque ideo nigrum esse album, si ita pronunciaret Romanus Pontifex, quod illum scio numquam facturum" (*Opera Omnia* [1706] IX,p.517). Iturrioz, J. (1970) MANR. 42:5-18.

SPIRITUAL DIARY

1.   The marginal numbers, in brackets, follow the Spanish Edition in his *Obras Completas* as prepared by Fr. Iparraguirre, which in turn follows the French edition prepared by Fr. Giuliani.

2.   "Our Lady" as in subsequent entries, the Trinity, a saint, etc., means the Mass he had celebrated that day. The liturgy in those days allowed more freedom than today. When nothing is mentioned, it means he had celebrated the Mass of the day.

3.   "no nada" says the original, meaning no revenue. The three options Ignatius considered were 1) no fixed revenue (*no nada*); 2) fixed revenues with no limit (*tener todo*); 3) partial fixed revenues in the churches and sacristies (*tener en parte*). Ignatius's election refers to numbers 1 and 3.

4.   "Sunday" is the fourth Sunday after Epiphany.

5.   This mark indicates Ignatius had some vision. He indicates the same with two lines.

6.   "scandal" : he had written and then crossed after scandal the word "*destruyendo*," meaning the Company if revenues were accepted.

7.   "*estante*" in the original means firm.

8.   "as I thought" (*pareciéndome*).Ignatius added this word giving an indication of his accuracy in narrating the signs.

9. "two mediators" means Our Lady and Jesus.

10. He had written "before" (*antes*) but for the sake of accuracy he added *desdel preparar* ("while preparing").

11. Ignatius distinguishes three times of preparation for Mass. The first begins as soon as he get out of bed. Some days, see n. 11, when he was ill, he made this preparation in bed. The second time is a brief period of calm prayer before Mass. This he calls "preparatory prayer." The third time covers the walk to the sacristy and getting dressed for Mass. These "times" may be clearly distinguished on February 15, (nos. 28-31) and March 1st. (n.91).

12. This is Ignatius' own recommendation in the *Exercises* put into practice. See *Exercises* n. 183.

13. This is an example of the "Three Colloquies" recommended in the *Exercises* nos. 62-64,147,156,168-199.

14. "I went through the elections," Ignatius had written before this phrase *a la noche* ("at night"), but he crossed it out.

15. "reasoning" does not give as vivid a meaning as the original *discurriendo*. The Spanish verb, as Iparraguirre suggests in this same note, indicates a movement or transit, a passage from one thing to another, one faculty to another. Ignatius used the same verb in the *Exercises*, in the colloquy of the first exercise. This *discurrir* is a work of labor of the exercitant and the exterior signs. It is a preparation to receive, not the cause of what is thought or appears.

16. "dense" according to Fr. Iparraguirre means "heavy with meaning, rich in content."

17. "consider and discern" are the two ways of election Ignatius refers to: *discurrir* and *discernir*. They are the second and third manner of election in the *Exercises*.

18. Iparraguirre on this note makes the important point that it represents the whole doctrine of the Trinity in its external manifestation: 1) mission given by Christ; 2) confirmation of this mission by the Spirit—who creates the inner gift of the spirit and the external signs; and 3) both as a confirmation of the manifestation of the Trinity in all its operations. Ignatius is obviously aware that his "text" is that of Christianity.

19. This is the first time a vision of the Spirit is mentioned. Ignatius, however, looks for the confirmation of the Three Persons, and so the election continues. According to the commentary of Fr. Iparraguirre on this note (*Obras Completas* p.346,n.31), it is mysterious, to say the least, that Ignatius crosses out having seen the Three Persons when in fact he only saw the Spirit. Apparently Ignatius saw the Spirit and felt the other Two Persons very closely. He could not understand why they did not confirm the election. It turns out it does not have to do with the election but with a fault of the saint, as it will be seen later on.

20. This is "the contemplation to attain love" of the *Exercises* in practice, (233-234).

21. In the Latin translation of the Diary Fr. Aldama lists the Franciscos Ignatius was in contact with while writing the *Diary*: Francisco Vanucci, treasurer of Paul III; Francisco Botelho, with whom he delt in matters of the Inquisition in Portugal; Francisco Alejandro, a convert Jew, who helped him very much in preaching the gospel amongst the Jews; Francisco de Lasso. (*Obras Completas*, p.346,n.36.)

22. Apparently the noise in the hall disturbed him, and he tried to stop it. Then the thought came to him, which he calls temptation, to have some

revenue. The house apparently was small and old and the noise disturbed Ignatius, though it was almost impossible to avoid noises in such a rickety place. See Ribadeneira, *Vida de San Ignacio*, 1.3 c.1.

23.   He takes the previous action of leaving prayer as a fault. He seems to recover from this in four days, for he celebrates again (n.43) Mass of the Trinity.

24.   He should have written "Tuesday and Wednesday." As in number 21 he should have written Wednesday instead of Tuesday and Thursday instead of Wednesday in n.23. Fr. Iparraguirre suggests he became confused with his own corrections.

25.   Of the Holy Trinity, it is presupposed.

26.   This ascending-descending scale of mediations and mediators looking for the signs he wants is a constant repetition in Ignatius, since his vision by the Cardoner river.

27.   See *Exercises* n. 61.

28.   As in the *Exercises* n.181 he sees first the advantages, then the disadvantages in following a course of action.

29.   "point" for Ignatius means here temptation as in n.22 as he immediately points out with the phrase "snares and obstacles of the enemy."

30.   See February 13, n.23.

31.   According to Fr. Iparraguirre, Ignatius is here concerned not only with the content of the oblation but also with the way it was offered. He later realized he was asking for things in a way not too pure or selfless.

32.   The commentators seem to agree Ignatius means here the end of a circle in the process of elections.

33.   Though he writes here "end," the circle of the election is not closed till March 12, n.153. The "reading" of signs of Ignatius is so skillful it might be useful to cover that reading. On n.11, February 9, he seems to have finished the election. On the following day he makes the oblation and on the 11th celebrates Mass of the Holy Spirit to offer the oblation that He may receive it. But in that Mass (n.14) he finds something is wrong. He repeats the election by the third mode on the following day as "something already agreed" (n.15). He has so many consolations and tears he considers the matter closed (n.16) except to give thanks (n.19). Then the matter of the noise comes up, and he abandons the Divine Persons while giving thanks (n.23). Thus he starts all over (n.23) looking for what he lost (n.25). This he does in three days from the 14th to the 17th (n.26-35) with more humility in his approach. He now uses only the Mediators. He finds again what he lost (n.42), and thus he said Mass of the Trinity and writes "end." While giving thanks a similar thing happens again, but this time is not his fault. He finds himself "dry" (n.44) and has to look for a new confirmation. Thus he thinks of fasting for three days but has to travel the election's way for a third time. Instead of giving thanks, he starts again electing.

34.   "Joy" is a chosen word of Ignatius (*regocijo*) which, according to the commentators, involved physical acts, like hugging himself, unable to hold the joy (*Obras Completas*, p.354,n.83).

35.   "favor" means the confirmation he was looking for.

36.   *dilatar el comer* has been translated as "postponing my meal" by some. We prefer the Spanish version of "fasting," for it seems to fit in better. (*Obras Completas*.p.355). See also *Exercises* n.87, in addition n.10.

37.   A double line was placed here by Ignatius in the *Diary* as indicating a separation.

38. This is the first Mass of the Trinity in a series of thirteen he will say. The last is on the 8th of March (n.134).

39. This is the first of a series of texts marked with dark lines as mentioned in the Introduction which are found in other writings of the saint. See *Autobiography* n.30.

40. Compare this to *Autobiography* n. 28.

41. See *Exercises* n. 60 on conservation and destruction.

42. See *Autobiography* n. 96 on the vision of the Storta.

43. Rome, March 1541. Then it was resolved the sacristies would have revenue. Ignatius, therefore, had to submit his decision to the society for their approval.

44. Ignatius keeps insisting on bringing the Trinity to agree to his way. He will keep insisting in nos. 76,78,110,112,118 but in a very different manner from the indignation of n.50.

45. "fire": A coal stove under his feet.

46. Carpi: Cardinal Rodolfo Pio de Carpi (1500-1564), a friend of the Jesuits.

47. Vicar: The Bishop, Vicar of Rome Felipe Archinto (1500-1558).

48. Trani: Cardinal Juan Domingo de Cupis, Archbishop of Trani and a benefactor of the Cathecumen house.

49. See *Autobiography* n.29.

50. See *Autobiography* n.44.

51. The original Spanish says at ten o'clock. In Rome in those days counting the hours started a half hour after sunset. At the beginning of March the first hour would be *our* 18:30. Thus ten o'clock then would be 4:30 a.m. now. (*Obras Completas*, p. 369,n.177).

52. Cardinal Juan Alvarez de Toledo (1488-1557) O.P., Bishop of Córdoba first (1539) and then of Burgos (1550). He then became Bishop of Santiago and Cardinal in 1538. He became the Inquisitor General and examined the *Exercises* by order of Paul III. He gave a very favorable report. He was a great friend of Ignatius. (*Obras Completas*, p. 371, n. 198).

53. See *Obras Completas* p. 375, n.222.

54. This is the process of descent used by Ignatius. The greater the descent, the greater the consolation (n.135).

55. This fire has been interpreted differently. (*Obras Completas* p. 377, n. 234).

56. See the note on desolation in the *Exercises* n.317.

57. The forty days for the election were over, so the saint becomes fidgety.

58. Twice Ignatius had believed he had finished. This third time, it is over. On the other two occasions his reading of the signs was forced by his expectations. The rest of the *Diary* is a clear lesson in the humility of reading the signs that are there and not those put there by our expectations.

59. This is a new part of the *Diary*. Fr. Codina explains in detail in MHSI, *Const.* I:108-109, the meaning of the code: a: tears *before* Mass; 1: tears *during* Mass; d: tears *after* Mass. On other codes see the Introduction.

60. Rule 7 of the second series of rules on the "Discernment of Spirits" of the *Exercises* n. 335.

AUTOBIOGRAPHY

1.   This prologue by Father Nadal was written, most probably, between 1561 and 1567. The Latin original may be seen in *Fontes narr.* I, 354-363. The greatest contributors to details of the life of Ignatius were, besides Fr. Nadal, Fr. Pedro de Ribadeneira, his official biographer, and Frs. Juan Alfonso de Polanco and Gonçalves da Camara.

2.   The Society of Jesus was officially confirmed by Paul III on the 27th of September, 1540. The *Spiritual Exercises* were approved by the same Pope on the 31st of July, 1548. During the years 1547 and 1550 Ignatius finished writing the *Constitutions*.

3.   Nadal was wrong; he should have said 1552, for in 1551 Nadal was in Sicily (*Obras Completas*, p. 87).

4.   Pontius Cogordan, French.

5.   On the 25th of March, 1552, Nadal returned to Sicily. In January of 1553 he was recalled to Rome, and in April he was sent to Spain and Portugal with the *Constitutions* and to visit those provinces of the Society.

6.   Nadal is wrong again. In 1553, Ignatius started to dictate his *Autobiography*.

7.   This occurred in 1558.

8.   The name of this Jesuit appears spelled in different forms: du Coudrey, du Codret, du Coudray, du Coudret; in Latin, Codretus; in Italian, Codreto or Coudreto. We follow here the one adopted by the Spanish and French editions of the *Autobiography*.

9.   The name of this part of the house of Rome was given because Francisco de Borja, Duke of Gandía, lived there in 1550-1551, when he visited Rome on the occasion of the Holy Year. Francisco de Borja had become a Jesuit on February 1, 1548, but his religious profession had not yet been made public.

10.   Fr. Alfonso de Polanco was born in Burgos, Spain, and joined the Society in 1541. In 1557, he was named Secretary of the Society, and he remained such while Ignatius, Laínez, and Francisco de Borja were Generals of the Society—that is, until 1573. He died in Rome in 1576.

11.   Pope Julius III wished to endow the Roman College with a fixed income, but it did not come through because of the death of this Pope in 1555. Cf. *MI, Epp.* VIII 664; *Chron.* V 12ss; *Fontes narr.* I 58 606-661; Ribadeneira, *De Actis* n. 37; *Fontes narr.* II 341-343.

13.   This took place on the 23rd of May, 1555.

14.   The original Spanish text ends here, and the rest is translated from the Latin. Cf. *Fontes narr.* I 348.

15.   According to Fr. Ribadeneira, "Though he (Ignatius) was very faithful as regards to substance, he was not so in relation to particulars and in relation to dates, for it was at the end of his old age when his memory was failing." MHSI *Epp.* Nadal III 540. This remark by Ribadeneira refers particularly to Ignatius's age. If at the age of 26 he was wounded, as we read here, then he was born in 1495, but as we also read in No. 30, he was 62 years old in 1555 and, therefore, he was born in 1493. Fr. Nadal, on the other hand, asserts the date of his birth to be in 1491. (*Fontes narr.* II 231). Apparently Ignatius made an error of memory, and the last date is the one believed to be the accurate one.

16.   The city of Pamplona, immortalized by Hemingway, is in the Northeast part of Spain.

17.   This practice was recommended by St. Thomas Aquinas (*In IV Sent.* XVII q. 3 a. 3 q. 2 sol. 2). It was practiced in the Middle Ages when there was no priest available.

18.   His name was Martín García de Loyola. The first born son, Juan Pérez de Loyola, had already died in Naples in 1496.

19.   The books he read in Spanish were the *Vida de Cristo* by Ludolfo de Sajonia (died, 1377), and the *Lives of the Saints* as in the *Leyenda Aurea* by Jacobo de Voragine (Varazze) (died, 1298 in Genoa). Cf. *Fontes narr.* II, p. 64 and pp. 186,234,404 and MHSI *Exercitia spiritualia*, pp. 38-46. The Spanish edition is by Fr. Gauberto M. Vagad.

20.   It has not been possible to establish who this lady was, and the hypotheses advanced are not very plausible. See *Obras Completas*, San Ignacio de Loyola, Biblioteca de Autores Cristianos, 1977, page 94, note 7.

21.   These experiences were the starting point for Ignatius' rules for the discernment of spirits that he later on wrote in the *Exercises*.

22.   This was the Carthusian house called Santa María de las Cuevas, on the outskirts of Seville. It does not exist today.

23.   He refers here to the Carthusian house, Miraflores (Burgos).

24.   Antonio Manrique de Lara, Duke of Nájera, from 1515 and Viceroy of Navarre from 1516 to 1521. Ignatius served under him while he was wounded at Pamplona. He died December 13, 1535. See Salazar y Castro, *Historia genealógica de la Casa de Lara* II, p. 170 and 175.

25.   This is a small town near Logroño and between this town and Nájera.

26.   His name was Juan Chanon, French; he used to confess the pilgrims as they came to Montserrat. See *MI Scripta* II 439-448. The knightly models of the time served both Ignatius de Loyola and Teresa de Avila. On Ignatius, see John F. Wickham "The Worldly Ideal of Iñigo de Loyola," *Thought*, 29:209-236, n.113, summer 1954.

27.   The mule served for a long time in the monastery, and the sword and dagger were also placed there, but they disappeared after a while. See *MI Scripta* de S. Ignatio I 725 and *MI Scripta* II 385.

28.   Apparently Ignatius intended to stay at Manresa for a few days, but he prolonged his stay for over 10 months from the 25th of March, 1522, to February 1523.

29.   See below, n.31. In time, Ignatius realized this sign was from the devil. See *Sumario Fontes Narrativae* I, p. 160, where Fr. Polanco gives account of this.

30.   The commentators have not been able to identify her.

31.   The Holy Trinity is the reality-image foundation of all Ignatius' spirituality. For a more detailed account of this reality-image, the reader should turn to the *Spiritual Diary*, especially to those texts that are bracketed by dark lines. It is obvious that many of these texts were lifted from the *Spiritual Diary* and relate to meditations performed by Ignatius on that day. In other words, the visions Ignatius talks about in the *Autobiography* do not occur as it were out of the blue but are linked to the efficiency and technologies of the *Spiritual Exercises*.

32.   The old monastery of St. Paul and Valldaura standing just above the Cardoner River.

33.   This is the statement that led Fr. Polanco to make Ignatius 63 years old at the time of his death (cf. M, *Fontes narr.* II 5125). Polanco later on changed

his mind as already stated in Footnote no. 15.

34.   This happened in 1535, as may be seen from Paragraph 91.

35.   In Paragraph 99 Ignatius also establishes that at this time he started the writing of the *Spiritual Exercises*.

36.   The name is Cardona and not Carmona as seen in many original Spanish texts. The Cardona family was one of the most noble families in Spain. The sister of the Duke of Cardona was married to Antonio Manrique de Lara, in whose service Ignatius had been for a while. (Cf. Salazar y Castro, *Historia genealógica de la Casa de Lara*, II, p. 176, and *Autobiografía*, p. 110, Footnote no. 25. For a fuller account of Ignatius' journey to Jerusalem, see James Broderick (1956) *St. Ignatius Loyola: The Pilgrim Years*. New York.

37.   This war was between Charles I of Spain and Frances I of France, who were fighting for Milan. Ignatius made this trip in February, 1524. The war was finally won by Charles I in the Battle of Pavia, where Frances I was made prisoner and taken to Madrid.

38.   Andrew Doria (1466-1560) came from Genoa. He was on the side of Frances I in 1522, but after his defeat at Pavia in 1525, he joined Pope Clement VII. Finally, in 1528, he joined the service of Charles I of Spain.

39.   Santa María del Mar—the most beautiful Gothic temple in Barcelona, by the seaport, built in 1383.

40.   Peter Lombard, also known as Magister Sententiarum, was the author of *Sententiarum Libri*, a systematic exposition of scholastic theology.

41.   Don Diego de Eguía was a priest born in Estella, in Navarre. He joined the Society of Jesus in 1540. For a while he was Ignatius' confessor. His brother, Esteban, also joined the Society. See *Fontes narr.* I 1103.

42.   Juan Reynalde, affectionately called Juanico because of his youth.

43.   This second investigation by the Inquisition happened on March 6, 1527 (*MI Scripta I*, p. 608). The documents on this investigation may be found in *MI Scripta I* 608-610, and in *MI Fontes documentales*, n. 71.

44.   Fonseca had founded in Salamanca the Colegio Mayor de Santiago for the benefit of the students without means.

45.   Around that time, that is between the 27th of June to the 13th of August, 1527, a theological conference had been convened at Valladolid to discuss 21 propositions from the works of Erasmus. Franciscans and Dominicans were the greatest adversaries of Erasmus in Spain (*OC*, p. 129, footnote 2).

46.   Martin Frías was the assistant to the bishop of Salamanca, Francisco de Bobadilla.

47.   According to a letter to Inés Pascual, Ignatius arrived in Paris on February 2, 1528. (*MI Epp.* I 74)

48.   The College of Montaigu was founded in the middle of the 14th century by the archbishop of Rouan, Gilles Aycelin de Montaigu. Ignatius studied humanities in this college between 1528 and 1529.

49.   Juan Castro (1485-1556), from the town of Burgos, improved his life through the intervention of Ignatius. He returned to Spain years later to become a Carthusian monk. Ignatius visited him in 1535.

50.   He went to Flanders in the years 1529, 1530, and 1531. It was during this last year that he travelled to London, as may be seen from Fr. Polanco's Latin life of Ignatius in *Fontes narr.* II, p. 556-558.

51.   See above text section numbers 54-55.

52. The time Ignatius spent studying in Paris was divided in the following manner: he studied grammar and humanities between February and April, 1528-1529; arts of philosophy between 1529-1530, 1530-1531, and 1531-1532. Between October 1532 and April 1533, he occupied himself with the written exercises required for the degree of Master of Arts. In 1533 and up to April 1535, he studied theology. In March 1535, he became a Master of Arts. (See *Scripta de S. Ignatio* II, 1-2, and *Fontes doc.*, n. 86.) The faculty of theology certified that he had studied there for about one year and a half. "Per unum annum cum dimidio"—this was the formula used at the University of Paris to show proficiency in theological studies., See *MI Scripta* II 2 and *MHSI Fabri Monumenta*, p. 6, where it shows that Peter Favre studied for over five years and received the same accreditation.

53. This is the substance of the famous vow of Montmartre, taken by Ignatius on August 15, 1554, with his first six companions: Francisco Javier, Pedro Fabro, Nicolás Bobadilla, Diego Laínez, Alfonso Salmerón, Simón Rodríguez. One year later when they renewed this vow, three other companions joined them: Claudio Jayo, Juan Coduri, and Pascasio Bröet. There is a short biographical summary of each one of them in *Fontes narr.* I, pp. 37-39, notes 21-31.

54. Martín García de Oñaz.

55. Diego de Hoces, born in Málaga, joined Ignatius very early. He died in 1538, and Ignatius saw his soul in heaven. (See Polanco in *Sumario*, n. 74, and in his Latin life of Ignatius, n. 91, *Fontes narr.* I 195, II 583.)

56. They were ordained the 24th of June, 1537. (See *MI Scripta* I, 543-546 and *Fontes documentales*, n. 103.)

57. Francis Xavier, Francisco Javier.

58. This young Spanish man met Ignatius when he left the employment of Cardinal Carafa. He later on joined the society and became a famous preacher.

59. This was the house of Quirino Garzoni, by a vineyard at Mount Pincio near a church called Trinita dei Monti.

60. Miguel Landívar, alias *Navarro*. He resented Francis Xavier's conversion and while at Paris tried to kill Ignatius. Later he seemed to change and either tried to enter the society or was in it for a short time. Ribadeneira, *De actis*, n. 19; *Fontes narr.* II, 332. *Obras Completas*, p. 160 n.

61. These two Spaniards sided with others against Ignatius and his companions. It was a violent persecution which Rome resolved in Ignatius' favor. *Obras Completas*, p. 161n.

Bibliography on Hermeneutics

ALBÁN,LAUREANO (1983) *Viaje Interminable*. Madrid: Ediciones Cultura Hispánica.

——, (1983) *The Endless Voyage*. Trans. Frederick Fornoff. Pittsburgh: International Poetry Forum.

ARISTOTLE (1941) *The Basic Works Of*. trans. W.C. Ross. Ed. Richard McKeon. New York: Random House.

BACHELARD, GASTON (1960) *The Poetics of Reverie*. Trans. Daniel Russell. Boston: Beacon Press.

——, (1947) *La Formation de l'esprit Scientifique*. Paris: Vrin.

——, (1940) *La Philosophie du nom*. Paris: P.U.F.

——, (1949) *Le Rationalisme applique*. Paris: P.U.F.

——, (1943) *L'Air et les songes*. Paris: Corti.

——, (1942) *L'Eau et les reves*. Paris: Corti.

——, (1948) *La Terre et les reveries de la volonté*. Paris: Corti.

——, (1938) *Psychoanalyse du feu*. Paris: Gallimard.

——, (1957) *La Poetique de l'Espace*. Paris: P.U.F.

——, (1939) *Lautriamont*. Paris: Corti.

BAKHTIN, L.M. (1981) *The Diologic Imagination: Four Essays*. Austin: The University of Texas Press.

BARTHES, ROLAND (1976) *Sade, Fourier, Loyola*. Trans. Richard Miller. New York: Hill & Wang.

BATAILLON, MARCEL (1950) *Erasmo y España*. Trans. Antonio Alatorre. Mexico: Fondo de Cultura Economica.

BOETHIUS (1967) *The Principles of Music*. Trans. Calvin Martin Bower. Ann Arbor, Michigan: University Microfilms.

BREMER, JOHN (1984) *The Polity*. Houston: Institute of Philosophy.

BROWN, RAYMOND E. (1977) *The Birth of the Messiah*. New York: Doubleday/ Image.

BYRON, WILLIAM (1978) *Cervantes, A Biography*. New York: Doubleday.

374

CASSIRER, E. (1957) *Philosophy of Symbolic Form, III: Phenomenology of Knowledge*. New Haven: Yale University Press.

CASEY, EDWARD (1976) *Imagining: A Phenomenological Study*. Bloomington: Indiana University Press.

———, (1976) "Comparative Phenomenology of Mental Activity: Memory, Hallucination, and Fantasy Contrasted with Imagination." *Research in Phenomenology* 6:1-25.

———, (1977) "Imagining and Remembering." *Review of Metaphysics* 31:187-209.

———, (1979) "Perceiving and Remembering," *Review of Metaphysics* 32:407-436.

Clanchy, E. (1979) *From Memory to Written Record*. Cambridge, Mass.: Harvard.

COMFORT, ALEX (1984) *Reality and Empathy*. Albany: State University of New York Press.

de Nicolás, Antonio T. (1971) *Four-Dimensional Man*. Bangalore: Dharmaram College.

———, (1976a) *Meditations through the Rg Veda*. Maine: Nicolas Hays.

———, (1976) *Avatāra: The Humanization of Philosophy through the Bhagavad Gītā*. Maine: Nicolas Hays.

———, (1980) "Notes on the Biology of Religion." *Journal of Social and Biological Structures* 3:219-225.

———, (1982) "Audial and Literary Cultures." *Journal of Social and Biological Structures* 5:269-288.

DE OSUNA, FRANCISCO (1981) *The Third Spiritual Alphabet*. Trans. Mary E. Giles. New York: Paulist Press.

DESCARTES, RENE (1961) *Meditations on First Philosophy*. Trans. L.J. Laffleur. New York: Bobbs-Merrill.

———, (1972) *Treatise of Man*. Trans. Thomas Steele Hall. Cambridge, Mass.: Harvard University Press.

DILTHEY, W. (1958) *Gesammelte Schriften, vol. 7, Der Aufbau der geschichtlichen Welt in den Geistenwissenschaften*. Leipzig and Berlin: Teubner.

DURAND,GILBERT (1969) *Les Structures Anthropologique de l'Imaginaire*. Paris: Bordas.

FEYERABEND, P. (1975) *Against Method*. London: New Left Press.

FICHTE, JOHANN GOTTLIEB (1971) *Fichtes Werke*. Berlin: Walter de Gruyter & Co.

FONTENROSE, JOSEPH (1959) *Python: A Study of Delphic Myth and Its Origin*. Berkeley: University of California Press.

GADAMER, HANS-GEORG (1976) *Philosophical Hermeneutics*. Trans. David E. Linge. Berkeley: University of California Press.

———, (1975) *Truth and Method*. Trans. Garret Barden, John Cumming. New York: Seabury Press.

HABERMAS, J. (1971) *Knowledge and Human Interests*. Trans. J.J. Shapiro. Boston: Beacon Press.

HALL, DAVID (1981) "Antonio de Nicolás and Ortega y Gasset." *Philosophy Today*. Vol. 25, n. 1/4, pp. 63-67.

———, (1973) *The Civilization of Experience*. New York: Fordham University Press.

HANSON, N.R. (1958) *Patterns of Discovery*. London: Cambridge University Press.

HAVELOCK, ERIC (1963) *Preface to Plato*. Cambridge: Harvard University.

HEELAN, PATRICK (1983) *Space Perception and the Philosophy of Science*. Berkeley: University of California Press.

———, (1979) "Music as Basic Metaphor and Deep Structure in Plato and in Ancient Cultures." *Journal of Social and Biological Structures* 2:279-91.

HEIDEGGER, M. (1962) *Being and Time*. Trans. J. Macquarrie and E. Robinson. New York: Harper & Row.

———, (1977) *The Question Concerning Technology and Other Essays*. New York: Harper Colophon.

HOHLER, T.P. (1982) *Imagination and Reflection: Intersubjectivity. Fichte's Grundlage of 1794*. The Hague: Nijhoff.

HUME, DAVID (1955) *An Inquiry Concerning Human Understanding*. New York: Bobbs-Merrill.

———, (1967) *A Treatise of Human Nature*. Oxford: Clarendon Press.

HUSSERL, E. (1931) *Ideas*. London: Allen and Unwin.

———, (1970a) *Logical Investigations*, 2 vols. Trans. J.N. Findlay. London: Routledge & Kegan Paul.

———, (1970b) *The Crisis of European Science and Transcendental Philosophy*. Evanston: Northwestern University Press.

IHDE, DON (1976) *Listening and Voice: A Phenomenology of Sound*. Athens: Ohio University Press.

———, (1977) *Experimental Phenomenology*. New York: Putnam.

IHDE, D. AND ZANER, R., EDT. (1975) *Interdisciplinary Phenomenology*. The Hague: Nijhoff.

JUNG, CARL-GUSTAV (1975) *Grundlagen der Alalytischen Psychologie*. Hamberg: Fisher Taschenbuch Verlag.

KANT, IMMANUEL (1781) *Critique of Pure Reason*. Trans. Norman Kemp Smith. London: Macmillan & Co. 1956.

KUHN, T.S. (1970) *The Structure of Scientific Revolutions*. 2nd ed. Chicago: University of Chicago Press.

LOCKE, J. (1689) *Essay Concerning Human Understanding*. Ed. Peter Niddich. Oxford: Clarendon Press 1975.

LÓPEZ ESTRADA, FRANCISCO (1980) "Siglos de Oro, Renacimiento." Vol. 2. *Historia y Crítica de la Literatura Española*. Barcelona: Editorial Critica.

MCCLAIN, ERNEST (1977) *The Myth of Invarience*. Maine: Nicolas Hays.

———, (1978) *The Pythagorean Plato*. Maine: Nicolas Hays.

———, (1981) *Meditations through the Quran*. Maine: Nicolas Hays.

MERLEAU-PONTY, M. (1962) *The Phenomenology of Perception*. Trans. Colin Smith. London: Routledge & Kegan Paul.

———, (1964) *The Primacy of Perception*. Ed. James Edie. Evanston: Northwestern University Press.

———, (1964) *The Visible and the Invisible*. Evanston: Northwestern University Press.

MUMFORD, L. (1963) *Technics and Civilization*. New York: Harcourt, Brace and World.

NEVILLE, ROBERT (1974) *The Cosmology of Freedom*. New Haven: Yale University Press.

———, (1980) *Creativity and God.* New York: Seabury Press.

———, (1981) *Reconstruction of Thinking.* Albany: State University of New York Press.

ONG, WALTER (1967) *The Presence of the Word.* New Haven: Yale University Press.

———, (1982) *Orality and Literacy: The Technologizing of the Word.* London: Methuen.

ORTEGA y GASSET, JOSÉ (1946) *Obras Completas*, 12 vols. Madrid: Revista de Occidente.

———, (1961) *Meditations on Quixote.* Trans. Evelyn Rugg and Diego Marín. New York: W.W. Norton & Co.

———, (1976) "The Forest." *Avatāra.* Trans. A.T. de Nicolás. Maine: Nicolas Hays.

———, (1941) *History as a System.* Trans. Helene Weyl. New York: W.W. Norton & Co.

———, (1969) *Some Lessons in Metaphysics.* Trans. Mildred Adams. New York: W.W. Norton & Co.

———, (1960) *What Is Philosophy?* Trans. Mildred Adams. New York: W.W. Norton & Co.

———, (1932) *The Revolt of the Masses.* Trans. Anonymous. New York: W.W. Norton & Co.

———, (1961) *The Modern Theme.* Trans. James Cleugh. New York: Harper Torchbooks.

———, (1946) *Concord and Liberty.* Trans. Helene Weyl. New York: W.W. Norton & Co.

———, (1944) *Mission of the University.* Trans. Howard Lee Nostrand. New York: W.W. Norton & Co.

———, (1971) *The Idea of Principle in Leibnitz and the Evolution of Deductive Theory.* Trans. Mildred Adams. New York: W.W. Norton & Co.

———, (1975) *Phenomenology and Art.* Trans. Philip W. Silver. New York: W.W. Norton & Co.

———, (1972) *Velazquez, Goya, and the Dehumanization of Art.* Trans. Alexis Brown. New York: W.W. Norton & Co.

———, (1958) *Man and Crisis.* New York: W.W. Norton & Co.

———, (1963) *Man and People.* New York: W.W. Norton & Co.

———, (1967) *Origin of Philosophy.* New York: W.W. Norton & Co.

PALMER, RICHARD (1969) *Hermeneutics: Interpretation Theory in Schleiermacher, Dilthey, Heidegger and Gadamer.* Evanston: Northwestern University Press.

PLATO (1961) *The Collected Dialogues Of.* Various Trans. Ed. Edith Hamilton, Huntington Cairns. New York: Bollingen Foundation.

RICOEUR, P. (1967) *The Symbolism of Evil.* Trans. E. Buchanan. New York: Harper & Row.

———, (1978) *The Philosophy of Paul Ricoeur: An Anthology of His Work.* Boston: Beacon.

———, (1980) *Hermeneutics and the Human Sciences.* Cambridge: Cambridge University Press.

RIVERS, ELIAS (1982) "Language and Reality in Quevedo's Sonnet." *Quevedo in Perspective.* Newark: Juan de la Cuesta.

ROMILLY, J. DE (1975) *Magic and Rhetoric in Ancient Greece*. Cambridge.: Harvard University Press.

RORTY, R. (1979) *Philosophy and the Mirror of Nature*. Princeton: Princeton University Press.

SAINT TERESA DE AVILA (1976) *The Collected Works*. Trans. Kieran Kavanaugh and Otilio Rodriguez. 2 vols. Washington: ICS Publications.

SAN IGNACIO DE LOYOLA (1977) *Obras Completas*. Ed. Ignacio Iparraguirre and Cándido Dalmases. Madrid: Biblioteca de Autores Cristianos.

SAN JUAN DE LA CRUZ (1960) *Vida y Obras de San Juan de la Cruz*. Madrid: Biblioteca de Autores Cristianos.

SPITZER, LEO (1963) *Classical and Christian Ideas of World Harmony*. Baltimore: The Johns Hopkins Press.

TREITLER, LEO (1981) "Oral, Written and Literary Process in the Transmission of Medieval Music." *Speculum*, 56.3:471-491.

———, (1984) "Orality and Literacy in the Music of the Middle Ages." in *Parergon*. Australia.

TURCHETTO, GERALD (1983) *Plato's Musical Imagination*. Ann Arbor: University Microfilms.

TURNER, F. (1983) "The Neural Lyre: Poetic Meter, the Brain and Time." *Journal of Social and Biological Structures* 8:277-307.

WILLIAMS, CH. (1939) *Descent of the Dove*. Michigan: William B. Eerdmans Publishing Co.

———, (1941) *Witchcraft*. London: Faber and Faber.

ZANER, R. (1970) *The Way of Phenomenology*. New York: Pegasus.

———, (1981) *The Context of Self*. Athens: Ohio University Press.

ZUM BRUNN, EMILIE (1969) *Le Dilemme de L'etre et du Néant chez Saint Augustin*. Paris: Centre National de la Recherche Scientifique.

———, (1978) "L'exégèse augustinienne de 'Ego sum qui sum' et la métaphysique de l'Exode." *Dieu de L'Etre*. Paris: Centre National de la Recherche Scientifique.

Selected Bibliography
on Ignatius de Loyola

The most complete bibliography on Ignatius for English readers is that
of Paul Begheyn, S.I., mentioned below. The present bibliography does
not include works already cited in the footnotes nor intends to be
exhaustive. It is only a selective bibliography concerned primarily with
the main texts of this volume intended as a general guide to the interested
reader. For the sake of accuracy it follows, in part, that of Begheyn. The
more advanced reader is advised to consult that bibliography.

1. BIBLIOGRAPHIES

BANGERT, WILLIAM V. (1976) *A Bibliographical Essay on the History of the
Society of Jesus*. St. Louis: Institute of Jesuit Sources.

BEGHEYN, PAUL (1981) *"A Bibliography on St. Ignatius' Spiritual Exercises".
Studies in the Spirituality of the Jesuits*. St. Louis: American Assistancy
Seminar on Jesuit Spirituality.

Catalogue de la Bibliothèque des Exercises. (1925-1926) CBE 92-99.

GILMONT, JEAN FRANCOIS, AND DAMAN, PAUL. (1958) *Bibliographie Ignatienne*
(1894-1957). Paris/Louvain: Desclee de Brouwer.

IPARRAGUIRRE, IGNACIO (1965) *Orientaciones Bibliográficas sobre San Ignacio
de Loyola*. I.2nd. ed. Rome: Institutum Historicum S.I.

POLGAR, LASZLO (1967) *Bibliography of the History of the Society of Jesus—
Bibliographie sur Geschichte der Gesellschaft Jesu*. Rome: Institutum
Historicum S.I.

RUIZ JURADO, MANUEL (1976) *La Bibliografía sobre los Ejercicios*. (1965-1975)
Rome:CIS.

———, (1977) *Orientaciones Bibliográficas sobre San Ignacio de Loyola*. II,
1965-1976. Rome: Institutum Historicum S.I.

STUMPF, E.J. (1956) "Ignatian Spirituality in English." *Woodstock Letters*.
85:441-444.

2. TEXTUAL EDITIONS: THE WRITINGS

A. *Critical Editions*

ALBAREDA, A. (1935) *S. Ingasia Montserrat.* Barcelona: Monestir de Montserrat.

BREMOND, H. (1929) *S. Ignace et les Exercices*: Vie Spirituelle, 20 (Supplement, May 1929) 79-123.

CODINA, A. (1926) *Los orígenes de los Ejercicios espirituales.* p. XVI and 309. Barcelona.

DELETURIA, P. (1521-1540) *Génesis de los Ejercicios de San Ignacio y su influjo en la fundación de la Compañía de Jesús.* Bilbao Mensajero.

DUDON, P. (1934) *S. Ignace de Loyola.* Paris: H. Champion

GILMONT, JEAN-FRANCOIS (1961) *Les ecrits spirituels des premiers jesuites. Inventaire commente.* Rome: Institutum Historicum S.I.

IPARRAGUIRRE, IGNACIO, & DALMASES, CÁNDIDO DE (1977) *Obras Completas de San Ignacio de Loyola.* 2nd. ed. Madrid: Biblioteca de Autores Cristianos.

JIMÉNEZ, J. (1969) *Formación progresiva de los Ejercicios ignacianos. Primera parte: Loyola y Montserrat.* Santiago: Universidad Catholica de Chile.

Monumenta Historica S.I. Exercitia spiritualia (1969) Rome: Institutum Historicum S. J.

Monumenta Historica S.I. Exercitia spir. et. eorum Directoria (1919) Madrid, p. 1282.

PINARD DE LA BOULLAYE, H. (1950) *Les étapes de rédaction des Exercises.* Paris: J. Vrin

RAHNER, I.H. (1947) *Ignatius von Loyola und das geschichtliche Werden seiner Frommigkeit.* Vienna: Herder & Herder

WATRIGANT, H. (1897) *La genese des Exercises spir.*: Etudes, 71, 506-592; 72, 195-216; 73, 199-229.

ZUBILLAGA, FELIX, & HANISCH, WALTER. (1971) *Guía manual de los documentos históricos de la Compañía de Jesús de los cien primeros volúmenes*, etc. Rome: Institutum Historicum S.I.

B. *Translations*

GANSS, GEORGE, tr. & ed. (1970) *The Constitutions of the Society of Jesus.* St. Louis: The Institute of Jesuit Sources.

O'CALLAGHAN, JOSEPH, tr., and Olin, John, ed. (1974) *The Autobiography of Saint Ignatius Loyola with Related Documents.* New York: Harper & Row.

OWEN, ALOYSIUS, tr. *Memories of Loyola. Man for All Seasons.* n.d. Available from the tr., St. Peter's College, Jersey City, N.J.

RAHNER, HUGO (1960) *Saint Ignatius Loyola: Letters to Women.* tr. Kathleen Pond & S.A.H. Weetman. New York: Herder & Herder.

YOUNG, WILLIAM J., tr. (1959) *Letters of St. Ignatius Loyola.* Chicago: Loyola University Press.

_____, tr. (1979) *The Spiritual Journal of St. Ignatius Loyola.* Rome: CIS.

3. THE SPIRITUAL EXERCISES

A. *Original Text*

Acta antiquissima a P. Ludovico Consalvio, S.I., ex ore Sancti excepta et a P. Hannibale Codretto, eiusdem S.I., in Latinum conversa: Acta Sanctorum Iulii, t. 7p. 634-645.

Acta quaedam P.N. Ingatii de Loyola primarii secundum Deum institutoris Societatis Iesu a Ludovico Consalvo ex eiusdem ore Sancti excepta. 1873 Parisiis typis Julii Le Clerc et Soc. (Selecta Bibliotheca Ignatiana. I).

CALVERAS, JOSEPHUS AND DE DALMASES, CANDIDUS, eds. (1969) *Exercitia spiritualia S. Ignatii et eorum Directoria*, Monumenta Ignatiana. Series secunda. Nova editio. Tomus I. Exercitia Spiritualia. Rome: Institutum Historicum Societatis Jesu.

Palabras de los Ejercicios. (1975) Rome: CIS.

B. Translations
English

A.L.P.D. (1893) *The Spiritual Exercises of St. Ignatius Arranged in Prayers. Tr. from the French.* London: Catholic Truth Society.

AMBRUZZI, ALOYSIUS (1923) *The Spiritual Exercises of Saint Ignatius, with a Commentary.* Mangalore: St. Aloysius' College.

CLEMENT, ABBE (1846) *The Spiritual Exercises.* Dublin: J. Duffy.

CORBISHLEY, THOMAS (1973) *The Spiritual Exercises of Saint Ignatius.* Wheathampstead: Anthony Clarke.

DELMAGE, LEWIS (1968) *The Spiritual Exercises of Saint Ignatius.* New York: J.F. Wagner.

[DEPLACE, CHARLES] (1860) *Manresa; or, the Spiritual Exercises of St. Ignatius.* [tr. from the Latin]. London: [publisher unknown].

FLEMING, DAVID L.,ed. (1981) *Notes on the Spiritual Exercises of St. Ignatius Loyola.* St. Louis: Review for Religious.

_____, (1978) *The Spiritual Exercises of St. Ignatius. A Literal Translation and a Contemporary Reading.* St. Louis: Institute of Jesuit Sources.

LATTEY, CUTHBERT (1928) *The Spiritual Exercises of Saint Ignatius. Literal Translation from the original Spanish by a Benedictine of Stanbrook.* St. Louis & London: B. Herder Book Co.

LEAHY, DANIEL (1956) "English Translations of the Spiritual Exercises." *Woodstock Letters* 85: 435-440.

LONGRIDGE, WILLIAM H. (1919) *The Spiritual Exercises of Saint Ignatius of Loyola. Tr. from the Spanish with a commentary and a translation of the Directorium* [sic] *in Exercitia.* London: Robert Scott.

MOORE, THOMAS H. (1948) *The Spiritual Exercises. Newly tr. from the original Spanish "autograph."* New York: Catholic Book Pub. Co.

MORRIS, JOHN (1880) *The Text of the Spiritual Exercises of Saint Ignatius. Tr. from the original Spanish.* London: Burns & Oates.

MOTTOLA, ANTHONY (1964) *The Spiritual Exercises of St. Ignatius.* Garden City: Image Books.

MULLAN, ELDER (1914) *The Spiritual Exercises of St. Ignatius of Loyola, tr. from the autograph.* New York: P.J. Kennedy & Sons.

O'CALLAGHAN, J.F., tr. (1974) *The Autobiography of St. Ignatius Loyola with Related Documents.* Introduction and notes of J.C. Colin. New York: Harper & Row.

O'CONNOR, J.F.X., ed. (1900) *The Autobiography of St. Ignatius.* New York: Benziger Brothers.

PUHL, LOUIS J. (1951) *The Spiritual Exercises of St. Ignatius. A New Translation Based on Studies in the Language of the Autograph.* Chicago: Loyola University Press.

RICKABY, JOSPEH (1915) *The Spiritual Exercises of St. Ignatius Loyola. Spanish and English, with a continuous commentary.* London: Burns.

RIX, E.M., tr. (1900) *The Testament of Ignatius Loyola.* With Preface by George Tyrrell, s.j. London.

SAINT OMER (1736) *The Spiritual Exercises of S. Ignatius Loyola* [tr. from the Latin]. Nicolas Joseph Le Febure.

SEAGER, CHARLES (1847) *The Spiritual Exercises of St. Ignatius of Loyola, translated from the authorized Latin: with extracts from the literal version and notes of. . .Father Roothaan.* London: C. Dolman.

SHIPLEY, ORBY (1870) *Spiritual Exercises of S. Ignatius of Loyola.* London: Longmans, Green, Reader & Dyer.

SINISCALCHI, L. (1864) *The Spiritual Exercises of St. Ignatius with Meditations and Prayers.* [tr. from the Italian]. Dublin.

YOUNG, WILLIAM J., tr. (1968) *St. Ignatius' own story as told to Luis Gonzales de Camara.* (Chicago, Regnery, 1956; new edition. With a sampling of his letters.) Chicago: Loyola University Press.

French

THIBAUT, EUGENE, tr., s.j. (1922) *Le Récit du Pèlerin.* Louvain: E. Desbarax
THIRY, A., ed., s.j. (1956) *Le Récit du Pèlerin.* Louvain: Desclee de Brouwer.

German

BOEHMER, HEINRICH, ed. (1902) *Die Bekenntnisse des Ignatius von Loyola.* Leipzig.

SCHNEIDER, BRUKHART, ed. (1963) *Der Bericht des Pilgers.* Second ed. Freiburg: Verlag Herder.

Italian

The editions of MHSI. (1904) *Scripta de S. Ignatio.* vol.1 & 1043; *Fontes narrativi de S. Ignatio.* vol.1.

Spanish

GONZALEZ DE CAMARA, P. LUIS, ed. (1943) *Autobiografía.* Buenos Aires: Ed. Cultural.

MARCH, JOSE M., ed., s.j. (1929) *San Ignacio de Loyola. Autobiografía y Constitución canónica de la Compañía de Jesús.* Barcelona: Herder.

VICTORIANO LARRAÑAGA, R.P., ed., s.j. (1947) *Obras completas de San Ignacio de Loyola.* Vol.1. Madrid: BAC.

4. GENERAL COMMENTARIES

A. Historical: General

BANGERT, WILLIAM V. (1972) *A History of the Society of Jesus.* St. Louis: The Institute of Jesuit Sources.

BRODRICK, JAMES (1941) *The Origin of the Jesuits.* New York: Longmans, Green, & Co.

———, (1956) *Saint Ignatius Loyola: The Pilgrim Years.* New York: Farrar, Straus & Cudahy.

BROU, ALEXANDRE (1949) *Ignatian Methods of Prayer.* tr. William J. Young. Milwaukee: Bruce Publishing Co.

BROU, ALEXANDRE (1952) *The Ignatian Way to God.* tr. William J. Young. Milwaukee: Bruce Publishing Co.

CHARMOT, FRANCOIS (1966) *Ignatius Loyola and Francis de Sales. Two Masters— One Spirituality.* tr. M. Renelle. St. Louis/London: Herder.

CLANCY, THOMAS H. (1976) *An Introduction to Jesuit Life. The Constitutions and History through 435 Years.* St. Louis: Institute of Jesuit Sources.

COGNET, LOUIS (1959) *Post-Reformation Spirituality.* tr. P. Hepburne Scott. New York: Hawthorn Books.

COLEMAN, GERALD D. (1974) *Religious Experience as Guide of Spiritual Living. A Study in Ignatius of Loyola and Karl Rahner, His Interpreter.* Toronto: Institute of Christian Thought.

DELUMEAU, JEAN (1977) *Catholicism between Luther and Voltaire.* Philadelphia: Westminster Press.

DUDON, PAUL (1949) *St. Ignatius of Loyola.* tr. William J. Young. Milwaukee: Bruce Publishing Co.

HOLLIS, CHRISTOPHER (1931) *St. Ignatius.* London: Sheed & Ward.

IPARRAGUIRRE, IGNACIO (1974) "The Ever Youthful and Dynamic Character of Ignatian Spirituality." *Communications from the International Service in Ignatian Spirituality* 1:1-22.

———, (1970) "Ignace de Loyola. Vie et oeuvres," *Dictionnaire de spiritualite ascetique et mystique* VII: 1267-1277, Paris.

KNOWLES, DAVID (1966) "The Jesuits," in: *From Pachomius to Ignatius. A Study on the Constitutional History of Religious Orders.* Oxford: Clarendon Press, pp. 61-68.

LEECH, KENNETH (1977) *Soul Friend: A Study of Spirituality.* London: Sheldon Press.

LETURIA, PEDRO DE (1957) *Estudios Ignacianos.* ed. Ignacio Iparraguirre. 2 vols. Rome: Institutum Historicum S.I.

———, (1949) *Iñigo de Loyola.* tr. Aloysius J. Owen. Syracuse: Le Moyne College.

OLIN, JOHN C. (1969) *The Catholic Reformation: Savonarola to Ignatius Loyola. Reform in the Church, 1495-1540.* New York: Harper & Row.

O'DONNELL, GODFREY (1976) "Contemplation." *The Way Supplement* 27:27-34.

PRZYWARA, ERICH. (1971) *The Divine Majesty.* tr. Thomas Corbishley. London: Collins.

PURCELL, MARY (1957) *The First Jesuit: St. Ignatius Loyola.* Westminster, Md.: Newman Press.

RAHNER, KARL (1957) "A Basic Ignatian Concept. Some Reflections on Obedience." *Woodstock Letters* 86:291-310.

RAHNER, HUGO (1968) "Ignatius the Theologian," in: *Ignatius the Theologian*, 1-31. London: Chapman.

———, "Ignatius and the Ascetic Tradition of the Fathers," in: *Ignatius the Theologian*, 32-52.

————, (1968) *The Spirituality of St. Ignatius Loyola. An Account of Its Historical Development*. tr. Francis J. Smith. Chicago: Loyola University Press.

————, (1975) *The Vision of St. Ignatius in the Chapel of La Storta*. Rome: CIS.

RAHNER, KARL (1967) "The Ignatian Mysticism of Joy in the World," in: *Theological Investigations*. III. pp. 277-293. Baltimore/London: Helicon Press/Darton, Longman & Todd.

————, (1968) "The Ever Greater Glory of God." *Woodstock Letters* 97: 390-393.

RAHNER, KARL, AND IMHOF, PAUL (1979) *Ignatius of Loyola*. New York: Collins Publishing Co.

RESTREPA, DARIO (1976) " 'Spiritual conversation' according to St. Ignatius of Loyola." *Communications* 6: 2-23.

SCHNITT, ROBERT L. (1979) "Ignatian Mysticism: A Mysticism of Action." *Journal of Dharma* 4: 126-142.

THOMPSON, FRANCIS (1962) *St. Ignatius Loyola*. London: Burns & Oates.

TONER, JULES J. (1982) *A Commentary on Saint Ignatius' Rules for the Discernment of Spirits*. St. Louis: The Inst. of Jesuit Sources.

B. *Historical: Exercises*

AMBRUZZI, L. (1943) *Sant' Ignazio. Gli esercizi spirituali*. Traduzione e commento. Firenze.

BARTHES, ROLAND (1976) "Loyola," in: *Sade, Fourier, Loyola*. pp. 38-75. New York: Hill & Wang.

BURNS, GEORGE S. (1966) *Dialogue and Decision: The Spiritual Exercises in the Light of Vatican II*. Montreal: Palm Publishers.

CALCAGNO, FR. (1936) *Ascetica ignaziana* p.I. Turin: Documenta.

CALVERAS, JOSÉ (1949) *The Harvest-Field of the Spiritual Exercises of Saint Ignatius*. tr. J.H. Gense. Bombay: Bambardekar.

————, (1950) *Qué fruto se ha de sacar de los Ejercicios espirituales de San Ignacio*, 2nd. ed. Barcelona: Juan Flors

CASANOVAS, I. (1945) *Comentario y explanación de los Ejercicios espirituales*. tr. from Catalan by Fr. Isla, t.1., Teoria-Directorio-Preparacion. Barcelona: Juan Flors.

CLARKE, THOMAS (1972) "The Ignatian Exercises: Contemplation and Discernment." *Review for Religious* 31:62-69.

COATHALEM, HERVE (1971) *Ignatian Insights. A Guide to the Complete Spiritual Exercises*. tr. Charles J. McCarthy. 2nd ed. Taiwan: Taichung Taiwan: Kuangchi Press (197 Chunghsiao Road).

CROWE, FREDERICK E. (1978) "Dialectic and the Ignatian Spiritual Exercises." *Science et Esprit* 30:111-127.

CODINA, ARTURO (1926) *Los orígenes de los Ejercicios Espirituales de S. Ignacio de Loyola*. Barcelona: Biblioteca Balmes.

CUENOT, CLAUDE (1969) "Teilhard and the Spiritual Exercises of Saint Ignatius." *The Teilhard Review* (1969/1970) 4:50-59.

CUSSON, G. (1970) "Ignace de Loyola. Les Exercices Spirituels." *Dictionnaire de spiritualite ascetique et mystique*. VII. 1306-2318. Paris.

DALMASES, CÁNDIDO DE (1966) "Father Calveras' Study of the Text of the Exercises." *Woodstock Letters* 95:234-235.

DE LA PALMA (1556-1641) *Camino espiritual de la manera que lo enseña el B.P.S. Ignacio en su libro de los Ejercicios.* Madrid: Apostolado de la Prensa, 1944.

DE PONLEVOY (1921) *Comentario a los Ejercicios,* Oña: Bilbao

DENIS, A. (1818-1892) *Commentarii in Exercitia spiritualia S.P.N. Ign.* 4 vols. Malinas, 1891-1893.

DIERTINS, I. (1626-1700) *Sensus Exercitiorum explanatus*, Turin, 1838.

ENGLISH, JOHN (1973) *Spiritual Freedom: From an Experience of the Ignatian Exercises to the Art of Spiritual Direction.* Guelph, Ontario: Loyola House.

ERHART, JOSEPH F.X. (1953) "Doctrine of Father Jerome Nadal on the Spiritual Exercises of St. Ignatius." *Woodstock Letters* 82:317-334.

ESPINOSA, CLEMENTE, ed. *Los ejercicios de San Ignacio de la luz del Vaticano II.* Madrid: BAC, n.280.

_____, (1966) *Problematic of the Spiritual Exercises Today. The Results of an International Enquiry.* pro manuscripto. Rome: Borgo S. Spirito 5.

EVENETT, H. OUTRAM (1968) "St. Ignatius and the Spiritual Exercises," in: *The Spirit of the Counter-Reformation.* pp. 43-66. Cambridge: University Press.

FERRUSOLA (1705-1771) *Ejercicios espirituales* (Manresa 1886).

FESSARD, GASTON (1966) *La dialectique des Exercices Spirituels de saint Ignace de Loyola.* I. *Liberte-Temps-Grace.* II. *Fondement-Peche-Orthodoxie.* Paris: Aubier.

FITZPATRICK, DANIEL J. (1976) *Confusion. Call. Commitment. The Spiritual Exercises and Religious Education.* New York: Alba House.

GAGLIARDI, A. (1535-1607) *Commentarii seu explanationes in Ex.* Bruges, 1882, VIII & 200.

GANSS, GEORGE E. (1969) "The Authentic Spiritual Exercises of St. Ignatius: Some Facts of History and Terminology Basic to Their Functional Efficacy Today." *Studies in the Spirituality of the Jesuits* I/2.

GILL, HENRY V. (1938) *Jesuit Spirituality: Leading Ideas of the Spiritual Exercises of St. Ignatius.* 2nd. ed. Dublin: M.H. Gill & Son, Ltd.

GONZÁLEZ, L. AND IPARRAGUIRRE, I. *Ejercicios espirituales. Comentario pastoral.* Madrid: BAC, n.245.

GOODIER, ALBAN (1940) *St. Ignatius Loyola and Prayer. As Seen in the Book of the Spiritual Exercises.* London: Burns & Oates.

GUTIÉRREZ, J. (1929) *Manual de los Ejercicios espirituales* 3rd. ed., Bilbao: Mensajero.

HOCHHAUS, RAPHAEL H. *Some notes to facilitate the personal study of the Spiritual Exercises.* Jersey City: PASE.

HUGH, G.A. (1960) "The Exercises for Individuals and for Groups." *Woodstock Letters* 89:127-148.

HUMMELAUER, FRANZ VON (1967) *The Plan of the Spiritual Exercises of Saint Ignatius of Loyola, from the "Puncta metationum et contemplationum S.P. Ignatii."* ed. J.P. Morán. Quezon City: Jesuit Mission Band.

IGLESIAS, E. (1946) *Ejercicios espirituales. Algunas notas para su mejor inteligencia.* Mexico: Editorial Jus.

IPARRAGUIRRE, IGNACIO (1967) *Comentarios de los Ejercicios Ingacianos. (Siglos XVI-XVIII) Ripertorio critico.* Rome: Institutum Historicum S.I.

————, (1959) *A Key to the Study of the Spiritual Exercises*. tr. J. Chianese. Calcutta: The Little Flower Press.

————, (1946-1973) *Historia de los Ejercicios de San Ignacio de Loyola*. 3 vols. Bilbao/Rome: Mensajero del Corazón de Jesús/Institutum Historicum S.I.

————, (1949) *Líneas directivas de los Ejercicios ignacianos*, Bilbao: Mensajero.

————, *The Spiritual Exercises: Treasure of Christian Asceticism*. tr. Aloysius J. Owen. Jersey City: PASE.

————, (1956) "St. Ignatius as Retreat-Master." *Ignatiana II* 209-211.

————, (1978) *Vocabulario de Ejercicios Espirituales: Ensayo de hermenéutica ignaciana*. Rome: CIS.

KELLY, HUGH (1956) "St. Ignatius and the Spiritual Exercises." *Studies* 45: 275-284.

KIRK, GERARD F. *The organic structure of the Spiritual Exercises according to Pere Gaston Fessard S.J.* Jersey City: PASE.

LEDRUS, MICHAEL (1975) *Themes for the Spiritual Exercises*. Dublin: Christian Life Communities Central Secretariat.

LEONARD, WILLIAM J. (1967) "Inner Dynamism of the Exercises." *20-26 Workshop 1967*.

LETURIA, PEDRO DE. "Génesis de los Ejercicios de S. Ignacio y su influjo en la fundación de la Compañía de Jesús," in: *Estudios Ignacianos II* 3-55.

LEWIS, JACQUES. *An Approach to the Spiritual Exercises: The Different Texts of the Spiritual Exercises*. Jersey City: PASE.

————, (1967) "The Sense of the Spiritual Exercises." *Woodstock Letters* 96:229-234.

MALATESTA, EDWARD J. (1975) "The Apostolate of the Spiritual Exercises." *The Way Supplement* 24:124-135.

MARCHETTI, O. (1945) *Gli esercizi*. I. Il pensiero ignaziano, Rome: CIS.

MARIN, CANUTO HILARIO (1941) *Spiritualia exercitia secundum Romanorum Pontificum documenta*. Barcelona: Lib. Religiosa.

MATTEZ, MARIE THERESE. *Feminine Experience of the Spiritual Exercises*. Jersey City: PASE.

MCCARTHY, C.J., tr. (1961) *Ignatian Insights. A Guide to the Complete Spiritual Exercises*. Taichung: Kuangchi.

MERCIER, V. (1838-1905) *Manual des Exercices de S. Ignace*, (Poitiers, 1896).

NEUMAYER, F. (1697-1765) *Via compendii ad perfectionem statui religioso competentem octi diurno itinere emetienda*. Augsburg, 1757.

NICOLAU, MIGUEL (1970) "Origen de los Ejercicios de San Ignacio." *Manresa* 42:270-294 and 377-396.

NONELL, J. (1916) *Ejercicios. Estudios sobre el texto. Estudios Ignacianos:* II:31-39.

OLSEN, GLENN W. (1979) "Lay spirituality ad maiorem Dei gloriam." *Communio. International Catholic Review*, 6:405-412.

PEETERS, LOUIS (1956) *An Ignatian Approach to Divine Union*. tr. Hilliard L. Brozowski. Milwaukee: Bruce.

PETERS, WILLIAM A. (1964) "The Hidden Force behind the Spiritual Exercises." *Fordham Study 1964*, 5-8.

————, (1964) "Meditation or Contemplation?" *Fordham Study 1964*, 9-13.

————, (1978) *The Spiritual Exercises of St. Ignatius: Exposition and Interpretation*. 2nd. ed. Rome: CIS.

PINARD DE LA BOULLAYE, HENRI (1950) *Exercices Spirituels selon la methode de Saint Ignace.* 4 vols. 7th ed. Paris: Beauchesne et ses Fils.

POUSSET, DEOUARD (1980) *Life in Faith and Freedom. An Essay Presenting Gaston Fessard's Analysis of the Dialectic of the Spiritual Exercises of St. Ignatius.* tr. Eugene L. Donahue. St. Louis: The Institute of Jesuit Sources.

RAHNER, HUGO (1956) "Notes on the Spiritual Exercises." tr. Louis Mounteer. *Woodstock Letters* 85:281-336.

RIEMAN, NICHOLAS (1973) "The Spiritual Exercises: Preparation and Preparatory Forms." *Progressio. Supplement I,* May, 1973.

ROOTHAAN, JOHN (1945) *How to Meditate.* tr. Louis J. Puhl. Westminster, Md.: The Newman Bookshop.

ROUSTANG, FRANCOIS (1966) *Growth in the Spirit.* tr. Kathleen Pond. New York: Sheed and Ward.

SOLANES, F. (1941) *Comentario a los Ejercicios espirituales de San Ignacio.* Barcelona: Juan Flors.

SUÁREZ, F. *De religione S.I.* 1.9 c.5-7: ed. Vives, t.16, pp. 1017-1045.

5. DIRECTORIES

AQUAVIVA, CLAUDIO (1925) *The Directory to the Spiritual Exercises.* Roehampton: Griffin.

AQUAVIVA, CLAUDIO (1919) "The Directory," in: W.H. Longridge, *The Spiritual Exercises of Saint Ignatius of Loyola... and a Translation of the Directorium in Exercitia.* pp. 269-351. London: Robert Scott.

BUSH, BERNARD AMD OWNE, ALOYSIUS, trs. *Autograph Directories of Saint Ignatius Loyola.* Jersey City: PASE.

CICCOLINI, ANTONIO (1966) *The Directory in Reference to the Spiritual Exercises,* in: *Commentary on the Spiritual Exercises of St. Ignatius of Loyola.* Quezon City: Jesuit Mission Band.

GARCÍA-CUEVA, MARCO; ENGH, MIKE; AND POPE, MICHAEL, trs. (1980) *Four Directories for the Spiritual Exercises of Saint Ignatius Loyola.* Berkeley: Jesuit School of Theology.

MONUMENTA IGNATIANA (1955) Series secunda. Tomus II. *Directoria Exercitiorum spiritualium (1540-1599).* ed. Ignatius Iparraguirre. Rome: Institutum Historicum Societatis Iesu.

THURSTON, HERBERS (1923) "The First Englishman to Make the Spiritual Exercises." *Month* 142:336-347.

Index